A Brief Survey of the Sociological Imagination

Third Edition

Edited by

STEVEN GERARDI

New York City College of Technology

Kendall Hunt
publishing company

Dedicated to Anna, Michael, Nikki-Ann
and Stephany

Contents

ation A Brief Survey of the Sociological Imagination A Brief Survey
ciological Imagination A Brief Survey of the Sociological Imagination
urvey of the Sociological Imagination A Brief Survey of the Sociologic
ation A Brief Survey of the Sociological Imagination A Brief Survey
ciological Imagination A Brief Survey of the Sociological Imagination

CHAPTER I

Émile Durkheim
(1858–1917)

Émile Durkheim's career centered on studying the forces that hold society together. Durkheim suggested that religion, philosophy, ideas, and morals are products of the social condition of humanity, and are expressed as social realities. These social concepts are seen by Durkheim as the "Collective Conscience" of a clan or group because they correspond to, and are at the root of, each member's judgments and actions.

Durkheim's work entitled *The Division of Labor* was an effort at treating facts of moral life according to the scientific method. Durkheim suggested in the book *The Rules of Sociological Method* that "social facts" can be treated as "things" and thus can be examined in terms of their "external observable properties". Durkheim viewed moral life as a principle, which consists of rules of action, that becomes transformed during social evolution because it corresponds to, and serves human needs.

Durkheim in *The Division of Labor* establishes a moral split between traditional and modern society. Durkheim's concept is that the moral collective character of modern society is just as natural as the collective activity of smaller societies during previous ages. He develops this concept by comparing and contrasting both the traditional and modern types of societies. He begins this argument with the concept that in simpler societies there is a strong definition of morality, which is an all-enveloping Collective Conscience. There are four areas by which the properties of the Collective Conscience can be analyzed. They are volume, intensity, rigidity, and the content of beliefs and values. Volume refers to the degree in which individuals hold identical attitudes, values, and beliefs. Intensity refers to the extent of the emotional and intellectual hold these beliefs and values exert over all individuals. Generally speaking, the stronger the intensity the more enveloping the Collective Conscience. Rigidity pertains to how clear the

definitions are of the beliefs and associated practices prescribed by the Collective Conscience. Lastly, content refers to the variable of change altering beliefs and values. For example, within earlier societies religion "pervaded everything" and now it is only a smaller portion of social life.

The traditional Collective Conscience according to Durkheim tends to be high in volume, intensity and rigidity, and its content is religious in character. The unity of such a society is a strongly defined set of values and beliefs, which ensure that the actions of all individuals conform to the common norms. Durkheim labels this type of society Mechanical Solidarity. This label in no way implies that this solidarity is artificial; rather it is analogous to a simple cell organism.

Within this solidarity every person is a microcosm of the collective type, and thus has restricted opportunity to develop individuality. The Dutch Amish may be seen as a modern day example of this form of Solidarity. All think, act, dress alike, and their religion holds them together. One may see the Orthodox Jews as an another example of such a solidarity.

This form of solidarity may be further marked by the nature of the punishment which is doled out when the person deviates from the rigidly specified behavior codes of the collective. According to Durkheim, within this form of solidarity the sanctions are repressive because the collective response to any transgression by a member is highly emotional and charged with anger and outrage.

The reader may recall that during the 1990s an American young man vandalized an automobile in Singapore (an example of a Mechanical Solidarity) and was sentenced to ten lashes with a bamboo cane. This transgression of the moral code incensed the people of Singapore and the young American was punished repressively. Moreover, the traditional societies typically have simple, segmental structure, consisting of units of families and/or clans all of which are the functional equal.

However, during social development these formerly separate communities become linked within a single economic system, which Durkheim labels Density. With the development of density the obligation of living in co-operation with one another arises. This development changes the moral homogeneity of the collective, because of the diversification of its form and by the accelerate growth of the division of labor. Durkheim labels this society Organic Solidarity.

Organic Solidarity consists of ties of cooperation between individuals and/or groups, which derive from their occupational interdependence within the division of labor. Therefore for Durkheim, one should view society as a conveyer belt mass production factory. If the person in first position does not do his/her job, the second positioned person cannot do his/hers. Therefore, we are dependent on each other to perform his/her job.

Although Durkheim draws a clear separation between these forms of solidarity, the main concept is that collective conscience within modern society is not eradicated completely. Rather, a transformed solidarity emerges which comprises a new moral ideal—that of the cult of the individual. This morality provides validation for the specialized division of labor because of the large numbers of individuals which occupy different positions within this form of solidarity. Hence, the more specialized the division of labor the more individualistic the people. The kind of work one does becomes his/her human identity producing ever increasing amounts of individuality. One may understand this concept clearly by understanding that in such a society we view individuals based upon the career they have achieved. Almost without fail if one goes to a party in which all are strangers the two questions asked concurrently

are—what is your name? What do you do? By understanding what a person does for a "living" we automatically place that person in a level of social status, based upon the social feedback that person does likewise.

As a result of this transformation, restitutive law replaces repressive sanctions which cover individual rights. The application of these laws requires specialized agencies to enforce them. Moreover, according to Durkheim, violation of these laws usually does not stimulate the collective anger or outrage. In keeping with the main theme of this book, Durkheim argues that the influence of repressive sanctions does not disappear altogether, but remains in the values embodied in the moral individual, rather than the collective. Of course, there is no returning to the traditional form once this transformation occurs. Also, according to Durkheim, at this present time the emergence of Organic Solidarity has not fully actualized. Perhaps, one should remember that during the earlier 2000s a Suffolk Long Island, New York, policeman was abusing his public power demanding that women drivers disrobe. This policeman was sentenced to five years in prison and was required to pay the woman $15,000 in fines. Therefore, each woman was entitled to $5,000 in restitution payments. The court suggested that for each of the three women whose civil liberties were violated, their forced nudity was seen as worth $5,000 by this judge. In a Mechanical Solidarity this policeman would have been punished repressively because the people would have been outraged.

Finally, Organic Solidarity tends to have a low sense of Volume, Intensity, Rigidity and the Content would be secular or public.

Durkheim in his work *The Elementary Forms of Religious Life* argues that the values and beliefs embodied in the morality were originally elaborated as religious ideas. The major propositions this work puts forth are the following: 1) religion is society, 2) representations created in religion are later transformed into human thought, 3) religious symbols are accorded and assigned respect, and 4) the existence of God is not essential to religion. Moreover, according to Durkheim, all moral phenomena are the product of society. Morality possesses a certain "sacred" quality, which is the polar opposite to the profane. The basic argument is that religion divides the universe into two parts—that which humanity considers part of the mundane world and that which is associated with special subjects possessing awe.

An example of this point is totemism. Durkheim sees totemism as the simplest form of religious systems. Within these systems there are three sacred objects: the emblem of the totem, the totem itself and the members of the totemic clan. Of these, according to Durkheim, the emblem is the most sacred because it is the symbol of the identity of the clan, and thus possesses the highest form of power. If this idea was to be placed into an equation it would look like this: sacred force = symbolic representation of society = social force diffused through the totemic object.

The major differences among the works of *Division of Labor* and *Elementary Forms of Religious Life* and *Suicide,* is that the study of suicide begins with a concrete problem and the others begin with concepts. Durkheim was interested, as was mentioned before, in various types of social integration and in social disorganization which weakened social bonds. He used rates of suicide as an index of social integration. He noticed that suicide rates were higher for Protestants than Catholics, higher for unmarried people than for married, higher for soldiers in peace than in times of war, and higher in times of both prosperity and recession than in times of economic stability. Durkheim reasoned that the differences in suicide rates must be a function of social organization. His direct emphasis was that motive for suicide was a social pathology and not a

personal act in the modern world, but based upon levels of social integration in society.

Recognizing that there is no single circumstance that explains suicide he identifies four forms of suicide, which act as an index of the various states of social integration. They are egoism, anomie, fatalism and altruism. Durkheim suggested that the degree to which individuals are integrated into a group could motivate these various forms of action.

Therefore, anomie for Durkheim signifies a socio-cultural absence of a sense of limits on its members. This absence provides a weak solidarity or integration, causing disorientation and aggression in society. Durkheim argues that because in a non-anomic society a normative sense of limits become in time, a person's second nature. Thus, the root of the individual's self-fulfillment and cooperative reciprocity, is maintained in balance.

On the other hand, excessive regulations or a "despot" setting repressive and oppressive limits to self-fulfillment and reciprocity causes fatalism. The so-called Cuban Boat People can be seen as an example of this form of suicide. Many Cuban's risked their lives in the South Atlantic Ocean during the hurricane season knowing that only one in ten of the Boat People make the ninety mile trip to Miami successfully.

Egoism refers to the state in which individualism is carried out to the extreme. According to Durkheim, this is the result of the individual being weakly attached to the social order. The October 7, 2003 *New York Times* report that women in Sweden who have cosmetic breast implant surgery are more likely to commit suicide than those who do not have this form of surgery can be seen as an example. They might be thinking, I need to look better with large breasts so I am seen as a woman. However, when this action does not ring true, suicide may be the recourse.

Finally, altruism refers to a state of excessive community, and is marked by a high sense of integration and solidarity. The so-called 911 homicide bombers can be seen as an example. Their cause is more important than their own lives.

Durkheim's key focus was to show how societies move from traditional to modern ages. For Durkheim the common social pa-thology found in an Organic Solidarity is Ano-mie. Anomie accounts for all imbalances, confusion, and contradictions (i.e. drug use and crime) of the transition of traditional to modern society as a result of rapid social change.

Anomy and Modern Life

Émile Durkheim

In this excerpt from his classic study of suicide, Emile Durkheim asserts that human aspiration, which is not bounded by nature as in other creatures, must be framed by limits imposed by society. Modern societies, however, have lost some of their moral power over the individual. The consequence is a societal condition of anomy (or anomie), which people experience as a lack of moral regulation. In the extreme, anomy prompts people to suicide; more generally, an anomic society contains people with weak and vacillating moral values who have difficulty reining in their own ambitions and desires.

No living being can be happy or even exist unless his needs are sufficiently proportioned to his means. In other words, if his needs require more than can be granted, or even merely something of a different sort, they will be under continual friction and can only function painfully. . . .

In the animal, at least in a normal condition, this equilibrium is established with automatic spontaneity because the animal depends on purely material conditions. All the organism needs is that the supplies of substance and energy constantly employed in the vital process should be periodically renewed by equivalent quantities; that replacement be equivalent to use. When the void created by existence in its own resources is filled, the animal, satisfied, asks nothing further. Its power of reflection is not sufficiently developed to imagine other ends than those implicit in its physical nature. . . .

This is not the case with man, because most of his needs are not dependent on his body or not to the same degree. . . . But how determine the quantity of well-being, comfort or luxury legitimately to be craved by a human being? Nothing appears in man's organic nor in his psychological constitution which sets a limit to such tendencies. The functioning of individual life does not require them to cease at one point rather than at another; the proof being that they have constantly increased since the beginnings of history, receiving more and more complete satisfaction, yet with no weakening of average health . . . . It is not human nature which can assign the variable limits necessary to our needs. They are thus unlimited so far as they depend on the individual alone. Irrespective of any external regulatory force, our capacity for feeling is in itself an insatiable and bottomless abyss.

But if nothing external can restrain this capacity, it can only be a source of torment to itself. Unlimited desires are insatiable by definition and insatiability is rightly considered a sign of morbidity. Being unlimited, they constantly and infinitely surpass the means at their command; they cannot be quenched. Inextinguishable thirst is constantly renewed torture. It has been claimed, indeed, that human activity naturally aspires beyond assignable limits and sets itself unattainable goals. But how can such an undetermined state be any more reconciled with the conditions of mental life than with the demands of physical life? All man's pleasure in acting, moving and exerting himself implies the sense that his efforts are not in vain and that by walking he has advanced. However, one does not advance when one walks toward no goal, or—which is the same thing—when his goal is infinity. Since the distance between us and it is always the same, whatever road we take, we might as well have made the motions without progress from the spot. Even our glances behind and our feelings of pride at the distance covered can cause only deceptive satisfaction, since the remaining distance is not proportionately reduced. To pursue a goal which is by definition unattainable is to condemn oneself to a state of perpetual unhappiness. Of course, man may hope contrary to all reason, and hope has its pleasures even when unreasonable. It may sustain him for a time; but it cannot survive the repeated disappointments of experience indefinitely. What more can the future offer him than the past, since he can never reach a tenable condition nor even approach the glimpsed ideal? Thus, the more one has, the more one wants, since satisfactions received only stimulate instead of filling needs. . . .

To achieve any other result, the passions first must be limited. Only then can they be harmonized with the faculties and satisfied. But since the individual has no way of limiting them, this must be done by some force exterior to him. A regulative force must play the same role for moral needs which the organism plays for physical needs. This means that the force can only be moral. The awakening of conscience interrupted the state of equilibrium of the animal's dormant existence; only conscience, therefore, can furnish the means to re-establish it. Physical restraint would be ineffective; hearts cannot be touched by physio-chemical forces. So far as the appetites are not automatically restrained by physiological mechanisms, they can be halted only by a limit that they recognize as just. Men would never consent to restrict their desires if they felt justified in passing the assigned limit. But, for reasons given above, they cannot assign themselves this law of justice. So they must receive it from an authority which they respect, to which they yield spontaneously. Either directly and as a whole, or through the agency of one of its organs, society alone can play this moderating role; for it is the only moral power superior to the individual, the authority of which he accepts. It alone has the power necessary to stipulate law and to set the point beyond which the passions must not go. . . .

. . . Man's characteristic privilege is that the bond he accepts is not physical but moral; that is, social. He is governed not by a material environment brutally imposed on him, but by a conscience superior to his own, the superiority of which he feels. Because the greater, better part of his existence transcends the body, he escapes the body's yoke, but is subject to that of society.

But when society is disturbed by some painful crisis or by beneficent but abrupt transitions, it is momentarily incapable of exercising this influence; thence come the sudden rises in the curve of suicides which we have pointed out above.

In the case of economic disasters, indeed, something like a declassification occurs which suddenly casts certain individuals into a lower state than their previous one. Then they must reduce their requirements, restrain their needs, learn greater self-control. All the advantages of social influence are lost so far as they are concerned; their moral education has to be recommenced. But society cannot adjust them instantaneously to this new life and teach them to practice the increased self-repression to which they are unaccustomed. So they are not adjusted to the condition forced on them, and its very prospect is intolerable; hence the suffering which detaches them from a reduced existence even before they have made trial of it.

It is the same if the source of the crisis is an abrupt growth of power and wealth. Then, truly, as the conditions of life are changed, the standard according to which needs were regulated can no longer remain the same; for it varies with social resources, since it largely determines the share of each class of producers. The scale is upset; but a new scale cannot be immediately improvised. Time is required for the public conscience to reclassify men and things. So long as the social forces thus freed have not regained equilibrium, their respective values are unknown and so all regulation is lacking for a time. The limits are unknown between the possible and the impossible, what is just and what is unjust, legitimate claims and hopes and those which are immoderate. Consequently, there is no restraint upon aspiration. . . . Appetites, not being controlled by a public opinion become disoriented, no longer recognize the limits proper to them. . . . With increased prosperity desires increase. At the very moment when traditional rules have lost their authority, the richer prize offered these appetites stimulates

them and makes them more exigent and impatient of control. The state of de-regulation or anomy is thus further heightened by passions being less disciplined, precisely when they need more disciplining. . . .

This explanation is confirmed by the remarkable immunity of poor countries. Poverty protects against suicide because it is a restraint in itself. No matter how one acts, desires have to depend upon resources to some extent; actual possessions are partly the criterion of those aspired to. So the less one has the less he is tempted to extend the range of his needs indefinitely. Lack of power, compelling moderation, accustoms men to it, while nothing excites envy if no one has superfluity. Wealth, on the other hand, by the power it bestows, deceives us into believing that we depend on ourselves only. Reducing the resistance we encounter from objects, it suggests the possibility of unlimited success against them. The less limited one feels, the more intolerable all limitation appears. Not without reason, therefore, have so many religions dwelt on the advantages and moral value of poverty. It is actually the best school for teaching self-restraint. Forcing us to constant self-discipline, it prepares us to accept collective discipline with equanimity, while wealth, exalting the individual, may always arouse the spirit of rebellion which is the very source of immorality. This, of course, is no reason why humanity should not improve its material condition. But though the moral danger involved in every growth of prosperity is not irremediable, it should not be forgotten.

If anomy never appeared except, as in the above instances, in intermittent spurts and acute crisis, it might cause the social suicide-rate to vary from time to time, but it would not be a regular, constant factor. In one sphere of social life, however—the sphere of trade and industry—it is actually in a chronic state.

For a whole century, economic progress has mainly consisted in freeing industrial relations from all regulation. Until very recently, it was the function of a whole system of moral forces to exert this discipline. First, the influence of religion was felt alike by workers and masters, the poor and the rich. It consoled the former and taught them contentment with their lot by informing them of the providential nature of the social order, that the share of each class was assigned by God himself, and by holding out the hope for just compensation in a world to come in return for the inequalities of this world. It governed the latter, recalling that worldly interests are not man's entire lot, that they must be subordinate to other and higher interests, and that they should therefore not be pursued without rule or measure. Temporal power, in turn, restrained the scope of economic functions by its supremacy over them and by the relatively subordinate role it assigned them. Finally, within the business world proper, the occupational groups by regulating salaries, the price of products and production itself, indirectly fixed the average level of income on which needs are partially based by the very force of circumstances. However, we do not mean to propose this organization as a model. Clearly it would be inadequate to existing societies without great changes. What we stress is its existence, the fact of its useful influence, and that nothing today has come to take its place.

Actually, religion has lost most of its power. And government, instead of regulating economic life, has become its tool and servant. The most opposite schools, orthodox economists and extreme socialists, unite to reduce government to the role of a more or less passive intermediary among the various social functions. The former wish to make it simply the guardian of individual contracts; the latter leave it the task of doing the collective bookkeeping, that is, of recording the demands of consumers, transmitting them to producers, inventorying the total revenue and distributing it according to a fixed formula. But both refuse it any power to subordinate other social organs to itself and to make them converge toward one dominant aim. On both sides nations are declared to have the single or chief purpose of achieving industrial prosperity; such is the implication of the dogma of economic materialism, the basis of both apparently opposed systems. And as these theories merely express the state of opinion, industry, instead of being still regarded as a means to an end transcending itself, has become the supreme end of individuals and societies alike. Thereupon the appetites thus excited have become freed of any limiting authority. By sanctifying them, so to speak, this apotheosis of well-being has placed them above all human law. Their restraint seems like a sort of sacrilege. For this reason, even the purely utilitarian regulation of them exercised by the industrial world itself through the medium of occupational groups has been unable to persist. Ultimately, this liberation of desires has been made worse by the very development of industry and the almost infinite extension of the market. So long as the producer could gain his profits only in his immediate neighborhood, the restricted amount of possible gain could not much overexcite ambition. Now that he may assume to have almost the entire world as his customer, how could passions accept their former confinement in the face of such limitless prospects?

Such is the source of the excitement predominating in this part of society, and which has thence extended to the other parts. There the state of crisis and anomy is constant and, so to speak, normal. From top to bottom of the ladder, greed is aroused without knowing where to find ultimate foothold. Nothing can calm it, since its goal is far beyond all it can attain. Reality seems valueless by comparison with the dreams of fevered imaginations; reality is therefore abandoned, but so too is possibility abandoned when it in turn becomes reality. A thirst arises for novelties, unfamiliar pleasures, nameless sensations, all of which lose their savor once known. Henceforth one has no strength to endure the least reverse. The whole fever subsides and the sterility of all the tumult is apparent, and it is seen that all these new sensations in their infinite quantity cannot form a solid foundation of happiness to support one during days of trial. The wise man, knowing how to enjoy achieved results without having constantly to replace them with others, finds in them an attachment to life in the hour of difficulty. But the man who has always pinned all his hopes on the future and lived with his eyes fixed upon it, has nothing in the past as a comfort against the present's afflictions, for the past was nothing to him but a series of hastily experienced stages. What blinded him to himself was his expectation always to find further on the happiness he had so far missed. Now he is stopped in his tracks; from now on nothing remains behind or ahead of him to fix his gaze upon. Weariness alone, moreover, is enough to bring disillusionment, for he cannot in the end escape the futility of an endless pursuit.

We may even wonder if this moral state is not principally what makes economic catastrophes of our day so fertile in suicides. In societies where a man is subjected to a healthy discipline, he submits more readily to the blows of chance. The necessary effort for sustaining a little more discomfort costs him relatively little, since he is used to discomfort and constraint. But when every constraint is hateful in itself, how can closer constraint not seem intolerable? There is no tendency to resignation in the feverish impatience of men's lives. When there is no other aim but to outstrip constantly the point arrived at, how painful to be thrown back! Now this very lack of

organization characterizing our economic condition throws the door wide to every sort of adventure. Since imagination is hungry for novelty, and ungoverned, it gropes at random. Setbacks necessarily increase with risks and thus crises multiply, just when they are becoming more destructive.

Yet these dispositions are so inbred that society has grown to accept them and is accustomed to think them normal. It is everlastingly repeated that it is man's nature to be eternally dissatisfied, constantly to advance, without relief or rest, toward an indefinite goal. The longing for infinity is daily represented as a mark of moral distinction, whereas it can only appear within unregulated consciences which elevate to a rule the lack of rule from which they suffer. The doctrine of the most ruthless and swift progress has become an article of faith. But other theories appear parallel with those praising the advantages of instability, which, generalizing the situation that gives them birth, declare life evil, claim that it is richer in grief than in pleasure and that it attracts men only by false claims. Since this disorder is greatest in the economic world, it has most victims there.

Industrial and commercial functions are really among the occupations which furnish the greatest number of suicides. . . . Almost on a level with the liberal professions, they sometimes surpass them; they are especially more afflicted than agriculture, where the old regulative forces still make their appearance felt most and where the fever of business has least penetrated. Here is best recalled what was once the general constitution of the economic order. And the divergence would be yet greater if, among the suicides of industry, employers were distinguished from workmen, for the former are probably most stricken by the state of anomy. The enormous rate of those with independent means (720 per million) sufficiently shows that the possessors of most comfort suffer most. Everything that enforces subordination attenuates the effects of this state. At least the horizon of the lower classes is limited by those above them, and for this same reason their desires are more modest. Those who have only empty space above them are almost inevitably lost in it, if no force restrains them.

Social Order and Control Via Close Social Ties: The Example of Suicide

Émile Durkheim

We have thus successively set up the three following propositions:

- Suicide varies inversely with the degree of integration of religious society.
- Suicide varies inversely with the degree of integration of domestic society.
- Suicide varies inversely with the degree of integration of political society.

This grouping shows that whereas these different societies [i.e., social groups or social contexts] have a moderating influence upon suicide, this is due not to special characteristics of each but to a characteristic common to all. Religion does not owe its efficacy to the special nature of religious sentiments, since domestic and political societies both produce the same effects when strongly integrated. This, moreover, we have already proved when studying directly the manner of action of different religions upon suicide. [Similarly], it is not the special nature of the domestic or political tie which can explain the immunity they confer, since religious society has the same advantage. The cause can only be found in a single quality possessed by all these social groups, though perhaps to varying degrees. The only quality satisfying this condition is that they are all strongly integrated social groups. So we reach the general conclusion: suicide varies inversely with the degree of integration of the social groups of which the individual forms a part.

But society cannot disintegrate without the individual simultaneously detaching himself from social life, without his own goals becoming preponderant over those of the community, in a word, without his personality tending to surmount the collective personality. The more weakened the groups to which he belongs, the less he depends upon them, the more he consequently depends only on himself and recognizes no other rules of conduct than what are founded on his private interests. If we agree to call this state egoism, in which the individual ego asserts itself to excess in the face of the social ego and at its expense, we may call egoistic the special type of suicide springing from excessive individualism.

But how can suicide have such an origin?

First of all, it can be said that, as collective force is one of the obstacles best calculated to restrain suicide, its weakening involves a development of suicide. When society is strongly integrated, it holds individuals under its control, considers them at its service and thus forbids them to dispose willfully of themselves. Accordingly it opposes their evading their duties to it through death. But how could society impose its supremacy upon them when they refuse to accept this subordination as legitimate? It no longer then possesses the requisite authority to retain them in their duty if they wish to desert; and conscious of its own weakness, it even recognizes their right to do freely what it can no longer prevent. So far as they are the admitted masters of their destinies, it is their privilege to end their lives. They, on their part, have no reason to endure life's suffering patiently. For they cling to life more resolutely when belonging to a group they love, so as not to betray interests they put before their own. The bond that unites them with the common cause attaches them to life and the lofty goal they envisage prevents their feeling personal troubles so deeply. There is, in short, in a cohesive and animated society a constant interchange of ideas and feelings from all to each and each to all, something like a mutual moral support, which instead of throwing the individual on his own resources, leads him to share in the collective energy and supports his own when exhausted.

Marital Status and Suicide

[Table 1.1 supports the proposition for "domestic society" by showing] . . . that marriage has indeed a preservative effect of its own against suicide.[1]

[In short,] . . . the family is the essential factor in the immunity of married persons, that is, the family as the whole group of parents and children. . . .

TABLE 1.1

Influence of the Family on Suicide by Sex

MEN

	Suicide Rate*	Coefficient of Preservation in Relation to Unmarried Men**
Unmarried men 45 years old	975	—
Husbands with children	336	2.9
Husbands without children	644	1.5
Unmarried men 60 years old	1,504	—
Widowers with children	937	1.6
Widowers without children	1,258	1.2

WOMEN

	Suicide Rate*	Coefficient of Preservation in Relation to Unmarried Women***
Unmarried women 42 years old	150	—
Wives with children	79	1.89
Wives without children	221	0.67
Unmarried women 60 years old	196	—
Widows with children	186	1.06
Widows without children	322	0.60

[*   Per million inhabitants of France, 1889–1891]
[** Ratio of unmarried men to each category of marital status]
[*** Ratio of unmarried women to each category of marital status]

Divorce and Suicide

In the *Annales de demographie internationale* (September 1882), Bertillon published a remarkable study of divorce, in which he proved the following proposition: throughout Europe the number of suicides varies with that of divorces and separations.

If the different countries are compared from this twofold point of view, this parallelism is apparent (see Table 1.2). Not only is the relation between the averages evident, but the single irregular detail of any importance is that of Holland, where suicides are not as frequent as divorces.

The law may be yet more vigorously verified we compare not different countries but different provinces of a single country. Notably, in Switzerland the agreement between the two series of phenomenon is striking (see Table 1.3). The Protestant cantons have the most divorces and also the most suicides. The mixed cantons follow, from both points of view and only then come the Catholic cantons. Within each group the same agreements appear. Among the Catholic cantons Solothurn and Inner Appenzell are marked by the high number of their suicide Freiburg, although Catholic and French, has a considerable number of both divorces and suicides. Finally the mixed cantons, with the one exception of Argau, are classed in exactly the same way in both respects.

TABLE 1.2

Comparison of European States from the Point of View of Both Divorce and Suicide

	Annual Divorces per 1,000 Marriages		Suicides per Million Inhabitants
Countries Where Divorce and Separation Are Rare			
Norway	0.54	(1875–80)	73
Russia	1.6	(1871–77)	30
England and Wales	1.3	(1871–79)	68
Scotland	2.1	(1871–81)	—
Italy	3.05	(1871–73)	31
Finland	3.9	(1875–79)	30.8
Averages	2.07		46.5
Countries Where Divorce and Separation Are of Average Frequency			
Bavaria	5.0	(1881)	90.5
Belgium	5.1	(1871–80)	68.5
Holland	6.0	(1871–80)	35.5
Sweden	6.4	(1871–80)	81
Baden	6.5	(1874–79)	156.6
France	7.5	(1871–79)	150
Wurttemberg	8.4	(1876–78)	162.4
Prussia	—		133
Averages	6.4		109.6
Countries Where Divorce and Separation Are Frequent			
Kingdom of Saxony	26.9	(1876–80)	299
Denmark	38	(1871–80)	258
Switzerland	47	(1876–80)	216
Averages	37.3		257

TABLE 1.3 TABLE 1.3 TABLE 1.3 **TABLE 1.3** TABLE 1.3 TABLE 1.3 TABLE 1.3

Comparison of Swiss Cantons from the Point of View of Divorce and Suicide

	Divorces and Separations per 1,000 Marriages	Suicides per Million		Divorces and Separations per 1,000 Marriages	Suicides per Million
I. Catholic Cantons					
French and Italian					
Tessino	7.6	57	Freiburg	15.9	119
Valais	4.0	47			
Averages	5.8	50	Averages	15.9	119
German					
Uri	—	60	Solothurn	37.7	205
Upper Unterwalden	4.9	20	Inner Appenzell	18.9	158
Lower Unterwalden	5.2	1	Zug	14.8	87
Schwyz	5.6	70	Luzern	13.0	100
Averages	3.9	37.7	Averages	21.1	137.5
II. Protestant Cantons					
French					
Neufchatel	42.4	560	Vaud	43.5	352
German					
Bern	47.2	229	Schaffhausen	106.0	602
Basel (city)	34.5	323	Outer Appenzell	100.7	213
Basel (country)	33.0	288	Glaris	83.1	127
			Zurich	80.0	288
Averages	38.2	280	Averages	92.4	307
III. Cantons Mixed as to Religion					
Argau	40.4	195	Geneva	70.5	360
Grisons	30.9	116	Saint Gall	57.6	179
Averages	36.9	155	Averages	64.0	269

The same comparison, if made between French departments, gives the same result. Having classified them in eight categories according to the importance of their suicidal mortality, we discovered that the groups thus formed were arranged in the same order as with reference to divorces and separations [see Table 1.4].

One must seek the cause of this remarkable relation, not in the organic predispositions of people but in the intrinsic nature of divorce. As our first proposition here we may assert: in all countries for which we have the necessary data, suicides of divorced people are immensely more numerous than those of other portions of the population [see Table 1.5].

Thus, divorced persons of both sexes kill themselves between three and four times as often as married persons, although younger (40 years in France as against 46 years), and considerably more often than widowed persons in spite of the aggravation resulting from the latter from their advanced age. What is the explanation? . . .

TABLE 1.4

Suicide and the Prevalence of Divorce and Separation in French Departments

	Suicides per Million	Average of Divorces and Separations per 1,000 Marriages
1st group (5 departments)	< 50	2.6
2nd group (18 departments)	51–75	2.9
3rd group (15 departments)	76–100	5.0
4th group (19 departments)	101–150	5.4
5th group (10 departments)	151–200	7.5
6th group (9 departments)	201–250	8.2
7th group (4 departments)	251–300	10.0
8th group (5 departments)	> 300	12.4

Now divorce implies a weakening of matrimonial regulation. Where it exists, and especially where law and custom permit its excessive practice, marriage is nothing but a weakened [shadow] of itself; it is an inferior form of marriage. It cannot produce its useful effects to the same degree. Its restraint upon desire is weakened; since it is more easily disturbed and superseded, it controls passion less and passion tends to rebel. It consents less readily to its assigned limit. The moral calmness and tranquility which were the husband's strength are less; they are replaced to some extent by an uneasiness which keeps a man from being satisfied with what he has. Besides, he is the less inclined to become attached to his present state as his enjoyment of it is not completely sure: the future is less certain. One cannot be strongly restrained by a chain which may be broken on one side at any moment. One cannot help looking beyond one's own position when the ground underfoot does not feel secure. Hence, in the countries where marriage is strongly tempered by divorce, the immunity of the married man is inevitably less. As he resembles the unmarried under his regime, he inevitably loses some of his own advantages. Consequently, the total number of suicides rises.[2]

TABLE 1.5

Suicides in a Million

		Unmarried above 15 Years		Married		Widowed		Divorced	
		Men	Women	Men	Women	Men	Women	Men	Women
Prussia	(1887–1889)*	360	120	430	90	1,471	215	1,875	290
Prussia	(1883–1890)*	388	129	498	100	1,552	194	1,952	328
Baden	(1885–1893)	458	93	460	85	1,172	171	1,328	—
Saxony	(1847–1858)	—	—	481	120	1,242	240	3,102	312
Saxony	(1876)	555.18[†]		821	146	—	—	3,252	389
Wurttemberg	(1846–1860)	—	—	226	52	530	97	1,298	281
Wurttemberg	(1873–1892)	251	—	218[†]		405[†]		796[†]	

*There appears to be some error in the figures for Prussia here.—Ed.
[†]Men and women combined.—Ed.

Notes

1. M. Bertillon . . . had already given the suicide-rate for the different categories of marital status with and without children. He found the following results:

Husbands w. children	205
Widowers w. children	526
Husbands w. no children	478
Widowers w. no children	1,004
Wives w. children	45
Widows w. children	104
Wives w. no children	158
Widows w. no children	238

These figures refer to [suicides per million and] the years 1861–68. Given the general increase in suicides, they confirm our own figures. . . [Ed. note: Only substantive footnotes are included in this selection.]

2. It will be objected that where marriage is not tempered by divorce the rigid obligation of monogamy may result in disgust. This result will of course follow if the moral character of the obligation is no longer felt. What actually matters in fact is not only that the regulation should exist, but that it should be accepted by the conscience. Otherwise, since this regulation no longer has moral authority and continues only through the force of inertia, it can no longer play any useful role. It chafes without accomplishing much.

Selected Readings

Emile Durkheim, 1858–1917: A Collection of Essays by Kurt H. Wolff.

Durkheim and the Social Anthropology of Culture, in Social Forces by James L. Peacock.

Moral Education: A Study in the Theory and Application of the Sociology of Education by Emile Durkheim, Paul Fauconnet, Herman Schnurer, Everett Wilson K.

The Division of Labor in Society by Emile B. Durkheim, George B. Simpson.

The Elementary Forms of the Religious Life by Emile Durkheim, Joseph Ward Swain.

Durkheim and Postmodern Culture by St.jepan G. Messtrovic.

Durkheim, Deviance and Development: Opportunities Lost and Regained, in Social Forces by T. Anthony Jones.

Durkheim and Sexual Anomie: A Comment on Tiryakian, in Social Forces by Philippe Besnard.

Durkheim and Women by Jennifer M. Lehmann.

Moral Integration and Political Inclusion: a Comparison of Durkheim's and Weber's Theories of Democracy, in Social Forces by Jeffrey Prater.

Mourning and the Making of a Sacred Symbol: Durkheim and the Lincoln Assassination, in Social Forces by Barry Schwartz.

Critical-Thinking Questions

1. What is the Collective Conscience of a Mechanical and Organic Solidarity?

2. What are the four scientific tools Durkheim uses to evaluate Collective Consciences?

3. What are the four forms of suicide and their related social integration?

CHAPTER II

Max Weber (1864–1920)

Max Weber's basic observation in sociology was the extensive influence religion had on aspects of social change, economic life, and the development of rationality or science and technology in modern society. Weber was a German sociologist who attempted to trace capitalism and science/technology through a vast comparative study of the world religions.

In *Economy and Society* Max Weber reveals his major concept of Rationality which is a historic-religious transformation process. The Principle of Rationality suggests that the degree to which a society displaces irrational thought with rational thought will make it stand as the most powerful nation during that historical point of time. For Weber this force accounts for the rise and fall of institutional structures, classes and parties or it is the force of social change. Rationality consists of two types of movements within social development—Substantive and Formal.

Substantive Rationality or the traditional society is characterized by personal relationships and is without the purely measured acts of economic calculable. According to Weber, substantive forms are rooted in the recurrent and normal needs of the workday, usually with a patriarchal figure as routine leader of daily chores.

According to Weber, a charismatic/patriarchal leader arises because he holds a specific gift of the body and spirit, which was believed also to be supernatural or given to him by God. Within this society the image of the world is based on concrete magic, and religious dogma centered on mystical experiences.

On the other hand, Formal Rationality is antagonistic to substantive or traditional rationality because formal rationality is a "modern state" with "advanced institutions" based on a "money economy" which has become synonymous with occidental development.

Formal Rationality embraces a bureaucratic authority both in the private economy and the political sectors, because of the objective discharge of business in a "precise, unambiguous, continuous manner, with as much speed as possible" creating order. This form of rationality for Weber, is the quintessence of legality.

Within Formal Rationality a process occurs which changes humanity's thinking and attitudes concerning the image of the world. Weber labels this historic-religious transformation disenchantment. Weber saw this process as a general trend in Western Civilization as being an iron cage, because in his view, there is no way out, no way of returning to a time in which the world would be viewed through magical or religious imagery. Moreover this transformation was blocked everywhere, except for Western Civilization, as a consequence of the survival of traditional, quasi-magical elements within the economic ethics of other world religions.

Disenchantment can be seen as the degree to which the magical elements of thought are displaced by that of the rational, intellectual and an objective articulation of the image of the world. The masteries of nature and the "mystic experience" to a large extent, progress to an intellectual, impersonal, calculating image based in rules and scientific laws. Hence, this attitude seeks the "meaning of inner-worldly occurrences" through empirical and scientific thought. Thus, it is pushing back religion and the supernatural into the realm of the irrational, reducing human relations to an objective and impersonal stance.

According to Weber, early on in the development of religious doctrines there is an important split into two forms which creates different forms of human identity, and thus different worldviews. He illustrates this point by a comparison of Asian and Western development. By contrast, Asian religious doctrine leads its followers in pursuit of world adjustment and world flight. This produces a human identity that is passive to the masteries of nature and world occurrences. On the other hand, Western salvation doctrine leads its followers in pursuit of world domination/ mastery and "inner worldliness," because God gives the people the responsibility of free choice. This free choice leads to science and technology because it gives the individual the power of choice and reason. This produces a human identity which is aggressive toward world events and the masteries of nature; thus, abandoning of the magical/mystical attitude for a systematic worldview of domination.

The Principle of Rationality has two outcomes: the first, is that empirical knowledge and technological know-how led to control of the world by Western Civilization through calculation. The second, is the intellectual elaboration of the world by taking a consistent and unified stance toward it, which becomes associated with the dominant culture in which people are treated impersonally and objectively becoming a way of life.

Finally, another area we do not usually associate with religious doctrine is capitalism. Weber in his work the *Protestant Work Ethic and the Spirit of Capitalism* states that the protestant sect of Calvinism changed Western Civilization by suggesting that hard work and the accumulation of wealth was in fact God's work. The more wealth one accumulates the more "good work" for God can be performed leading to eternal life at the right hand of God.

John Calvin and his followers believed in predestination, but no one knows their faith. In an effort to fulfil their destiny, this group found it necessary to work hard, accumulate wealth, invest this wealth to gain more wealth, and so on, leading to the basis of American Capitalism; for in Europe this Christian sect was persecuted and found themselves leaving Europe and settling in what is now the United States of America, bringing with them their religious beliefs, becoming the majority in the United States. Men like Benjamin Franklin and Abraham Lincoln who influenced the growth and philosophy of the United States were all Calvinist. Today, the idea of capitalism is part and parcel of the American identity. As Americans we are always thinking in terms of capitalism, even if we are not working on Wall Street. Education is viewed by many Americans as an investment in their and/or their children's future. Indeed, our society places a large proportion of wealth in the investment of education. The axiom is invest in education today for a better job or working conditions in the future; in fact society sees education as making for a better citizen and individual.

So to sum up, Weber saw religion as the most important aspect of human social life for it creates human identity which can change the course of history.

The Disenchantment of Modern Life

Max Weber

In this excerpt from a speech, Science as a Vocation, delivered at Munich University in 1918, Weber claims that the rise of science has changed our way of thinking about the world. Where, in the past, humans confronted a world of mystical forces beyond our comprehension, now we assume that all things yield to human comprehension. Thus, Weber concludes, the world has become disenchanted. Notice, however, that something is lost in the process for, unlike the churches of the past, science can provide no answer to questions of ultimate meaning in life.

Scientific progress is a fraction, the most important fraction, of the process of intellectualization which we have been undergoing for thousands of years and which nowadays is usually judged in such an extremely negative way. Let us first clarify what this intellectualist rationalization, created by science and by scientifically oriented technology, means practically.

Does it mean that we, today, for instance, everyone sitting in this hall, have a greater knowledge of the conditions of life under which we exist than has an American Indian or a Hottentot? Hardly. Unless he is a physicist, one who rides on the streetcar has no idea how the car happened to get into motion. And he does not need to know. He is satisfied that he may "count" on the behavior of the streetcar, and he orients his conduct according to this expectation; but he knows nothing about what it takes to produce such a car so that it can move. The savage knows incomparably more about his tools. When we spend money today I bet that even if there are colleagues of political economy here in the hall, almost every one of them will hold a different answer in readiness to the question: How does it happen that one can buy something for money—sometimes more and sometimes less? The savage knows what he does in order to get his daily food and which institutions serve him in this pursuit. The increasing intellectualization and rationalization do *not*, therefore, indicate an increased and general knowledge of the conditions under which one lives.

It means something else, namely, the knowledge or belief that if one but wished one *could* learn it at any time. Hence, it means that principally there are no mysterious incalculable forces that come into play, but rather that one can, in principle, master all things by calculation. This means that the world is disenchanted. One need no longer have recourse to magical means in order to master or implore the spirits, as did the savage, for whom such mysterious powers existed. Technical means and calculations perform the service. This above all is what intellectualization means. . . .

Science today is a "vocation" organized in special disciplines in the service of self-clarification and knowledge of interrelated facts. It is not the gift of grace of seers and prophets dispensing sacred values and revelations, nor does it partake of the contemplation of sages and philosophers about the meaning of the universe. This, to be sure, is the inescapable condition of our historical situation. We cannot evade it so long as we remain true to ourselves. And if Tolstoi's question recurs to you: As science does not, who is to answer the question: "What shall we do, and, how shall we arrange our lives?" or, in the words used here tonight: "Which of the warring gods should we serve? Or should we serve perhaps an entirely different god, and who is he?" then one can say that only a prophet or a savior can give the answers. . . .

To the person who cannot bear the fate of the times like a man, one must say: May he rather return silently, without the usual publicity build-up of renegades, but simply and plainly. The arms of the old churches are opened widely and compassionately for him. After all, they do not make it hard for him. One way or another he has to bring his "intel-lectual sacrifice"—that is inevitable. If he can really do it, we shall not rebuke him. For such an intellectual sacrifice in favor of an unconditional religious devotion is ethically quite a different matter than the evasion of the plain duty of intellectual integrity, which sets in if one lacks the courage to clarify one's own ultimate standpoint and rather facilitates this duty by feeble relative judgments. In my eyes, such religious return stands higher than the academic prophecy, which does not clearly realize that in the lecture-rooms of the university no other virtue holds but plain intellectual integrity: Integrity, however, compels us to state that for the many who today tarry for new prophets and saviors, the situation is the same as resounds in the beautiful Edomite watchman's song of the period of exile that has been included among Isaiah's oracles:

> *He calleth to me out of Seir, Watchman, what of the night? The watchman said, The morning cometh, and also the night: if ye will enquire, enquire ye: return, come.*

The people to whom this was said has enquired and tarried for more than two millennia, and we are shaken when we realize its fate. From this we want to draw the lesson that nothing is gained by yearning and tarrying alone, and we shall act differently. We shall set to work and meet the "demands of the day," in human relations as well as in our vocation. This, however, is plain and simple, if each finds and obeys the demon who holds the fibers of his very life.

The Protestant Ethic and the Spirit of Capitalism

— Max Weber

In perhaps his most well-known treatise, Max Weber argues that a major factor in the development of the capitalist economic system was the distinctive world view of early, ascetic Protestantism, especially Calvinism and Puritanism. In this excerpt from his classic analysis, Weber explains that religious ideas about work and materials initially fostered capitalism s growth; ultimately, he concludes, capitalism was able to stand on its own without religious supports.

A product of modern European civilization, studying any problem of universal history, is bound to ask himself to what combination of circumstances the fact should be attributed that in Western civilization, and in Western civilization only, cultural phenomena have appeared which (as we like to think) lie in a line of development having *universal* significance and value. . . . All over the world there have been merchants, wholesale and retail, local and engaged in foreign trade. . . .

But in modern times the Occident has developed, in addition to this, a very different form of capitalism which has appeared nowhere else: the rational capitalistic organization of (formally) free labour. Only suggestions of it are found elsewhere. Even the organization of unfree labour reached a considerable degree of rationality only on plantations and to a very limited extent in the *Ergasteria* of antiquity. In the manors, manorial workshops, and domestic industries on estates with serf labour it was probably somewhat less developed. Even real domestic industries with free labour have definitely been proved to have existed in only a few isolated cases outside the Occident. . . .

Rational industrial organization, attuned to a regular market, and neither to political nor irrationally speculative opportunities for profit, is not, however, the only peculiarity of Western capitalism. The modern rational organization of the capitalistic enterprise would not have been possible without two other important factors in its development: the separation of business from the household, which completely dominates modern economic life, and closely connected with it, rational bookkeeping . . . .

Hence in a universal history of culture the central problem for us is not, in the last analysis, even from a purely economic viewpoint, the development of capitalistic activity as such, differing in different cultures only in form: the adventurer type, or capitalism in trade, war, politics, or administration as sources of gain. It is rather the origin of this sober bourgeois capitalism with its rational organization of free labour. Or in terms of cultural history, the problem is that of the origin of the Western bourgeois class and of its peculiarities, a problem which is certainly closely connected with that of the origin of the capitalistic organization of labour, but is not quite the same thing. For the bourgeois as a class existed prior to the development of the peculiar modern form of capitalism, though, it is true, only in the Western Hemisphere.

Now the peculiar modern Western form of capitalism has been, at first sight, strongly influenced by the development of technical possibilities. Its rationality is today essentially dependent on the calculability of the most important technical factors. But this means fundamentally that it is dependent on the peculiarities of modern science, especially the natural sciences based on mathematics and exact and rational experiment. On the other hand, the development of these sciences and of the technique resting upon them now receives important stimulation from these capitalistic interests in its practical economic application. It is true that the origin of Western science cannot be attributed to such interests. Calculation, even with decimals, and algebra have been carried on in India, where the decimal system was invented. But it was only made use of by developing capitalism in the West, while in India it led to no modern arithmetic or bookkeeping. Neither was the origin of mathematics and mechanics determined by capitalistic interests. But the *technical* utilization of scientific knowledge, so important for the living conditions of the mass of people, was certainly encouraged by economic considerations, which were extremely favourable to it in the Occident. But this encouragement was derived from the peculiarities of the social structure of the Occident. We must hence ask, from *what* parts of that structure was it derived, since not all of them have been of equal importance?

Among those of undoubted importance are the rational structures of law and of administration. For modern rational capitalism has need, not only of the technical means of production, but of a calculable legal system and of administration in terms of formal rules. Without it adventurous and speculative trading capitalism and all sorts of politically determined capitalisms are possible, but no rational enterprise under individual initiative, with fixed capital and certainty of calculations. Such a legal system and such administration have been available for economic activity in a comparative state of legal and formalistic perfection only in the Occident. We must hence inquire where that law came from. Among other circumstances, capitalistic interests have in turn undoubtedly also helped, but by no means alone nor even principally, to prepare the way for the predominance in law and administration of a class of jurists specially trained in rational law. But these interests did not themselves create that law. Quite different forces were at work in this development. And why did not the capitalistic interests do the same in China or India? Why did not the scientific, the artistic, the political, or the economic development there enter upon that path of rationalization which is peculiar to the Occident?

For in all the above cases it is a question of the specific and peculiar rationalism of Western culture. . . . It is hence our first concern to work out and to explain genetically the special peculiarity of Occidental rationalism, and within this field that of the modern Occidental form. Every such attempt at explanation must, recognizing the fundamental importance of the economic factor, above all take account of the economic conditions. But at the same time the opposite correlation must not be left out of consideration. For though the development of economic rationalism is partly dependent on rational technique and law, it is at the same time determined by the ability and disposition of men to adopt certain types of practical rational conduct. When these types have been obstructed by spiritual obstacles, the development of rational economic conduct has also met serious inner resistance. The magical and religious forces, and the ethical ideas of duty based upon them, have in the past always been among the most important formative influences on conduct. In the studies collected here we shall be concerned with these forces.

Two older essays have been placed at the beginning which attempt, at one important point, to approach the side of the problem which is generally most difficult to grasp: the influence of certain religious ideas on the development of an economic spirit, or the *ethos* of an economic system. In this case we are dealing with the connection of the spirit of modern economic life with the rational ethics of ascetic Protestantism. Thus we treat here only one side of the causal chain. . . .

. . . [T]hat side of English Puritanism which was derived from Calvinism gives the most consistent religious basis for the idea of the calling. . . . For the saints' everlasting rest is in the next world; on earth man must, to be certain of his state of grace, "do the works of him who sent him, as long as it is yet day." Not leisure and enjoyment, but only activity serves to increase the glory of God according to the definite manifestations of His will.

Waste of time is thus the first and in principle the deadliest of sins. The span of human life is infinitely short and precious to make sure of one's own election. Loss of time through sociability, idle talk, luxury, even more sleep than is necessary for health, six to at most eight hours, is worthy of absolute moral condemnation. It does not yet hold, with Franklin, that time is money, but the proposition is true in a certain spiritual sense. It is infinitely valuable because every hour lost is lost to labour for the glory of God. Thus inac-

tive contemplation is also valueless, or even directly reprehensible if it is at the expense of one's daily work. . . .

[T]he same prescription is given for all sexual temptation as is used against religious doubts and a sense of moral unworthiness: "Work hard in your calling." But the most important thing was that even beyond that labour came to be considered in itself the end of life, ordained as such by God. St. Paul's "He who will not work shall not eat" holds unconditionally for everyone. Unwillingness to work is symptomatic of the lack of grace.

Here the difference from the mediæval viewpoint becomes quite evident. Thomas Aquinas also gave an interpretation of that statement of St. Paul. But for him labour is only necessary *naturali ratione* for the maintenance of individual and community. Where this end is achieved, the precept ceases to have any meaning. Moreover, it holds only for the race, not for every individual. It does not apply to anyone who can live without labour on his possessions, and of course contemplation, as a spiritual form of action in the Kingdom of God, takes precedence over the commandment in its literal sense. Moreover, for the popular theology of the time, the highest form of monastic productivity lay in the increase of the *Thesaurus ecclesli* through prayer and chant.

. . . For everyone without exception God's Providence has prepared a calling, which he should profess and in which he should labour. And this calling is not, as it was for the Lutheran, a fate to which he must submit and which he must make the best of, but God's commandment to the individual to work for the divine glory. This seemingly subtle difference had far-reaching psychological consequences, and became connected with a further development of the providential interpretation of the economic order which had begun in scholasticism.

It is true that the usefulness of a calling, and thus its favour in the sight of God, is measured primarily in moral terms, and thus in terms of the importance of the goods produced in it for the community. But a further, and, above all, in practice the most important, criterion is found in private profitableness. For if that God, whose hand the Puritan sees in all the occurrences of life, shows one of His elect a chance of profit, he must do it with a purpose. Hence the faithful Christian must follow the call by taking advantage of the opportunity. "If God show you a way in which you may lawfully get more than in another way (without wrong to your soul or to any other), if you refuse this, and choose the less gainful way, you cross one of the ends of your calling, and you refuse to be God's steward, and to accept His gifts and use them for Him when He requireth it: you may labour to be rich for God, though not for the flesh and sin." . . .

The superior indulgence of the *seigneur* and the parvenu ostentation of the *nouveau riche* are equally detestable to asceticism. But, on the other hand, it has the highest ethical appreciation of the sober, middle-class, self-made man. "God blesseth His trade" is a stock remark about those good men who had successfully followed the divine hints. The whole power of the God of the Old Testament, who rewards His people for their obedience in this life, necessarily exercised a similar influence on the Puritan who . . . compared his own state of grace with that of the heroes of the Bible. . . .

Although we cannot here enter upon a discussion of the influence of Puritanism in all . . . directions, we should call attention to the fact that the toleration of pleasure in cultural goods, which contributed to purely aesthetic or athletic enjoyment, certainly always ran up against one characteristic limitation: They must not cost anything. Man is only a trustee of the goods which have come to him through God's grace. He must, like the servant in the parable, give an account of every penny entrusted to him, and it is at least hazardous to spend any of it for a purpose which does not serve the glory of God but only one's own enjoyment. What person, who keeps his eyes open, has not met representatives of this viewpoint even in the present? The idea of a man's duty to his possessions, to which he subordinates himself as an obedient steward, or even as an acquisitive machine, bears with chilling weight on his life. The greater the possessions the heavier, if the ascetic attitude toward life stands the test, the feeling of responsibility for them, for holding them undiminished for the glory of God and increasing them by restless effort. The origin of this type of life also extends in certain roots, like so many aspects of the spirit of capitalism, back into the Middle Ages. But it was in the ethic of ascetic Protestantism that it first found a consistent ethical foundation. Its significance for the development of capitalism is obvious.

This worldly Protestant asceticism, as we may recapitulate up to this point, acted powerfully against the spontaneous enjoyment of possessions; it restricted consumption, especially of luxuries. On the other hand, it had the psychological effect of freeing the acquisition of goods from the inhibitions of traditionalistic ethics. It broke the bonds of the impulse of acquisition in that it not only legalized it, but (in the sense discussed) looked upon it as directly willed by God. . . .

As far as the influence of the Puritan outlook extended, under all circumstances—and this is, of course, much more important than the mere encouragement of capital accumulation—it favoured the development of a rational bourgeois economic life; it was the most important, and above all the only consistent influence in the development of that life. It stood at the cradle of the modern economic man.

To be sure, these Puritanical ideals tended to give way under excessive pressure from the temptations of wealth, as the Puritans themselves knew very well. With great regularity we find the most genuine adherents of Puritanism among the classes which were rising from a lowly status, the small bourgeois and farmers while the *beati possidentes,* even among Quakers, are often found tending to repudiate the old ideals. It was the same fate which again and again befell the predecessor of this worldly asceticism, the monastic asceticism of the Middle Ages. In the latter case when rational economic activity had worked out its full effects by strict regulation of conduct and limitation of consumption, the wealth accumulated either succumbed directly to the nobility, as in the time before the Reformation, or monastic discipline threatened to break down, and one of the numerous reformations became necessary.

In fact the whole history of monasticism is in a certain sense the history of a continual struggle with the problem of the secularizing influence of wealth. The same is true on a grand scale of the worldly asceticism of Puritanism. The great revival of Methodism, which preceded the expansion of English industry toward the end of the eighteenth century, may well be compared with such a monastic reform. We may hence quote here a passage from John Wesley himself which might well serve as a motto for everything which has been said above. For it shows that the leaders of these ascetic movements understood the seemingly paradoxical relationships which we have here analysed perfectly well, and in the same sense that we have given them. He wrote:

I fear, wherever riches have increased, the essence of religion has decreased in the same proportion. Therefore I do not see how it is possible, in the nature of things, for any revival of true religion to continue long. For religion must necessarily produce both industry and frugality, and these cannot but produce riches. But as riches increase, so will pride, anger, and love of the world in all its branches. How then is it possible that Methodism, that is, a religion of the heart, though it flourishes now as a green bay tree, should continue in this state? For the Methodists in every place grow diligent and frugal; consequently they increase in goods. Hence they proportionately increase in pride, in anger, in the desire of the flesh, the desire of the eyes, and the pride of life. So, although the form of religion remains, the spirit is swiftly vanishing away. Is there no way to prevent this this continual decay of pure religion? We ought not to prevent people from being diligent and frugal; we must exhort all Christians to gain all they can, and to save all they can, that is, in effect, to grow rich.

As Wesley here says, the full economic effect of those great religious movements, whose significance for economic development lay above all in their ascetic educative influence, generally came only after the peak of the purely religious enthusiasm was past. Then the intensity of the search for the Kingdom of God commenced gradually to pass over into sober economic virtue; the religious roots died out slowly, giving way to utilitarian worldliness. Then, as Dowden puts it, as in *Robinson Crusoe,* the isolated economic man who carries on missionary activities on the side takes the place of the lonely spiritual search for the Kingdom of Heaven of Bunyan's pilgrim, hurrying through the marketplace of Vanity. . . .

A specifically bourgeois economic ethic had grown up. With the consciousness of standing in the fullness of God's grace and being visibly blessed by Him, the bourgeois business man, as long as he remained within the bounds of formal correctness, as long as his moral conduct was spotless and the use to which he put his wealth was not objectionable, could follow his pecuniary interests as he would and feel that he was fulfilling a duty in doing so. The power of religious asceticism provided him in addition with sober, conscientious, and unusually industrious workmen, who clung to their work as to a life purpose willed by God.

Finally, it gave him the comforting assurance that the unequal distribution of the goods of this world was a special dispensation of Divine Providence, which in these differences, as in particular grace, pursued secret ends unknown to men. . . .

One of the fundamental elements of the spirit of modern capitalism, and not only of that but of all modern culture: Rational conduct on the basis of the idea of the calling, was born—that is what this discussion has sought to demonstrate—from the spirit of Christian asceticism. One has only to reread the passage from Franklin, quoted at the beginning of this essay, in order to see that the essential elements of the attitude which was there called the spirit of capitalism are the same as what we have just shown to be the content of the Puritan worldly asceticism, only without the religious basis, which by Franklin's time had died away. . . .

Since asceticism undertook to remodel the world and to work out its ideals in the world, material goods have gained an increasing and finally an inexorable power over the lives of men as at no previous period in history. Today the spirit of religious asceticism—whether finally, who knows?—has escaped from the cage. But victorious capitalism, since it rests on mechanical foundations, needs its support no longer. The rosy blush of its laughing heir, the Enlightenment, seems also to be irretrievably fading, and the idea of duty in one's calling prowls about in our lives like the ghost of dead religious beliefs. Where the fulfilment of the calling cannot directly be related to the highest spiritual and cultural values, or when, on the other hand, it need not be felt simply as economic compulsion, the individual generally abandons the attempt to justify it at all. In the field of its highest development, in the United States, the pursuit of wealth, stripped of its religious and ethical meaning, tends to become associated with purely mundane passions, which often actually give it the character of sport.

No one knows who will live in this cage in the future, or whether at the end of this tremendous development entirely new prophets will arise, or there will be a great rebirth of old ideas and ideals, or, if neither, mechanized petrification, embellished with a sort of convulsive self-importance. For of the last stage of this cultural development, it might well be truly said: "Specialists without spirit, sensualists without heart; this nullity imagines that it has attained a level of civilization never before achieved."

But this brings us to the world of judgments of value and of faith, with which this purely historical discussion need not be burdened. . . .

Here we have only attempted to trace the fact and the direction of its influence to their motives in one, though a very important point. But it would also further be necessary to investigate how Protestant Asceticism was in turn influenced in its development and its character by the totality of social conditions, especially economic. The modern man is in general, even with the best will, unable to give religious ideas a significance for culture and national character which they deserve. But it is, of course, not my aim to substitute for a one-sided materialistic an equally one-sided spiritualistic causal interpretation of culture and of history. Each is equally possible, but each, if it does not serve as the preparation, but as the conclusion of an investigation, accomplishes equally little in the interest of historical truth.

The Characteristics of Bureaucracy

Max Weber

According to Max Weber, human societies have historically been oriented by tradition of one kind or another. Modernity, in contrast, is marked by a different form of human consciousness: a rational world view. For Weber, there is no clearer expression of modern rationality than bureaucracy. In this selection, Weber identifies the characteristics of this organizational form.

Modern officialdom functions in the following specific manner:

I. There is the principle of fixed and official jurisdictional areas, which are generally ordered by rules, that is, by laws or administrative regulations. (1) The regular activities required for the purposes of the bureaucratically governed structure are distributed in a fixed way as official duties. (2) The authority to give the commands required for the discharge of these duties is distributed in a stable way and is strictly delimited by rules concerning the coercive means, physical, sacerdotal, or otherwise, which may be placed at the disposal of officials. (3) Methodical provision is made for the regular and continuous fulfillment of these duties and for the execution of the corresponding rights; only persons who have the generally regulated qualifications to serve are employed.

In public and lawful government these three elements constitute "bureaucratic authority." In private economic domination, they constitute bureaucratic "management." Bureaucracy, thus understood, is fully developed in political and ecclesiastical communities only in the modern state, and, in the private economy, only in the most advanced institutions of capitalism. Permanent and public office authority, with fixed jurisdiction, is not the historical rule but rather the exception. This is so even in large political structures such as those of the ancient Orient, the Germanic, and Mongolian empires of conquest, or of many feudal structures of state. In all these cases, the ruler executes the most important measures through personal trustees, table-companions, or court-servants. Their commissions and authority are not precisely delimited and are temporarily called into being for each case.

II. The principles of office hierarchy and of levels of graded authority mean a firmly ordered system of super- and subordination in which there is a supervision of the lower offices by the higher ones. Such a system offers the governed the possibility of appealing the decision of a lower office to its higher authority, in a definitely regulated manner. With the full development of the bureaucratic type, the office hierarchy is monocratically organized. The principle of hierarchical office authority is found in all bureaucratic structures: in state and ecclesiastical structures as well as in large party organizations and private enterprises. It does not matter for the character of bureaucracy whether its authority is called "private" or "public."

When the principle of jurisdictional "competency" is fully carried through, hierarchical subordination—at least in public office—does not mean that the "higher" authority is simply authorized to take over the business of the "lower." Indeed, the opposite is the rule. Once established and having fulfilled its task, an office tends to continue in existence and be held by another incumbent.

III. The management of the modern office is based upon written documents ("the files"), which are preserved in their original or draft form. There is, therefore, a staff of subaltern officials and scribes of all sorts. The body of officials actively engaged in a "public" office, along with the respective apparatus of material implements and the files, make up a "bureau." In private enterprise, "the bureau" is often called "the office."

In principle, the modern organization of the civil service separates the bureau from the private domicile of the official, and, in general, bureaucracy segregates official activity as something distinct from the sphere of private life. Public monies and equipment are divorced from the private property of the official. . . . In principle, the executive office is separated from the household, business from private correspondence, and business assets from private fortunes. The more consistently the modern type of business management has been carried through, the more are these separations the case. The beginnings of this process are to be found as early as the Middle Ages.

It is the peculiarity of the modern entrepreneur that he conducts himself as the "first official" of his enterprise, in the very same way in which the ruler of a specifically modern bureaucratic state spoke of himself as "the first servant" of the state. The idea that the bureau activities of the state are intrinsically different in character from the management of private economic offices is a continental European notion and, by the way of contrast, is totally foreign to the American way.

IV. Office management, at least all specialized office management—and such management is distinctly modern—usually presupposes a thorough and expert training. This increasingly holds for the modern executive and employee of private enterprises, in the same manner as it holds for the state official.

V. When the office is fully developed, official activity demands the full working capacity of the official, irrespective of the fact that his obligatory time in the bureau may be firmly delimited. In the normal case, this is only the product of a long development, in the public as well as in the private office. Formerly, in all cases, the normal state of affairs was reversed: Official business was discharged as a secondary activity.

VI. The management of the office follows general rules, which are more or less stable, more or less exhaustive, and which can be learned. Knowledge of these rules represents a special technical learning which the officials possess. It involves jurisprudence, or administrative or business management.

The reduction of modern office management to rules is deeply embedded in its very nature. The theory of modern public administration, for instance, assumes that the authority to order certain matters by decree—which has been legally granted to public authorities—does not entitle the bureau to regulate the matter by commands given for each case, but only to regulate the matter abstractly. This stands in extreme contrast to the regulation of all relationships through individual privileges and bestowals of favor, which is absolutely dominant in patrimonialism, at least insofar as such relationships are not fixed by sacred tradition.

All this results in the following for the internal and external position of the official.

I. Office holding is a "vocation." This is shown, first, in the requirement of a firmly prescribed course of training, which demands the entire capacity for work for a long period of time, and in the generally prescribed and special examinations which are prerequisites of employment. Furthermore, the position of the official is in the nature of a duty. This determines the internal structure of his relations, in the following manner: Legally and actually, office holding is not considered a source to be exploited for rents or emoluments, as was normally the case during the Middle Ages and frequently up to the threshold of recent times. . . . Entrances into an office, including one in the private economy, is considered an acceptance of a specific obligation of faithful management in return for a secure existence. It is decisive for the specific nature of modern loyalty to an office that, in the pure type, it does not establish a relationship to a *person*, like the vassal's or disciple's faith in feudal or in patrimonial relations and authority. Modern loyalty is devoted to impersonal and functional purposes. . . .

II. The personal position of the official is patterned in the following way:

(1) Whether he is in a private office or a public bureau, the modern official always strives and usually enjoys a distinct *social esteem* as compared with the governed. His social position is guaranteed by the prescriptive rules of rank order and, for the political official, by special definitions of the criminal code against "insults of officials" and "contempt" of state and church authorities.

The actual social position of the official is normally highest where, as in old civilized countries, the following conditions prevail: a strong demand for administration by trained experts; a strong and stable social differentiation, where the official predominantly derives from socially and economically privileged strata because of the social distribution of power; or where the costliness of the required training and status conventions are binding upon him. The possession of educational certificates—to be discussed elsewhere—are usually linked with qualification for office. Naturally, such certificates or patents enhance the "status element" in the social position of the official. . . .

Usually the social esteem of the officials as such is especially low where the demand for expert administration and the dominance of status conventions are weak. This is especially the case in the United States; it is often the case in new settlements by virtue of their wide fields for profit-taking and the great instability of their social stratification.

(2) The pure type of bureaucratic official is *appointed* by a superior authority. An official elected by the governed is not a purely bureaucratic figure. Of course, the formal existence of an election does not by itself mean that no appointment hides behind the election—in the state, especially, appointment by party chiefs. Whether or not this is the case does not depend upon legal statutes but upon the way in which the party mechanism functions. Once firmly organized, the parties can turn a formally free election into the mere acclamation of a candidate designated by the party chief. As a rule, however, a formally free election is turned into a fight, conducted according to definite rules, for votes in favor of one of two designated candidates. . . .

(3) Normally, the position of the official is held for life, at least in public bureaucracies; and this is increasingly the case for all similar structures. As a factual rule, *tenure for life* is presupposed, even where the giving of notice or periodic reappointment occurs. In contrast to the worker in a private enterprise, the official normally holds tenure. Legal or actual

life-tenure, however, is not recognized as the official's right to the possession of office, as was the case with many structures of authority in the past. Where legal guarantees against arbitrary dismissal of transfer are developed, they merely serve to guarantee a strictly objective discharge of specific office duties free from all personal considerations. . . .

(4) The official receives the regular *pecuniary* compensation of a normally fixed *salary* and the old age security provided by a pension. The salary is not measured like a wage in terms of work done, but according to "status," that is, according to the kind of function (the "rank") and, in addition, possibly, according to the length of service. The relatively great security of the official's income, as well as the rewards of social esteem, make the office a sought-after position. . . .

(5) The official is set for a *"career"* within the hierarchical order of the public service. He moves from the lower, less important, and lower paid to the higher positions. The average official naturally desires a mechanical fixing of the conditions of promotion: if not of the offices, at least of the salary levels. He wants these conditions fixed in terms of "seniority," or possibly according to grades achieved in a developed system of expert examinations. . . .

Selected Readings

Max Weber by H.S. Miller.

Basic Concepts in Sociology by Max Weber.

The Theory of Social and Economic Organization by Max Weber.

The Rational and Social Foundations of Music by Max Weber.

Max Weber's Political Sociology: A Pessimistic Vision of a Rationalized World by Ronald M. Classman, Vat Murmur.

Max Weber and German Politics: A Study in Political Sociology by J. P. Mayer. Aspects of the Rise of Economic Individualism: A Criticism of Max Weber and His School by H.M. Robertson.

Religion and Economic Action: A Critique of Max Weber by Kurt Samuelsson, E. Geoffrey French, D.C. Coleman.

The Classical Roots of Ethnomethodology: Durkheim, Weber, and Garfinkel by Richard A. Hilbert.

Legitimation of Social Rights and the Western Welfare State: A Weberian Perspective by Kathi V. Friedman.

Rationalization and Natural Law: Max Weber's and Ernst Troeltsch's Interpretation of the Medieval Doctrine of Natural Law, in The Review of Metaphysics by Ludger Honnefelder.

The Sociology of Economic Life by Mark Granovetter, Richard Swedberg.

Max Weber on the ethical irrationality of political leadership, in Sociology by Nicholas Gane.

The Weber Thesis Reexamined, in Church history by Winthrop S. Hudson.

Critical-Thinking Questions

1. What is the Principle of Rationality?

2. How did science and technology arise?

3. What is the spirit of capitalism?

CHAPTER III

Karl Marx
(1818–1883)

Karl Marx, along with Friedrich Engels (1820–1895), developed the concept of communism. Although many of these ideas are bankrupt today, the concept of Alienated humanity is alive and well in American sociology and has become the cornerstone of Conflict Theory. Conflict Theory has been used by all of the so-called "movements" in the United States of America to suggest that society reduces humans in many cases to objects, and there must be a redress. The Labor movement, the Civil Rights movement, the women's movement, and the gay rights movement have all employed this form of social redress.

Marx saw the modern capitalist society as an historical process of oppression and alienation. Marx believed that all of human history is the collective creative activity of humanity, the existence of living individuals, their physical organization, and their relationship to nature and the need to mold nature. Moreover, Marx's philosophy of "Historical Materialism" incorporates in a capsule the idea that history is not merely an accumulation of accidents or deeds of great men as many historians argue, but the development of the human race through labor and productive forces.

Marx develops an important concept concerning modern society, which he viewed as also being a historical process, which he labels Alienation or Estrangement of Labor. Alienation, for Marx, means that humanity does not experience itself as the acting agent in its attempt to own the objects of their labor. Essentially objects, even though they may be objects of the workers own creation, stand above and against them because they belong to another. Hence, alienation is experiencing the world and oneself passively, as the subject/individual separated from the object he/she has created based upon the perversion of labor into a meaningless crippling productive force.

Marx also argued that labor under capitalism appears only as a means of sustaining life; it is no longer a creative activity by which humanity develops itself. For Marx this is a contradiction of the nature of humanity because the economic condition of humanity has become more powerful than the individual, and the task of human nature is to control economic conditions.

As was mentioned earlier, the worker is alienated from the object of his/her creation because the product of his labor belongs to another. According to Marx, the worker creates this relationship of the other person or capitalist who does not work and is outside the work process, and creates the relationship of the worker to the work. Moreover, the worker's product is not a reflection of himself/herself, but something removed from him/her and which stands against the worker as an alienated force. Marx argued that when labor is creative, this energy is returned to the worker not only as a product but as the humanized form created from raw substances provided by nature. Such creations act as confirmation of his/her individuality and latent potential.

However, as a result of alienated labor and its relationships, the product of labor is labor transformed into an object solely owned by the capitalist which stands above the worker and is utilized in the same way as any other object of capital. This historical transformation alienates the worker from himself/herself, from the product of his/her own making and from other persons.

Furthermore, Marx argues that a person is not only alienated from him/herself, but from the essence of humanity or their species-being. The nature of the species-being has emerged from nature over the darkness of time, as have animals. However, humanity transforms, develops and changes their world, and hence is the past, present and future;

whereas, the species-nature of animals is rooted in the internal repetition of activities, accepting what nature has to offer. However, alienated labor also perverts this human character or species-being into a means of existence, rather than a free, conscious creative activity. He suggests that as a result of alienated labor, humanity feels free only to act in its most animal functions, because alienated labor now appears as a means of satisfying needs in order to maintain physical existence. Rather than a free creative activity, this existence decreases humanities advantage over animals because humanities is reduced to an animal by working at maintaining its physical needs and not its free creative needs. Marx argues that productive life is species life because it is humanity's conscious transformation of the outside world into his self-identity, which resides in the whole free conscious activity character of the species.

Private property for Marx is the all summarized expression of alienated labor because it includes the relation of the worker transformed into a commodity. For Marx alienation is based in private property, as a result of the historical social division of labor of the haves and have-nots, which destroys unity and produces inequalities. These inequalities over time become interlinked with the history of the division of labor within "manufacturing" producing the same effect, that of the haves and have-nots.

Additionally, for the capitalist labor is capital. The capitalist sees capital as a value, which must be constantly increased by surplus. This mind-set Marx sees as rooted in the private appropriation of surplus value.

The theory of surplus value assumes that the worker in the capitalist system only appears to be selling his/her labor for a fair exchange of wages. However, the capitalist is not forced to buy labor-power on a continuous basis, but only when it is profitable to do so. On the other hand, the worker is under the "economic compulsion" to sell labor, because he/she doesn't have access to large scale resources, reserves of money or the means of production which would enable him/her to survive long periods of time. This lack of resources places him/her in a subordinate role.

In this subordinate role the workers are forced to sell their labor in the market place for consumption. The worker sells his/her labor power or the capacity to work for a length of time as a commodity to the capitalist, the workers labor power is owned by the capitalist as any other commodity might be and thus is assigned a specific value. A commodity for Marx must first satisfy a need; it must be useful or have a use-value. Labor power for the capitalist labor has a double capacity. One capacity is to transfer into the product the value of the raw materials and machines into a new value or exchange-value. This new value develops in the process of production in which the worker produces value over and above the value of their own labor power, their wages and the quantity of consumer goods necessary to keep the worker and his children in condition to continue to work at a given level of intensity. Marx labels this surplus value. Surplus value is the total value of the products over the sum of values of its parts (raw material and machines), and is obtained solely from human labor power on the product, which expends more labor time than necessary for the maintenance of the worker's life.

Moreover, because commodities are so vastly different, nothing within the commodity is comparable except for consumption. However, the "exchange-value" of commodities are measured based on a common value, which is the human labor spent on the product.

Additionally, during the historical transformation of creative labor to alienated labor, money is also transformed into capital. The more capital the more money for the capitalist not only to add to his/her purchasing power of consumer goods, but also adds more machines, more raw materials and most importantly more labor power. According to Marx the more labor power, the more products can be produced, satisfying the capitalist quest for the "primitive accumulation" of wealth.

In summary labor under capitalism is seen by Marx as an historical development which is the negation of its own principle that of the creative activity through which humanity makes itself. Instead alienated labor converts humanity into a mechanized partial function of the production process, which dominates and confronts the individual as an alien force.

Marx suggests that as the value of things increases there is a direct decrease in the value of humanity. The "end-product" is always more valuable than the sum of its parts. Hence, since human labor is one of these parts, humanity itself devaluates.

Alienated Labor

The human species, argues Karl Marx, is social by nature and expresses that social nature in the act of production. But within the capitalist economic system, Marx claims, the process of production does not affirm human nature but denies it. The result is what he terms "alienated labor."

. . .[We] have shown that the worker sinks to the level of a commodity, and to a most miserable commodity; that the misery of the worker increases with the power and volume of his production; that the necessary result of competition is the accumulation of capital in a few hands, and thus a restoration of monopoly in a more terrible form; and finally that the distinction between capitalist and landlord, and between agricultural laborer and industrial worker, must disappear, and the whole of society divide into the two classes of property *owners* and *propertyless* workers. . . .

Thus we have now to grasp the real connexion between this whole system of alienation—private property, acquisitiveness, the separation of labor, capital and land, exchange and competition, value and the devaluation of man, monopoly and competition—and the system of *money*. . . .

We shall begin from a *contemporary* economic fact. The worker becomes poorer the more wealth he produces and the more his production increases in power and extent. The worker becomes an ever cheaper commodity the more goods he creates. The *devaluation* of the human world increases in direct relation with the *increase in value* of the world of things. Labor does not only create goods; it also produces itself and the worker as a *commodity*, and indeed in the same proportion as it produces goods.

This fact simply implies that the object produced by labor, its product, now stands opposed to it as an *alien being*, as a *power independent* of the producer. The product of labor is labor which has been embodied in an object and turned into a physical thing; this product is an *objectification* of labor. The performance of work is at the same time its objectification. The performance of work appears in the sphere of political economy as a *vitiation*[1] of the worker, objectification as a *loss* and as *servitude to the object*, and appropriation as *alienation*.

So much does the performance of work appear as vitiation that the worker is vitiated to the point of starvation. So much does objectification appear as loss of the object that the worker is deprived of the most essential things not only of life but also of work. Labor itself becomes an object which he can acquire only by the greatest effort and with unpredictable interruptions. So much does the appropriation of the object appear as alienation that the more objects the worker produces the fewer he can possess and the more he falls under the domination of his product, of capital.

All these consequences follow from the fact that the worker is related to the *product of his labor* as to an *alien* object. For it is clear on this presupposition that the more the worker expends himself in work the more powerful becomes the world of objects which he creates in face of himself, the poorer he becomes in his inner life, and the less he belongs to himself. It is just the same as in religion. The more of himself man attributes to God the less he has left in himself. The worker puts his life into the object, and his life then belongs no longer to himself but to the object. The greater his activity, therefore, the less he possesses. What is embodied in the product of his labor is no longer his own. The greater this product is, therefore, the more he is diminished. The *alienation* of the worker in his product means not only that his labor becomes an object, assumes an *external* existence, but that it exists independently, *outside himself,* and alien to him, and that it stands opposed to him as an autonomous power. The life which he has given to the object sets itself against him as an alien and hostile force.

Let us now examine more closely the phenomenon of *objectification;* the worker's production and the *alienation* and *loss* of the object it produces, which is involved in it. The worker can create nothing without *nature,* without the *sensuous external world.* The latter is the material in which his labor is realized, in which it is active, out of which and through which it produces things.

But just as nature affords the *means of existence* of labor, in the sense that labor cannot *live* without objects upon which it can be exercised, so also it provides the *means of existence* in a narrower sense; namely the means of physical existence for the *worker* himself. Thus, the more the worker *appropriates* the external world of sensuous nature by his labor the more he deprives himself of *means of existence,* in two respects: First, that the sensuous external world becomes progressively less an object belonging to his labor or a means of existence of his labor, and secondly, that it becomes progressively less a means of existence in the direct sense, a means for the physical subsistence of the worker.

In both respects, therefore, the worker becomes a slave of the object; first, in that he receives an *object of work,* i.e., receives *work,* and secondly, in that he receives *means of subsistence.* Thus the object enables him to exist, first as a *worker* and secondly, as a *physical subject.* The culmination of this enslavement is that he can only maintain himself as a *physical subject* so far as he is a *worker,* and that it is only as a *physical subject* that he is a worker.

(The alienation of the worker in his object is expressed as follows in the laws of political economy: The more the worker produces the less he has to consume; the more value he creates the more worthless he becomes; the more refined his product the more crude and misshapen the worker; the more civilized the product the more barbarous the worker; the more powerful the work the more feeble the worker; the more the work manifests intelligence the more the worker declines in intelligence and becomes a slave of nature.)

Political economy conceals the alienation in the nature of labor insofar as it does not examine the direct relationship between the worker (work) and production. Labor certainly produces marvels for the rich but it produces privation for the worker. It produces palaces, but hovels for the worker. It produces beauty, but deformity for the worker. It replaces labor by machinery, but it casts some of the workers back into a barbarous kind of work and turns the others into machines. It produces intelligence, but also stupidity and cretinism for the workers.

The direct relationship of labor to its products is the relationship of the worker to the objects of his production. The relationship of property owners to the objects of production and to production itself is merely a *consequence* of this first relationship and confirms it. We shall consider this second aspect later.

Thus, when we ask what is the important relationship of labor, we are concerned with the relationship of the *worker* to production.

So far we have considered the alienation of the worker only from one aspect; namely, *his relationship with the products of his labor.* However, alienation appears not merely in the result but also in the *process of production,* within *productive activity* itself. How could the worker stand in an alien relationship to the product of his activity if he did not alienate himself in the act of production itself? The product is indeed only the *résumé* of activity, of production. Consequently, if the product of labor is alienation, production itself must be active alienation— the alienation of activity and the activity of alienation. The alienation of the object of labor merely summarizes the alienation in the work activity itself.

What constitutes the alienation of labor? First, that the work is *external* to the worker, that it is not part of his nature; and that, consequently, he does not fulfill himself in his work but denies himself, has a feeling of misery rather than well-being, does not develop freely his mental and physical energies but is physically exhausted and mentally debased.

The worker, therefore, feels himself at home only during his leisure time, whereas at work he feels homeless. His work is not voluntary but imposed, *forced labor.* It is not the satisfaction of a need, but only a *means* for satisfying other needs. Its alien character is clearly shown by the fact that as soon as there is no physical or other compulsion it is avoided like the plague. External labor, labor in which man alienates himself, is a labor of self-sacrifice, of mortification. Finally, the external character of work for the worker is shown by the fact that it is not his own work but work for someone else, that in work he does not belong to himself but to another person. . . .

We arrive at the result that man (the worker) feels himself to be freely active only in his animal functions—eating, drinking, and procreating, or at most also in his dwelling and in personal adornment—while in his human functions he is reduced to an animal. The animal becomes human and the human becomes animal.

Eating, drinking, and procreating are of course also genuine human functions. But abstractly considered, apart from the environment of human activities, and turned into final and sole ends, they are animal functions.

We have now considered the act of alienation of practical human activity, labor, from two aspects: (1) the relationship of the worker to the *product of labor* as an alien object which dominates him. This relationship is at the same time the relationship to the sensuous external world, to natural objects, as an alien and hostile world; (2) the relationship of labor to the *act of production* within *labor.* This is the relationship of the worker to his own activity as something alien and not belonging to him, activity as suffering (passivity), strength as powerlessness, creation as emasculation, the *personal* physical and mental energy of the worker, his personal life (for what is life but activity?), as an activity which is directed against himself, independent of him and not belonging to him. This is *self-alienation* as against the [afore]mentioned alienation of the *thing*.

We have now to infer a third characteristic of *alienated labor* from the two we have considered.

Man is a species-being not only in the sense that he makes the community (his own as well as those of other things) his object both practically and theoretically, but also (and this is simply another expression for the same thing) in the sense that he treats himself as the present, living species, as a *universal* and consequently free being.

Species-life, for man as for animals, has its physical basis in the fact that man (like animals) lives from inorganic nature, and since man is more universal than an animal so the range of inorganic nature from which he lives is more universal. Plants, animals, minerals, air, light, etc. constitute, from the theoretical aspect, a part of human consciousness as objects of natural science and art; they are man's spiritual inorganic nature, his intellectual means of life, which he must first prepare for enjoyment and perpetuation. So also, from the practical aspect, they form a part of human life and activity. In practice man lives only from these natural products, whether in the form of food, heating, clothing, housing, etc. The universality of man appears in practice in the universality which makes the whole of nature into his inorganic body: (1) as a direct means of life; and equally (2) as the material object and instrument of his life activity. Nature is the inorganic body of man; that is to say nature, excluding the human body itself. To say that man *lives* from nature means that nature is his *body* with which he must remain in a continuous interchange in order not to die. The statement that the physical and mental life of man, and nature, are interdependent means simply that nature is interdependent with itself, for man is a part of nature.

Since alienated labor (1) alienates nature from man; and (2) alienates man from himself, from his own active function, his life activity; so it alienates him from the species. It makes *species-life* into a means of individual life. In the first place it alienates species-life and individual life, and secondly, it turns the latter, as an abstraction, into the purpose of the former, also in its abstract and alienated form.

For labor, *life activity, productive life*, now appear to man only as *means* for the satisfaction of a need, the need to maintain his physical existence. Productive life is, however, species-life. It is life creating life. In the type of life activity resides the whole character of a species, its species-character; and free, conscious activity is the species-character of human beings. Life itself appears only as a *means of life*.

The animal is one with its life activity. It does not distinguish the activity from itself. It is *its activity*. But man makes his life activity itself an object of his will and consciousness. He has a conscious life activity. It is not a determination with which he is completely identified. Conscious life activity distinguishes man from the life activity of animals. Only for this reason is he a species-being. Or rather, he is only a self-conscious being, i.e., his own life is an object for him, because he is a species-being. Only for this reason is his activity free activity. Alienated labor reverses the relationship, in that man because he is a self-conscious being makes his life activity, his *being*, only a means for his *existence*.

Note

1.   Debasement.

Manifesto of the Communist Party

Karl Marx and Friedrich Engels

Karl Marx, collaborating with Friedrich Engels, produced the "Manifesto" in 1848. This document is a well-known statement about the origin of social conflict in the process of material production. The ideas of Marx and Engels have been instrumental in shaping the political lives of more than one-fifth of the world's population, and, of course, they have been instrumental in the development of the social-conflict paradigm in sociology.

Bourgeois and Proletarians[1]

The history of all hitherto existing society[2] is the history of class struggles.

Freeman and slave, patrician and plebeian, lord and serf, guild-master[3] and journeyman, in a word, oppressor and oppressed, stood in constant opposition to one another, carried on an uninterrupted, now hidden, now open fight, a fight that each time ended, either in a revolutionary reconstitution of society at large, or in the common ruin of the contending classes.

In the earlier epochs of history, we find almost everywhere a complicated arrangement of society into various orders, a manifold gradation of social rank. In ancient Rome we have patricians, knights, plebeians, slaves; in the Middle Ages, feudal lords, vassals, guild-masters, journeymen, apprentices, serfs; in almost all of these classes, again, subordinate gradations.

The modern bourgeois society that has sprouted from the ruins of feudal society has not done away with class antagonisms. It has but established new classes, new conditions of oppression, new forms of struggle in place of the old ones.

Our epoch, the epoch of the bourgeoisie, possesses, however, this distinctive feature; it has simplified the class antagonisms. Society as a whole is more and more splitting up into two great hostile camps, into two great classes directly facing each other: Bourgeoisie and Proletariat.

From the serfs of the Middle Ages sprang the chartered burghers of the earliest towns. From these burgesses the first elements of the bourgeoisie were developed.

The discovery of America, the rounding of the Cape, opened up fresh ground for the rising bourgeoisie. The East Indian and Chinese markets, the [colonization] of America, trade with the colonies, the increase in the means of

From *Manifesto of the Communist Party,* Part I, by Karl Marx and Friedrich Engels.

exchange and in commodities generally, gave to commerce, to navigation, to industry, an impulse never before known, and thereby, to the revolutionary element in the tottering feudal society, a rapid development.

The feudal system of industry, under which industrial production was monopolized by close guilds, now no longer sufficed for the growing wants of the new markets. The manufacturing system took its place. The guild-masters were pushed on one side by the manufacturing middle class; division of labor between the different corporate guilds vanished in the face of division of labor in each single workshop.

Meantime the markets kept ever growing, the demand, ever rising. Even manufacture no longer sufficed. Thereupon, steam and machinery revolutionized industrial production. The place of manufacture was taken by the giant, Modern Industry, the place of the industrial middle class, by industrial millionaires, the leaders of whole industrial armies, the modern bourgeois.

Modern industry has established the world-market, for which the discovery of America paved the way. This market has given an immense development to commerce, to navigation, to communication by land. This development has, in its turn, reacted on the extension of industry; and in proportion as industry, commerce, navigation, railways extended, in the same proportion the bourgeoisie developed, increased its capital, and pushed into the background every class handed down from the Middle Ages.

We see, therefore, how the modern bourgeoisie is itself the product of a long course of development, of a series of revolutions in the modes of production and of exchange.

Each step in the development of the bourgeoisie was accompanied by a corresponding political advance of that class. An oppressed class under the sway of the feudal nobility, an armed and self-governing association in the mediaeval commune,[4] here independent urban republic (as in Italy and Germany), there taxable "third estate" of the monarchy (as in France), afterwards, in the period of manufacture proper, serving either the semi-feudal or the absolute monarchy as a counterpoise against the nobility, and, in fact, corner-stone of the great monarchies in general, the bourgeoisie has at last, since the establishment of modern industry and of the world-market, conquered for itself, in the modern representative State, exclusive political sway. The executive of the modern State is but a committee for managing the common affairs of the whole bourgeoisie.

The bourgeoisie, historically, has played a most revolutionary part.

The bourgeoisie, wherever it has got the upper hand, has put an end to all feudal, patriarchal, idyllic relations. It has pitilessly torn asunder the motley feudal ties that bound man to his "natural superiors," and has left remaining no other nexus between man and man than naked self-interest, than callous "cash payment." It has drowned the most heavenly ecstasies of religious fervour, of chivalrous enthusiasm, of philistine sentimentalism, in the icy water of egotistical calculation. It has resolved personal worth into exchange value, and in place of the numberless indefeasible chartered freedoms, has set up that single, unconscionable freedom— Free Trade. In one word, for exploitation, veiled by religious and political illusions, it has substituted naked, shameless, direct, brutal exploitation.

The bourgeoisie has stripped of its halo every occupation hitherto honoured and looked up to with reverent awe. It has converted the physician, the lawyer, the priest, the poet, the man of science, into its paid [wage-laborers].

The bourgeoisie has torn away from the family its sentimental veil, and has reduced the family relation to a mere money relation.

The bourgeoisie has disclosed how it came to pass that the brutal display of vigour in the Middle Ages, which reactionists so much admire, found its fitting complement in the most slothful indolence. It has been the first to show what man's activity can bring about. It has accomplished wonders far surpassing Egyptian pyramids, Roman aqueducts, and Gothic cathedrals; it has conducted expeditions that put in the shade all former Exoduses of nations and crusades.

The bourgeoisie cannot exist without constantly revolutionizing the instruments of production, and thereby the relations of production, and with them the whole relations of society. Conservation of the old modes of production in unaltered form, was, on the contrary, the first condition of existence for all earlier industrial classes. Constant revolutionizing of production, uninterrupted disturbance of all social conditions, everlasting uncertainty and agitation distinguish the bourgeois epoch from all earlier ones. All fixed, fast-frozen relations, with their train of ancient and venerable prejudices and opinions, are swept away, all new-formed ones become antiquated before they can ossify. All that is solid melts into air, all that is holy is profaned, and man is at last compelled to face with sober senses, his real conditions of life, and his relations with his kind.

The need of a constantly expanding market for its products chases the bourgeoisie over the whole surface of the globe. It must nestle everywhere, settle everywhere, establish [connections] everywhere.

The bourgeoisie has through its exploitation of the world-market given a cosmopolitan character to production and consumption in every country. To the great chagrin of reactionists, it has drawn from under the feet of industry the national ground on which it stood. All old-established national industries have been destroyed or are daily being destroyed. They are dislodged by new industries, whose introduction becomes a life and death question for all civilised nations, by industries that no longer work up indigenous raw material, but raw material drawn from the remotest zones; industries whose products are consumed, not only at home, but in every quarter of the globe. In place of the old wants, satisfied by the productions of the country, we find new wants, requiring for their satisfaction the products of distant lands and climes. In place of the old local and national seclusion and self-sufficiency, we have intercourse in every direction, universal interdependence of nations. And as in material, so also in intellectual production. The intellectual creations of individual nations become common property. National one-sidedness and narrow-mindedness become more and more impossible, and from the numerous national and local literatures there arises a world-literature.

The bourgeoisie, by the rapid improvement of all instruments of production, by the immensely facilitated means of communication, draws all, even the most barbarian, nations into civilization. The cheap prices of its commodities are the heavy artillery with which it batters down all Chinese walls, with which it forces the barbarians' intensely obstinate hatred of foreigners to capitulate. It compels all nations, on pain of extinction, to adopt the bourgeois mode of production; it compels them to introduce what it calls civilization into their midst, i.e., to become bourgeois themselves. In a word, it creates a world after its own image.

The bourgeoisie has subjected the country to the rule of the towns. It has created enormous cities, has greatly increased the urban population as compared with the rural, and has thus rescued a considerable part of the population from the idiocy of rural life. Just as it has made the country dependent on the towns, so it has made barbarian and semi-barbarian countries dependent on the civilised ones, nations of peasants on nations of bourgeois, the East on the West.

The bourgeoisie keeps more and more doing away with the scattered state of the population, of the means of production, and of property. It has agglomerated population, centralized means of production, and has concentrated property in a few hands. The necessary consequence of this was political centralization. Independent, or but loosely connected provinces, with separate interests, laws, governments and systems of taxation, became lumped together in one nation, with one government, one code of laws, one national class-interest, one frontier and one customs-tariff.

The bourgeoisie, during its rule of scarce one hundred years, has created more massive and more colossal productive forces than have all preceding generations together. Subjection of Nature's forces to man, machinery, application of chemistry to industry and agriculture, steam-navigation, railways, electric telegraphs, clearing of whole continents for cultivation, canalization of rivers, whole populations conjured out of the ground—what earlier century had even a presentiment that such productive forces slumbered in the lap of social labor?

We see then: The means of production and of exchange on whose foundation the bourgeoisie built itself up, were generated in feudal society. At a certain stage in the development of these means of production and of exchange, the conditions under which feudal society produced and exchanged, the feudal organization of agriculture and manufacturing industry, in one word, the feudal relations of property became no longer compatible with the already developed productive forces; they became so many fetters. They had to burst asunder; they were burst asunder.

Into their places stepped free competition, accompanied by a social and political constitution adapted to it, and by the economical and political sway of the bourgeois class.

A similar movement is going on before our own eyes. Modern bourgeois society with its relations of production, of exchange and of property, a society that has conjured up such gigantic means of production and of exchange, is like the sorcerer, who is no longer able to control the powers of the nether world whom he has called up by his spells. For many a decade past the history of industry and commerce is but the history of the revolt of modern productive forces against modern conditions of production, against the property relations that are the conditions for the existence of the bourgeoisie and of its rule. It is enough to mention the commercial crises that by their periodical return put on its trial, each time more threateningly, the existence of the entire bourgeois society. In these crises a great part not only of the existing products, but also of the previously created productive forces, are periodically destroyed. In these crises there breaks out an epidemic that, in all earlier epochs, would have seemed an absurdity—the epidemic of overproduction. Society suddenly finds itself put back into a state of momentary barbarism; it appears as if a famine, a universal war of devastation had cut off the supply of every means of subsistence; industry and commerce seem to be destroyed; and why? Because there is too much civilization, too much means of subsistence, too much industry, too much commerce. The productive forces at the disposal of society no longer tend to further the development of the conditions of bourgeois property; on the contrary, they have become too powerful for these conditions, by which they are fettered, and so soon as they overcome these fetters, they bring disorder into the whole of bourgeois society, endanger the existence of bourgeois property. The conditions of bourgeois society are too narrow to comprise the wealth created by them. And how does the bourgeoisie get over these crises? On the one hand by enforced destruction of a mass of productive forces; on the other, by the conquest of new markets, and by the more thorough exploitation of the old ones. That is to say, by paving the way for more extensive and more destructive crises, and by diminishing the means whereby crises are prevented.

The weapons with which the bourgeoisie felled feudalism to the ground are now turned against the bourgeoisie itself.

But not only has the bourgeoisie forged the weapons that bring death to itself; it has also called into existence the men who are to wield those weapons—the modern working class—the proletarians.

In proportion as the bourgeoisie, i.e., capital, is developed, in the same proportion is the proletariat, the modern working class, developed, a class of laborers, who live only so long as they find work, and who find work only so long as their labor increases capital. These laborers, who must sell themselves piecemeal, are a commodity, like every other article of commerce, and are consequently exposed to all the vicissitudes of competition, to all the fluctuations of the market.

Owing to the extensive use of machinery and to division of labor, the work of the proletarians has lost all individual character, and, consequently, all charm for the workman. He becomes an appendage of the machine, and it is only the most simple, most monotonous and most easily acquired knack that is required of him. Hence, the cost of production of a workman is restricted, almost entirely, to the means of subsistence that he requires for his maintenance, and for the propagation of his race. But the price of a commodity, and also of labor, is equal to its cost of production. In proportion, therefore, as the repulsiveness of the work increases, the wage decreases. Nay more, in proportion as the use of machinery and division of labor increases, in the same proportion the burden of toil also increases, whether by prolongation of the working hours, by increase of the work enacted in a given time, or by increased speed of the machinery, etc.

Modern industry has converted the little workshop of the patriarchal master into the great factory of the industrial capitalist. Masses of laborers, crowded into the factory, are organized like soldiers. As privates of the industrial army they are placed under the command of a perfect hierarchy of officers and sergeants. Not only are they the slaves of the bourgeois class, and of the bourgeois State, they are daily and hourly enslaved by the machine, by the over-looker, and, above all, by the individual bourgeois manufacturer himself. The more openly this despotism proclaims gain to be its end and aim, the more petty, the more hateful and the more embittering it is.

The less the skill and exertion or strength implied in manual labor, in other words, the more modern industry becomes developed, the more is the labor of men superseded by that of women. Differences of age and sex have no longer any distinctive social validity for the working class. All are instruments of labor, more or less expensive to use, according to their age and sex.

No sooner is the exploitation of the laborer by the manufacturer, so far, at an end, that he receives his wages in cash, than he is set upon by the other portions of the bourgeoisie, the landlord, the shopkeeper, the pawnbroker, etc.

The lower strata of the middle class—the small tradespeople, shopkeepers, and retired tradesmen generally, the handicraftsmen and peasants—all these sink gradually into the proletariat, partly because their diminutive capital does not suffice for the scale on which Modern Industry is carried on, and is swamped in the competition with the large capitalists, partly because their specialised skill is rendered worthless by new methods of production. Thus the proletariat is recruited from all classes of the population.

The proletariat goes through various stages of development. With its birth begins its struggle with the bourgeoisie. At first the contest is carried on by individual laborers, then by the workpeople of a factory, then by the operatives of one trade, in one locality, against the individual bourgeois who directly exploits them. They direct their attacks not against the bourgeois conditions of production, but against the instruments of production themselves; they destroy imported wares that compete with their labor, they smash to pieces machinery, they set factories ablaze, they seek to restore by force the vanished status of the workman of the Middle Ages.

At this stage the laborers still form an incoherent mass scattered over the whole country, and broken up by their mutual competition. If anywhere they unite to form more compact bodies, this is not yet the consequence of their own active union, but of the union of the bourgeoisie, which class, in order to attain its own political ends, is compelled to set the whole proletariat in motion, and is moreover yet, for a time, able to do so. At this stage, therefore, the proletarians do not fight their enemies, but the enemies of their enemies, the remnants of absolute monarchy, the landowners, the non-industrial bourgeois, the petty bourgeoisie. Thus the whole historical movement is concentrated in the hands of the bourgeoisie; every victory so obtained is a victory for the bourgeoisie.

But with the development of industry the proletariat not only increases in number, it becomes concentrated in greater masses, its strength grows, and it feels that strength more. The various interests and conditions of life within the ranks of the proletariat are more and more equalized, in proportion as machinery obliterates all distinctions of labor, and nearly everywhere reduces wages to the same low level. The growing competition among the bourgeois, and the resulting commercial crises, make the wages of the workers ever more fluctuating. The unceasing improvement of machinery, ever more rapidly developing, makes their livelihood more and more precarious; the collisions between individual workmen and individual bourgeois take more

and more the character of collisions between two classes. Thereupon the workers begin to form combinations (Trades' Unions) against the bourgeois; they club together in order to keep up the rate of wages; they found permanent associations in order to make provision beforehand for these occasional revolts. Here and there the contest breaks out into riots.

Now and then the workers are victorious, but only for a time. The real fruit of their battles lies, not in the immediate result, but in the ever expanding union of the workers. This union is helped on by the improved means of communication that are created by modern industry, and that place the workers of different localities in contact with one another. It was just this contact that was needed to centralize the numerous local struggles, all of the same character, into one national struggle between classes. But every class struggle is a political struggle. And that union, to attain which the burghers of the Middle Ages, with their miserable highways, required centuries, the modern proletarians, thanks to railways, achieve in a few years.

This organization of the proletarians into a class, and consequently into a political party, is continually being upset again by the competition between the workers themselves. But it ever rises up again, stronger, firmer, mightier. It compels legislative recognition of particular interests of the workers, by taking advantage of the divisions among the bourgeoisie itself. Thus the ten-hours'-bill in England was carried.

Altogether collisions between the classes of the old society further, in many ways, the course of development of the proletariat. The bourgeoisie finds itself involved in a constant battle. At first with the aristocracy; later on, with those portions of the bourgeoisie itself, whose interests have become antagonistic to the progress of industry; at all times, with the bourgeoisie of foreign countries. In all these battles it sees itself compelled to appeal to the proletariat, to ask for its help, and thus, to drag it into the political arena. The bourgeoisie itself, therefore, supplies the proletariat with its own elements of political and general education, in other words, it furnishes the proletariat with weapons for fighting the bourgeoisie.

Further, as we have already seen, entire sections of the ruling classes are, by the advance of industry, precipitated into the proletariat, or are at least threatened in their conditions of existence. These also supply the proletariat with fresh elements of enlightenment and progress.

Finally, in times when the class-struggle nears the decisive hour, the process of dissolution going on within the ruling class, in fact within the whole range of old society, assumes such a violent, glaring character, that a small section of the ruling class cuts itself adrift, and joins the revolutionary class, the class that holds the future in its hands. Just as, therefore, at an earlier period, a section of the nobility went over to the bourgeoisie, so now a portion of the bourgeoisie goes over to the proletariat, and in particular, a portion of the bourgeois ideologists, who have raised themselves to the level of comprehending theoretically the historical movements as a whole.

Of all the classes that stand face to face with the bourgeoisie today, the proletariat alone is a really revolutionary class. The other classes decay and finally disappear in the face of modern industry; the proletariat is its special and essential product.

The lower-middle class, the small manufacturer, the shopkeeper, the artisan, the peasant, all these fight against the bourgeoisie, to save from extinction their existence as fractions of the middle class. They are therefore not revolutionary, but conservative. Nay more, they are reactionary, for they try to roll back the wheel of history. If by chance they are revolutionary, they are so, only in view of their impending transfer into the proletariat, they thus defend not their present, but their future interests, they desert their own standpoint to place themselves at that of the proletariat.

The "dangerous class," the social scum, that passively rotting mass thrown off by the lowest layers of old society, may, here and there, be swept into the movement by a proletarian revolution; its conditions of life, however, prepare it far more for the part of a bribed tool of reactionary intrigue.

In the conditions of the proletariat, those of old society at large are already virtually swamped. The proletarian is without property; his relation to his wife and children has no longer anything in common with the bourgeois family-relations; modern industrial labor, modern subjection to capital, the same in England as in France, in America as in Germany, has stripped him of every trace of national character. Law, morality, religion, are to him so many bourgeois prejudices, behind which lurk in ambush just as many bourgeois interests.

All the preceding classes that got the upper hand sought to fortify their already acquired status by subjecting at large to their conditions of appropriation. The proletarians cannot become masters of the productive forces of society, except by abolishing their own previous mode of appropriation, and thereby also every other previous mode of appropriation. They have nothing of their own to secure and to fortify; their mission is to destroy all previous securities for, and insurances of, individual property.

All previous historical movements were movements of minorities, or in the interest of minorities. The proletarian movement is the self-conscious, independent movement of the immense majority, in the interest of the immense majority. The proletariat, the lowest stratum of our present society, cannot stir, cannot raise itself up, without the whole superincumbent strata of official society being sprung into the air.

Though not in substance, yet in form, the struggle of the proletariat with the bourgeoisie is at first a national struggle. The proletariat of each country must, of course, first of all settle matters with its own bourgeoisie.

In depicting the most general phases of the development of the proletariat, we traced the more or less veiled civil war, raging within existing society, up to the point where that war breaks out into open revolution, and where the violent overthrow of the bourgeoisie, lays the foundation for the sway of the proletariat.

Hitherto, every form of society has been based, as we have already seen, on the antagonism of oppressing and oppressed classes. But in order to oppress a class, certain conditions must be assured to it under which it can, at least, continue its slavish existence. The serf, in the period of serfdom, raised himself to membership in the commune, just as the petty bourgeois, under the yoke of feudal absolutism, managed to develop into a bourgeois. The modern laborer, on the contrary, instead of rising with the progress of industry, sinks deeper and deeper below the conditions of existence of his own class. He becomes a pauper, and pauperism develops more rapidly than population and wealth. And here it becomes evident, that the bourgeoisie is unfit any longer to be the ruling class in society, and to impose its conditions of existence upon society as an overriding law. It is unfit to rule, because it is incompetent to assure an existence to its slave within his slavery, because it cannot help letting him sink into such a state, that it has to feed him, instead of being fed by him. Society can no longer live under this bourgeoisie, in other words, its existence is no longer compatible with society.

The essential condition for the existence, and for the sway of the bourgeois class, is the formation and augmentation of capital; the condition for capital is wage-labor. Wage-labor rests exclusively on competition between the laborers. The advance of industry, whose involuntary promoter is the bourgeoisie, replaces the isolation of the laborers, due to competition, by their involuntary combination, due to association. The development of modern industry, therefore, cuts from under its feet the very foundation on which the bourgeoisie produces and appropriates products. What the bourgeoisie therefore produces, above all, are its own grave-diggers. Its fall and the victory of the proletariat are equally inevitable.

Notes

1. By *bourgeoisie* is meant the class of modern capitalists, owners of the means of social production and employers of wage-labor. By *proletariat*, the class of modern wage-laborers who, having no means of production of their own, are reduced to selling their labor-power in order to live.

2. That is, all written history. In 1847, the pre-history of society, the social organization existing previous to recorded history, was all but unknown. Since then, Haxthausen discovered common ownership of land in Russia. Maurer proved it to be the social foundation from which all Teutonic races started in history, and by and by village communities were found to be, or to have been, the primitive form of society everywhere from India to Ireland. The inner organization of this primitive Communistic society was laid bare, in its typical form, by Morgan's crowning discovery of the true nature of the gens and its relation to the tribe. With the dissolution of these primaeval communities society begins to be differentiated into separate and finally antagonistic classes. I have attempted to retrace this process of dissolution in "Der Ursprung der Familie, des Privateigenthums und des Staats," 2d ed. Stuttgart 1886.

3. Guild-master, that is, a full member of a guild, a master within, not a head of, a guild.

4. "Commune" was the name taken, in France, by the nascent towns even before they had conquered from their feudal lords and masters, local self-government and political

rights as "the Third Estate." Generally speaking, for the economical development of the bourgeoisie, England is here taken as the typical country, for its political development, France.

Selected Readings

Karl Marx: The Story of His Life by Franz Mehring.

Karl Marx by Murray Wolfson.

Introduction to Marx and Engels: A Critical Reconstruction by Richard Schmitt. The Marxist System: Economic, Political, and Social Perspectives by Robert Freedman.

The Philosophical Foundations of Marxism by Louis Dupre.

The Ethical Foundations of Marxism by Eugene Kamenka.

Marx, a Radical Critique by Alan Carter.

A Reappraisal of Marxian Economics by Murray Wolfson.

Marx's Concept of Man by Erich Fromm, Karl Marx, T. B. Bottomore.

Capital, The Communist Manifesto, and Other Writings by Karl Marx, Max Eastman.

Karl Marx: The Essential Writings by Karl Marx, Frederic L. Bender.

The Poverty of Philosophy by Karl Marx.

A Contribution to the Critique of Political Economy by Karl Marx, N. I. Stone. The Class Struggles in France, 1848–1850 by Karl Marx.

Critical-Thinking Questions

1. What is creative labor?

2. What is alienated labor?

3. What is the Theory of Surplus Value?

tion A Brief Survey of the Sociological Imagination A Brief Survey
iological Imagination A Brief Survey of the Sociological Imagination
rvey of the Sociological Imagination A Brief Survey of the Sociologic
tion A Brief Survey of the Sociological Imagination A Brief Survey
iological Imagination A Brief Survey of the Sociological Imagination
rvey of the Sociologic

CHAPTER IV

Georg Simmel (1858–1918)

tion A Brief Survey of the Sociological Imagination A Brief Survey
iological Imagination A Brief Survey of the Sociological Imagination
rvey of the Sociological Imagination A Brief Survey of the Sociologic
tion A Brief Survey of the Sociological Imagination A Brief Survey
iological Imagination A Brief Survey of the Sociological Imagination
rvey of the Sociological Imagination A Brief Survey of the Sociologic
tion A Brief Survey of the Sociological Imagination A Brief Survey
iological Imagination A Brief Survey of the Sociological Imagination
rvey of the Sociological Imagination A Brief Survey of the Sociologic
tion A Brief Survey of the Sociological Imagination A Brief Survey
iological Imagination A Brief Survey of the Sociological Imagination
rvey of the Sociological Imagination A Brief Survey of the Sociologic

Simmel's sociology is generally centered around society and the individual and the perceptive analyses of city life and the money economy. Simmel's writings deal with individuals and their relationship to things as well as the individual's subjective understanding of the interaction with others. Additionally, Simmel was the first to employ the social role as an analytical concept. *The Stranger* as a sociological type is an example of this analytical approach.

In *The Stranger*, Simmel argues that in all human relationships there is a unity of nearness and remoteness, indifference and involvement. *The Stranger* is close in a natural, social and general human sense. But these common features only connect us because we all are a part of the human family. As a group member the stranger is both near and far at the same time. This nearness and farness produces tensions only when the Stranger displays his/her social difference (i.e. race, religion, city vs. country dweller, etc.). Simmel supports this point by identifying the social position of the Jew in Europe and the Beede tax. The Jew under the Beede tax had to pay a fixed tax per single person. On the other hand, for Christian citizens the tax was based on his changing fortune. Simmel refers to this social position because historically Europe has a long tradition of being Christian. Hence, in Europe the Jew was seen as a stranger as a result of his/her religious doctrine. Thus, this taxation policy discriminated based on the religious strangeness of the Jew in Europe.

Another area in which Simmel explores the individual and the social role is in the varying degrees in which domination and freedom exists within social relationships. Simmel argues that within a relationship of subordination, even for the person who is the most subordinate within the relationship, the exclusion of spontaneity is rare. "Having no choice," as Simmel puts it, is relative and is a condition based upon the desire to escape from the consequences, if one should decide to disobey. Thus one's freedom in the subordinate position can only be destroyed according to Simmel by physical violation, in all other cases this relationship "demands a price for the realization of freedom" which one may or may not be willing to pay.

Simmel argues that the super-subordinated relationship also plays an important role in social life. This relationship came into existence because people are mutually obligated to one another. Thus for Simmel, the ruler including the unconditional ruler has a mutual contract with his subjects. However, this relationship is a co-existing structure of domination. Simmel argues that in the leader/led relationship, the leader is also led. Simmel argues that the "master is the slave of his slave", because the leader is forced to "listen and guess" what the tendencies of the multitudes might be.

In the *Metropolis and Mental Life* Simmel argues that in modern life individuals must adjust to external forces, and at the same time humanity makes its environment. The psychological formation of the Metropolitan individual is based in the intensification of the nervous stimulation. The city is always producing "onrushing" impressions for which the individual must act with his head and not with his heart, as might be found in small town life. Thus, Metropolitan life for Simmel fosters the predominance of intelligence.

Intellectuality for Simmel is seen as a way of persevering the subject life over the overwhelming power of the city and Metropolis life. Moreover, the metropolis has always been the seat of the money economy. The money economy and the dominance of the intellect are connected for Simmel, and they share a "matter-of-fact" attitude in dealing with humanity, things and formal justice. Money, according to Simmel, reduces all things including individuality to how much? The money economy dominates the Metropolis and hence the matter-of-fact attitude of the city.

Hence, the modern mind has become more and more calculating because of the money economy. The modern mind as a result, transforms all of the world into math formulas to fix every part of the world.

Simmel suggests that the money economy in Metropolis life is the common denominator of all values and "colors or rather discolors" all things including social interaction. And yet, all that is negative about metropolis life, there is a positive factor, the rise of the individual. Metropolitan life provides individual independence and the elaboration of individuality itself. Metropolis life in fact provides the arena for the stimuli and for the development of the individual and the psychic existence of individuality.

The Metropolis and Mental Life

In this, one of his best-known essays, Simmel examines what might be called the "spiritual condition" of the modern world. His focus is the city, in which forces of modernity—including anonymity, a detached sophistication, and a preoccupation with commercial matters—are most clearly evident. Note that Simmel finds reason both to praise this new world and to warn of its ability to destroy our humanity.

The deepest problems of modern life derive from the claim of the individual to preserve the autonomy and individuality of his existence in the face of overwhelming social forces, of historical heritage, of external culture, and of the technique of life. The fight with nature which primitive man has to wage for his *bodily* existence attains in this modern form its latest transformation. The eighteenth century called upon man to free himself of all the historical bonds in the state and in religion, in morals and in economics. Man's nature, originally good and common to all, should develop unhampered. In addition to more liberty, the nineteenth century demanded the functional specialization of man and his work; this specialization makes one individual incomparable to another, and each of them indispensable to the highest possible extent. However, this specialization makes each man the more directly dependent upon the supple-mentary activities of all others. Nietzsche sees the full development of the individual conditioned by the most ruthless struggle of individuals; socialism believes in the suppression of all competition for the same reason. Be that as it may, in all these positions the same basic motive is at work: The person resists to being leveled down and worn out by a social-technological mechanism. An inquiry into the inner meaning of specifically modern life and its products, into the soul of the cultural body, so to speak, must seek to solve the equation which structures like the metropolis set up between the individual and the superindividual contents of life. Such an inquiry must answer the question of how the personality accommodates itself in the adjustments to external forces. This will be my task today.

The psychological basis of the metropolitan type of individuality consists in the *intensification of nervous stimulation* which re-

Reprinted with permission of The Free Press, a Division of Simon & Schuster Adult Publishing Group, from *The Sociology of Georg Simmel,* translated and edited by Kurt H. Wolff. Copyright © 1950 by The Free Press. Copyright © renewed 1978 by The Free Press. All rights reserved.

sults from the swift and uninterrupted change of outer and inner stimuli. Man is a differentiating creature. His mind is stimulated by the difference between a momentary impression and the one which preceded it. Lasting impressions, impressions which differ only slightly from one another, impressions which take a regular and habitual course and show regular and habitual contrasts—all these use up, so to speak, less consciousness than does the rapid crowding of changing images, the sharp discontinuity in the grasp of a single glance, and the unexpectedness of onrushing impressions. These are the psychological conditions which the metropolis creates. With each crossing of the street, with the tempo and multiplicity of economic, occupational and social life, the city sets up a deep contrast with small town and rural life with reference to the sensory foundations of psychic life. The metropolis exacts from man as a discriminating creature a different amount of consciousness than does rural life. Here the rhythm of life and sensory mental imagery flows more slowly, more habitually, and more evenly. Precisely in this connection the sophisticated character of metropolitan psychic life becomes understandable—as over against small town life, which rests more upon deeply felt and emotional relationships. These latter are rooted in the more unconscious layers of the psyche and grow most readily in the steady rhythm of uninterrupted habituations. The intellect, however, has its locus in the transparent, conscious, higher layers of the psyche; it is the most adaptable of our inner forces. In order to accommodate to change and to the contrast of phenomena, the intellect does not require any shocks and inner upheavals; it is only through such upheavals that the more conservative mind could accommodate to the metropolitan rhythm of events. Thus the metropolitan type of man—which, of course, exists in a thousand individual variants—develops an organ protecting him against the threatening currents and discrepancies of his external environment which would uproot him. He reacts with his head instead of his heart. In this an increased awareness assumes the psychic prerogative. Metropolitan life, thus, underlies a heightened awareness and a predominance of intelligence in metropolitan man. The reaction to metropolitan phenomena is shifted to that organ which is least sensitive and quite remote from the depth of the personality. Intellectuality is thus seen to preserve subjective life against the overwhelming power of metropolitan life, and intellectuality branches out in many directions and is integrated with numerous discrete phenomena.

The metropolis has always been the seat of the money economy. Here the multiplicity and concentration of economic exchange gives an importance to the means of exchange which the scantiness of rural commerce would not have allowed. Money economy and the dominance of the intellect are intrinsically connected. They share a matter-of-fact attitude in dealing with men and with things; and, in this attitude, a formal justice is often coupled with an inconsiderate hardness. The intellectually sophisticated person is indifferent to all genuine individuality, because relationships and reactions result from it which cannot be exhausted with logical operations. In the same manner, the individuality of phenomena is not commensurate with the pecuniary principle. Money is concerned only with what is common to all: It asks for the exchange value, it reduces all quality and individuality to the question: How much? All intimate emotional relations between persons are founded in their individuality, whereas in rational relations man is reckoned with like a number, like an element which is in itself indifferent. Only the objective measurable achievement is of interest. Thus metropolitan man reckons with his merchants and customers, his domestic servants and often even with persons with whom he is obliged to have social intercourse. These features of intellectuality contrast with the nature of the small circle in which the inevitable knowledge of individuality as inevitably produces a warmer tone of behavior, a behavior which is beyond a mere objective balancing of service and return. In the sphere of the economic psychology of the small group it is of importance that under primitive conditions production serves the customer who orders the goods, so that the producer and the consumer are acquainted. The modern metropolis, however, is supplied almost entirely by production for the market, that is, for entirely unknown purchasers who never personally enter the producer's actual field of vision. Through this anonymity the interests of each party acquire an unmerciful matter-of-factness; and the intellectually calculating economic egoisms of both parties need not fear any deflection because of the imponderables of personal relationships. The money economy dominates the metropolis; it has displaced the last survivals of domestic production and the direct barter of goods; it minimizes, from day to day, the amount of work ordered by customers. The matter-of-fact attitude is obviously so intimately interrelated with the money economy, which is dominant in the metropolis, that nobody can say whether the intellectualistic mentality first promoted the money economy or whether the latter determined the former. The metropolitan way of life is certainly the most fertile soil for this reciprocity, a point which I shall document merely by citing the dictum of the most eminent English constitutional historian: Throughout the whole course of English history, London has never acted as England's heart but often as England's intellect and always as her moneybag!

In certain seemingly insignificant traits, which lie upon the surface of life, the same psychic currents characteristically unite. Modern mind has become more and more calculating. The calculative exactness of practical life which the money economy has brought about corresponds to the ideal of natural science: to transform the world into an arithmetic problem, to fix every part of the world by mathematical formulas. Only money economy has filled the days of so many people with weighing, calculating, with numerical determinations, with a reduction of qualitative values to quantitative ones. Through the calculative nature of money a new precision, a certainty in the definition of identities and differences, an unambiguousness in agreements and arrangements has been brought about in the relations of life-elements—just as externally this precision has been effected by the universal diffusion of pocket watches. However, the conditions of metropolitan life are at once cause and effect of this trait. The relationships and affairs of the typical metropolitan usually are so varied and complex that without the strictest punctuality in promises and services the whole structure would break down into an inextricable chaos. Above all, this necessity is brought about by the aggregation of so many people with such differentiated interests, who must integrate their relations and activities into a highly complex organism. If all clocks and watches in Berlin would suddenly go wrong in different ways, even if only by one hour, all economic life and communication of the city would be disrupted for a long time. In addition an apparently mere external factor, long distances, would make all waiting and broken appointments result in an ill-afforded waste of time. Thus, the technique of metropolitan life is unimaginable without the most punctual integration of all activities and mutual relations into a stable and impersonal time schedule. Here again the general conclusions of this entire task of reflection become obvious, namely, that from each point on the surface of existence—however closely attached to the surface alone—one may drop a sounding into the depth of the psyche so that all the most banal externalities of life finally are connected with the ultimate decisions concerning the meaning and style of life. Punctuality, calculability, exactness are forced upon life by the complexity and extension of metropolitan existence and are not only most intimately connected with its money economy and intellectualistic character. These traits must also color the contents of life and favor the exclusion of those irrational, instinctive, sovereign traits and impulses which aim at determining the mode of life from within, instead of receiving the general and precisely schematized form of life from without. . . .

The same factors which have thus coalesced into the exactness and minute precision of the form of life have coalesced into a structure of the highest impersonality; on the other hand, they have promoted a highly personal subjectivity. There is perhaps no psychic phenomenon which has been so unconditionally reserved to the metropolis as has the blasé attitude. The blasé attitude results first from the rapidly changing and closely compressed contrasting stimulations of the nerves. From this, the enhancement of metropolitan intellectuality, also, seems originally to stem. Therefore, stupid people who are not intellectually alive in the first place usually are not exactly blasé. A life in boundless pursuit of pleasure makes one blasé because it agitates the nerves to their strongest reactivity for such a long time that they finally cease to react at all. In the same way, through the rapidity and contradictoriness of their changes, more harmless impressions force such violent responses, tearing the nerves so brutally hither and thither that their last reserves of strength are spent; and if one remains in the same milieu they have no time to gather new strength. An incapacity thus emerges to react to new sensations with the appropriate energy. This constitutes that blasé attitude which, in fact, every metropolitan child shows when compared with children of quieter and less changeable milieus.

This physiological source of the metropolitan blasé attitude is joined by another source which flows from the money economy. The essence of the blasé attitude consists in the blunting of discrimination. This does not mean that the objects are not perceived, as is the case with the half-wit, but rather that the meaning and differing values of things, and thereby the things themselves, are experienced as insubstantial. They appear to the blasé person in an evenly flat and gray tone; no one object deserves preference over any other. This mood is the faithful subjective reflection of the completely internalized money economy. By being the equivalent to all the manifold things in one and the same way, money becomes the most frightful leveler. For money expresses all qualitative differences of things in terms of "how much?" Money, with all its colorlessness and indifference, becomes the common denominator of all values; irreparably it hollows out the core of things, their individuality, their specific value, and their incomparability. All things float with equal specific gravity in the constantly moving stream of money. All things lie on the same level and differ from one another only in the size of the area which they cover. In the individual case this coloration, or rather discoloration, of things through their money equivalence may be unnoticeably minute. However, through the relations of the rich to the objects to be had for money, perhaps even through the total character which the mentality of the contemporary public everywhere imparts to these objects, the exclusively pecuniary evaluation of objects has become quite considerable. The large cities, the main seats of the money exchange, bring the purchasability of things to the fore much more impressively than do smaller localities. That is why cities are also the genuine locale of the blasé attitude. In the blasé attitude the concentration of men and things stimulate the nervous system of the individual to its highest achievement so that it attains its peak. Through the mere quantitative intensification of the same conditioning factors this achievement is transformed into its opposite and appears in the peculiar adjustment of the blasé attitude. In this phenomenon the nerves find in the refusal to react to their stimulation the last possibility of accommodating to the contents and forms of metropolitan life. The self-preservation of certain personalities is brought at the price of devaluating the whole objective world, a devaluation which in the end unavoidably drags one's own personality down into a feeling of the same worthlessness.

Whereas the subject of this form of existence has to come to terms with it entirely for himself, his self-preservation in the face of the large city demands from him a no less negative behavior of a social nature. This mental attitude of metropolitans toward one another we may designate, from a formal point of view, as reserve. If so many inner reactions were responses to the continuous external contacts with innumerable people as are those in the small town, where one knows almost everybody one meets and where one has a positive relation to almost everyone, one would be completely atomized internally and come to an unimaginable psychic state. Partly this psychological fact, partly the right to distrust which men have in the face of the touch-and-go elements of metropolitan life, necessitates our reserve. As a result of this reserve we frequently do not even know by sight those who have been our neighbors for years. And it is this reserve which in the eyes of the small-town people makes us appear to be cold and heartless. Indeed, if I do not deceive myself, the inner aspect of this outer reserve is not only indifference but, more often than we are aware, it is a slight aversion, a mutual strangeness and repulsion, which will break into hatred and fight at the moment of a closer contact, however caused. The whole inner organization of such an extensive communicative life rests upon an extremely varied hierarchy of sympathies, indifferences, and aversions of the briefest as well as of the most permanent nature. The sphere of indifference in this hierarchy is not as large as might appear on the surface. Our psychic activity still responds to almost every impression of somebody else with a somewhat distinct feeling. The unconscious, fluid, and changing character of this impression seems to result in a state of indifference. Actually this indifference would be just as unnatural as the diffusion of indiscriminate mutual suggestion would be unbearable. From both these typical dangers of the metropolis, indifference and indiscriminate suggestibility, antipathy protect us. A latent antipathy and the preparatory stage of practical antagonism affect the distances and aversions without which this mode of life could not at all be led. The extent and the mixture of this style of life, the rhythm of its emergence and disappearance, the forms in which it is satisfied—all these, with the unifying motives in the narrower sense, form the inseparable whole of the metropolitan style of life. What appears in the metropolitan style of life directly as dissociation is in reality only one of its elemental forms of socialization.

This reserve with its overtone of hidden aversion appears in turn as the form or the cloak of a more general mental phenomenon of the metropolis: It grants to the individual a kind and an amount of personal freedom which has no analogy whatsoever under other conditions. The metropolis goes back to one of the large developmental tendencies of social life as such, to one of the few tendencies for which an approximately universal formula can be discovered. The earliest phase of social formations found in historical as well as in contemporary social structures is this: a relatively small circle firmly closed against neighboring, strange, or in some way antagonistic circles. However, this circle is closely coherent and allows its individual members only a narrow field for the development of unique qualities and free, self-responsible movements. Political and kinship groups, parties and religious associations begin in this way. The self-preservation of very young associations requires the establishment of strict boundaries and a centripetal unity. Therefore they cannot allow the individual freedom and unique inner and outer development. From this stage social development proceeds at once in two different, yet corresponding, directions. To the extent to which the group grows—numerically, spatially, in significance and in content of life—to the same degree the group's direct, inner unity loosens, and the rigidity of the original demarcation against others is softened through mutual relations and connections. At the same time, the individual gains freedom of movement, far beyond the first jealous delimitation. The individual also gains a specific individuality to which the division of labor in the enlarged group gives both occasion and necessity. . . .

It is not only the immediate size of the area and the number of persons which, because of the universal historical correlation between the enlargement of the circle and the personal inner and outer freedom, has made the metropolis the locale of freedom. It is rather in transcending this visible expanse that any given city becomes the seat of cosmopolitanism. The horizon of the city expands in a manner comparable to the way in which wealth develops; a certain amount of property increases in a quasi-automatical way in ever more rapid progression. As soon as a certain limit has been passed, the economic, personal, and intellectual relations of the citizenry, the sphere of intellectual predominance of the city over its hinterland, grow as in geometrical progression. Every gain in dynamic extension becomes a step, not for an equal, but for a new and larger extension. From every thread spin-

ning out of the city, ever new threads grow as if by themselves, just as within the city the unearned increment of ground rent, through the mere increase in communication, brings the owner automatically increasing profits. At this point, the quantitative aspect of life is transformed directly into qualitative traits of character. The sphere of life of the small town is, in the main, self-contained and autarchic. For it is the decisive nature of the metropolis that its inner life overflows by waves into a far-flung national or international area. . . .

The most profound reason, however, why the metropolis conduces to the urge for the most individual personal existence—no matter whether justified and successful—appears to me to be the following: The development of modern culture is characterized by the preponderance of what one may call the "objective spirit" over the "subjective spirit." This is to say, in language as well as in law, in the technique of production as well as in art, in science as well as in the objects of the domestic environment, there is embodied a sum of spirit. The individual in his intellectual development follows the growth of this spirit very imperfectly and at an ever increasing distance. If, for instance, we view the immense culture which for the last hundred years has been embodied in things and in knowledge, in institutions and in comforts, and if we compare all this with the cultural progress of the individual during the same period—at least in high status groups—a frightful disproportion in growth between the two becomes evident. Indeed, at some points we notice a retrogression in the culture of the individual with reference to spirituality, delicacy, and idealism. This discrepancy results essentially from the growing division of labor. For the division of labor demands from the individual an ever more one-sided accomplishment, and the greatest advance in a one-sided pursuit only too frequently means dearth to the personality of the individual. In any case, he can cope less and less with the overgrowth of objective culture. The individual is reduced to a negligible quantity, perhaps less in his consciousness than in his practice and in the totality of his obscure emotional states that are derived from this practice. The individual has become a mere cog in an enormous organization of things and powers which tear from his hands all progress, spirituality, and value in order to transform them from their subjective form into the form of a purely objective life. It needs merely to be pointed out that the metropolis is the genuine arena of this culture which outgrows all personal life. Here in buildings and educational institutions, in the wonders and comforts of space-conquering technology, in the formations of community life, and in the visible institutions of the state, is offered such an overwhelming fullness of crystallized and impersonalized spirit that the personality, so to speak, cannot maintain itself under its impact. On the one hand, life is made infinitely easy for the personality in that stimulations, interests, uses of time, and consciousness are offered to it from all sides. They carry the person as if in a stream, and one needs hardly to swim for oneself. On the other hand, however, life is composed more and more of these impersonal contents and offerings which tend to displace the genuine personal colorations and incomparabilities. This results in the individual's summoning the utmost in uniqueness and particularization, in order to preserve his most personal core. He has to exaggerate this personal element in order to remain audible even to himself. . . .

The Stranger

If wandering is the liberation from every given point in space, and thus the conceptional opposite to fixation at such a point, the sociological form of the "stranger" presents the unity, as it were, of these two characteristics. This phenomenon too, however, reveals that spatial relations are only the condition, on the one hand, and the symbol, on the other, of human relations. The stranger is thus being discussed here, not in the sense often touched upon in the past, as the wanderer who comes today and goes tomorrow, but rather as the person who comes today and stays tomorrow. He is, so to speak, the *potential* wanderer: although he has not moved on, he has not quite overcome the freedom of coming and going. He is fixed within a particular spatial group, or within a group whose boundaries are similar to spatial boundaries. But his position in this group is determined, essentially, by the fact that he has not belonged to it from the beginning, that he imports qualities into it, which do not and cannot stem from the group itself.

The unity of nearness and remoteness involved in every human relation is organized, in the phenomenon of the stranger, in a way which may be most briefly formulated by saying that in the relationship to him, distance means that he, who is close by, is far, and strangeness means that he, who also is far, is actually near. For, to be a stranger is naturally a very positive relation; it is a specific form of interaction. The inhabitants of Sirius are not really strangers to us, at least not in any sociologically relevant sense: they do not exist for us at all; they are beyond far and near. The stranger, like the poor and like sundry "inner enemies," is an element of the group itself. His position as a full-fledged member involves both being outside it and confronting it. The following statements, which are by no means intended as exhaustive, indicate how elements which increase distance and repel, in the relations of and with the stranger produce a pattern of coordination and consistent interaction.

Throughout the history of economics the stranger everywhere appears as the trader, or the trader as stranger. As long as economy is essentially self-sufficient, or products are exchanged within a spatially narrow group, it needs no middleman: a trader is only required for products that originate outside the group. Insofar as members do not leave the circle in order to buy these necessities—in which case *they* are the "strange" merchants in that outside territory—the trader *must* be a stranger, since nobody else has a chance to make a living.

This position of the stranger stands out more sharply if he settles down in the place of his activity, instead of leaving it again: in innumerable cases even this is possible only if he can live by intermediate trade. Once an

Reprinted with the permission of The Free Press, a Division of Simon & Schuster Adult Publishing Group, from *The Sociology of Georg Simmel,* translated and edited by Kurt H. Wolff. Copyright © 1950 by The Free Press. Copyright © renewed 1978 by The Free Press. All rights reserved.

economy is somehow closed, the land is divided up, and handicrafts are established that satisfy the demand for them, the trader, too, can find his existence. For in trade, which alone makes possible unlimited combinations, intelligence always finds expansions and new territories, an achievement which is very difficult to attain for the original producer with his lesser mobility and his dependence upon a circle of customers that can be increased only slowly. Trade can always absorb more people than primary production; it is, therefore, the sphere indicated for the stranger, who intrudes as a supernumerary, so to speak, into a group in which the economic positions are actually occupied—the classical example is the history of European Jews. The stranger is by nature no "owner of soil"—soil not only in the physical, but also in the figurative sense of a life-substance which is fixed, if not in a point in space, at least in an ideal point of the social environment. Although in more intimate relations, he may develop all kinds of charm and significance, as long as he is considered a stranger in the eyes of the other, he is not an "owner of soil." Restriction to intermediary trade, and often (as though sublimated from it) to pure finance, gives him the specific character of *mobility*. If mobility takes place within a closed group, it embodies that synthesis of nearness and distance which constitutes the formal position of the stranger. For, the fundamentally mobile person comes in contact, at one time or another, with every individual, but is not organically connected, through established ties of kinship, locality, and occupation, with any single one.

Another expression of this constellation lies in the objectivity of the stranger. He is not radically committed to the unique ingredients and peculiar tendencies of the group, and therefore approaches them with the specific attitude of "objectivity." But objectivity does not simply involve passivity and detachment; it is a particular structure composed of distance and nearness, indifference and involvement. I refer to the discussion (in the chapter on "Superordination and Subordination"[1]) of the dominating positions of the person who is a stranger in the group; its most typical instance was the practice of those Italian cities to call their judges from the outside, because no native was free from entanglement in family and party interests.

With the objectivity of the stranger is connected, also, the phenomenon touched upon above,[2] although it is chiefly (but not exclusively) true of the stranger who moves on. This is the fact that he often receives the most surprising openness—confidences which sometimes have the character of a confessional and which would be carefully withheld from a more closely related person. Objectivity is by no means non-participation (which is altogether outside both subjective and objective interaction), but a positive and specific kind of participation—just as the objectivity of a theoretical observation does not refer to the mind as a passive *tabula rasa* on which things inscribe their qualities, but on the contrary, to its full activity that operates according to its own laws, and to the elimination, thereby, of accidental dislocations and emphases, whose individual and subjective differences would produce different pictures of the same object.

Objectivity may also be defined as freedom: the objective individual is bound by no commitments which could prejudice his perception, understanding, and evaluation of the given. The freedom, however, which allows the stranger to experience and treat even his close relationships as though from a bird's-eye view, contains many dangerous possibili-

---

[1] Pp. 216–221 above.—Tr.
[2] On pp. 500–502 of the same chapter from which the present *"Exkurs"* is taken (IX, *"Der Raum und die räumlichen Ordnungen der Gesellschaft,"* Space and the Spatial Organization of Society). The chapter itself is not included in this volume.—Tr.

ties. In uprisings of all sorts, the party attacked has claimed, from the beginning of things, that provocation has come from the outside, through emissaries and instigators. Insofar as this is true, it is an exaggeration of the specific role of the stranger: he is freer, practically and theoretically; he surveys conditions with less prejudice; his criteria for them are more general and more objective ideals; he is not tied down in his action by habit, piety, and precedent.[3]

Finally, the proportion of nearness and remoteness which gives the stranger the character of objectivity, also finds practical expression in the more *abstract nature* of the relation to him. That is, with the stranger one has only certain *more general* qualities in common, whereas the relation to more organically connected persons is based on the commonness of specific differences from merely general features. In fact, all somehow personal relations follow this scheme in various patterns. They are determined not only by the circumstance that certain common features exist among the individuals, along with individual differences, which either influence the relationship or remain outside of it. For, the common features themselves are basically determined in their effect upon the relation by the question whether they exist only between the participants in this particular relationship, and thus are quite general in regard to this relation, but are specific and incomparable in regard to everything outside of it—or whether the participants feel that these features are common to them because they are common to a group, a type, or mankind in general. In the case of the second alternative, the effectiveness of the common features becomes diluted in proportion to the size of the group composed of members who are similar in this sense. Although the commonness functions as their unifying basis, it does not make *these* particular persons interdependent on one another, because it could as easily connect everyone of them with all kinds of individuals other than the members of his group. This too, evidently, is a way in which a relationship includes both nearness and distance at the same time: to the extent to which the common features are general, they add, to the warmth of the relation founded on them, an element of coolness, a feeling of the contingency of precisely *this* relation—the connecting forces have lost their specific and centripetal character.

In the relation to the stranger, it seems to me, this constellation has an extraordinary and basic preponderance over the individual elements that are exclusive with the particular relationship. The stranger is close to us, insofar as we feel between him and ourselves common features of a national, social, occupational, or generally human, nature. He is far from us, insofar as these common features extend beyond him or us, and connect us only because they connect a great many people.

A trace of strangeness in this sense easily enters even the most intimate relationships. In the stage of first passion, erotic relations strongly reject any thought of generalization: the lovers think that there has never been a love like theirs; that nothing can be compared either to the person loved or to the feelings for that person. An estrangement—whether as cause or as consequence it is difficult to decide—usually comes at the moment when this

---

[3]But where the attacked make the assertion falsely, they do so from the tendency of those in higher position to exculpate inferiors, who, up to the rebellion, have been in a consistently close relation with them. For, by creating the fiction that the rebels were not really guilty, but only instigated, and that the rebellion did not really start with *them*, they exonerate themselves, inasmuch as they altogether deny all real grounds for the uprising.

feeling of uniqueness vanishes from the relationship. A certain skepticism in regard to its value, in itself and for them, attaches to the very thought that in their relation, after all, they carry out only a generally human destiny; that they experience an experience that has occurred a thousand times before; that, had they not accidentally met their particular partner, they would have found the same significance in another person.

Something of this feeling is probably not absent in any relation, however close, because what is common to two is never common to them alone, but is subsumed under a general idea which includes much else besides, many *possibilities* of commonness. No matter how little these possibilities become real and how often we forget them, here and there, nevertheless, they thrust themselves between us like shadows, like a mist which escapes every word noted, but which must coagulate into a solid bodily form before it can be called jealousy. In some cases, perhaps the more general, at least the more unsurmountable, strangeness is not due to different and ununderstandable matters. It is rather caused by the fact that similarity, harmony, and nearness are accompanied by the feeling that they are not really the unique property of this particular relationship: they are something more general, something which potentially prevails between the partners and an indeterminate number of others, and therefore gives the relation, which alone was realized, no inner and exclusive necessity.

On the other hand, there is a kind of "strangeness" that rejects the very commonness based on something more general which embraces the parties. The relation of the Greeks to the Barbarians is perhaps typical here, as are all cases in which it is precisely general attributes, felt to be specifically and purely human, that are disallowed to the other. But "stranger," here, has no positive meaning; the relation to him is a non-relation; he is not what is relevant here, a member of the group itself.

As a group member, rather, he is near and far *at the same time,* as is characteristic of relations founded only on generally human commonness: But between nearness and distance, there arises a specific tension when the consciousness that only the quite general is common, stresses that which is not common. In the case of the person who is a stranger to the country, the city, the race, etc., however, this non-common element is once more nothing individual, but merely the strangeness of origin, which is or could be common to many strangers. For this reason, strangers are not really conceived as individuals, but as strangers of a particular type: the element of distance is no less general in regard to them than the element of nearness.

This form is the basis of such a special case, for instance, as the tax levied in Frankfort and elsewhere upon medieval Jews. Whereas the *Beede* [tax] paid by the Christian citizen changed with the changes of his fortune, it was fixed once for all for every single Jew. This fixity rested on the fact that the Jew had his social position as a *Jew,* not as the individual bearer of certain objective contents. Every other citizen was the owner of a particular amount of property, and his tax followed its fluctuations. But the Jew as a taxpayer was, in the first place, a Jew, and thus his tax situation had an invariable element. This same position appears most strongly, of course, once even these individual characterizations (limited though they were by rigid invariance) are omitted, and all strangers pay an altogether equal head-tax.

In spite of being inorganically appended to it, the stranger is yet an organic member of the group. Its uniform life includes the specific conditions of this element. Only we do not know how to designate the peculiar unity of this position other than by saying that it is composed of certain measures of nearness and distance. Although some quantities of them characterize all relationships, a *special* proportion and reciprocal tension produce the particular, formal relation to the "stranger."

Selected Readings

Experience and Culture: The Philosophy of Georg Simmel by Rudolph H. Weingartner.

Georg Simmel, 1858–1918: A Collection of Essays, with Translations and a Bibliography (1959) by Kurt H. Wolff.

The Social Theory of Georg Simmel (1925) by Nicholas J. Spykman.

Georg Simmel's Concept of the Stranger and Intercultural Communication Research, in Communication Theory by Everett M. Rogers.

Communication and Social Order (includes "Georg Simmel's Search for an Autonomous Form of Sociability") by Hugh Dalziel Duncan.

The development of Sociology (1936) (includes "The 'Formal Sociology' of Simmel and Von Wiese") by Floyd Nelson House.

Sociological Theory: Present-Day Sociology From the Past (includes "Superiority and Subordination in Social Relationships," "Knowledge and Ignorance," and other articles by Georg Simmel) by Edgar F. Borgatta, Henry J. Meyer.

From Ghetto to Emancipation: Historical and Contemporary Reconsiderations of the Jewish Community (includes "Georg Simmel and the Crisis of Culture") by David N. Myers, William V. Rowe.

Being Urban: A Sociology of City Life (includes "Georg Simmel: The Metropolis and Mental Life") by David A. Karp, Gregory P. Stone, William C. Yoels. American Social Psychology: Its Origins, Development, and European Background (1932) (includes "Georg Simmel and More Recent Developments") by Fay Berger Karpf, Ellsworth Faris.

Critical-Thinking Questions

1. Who is the stranger?

2. What accounts for the matter-of-fact attitude?

3. What accounts for intellectual growth in the city?

CHAPTER V

George Herbert Mead (1863–1931)

George Herbert Mead, an American sociologist and a member of the so-called pragmatic approach sets out to extend the scientific method to all areas of study. All ideas and methods are treated as hypotheses that can be tested for the ability to solve a problem. The theorist in this tradition turn to the individual action as the central point of sociological analysis or symbolic interaction.

Symbolic interaction rests in the analysis of: 1) how human beings act toward things based on the meaning things have for them, 2) how the meaning of such things arise out of social interaction, 3) how people act toward the other person with regard to the thing, 4) how these meanings are processed and modified through thought and the interpretative process, 5) how meanings of self and social products are created and formed through the process of communications.

Mead, one of the major theorists in this tradition expands Gorge Horton Cooley's Looking Glass Self. The Looking Glass Self is the behavior of others and acts as the mirror in which individuals see themselves. Mead's work entitled *The Mind, Self and Society* centers around the interplay of the human mind and society. He identifies distinctive qualities of self-development, which includes a social entity emerging, developed and shaped by social interaction. The second is the individual perception of self. According to Mead for self to emerge there has to be a means by which the individual takes on an objective, impersonal attitude toward him/herself. Language is the means by which this impersonal position takes place because the individual hears his/her own significant symbols in an objective manner, by processing an objective view of his/her own thoughts and utterances. Hence, it is through the use of symbols that the individual becomes an object to him/herself.

Additionally, role-play and games influence the development of Self. For Mead role-play does not have formal rules. Role-playing places the individual in the place of the other, from which he/she can get a view of self from that role.

Games have formal rules and facilitate further development toward the development of self because the individuals learn to play games and to synchronize groups and rules which later act as a model for social action. Thus, games provide an important transition from childhood to adulthood.

Mead identifies two concepts of self-development—"I" and the "Me". The "I," according to Mead is the unique sense of self, and the "ME" is the social concept of self. The basis is "what I am versus what I am seen as by others."

Symbolic Interactionist study the day-to-day, moment by moment lived experiences of the individual and his/her cognition of these experiences as the focal point of sociological analysis. Indeed, social life is so mundane that the investigator has to make a special effort to notice a social phenomenon, let alone perceive its significance to the social situation. This form of behavioral investigation is referred to as Mundane Knowledge.

The Self

George Herbert Mead

The self is not the body but arises in social experience. Explaining this insight is perhaps the greatest contribution of George Herbert Mead. Mead argues that the basic shape of our personalities is derived from the social groupings in which we live. Note, too, that even the qualities that distinguish each of us from others emerge only within a social community.

In our statement of the development of intelligence we have already suggested that the language process is essential for the development of the self. The self has a character which is different from that of the physiological organism proper. The self is something which has a development; it is not initially there, at birth, but arises in the process of social experience and activity, that is, develops in the given individual as a result of his relations to that process as a whole and to other individuals within that process. . . .

We can distinguish very definitely between the self and the body. The body can be there and can operate in a very intelligent fashion without there being a self involved in the experience. The self has the characteristic that it is an object to itself, and that characteristic distinguishes it from other objects and from the body. It is perfectly true that the eye can see the foot, but it does not see the body as a whole. We cannot see our backs; we can feel certain portions of them, if we are agile, but we cannot get an experience of our whole body. There are, of course, experiences which are somewhat vague and difficult of location, but the bodily experiences are for us organized about a self. The foot and hand belong to the self. We can see our feet, especially if we look at them from the wrong end of an opera glass, as strange things which we have difficulty in recognizing as our own. The parts of the body are quite distinguishable from the self. We can lose parts of the body without any serious invasion of the self. The mere ability to experience different parts of the body is not different from the experience of a table. The table presents a different feel from what the hand does when one hand feels another, but it is an experience of something with which we come definitely into contact. The body does not experience itself as a whole, in the sense in which the self in some way enters into the experience of the self.

It is the characteristic of the self as an object to itself that I want to bring out. This characteristic is represented in the word "self," which is a reflexive, and indicates that which can be both subject and object. This type of object is essentially different from other objects, and in the past it has been distinguished as conscious, a term which indicates an experience with, an experience of, one's self. It was assumed that consciousness in some way carried this capacity of being an object to itself. In giving a behavioristic statement of consciousness we have to look for some sort of experience in which the physical organism can become an object to itself.[1]

When one is running to get away from someone who is chasing him, he is entirely occupied in this action, and his experience may be swallowed up in the objects about him, so that he has, at the time being, no consciousness of self at all. We must be, of course, very completely occupied to have that take place, but we can, I think, recognize that sort of a possible experience in which the self does not enter. We can, perhaps, get some light on that situation through those experiences in which in very intense action there appear in the experience of the individual, back of this intense action, memories and anticipations. Tolstoi as an officer in the war gives an account of having pictures of his past experience in the midst of his most intense action. There are also the pictures that flash into a person's mind when he is drowning. In such instances there is a contrast between an experience that is absolutely wound up in outside activity in which the self as an object does not enter, and an activity of memory and imagination in which the self is the principal object. The self is then entirely distinguishable from an organism that is surrounded by things and acts with reference to things, including parts of its own body. These latter may be objects like other objects, but they are just objects out there in the field, and they do not involve a self that is an object to the organism. This is, I think, frequently overlooked. It is that fact which makes our anthropomorphic reconstructions of animal life

so fallacious. How can an individual get outside himself (experientially) in such a way as to become an object to himself? This is the essential psychological problem of selfhood or of self-consciousness; and its solution is to be found by referring to the process of social conduct or activity in which the given person or individual is implicated. The apparatus of reason would not be complete unless it swept itself into its own analysis of the field of experience; or unless the individual brought himself into the same experiential field as that of the other individual selves in relation to whom he acts in any given social situation. Reason cannot become impersonal unless it takes an objective, noneffective attitude toward itself; otherwise we have just consciousness, not *self*-consciousness. And it is necessary to rational conduct that the individual should thus take an objective, impersonal attitude toward himself, that he should become an object to himself. For the individual organism is obviously an essential and important fact or constituent element of the empirical situation in which it acts; and without taking objective account of itself as such, it cannot act intelligently, or rationally.

The individual experiences himself as such, not directly, but only indirectly, from the particular standpoints of other individual members of the same social group, or from the generalized standpoint of the social group as a whole to which he belongs. For he enters his own experience as a self or individual, not directly or immediately, not by becoming a subject to himself, but only insofar as he first becomes an object to himself just as other individuals are objects to him or in his experience; and he becomes an object to himself only by taking the attitudes of other individuals toward himself within a social environment or context of experience and behavior in which both he and they are involved.

The importance of what we term "communication" lies in the fact that it provides a form of behavior in which the organism or the individual may become an object to himself. It is that sort of communication which we have been discussing—not communication in the sense of the cluck of the hen to the chickens, or the bark of a wolf to the pack, or the lowing of a cow, but communication in the sense of significant symbols, communication which is directed not only to others but also to the individual himself. So far as that type of communication is a part of behavior it at least introduces a self. Of course, one may hear without listening; one may see things that he does not realize; do things that he is not really aware of. But it is where one does respond to that which he addresses to another and where that response of his own becomes a part of his conduct, where he not only hears himself but responds to himself, talks and replies to himself as truly as the other person replies to him, that we have behavior in which the individuals become objects to themselves. . . .

The self, as that which can be an object to itself, is essentially a social structure, and it arises in social experience. After a self has arisen, it in a certain sense provides for itself its social experiences, and so we can conceive of an absolutely solitary self. But it is impossible to conceive of a self arising outside of social experience. When it has arisen we can think of a person in solitary confinement for the rest of his life, but who still has himself as a companion, and is able to think and to converse with himself as he had communicated with others. That process to which I have just referred, of responding to one's self as another responds to it, taking part in one's own conversation with others, being aware of what one is saying and using that awareness of what one is saying to determine what one is going to say thereafter—that is a process with which we are all familiar. We are continually following up our own address to other persons by an understanding of what we are saying, and using that understanding in the direction of our continued speech. We are finding out what we are going to say, what we are going to do, by saying and doing, and in the process we are continually controlling the process itself. In the conversation of gestures what we say calls out a certain response in another and that in turn changes our own action, so that we shift from what we started to do because of the reply the other makes. The conversation of gestures is the beginning of communication. The individual comes to carry on a conversation of gestures with himself. He says something, and that calls out a certain reply in himself which makes him change what he was going to say. One starts to say something, we will presume an unpleasant something, but when he starts to say it he realizes it is cruel. The effect on himself of what he is saying checks him; there is here a conversation of gestures between the individual and himself. We mean by significant speech that the action is one that affects the individual himself, and that the effect upon the individual himself is part of the intelligent carrying-out of the conversation with others. Now we, so to speak, amputate that social phase and dispense with it for the time being, so that one is talking to one's self as one would talk to another person.[2]

This process of abstraction cannot be carried on indefinitely. One inevitably seeks an audience, has to pour himself out to somebody. In reflective intelligence one thinks to act, and to act solely so that this action remains a part of a social process. Thinking becomes preparatory to social action. The very process of thinking is, of course, simply an inner conversation that goes on, but it is a conversation of gestures which in its completion implies the expression of that which one thinks to an audience. One separates the significance of what he is saying to others from the actual speech and gets it ready before saying it. He thinks it out, and perhaps writes it in the form of a book; but it is still a part of social intercourse in which one is addressing other persons and at the same time addressing one's self, and in which one controls the address to other persons by the response made to one's own gesture. That the person should be responding to himself is necessary to the self, and it is this sort of social conduct which provides behavior within which that self appears. I know of no other form of behavior than the linguistic in which the individual is an object to himself, and, so far as I can see, the individual is not a self in the reflexive sense unless he is an object to himself. It is this fact that gives a critical importance to communication, since this is a type of behavior in which the individual does so respond to himself.

We realize in everyday conduct and experience that an individual does not mean a great deal of what he is doing and saying. We frequently say that such an individual is not himself. We come away from an interview with a realization that we have left out important things, that there are parts of the self that did not get into what was said. What determines the amount of the self that gets into communication is the social experience itself. Of course, a good deal of the self does not need to get expression. We carry on a whole series of different relationships to different people. We are one thing to one man and another thing to another. There are parts of the self which exist only for the self in relationship to itself. We divide ourselves up in all sorts of different selves with reference to our acquaintances. We discuss politics with one and religion with another. There are all sorts of different selves answering to all sorts of different social reactions. It is the social process itself that is responsible for the appearance of the self; it is not there as a self apart from this type of experience.

A multiple personality is in a certain sense normal, as I have just pointed out. . . .

The unity and structure of the complete self reflects the unity and structure of the so-cial process as a whole; and each of the elementary selves of which it is composed reflects the unity and structure of one of the various aspects of that process in which the individual is implicated. In other words, the various elementary selves which constitute, or are organized into, a complete self are the various aspects of the structure of that complete self answering to the various aspects of the structure of the social process as a whole; the structure of the complete self is thus a reflection of the complete social process. The organization and unification of a social group is identical with the organization and unification of any one of the selves arising within the social process in which that group is engaged, or which it is carrying on.[3]

. . . Another set of background factors in the genesis of the self is represented in the activities of play and the game. . . . We find in children . . . imaginary companions which a good many children produce in their own experience. They organize in this way the responses which they call out in other persons and call out also in themselves. Of course, this playing with an imaginary companion is only a peculiarly interesting phase of ordinary play. Play in this sense, especially the stage which precedes the organized games, is a play at something. A child plays at being a mother, at being a teacher, at being a policeman; that is, it is taking different roles, as we say. We have something that suggests this in what we call the play of animals: A cat will play with her kittens, and dogs play with each other. Two dogs playing with each other will attack and defend, in a process which if carried through would amount to an actual fight. There is a combination of responses which checks the depth of the bite. But we do not have in such a situation the dogs taking a definite role in the sense that a child deliberately takes the role of another. This tendency on the part of children is what we are working with in the kindergarten where the roles which the children assume are made the basis for training. When a child does assume a role he has in himself the stimuli which call out that particular response or group of responses. He may, of course, run away when he is chased, as the dog does, or he may turn around and strike back just as the dog does in his play. But that is not the same as playing at something. Children get together to "play Indian." This means that the child has a certain set of stimuli that call out in itself the responses that they would call out in others, and which answer to an Indian. In the play period the child utilizes his own responses to these stimuli which he makes use of in building a self. The response which he has a tendency to make to these stimuli organizes them. He plays that he is, for instance, offering himself something, and he buys it; he gives a letter to himself and takes it away; he addresses himself as a parent, as a teacher; he arrests himself as a policeman. He has a set of stimuli which call out in himself the sort of responses they call out in others. He takes this group of responses and organizes them into a certain whole. Such is the simplest form of being another to one's self. It involves a temporal situation. The child says something in one character and responds in another character, and then his responding in another character is a stimulus to himself in the first character, and so the conversation goes on. A certain organized structure arises in him and in his other which replies to it, and these carry on the conversation of gestures between themselves.

If we contrast play with the situation in an organized game, we note the essential difference that the child who plays in a game must be ready to take the attitude of everyone else involved in that game, and that these different roles must have a definite relationship to each other. Taking a very simple game such as hide-and-seek, everyone with the exception of the one who is hiding is a person who is hunting. A child does not require more than the person who is hunted and the one who is hunting. If a child is playing in the first sense he just goes on playing, but there is no basic organization gained. In that early stage he passes from one another just as a whim takes him. But in a game where a number of individuals are involved, then the child taking one role must be ready to take the role of everyone else. If he gets in a ball game he must have the responses of each position involved in his own position. He must know what everyone else is going to do in order to carry out his own play. He has to take all of these roles. They do not all have to be present in consciousness at the same time, but at some moments he has to have three or four individuals present in his own attitude, such as the one who is going to throw the ball, the one who is going to catch it, and so on. These responses must be, in some degree, present in his own make-up. In the game, then, there is a set of responses of such others so organized that the attitude of one calls out the appropriate attitudes of the other.

This organization is put in the form of the rules of the game. Children take a great interest in rules. They make rules on the spot in order to help themselves out of difficulties. Part of the enjoyment of the game is to get these rules. Now, the rules are the set of responses which a particular attitude calls out. You can demand a certain response in others if you take a certain attitude. These responses are all in yourself as well. There you get an organized set of such responses as that to which I have referred, which is something more elaborate than the roles found in play. Here there is just a set of responses that follow on each other indefinitely. At such a stage we speak of a child as not yet having a fully developed self. The child responds in a fairly intelligent fashion to the immediate stimuli that come to him, but they are not organized. He does not organize his life as we would like to have him do, namely, as a whole. There is just a set of responses of the type of play. The child reacts to a certain stimulus, and the reaction is in himself that is called out in others, but he is not a whole self. In his game he has to have an organization of these roles; otherwise he cannot play the game. The game represents the passage in the life of the child from taking the role of others in play to the organized part that is essential to self-consciousness in the full sense of the term.

. . . The fundamental difference between the game and play is that in the former the child must have the attitude of all the others involved in that game. The attitudes of the other players which the participant assumes organize into a sort of unit, and it is that organization which controls the response of the individual. The illustration used was of a person playing baseball. Each one of his own acts is determined by his assumption of the action of the others who are playing the game. What he does is controlled by his being everyone else on that team, at least insofar as those attitudes affect his own particular response. We get then an "other" which is an organization of the attitudes of those involved in the same process.

The organized community or social group which gives to the individual his unity of self may be called "the generalized other." The attitude of the generalized other is the attitude of the whole community.[4] Thus, for example, in the case of such a social group as a ball team, the team is the generalized other insofar as it enters—as an organized process or social activity—into the experience of any one of the individual members of it.

If the given human individual is to develop a self in the fullest sense, it is not sufficient for him merely to take the attitudes of other human individuals toward himself and toward one another within the human social process, and to bring that social process as a whole into his individual experience merely in these terms: He must also, in the same way that he takes the attitudes of other individuals toward himself and toward one another, take their attitudes toward the various phases or aspects of the common social activity or set of social undertakings in which, as members of an organized society or social group, they are all engaged; and he must then, by generalizing these individual attitudes of that organized society or social group itself, as a whole, act toward different social projects which at any given time it is carrying out, or toward the various larger phases of the general social process which constitutes its life and of which these projects are specific manifestations. This getting of the broad activities of any given social whole or organized society as such within the experiential field of any one of the individuals involved or included in that whole is, in other words, the essential basis and prerequisite of the fullest development of that individual's self: Only insofar as he takes the attitudes of the organized social group to which he belongs toward the organized, cooperative social activity or set of such activities in which that group as such is engaged, does he develop a complete self or possess the sort of complete self he has developed. And on the other hand, the complex cooperative processes and activities and institutional functionings of organized human society are also possible only insofar as every individual involved in them or belonging to that society can take the general attitudes of all other such individuals with reference to these processes and activities and institutional functionings, and to the organized social whole of experiential relations and interactions thereby constituted—and can direct his own behavior accordingly.

It is in the form of the generalized other that the social process influences the behavior of the individuals involved in it and carrying it on, i.e., that the community exercises control over the conduct of its individual members; for it is in this form that the social process or community enters as a determining factor into the individual's thinking. In abstract thought the individual takes the attitude of the generalized other[5] toward himself, without reference to its expression in any particular other individuals; and in concrete thought he takes that attitude insofar as it is expressed in the attitudes toward his behavior of those other individuals with whom he is involved in the given social situation or act. But only by taking the attitude of the generalized other toward himself, in one or another of these ways, can he think at all; for only thus can thinking—or the internalized conversation of gestures which constitutes thinking—occur. And only through the taking by individuals of the attitude or attitudes of the generalized other toward themselves is the existence of a universe of discourse, as that system of common or social meanings which thinking presupposes at its context, rendered possible.

. . . I have pointed out, then, that there are two general stages in the full development of the self. At the first of these stages, the individual's self is considered simply by an organization of the particular attitudes of other individuals toward himself and toward one another in the specific social acts in which he participates with them. But at the second stage in the full development of the individual's self that self is constituted not only by an organization of these particular individual attitudes, but also by an organization of the social attitudes of the generalized other or the social group as a whole to which he belongs. . . . So the self reaches its full development by organizing these individual attitudes of others into the organized social or group attitudes, and by thus becoming an individual reflection of the general systematic pattern of social or group behavior in which it and the others are all involved—a pattern which enters as a whole into the individual's experience in terms of these organized group attitudes which, through the mechanism of his central nervous system, he takes toward himself, just as he takes the individual attitudes of others.

. . . A person is a personality because he belongs to a community, because he takes over the institutions of that community into his own conduct. He takes its language as a medium by which he gets his personality, and then through a process of taking the different roles that all the others furnish he comes to get the attitude of the members of the community. Such, in a certain sense, is the structure of a man's personality. There are certain common responses which each individual has toward certain common things, and insofar as those common responses are awakened in the individual when he is affecting other persons he arouses his own self. The structure, then, on which the self is built is this response which is common to all, for one has to be a member of a community to be a self. Such responses are abstract attitudes, but they constitute just what we term a man's character. They give him what we term his principles, the acknowledged attitudes of all members of the community toward what are the values of that community. He is putting himself in the place of the generalized other, which represents the organized responses of all the members of the group. It is that which guides conduct controlled by principles, and a person who has such an organized group of responses is a man who we say has character, in the moral sense.

. . . I have so far emphasized what I have called the structures upon which the self is constructed, the framework of the self, as it were. Of course we are not only what is common to all: Each one of the selves is different from everyone else; but there has to be such a common structure as I have sketched in order that we may be members of a community at all. We cannot be ourselves unless we are also members in whom there is a community of attitudes which control the attitudes of all. We cannot have rights unless we have common attitudes. That which we have acquired as self-conscious persons makes us such members of society and gives us selves. Selves can only exist in definite relationships to other selves. No hard-and-fast line can be drawn between our own selves and the selves of others, since our own selves exist and enter as such into our experience only insofar as the selves of others exist and enter as such into our experience also. The individual possesses a self only in relation to the selves of the other members of his social group; and the structure of his self expresses or reflects the general behavior pattern of this social group to which he belongs, just as does the structure of the self of every other individual belonging to this social group.

Notes

1. Man's behavior is such in his social group that he is able to become an object to himself, a fact which constitutes him a more advanced product of evolutionary development than are the lower animals. Fundamentally it is this social fact—and not his alleged possession of a soul or mind with which he, as an individual, has been mysteriously and supernaturally endowed, and with which the lower animals have not been endowed—that differentiates him from them.

2. It is generally recognized that the specifically social expressions of intelligence, or the exercise of what is often called "social intelligence," depend upon the given individual's ability to take the roles of, or "put himself in the place of," the other individuals implicated with him in given social situations; and upon his consequent sensitivity to their attitudes toward himself and toward one another. These specifically social expressions of intelligence, of course, acquire unique significance in terms of our view that the whole nature of intelligence is social to the very core—that this putting of one's self in the places of others, this taking by one's self of their roles or attitudes, is not merely one of the various aspects or expressions of intelligence or intelligent behavior, but is the very essence of its character. Spearman's "X factor" in intelligence—the unknown factor

which, according to him, intelligence contains—is simply (if our social theory of intelligence is correct) this ability of the intelligent individual to take the attitude of the other, or the attitudes of others, thus realizing the significations or grasping the meanings of the symbols or gestures in terms of which thinking proceeds; and thus being able to carry on with himself the internal conversation with these symbols or gestures which thinking involves.

3. The unity of the mind is not identical with the unity of the self. The unity of the self is constituted by the unity of the entire relational pattern of social behavior and experience in which the individual is implicated, and which is reflected in the structure of the self; but many of the aspects or features of this entire pattern do not enter into consciousness, so that the unity of the mind is in a sense an abstraction from the more inclusive unity of the self.

4. It is possible for inanimate objects, no less than for other human organisms, to form parts of the generalized and organized—the completely socialized—other for any given human individual, insofar as he responds to such objects socially or in a social fashion (by means of the mechanism of thought, the internalized conversation of gestures). Any thing—any object or set of objects, whether animate or inanimate, human or animal, or merely physical—toward which he acts, or to which he responds, socially, is an element in what for him is the generalized other; by taking the attitudes of which toward himself he becomes conscious of himself as an object or individual, and thus develops a self or personality. Thus, for example, the cult, in its primitive form, is merely the social embodiment of the relation between the given social group or community and its physical environment—an organized social means, adopted by the individual members of that group or community, of entering into social relations with that environment, or (in a sense) of carrying on conversations with it; and in this way that environment becomes part of the total generalized other for each of the

individual members of the given social group or community.

5. We have said that the internal conversation of the individual with himself in terms of words or significant gestures—the conversation which constitutes the process or activity of thinking—is carried on by the individual from the standpoint of the "generalized other." And the more abstract that conversation is, the more abstract thinking happens to be, the further removed is the generalized other from any connection with particular individuals. It is especially in abstract thinking, that is to say, that the conversation involved is carried on by the individual with the generalized other, rather than with any particular individuals. Thus it is, for example, that abstract concepts are concepts stated in terms of the attitudes of the entire social group or community; they are stated on the basis of the individual's consciousness of the attitudes of the generalized other toward them, as a result of his taking these attitudes of the generalized other and then responding to them. And thus it is also that abstract propositions are stated in a form which anyone—any other intelligent individual—will accept.

The Presentation of Self

Face-to-face interaction is a complex process by which people both convey and receive information about each other. In this selection, Erving Goffman presents basic observations about how everyone tries to influence how others perceive them. In addition, he suggests ways in which people can evaluate how honestly others present themselves.

When an individual enters the presence of others, they commonly seek to acquire information about him or to bring into play information about him already possessed. They will be interested in his general socio-economic status, his conception of self, his attitude toward them, his competence, his trustworthiness, etc. Although some of this information seems to be sought almost as an end in itself, there are usually quite practical reasons for acquiring it. Information about the individual helps to define the situation, enabling others to know in advance what he will expect of them and what they may expect of him. Informed in these ways, the others will know how best to act in order to call forth a desired response from him.

For those present, many sources of information become accessible and many carriers (or "sign-vehicles") become available for conveying this information. If unacquainted with the individual, observers can glean clues from his conduct and appearance which allow them to apply their previous experience with indi-viduals roughly similar to the one before them or, more important, to apply untested stereotypes to him. They can also assume from past experience that only individuals of a particular kind are likely to be found in a given social setting. They can rely on what the individual says about himself or on documentary evidence he provides as to who and what he is. If they know, or know of, the individual by virtue of experience prior to the interaction, they can rely on assumptions as to the persistence and generality of psychological traits as a means of predicting his present and future behavior.

However, during the period in which the individual is in the immediate presence of the others, few events may occur which directly provide the others with the conclusive information they will need if they are to direct wisely their own activity. Many crucial facts lie beyond the time and place of interaction or lie concealed within it. For example, the "true" or "real" attitudes, beliefs, and emotions of the individual can be ascertained only indirectly, through his avowals or through what appears to be involuntary expressive behavior. Similarly, if the individual offers the others a product or service, they will often find that during the interaction there will be no time and place immediately available for eating the pudding that the proof can be found in. They will be forced to accept some events as conventional or natural signs of something not directly available to the senses. In Ichheiser's terms,[1] the individual will have to act so that he intentionally or unintentionally *expresses* himself, and the others will in turn have to be *impressed* in some way by him.

The expressiveness of the individual (and therefore his capacity to give impressions) appears to involve two radically different kinds of sign activity: the expression that he *gives,* and the expression that he *gives off.* The first involves verbal symbols or their substitutes which he uses admittedly and solely to convey the information that he and the others are known to attach to these symbols. This is communication in the traditional and narrow sense. The second involves a wide range of action that others can treat as symptomatic of the actor, the expectation being that the action was performed for reasons other than the information conveyed in this way. As we shall have to see, this distinction has an only initial validity. The individual does of course intentionally convey misinformation by means of both of these types of communication, the first involving deceit, the second feigning.

. . . Let us now turn from the others to the point of view of the individual who presents himself before them. He may wish them to think highly of him, or to think that he thinks highly of them, or to perceive how in fact he feels toward them, or to obtain no clear-cut impression; he may wish to ensure sufficient harmony so that the interaction can be sustained, or to defraud, get rid of, confuse, mislead, antagonize, or insult them. Regardless of the particular objective which the individual

has in mind and of his motive for having this objective, it will be in his interests to control the conduct of the others, especially their responsive treatment of him. This control is achieved largely by influencing the definition of the situation which the others come to formulate, and he can influence this definition by expressing himself in such a way as to give them the kind of impression that will lead them to act voluntarily in accordance with his own plan. Thus, when an individual appears in the presence of others, there will usually be some reason for him to mobilize his activity so that it will convey an impression to others which it is in his interests to convey. Since a girl's dormitory mates will glean evidence of her popularity from the calls she receives on the phone, we can suspect that some girls will arrange for calls to be made, and Willard Waller's finding can be anticipated:

> It has been reported by many observers that a girl who is called to the telephone in the dormitories will often allow herself to be called several times, in order to give all the other girls ample opportunity to hear her paged.[2]

Of the two kinds of communication—expressions given and expressions given off—this report will be primarily concerned with the latter, with the more theatrical and contextual kind, the nonverbal, presumably unintentional kind, whether this communication be purposely engineered or not. As an example of what we must try to examine, I would like to cite at length a novelistic incident in which Preedy, a vacationing Englishman, makes his first appearance on the beach of his summer hotel in Spain:

> But in any case he took care to avoid catching anyone's eye. First of all, he had to make it clear to those potential companions of his holiday that they were of no concern to him whatsoever. He stared

through them, round them, over them— eyes lost in space. The beach might have been empty. If by chance a ball was thrown his way, he looked surprised; then let a smile of amusement lighten his face (Kindly Preedy), looked round dazed to see that there were people on the beach, tossed it back with a smile to himself and not a smile at the people, and then resumed carelessly his nonchalant survey of space.

But it was time to institute a little parade, the parade of the Ideal Preedy. By devious handlings he gave any who wanted to look a chance to see the title of his book—a Spanish translation of Homer, classic thus, but not daring, cosmopolitan too—and then gathered together his beach-wrap and bag into a neat sand-resistant pile (Methodical and Sensible Preedy), rose slowly to stretch at ease his huge frame (Big-Cat Preedy), and tossed aside his sandals (Carefree Preedy, after all).

The marriage of Preedy and the sea! There were alternative rituals. The first involved the stroll that turns into a run and a dive straight into the water, thereafter smoothing into a strong splashless crawl towards the horizon. But of course not really to the horizon. Quite suddenly he would turn on to his back and thrash great white splashes with his legs, somehow thus showing that he could have swum further had he wanted to, and then would stand up a quarter out of water for all to see who it was.

The alternative course was simpler, it avoided the cold-water shock and it avoided the risk of appearing too high-spirited. The point was to appear to be so used to the sea, the Mediterranean, and this particular beach, that one might as well be in the sea as out of it. It in-

volved a slow stroll down and into the edge of the water—not even noticing his toes were wet, land and water all the same to him!—with his eyes up at the sky gravely surveying portents, invisible to others, of the weather (Local Fisherman Preedy).[3]

The novelist means us to see that Preedy is improperly concerned with the extensive impressions he feels his sheer bodily action is giving off to those around him. We can malign Preedy further by assuming that he has acted merely in order to give a particular impression, that this is a false impression, and that the others present receive either no impression at all, or, worse still, the impression that Preedy is affectedly trying to cause them to receive this particular impression. But the important point for us here is that the kind of impression Preedy thinks he is making is in fact the kind of impression that others correctly and incorrectly glean from someone in their midst. . . .

There is one aspect of the others' response that bears special comment here. Knowing that the individual is likely to present himself in a light that is favorable to him, the others may divide what they witness into two parts; a part that is relatively easy for the individual to manipulate at will, being chiefly his verbal assertions, and a part in regard to which he seems to have little concern or control, being chiefly derived from the expressions he gives off. The others may then use what are considered to be the ungovernable aspects of his expressive behavior as a check upon the validity of what is conveyed by the governable aspects. In this a fundamental asymmetry is demonstrated in the communication process, the individual presumably being aware of only one stream of his communication, the witnesses of this stream and one other. For example, in Shetland Isle one crofter's wife, in serving native dishes to a visitor from the mainland of

Britain, would listen with a polite smile to his polite claims of liking what he was eating; at the same time she would take note of the rapidity with which the visitor lifted his fork or spoon to his mouth, the eagerness with which he passed food into his mouth, and the gusto expressed in chewing the food, using these signs as a check on the stated feelings of the eater. The same woman, in order to discover what one acquaintance (A) "actually" thought of another acquaintance (B), would wait until B was in the presence of A but engaged in conversation with still another person (C). She would then covertly examine the facial expressions of A as he regarded B in conversation with C. Not being in conversation with B, and not being directly observed by him, A would sometimes relax usual constraints and tactful deceptions, and freely express what he was "actually" feeling about B. This Shetlander, in short, would observe the unobserved observer.

Now given the fact that others are likely to check up on the more controllable aspects of behavior by means of the less controllable, one can expect that sometimes the individual will try to exploit this very possibility, guiding the impression he makes through behavior felt to be reliably informing.[4] For example, in gaining admission to a tight social circle, the participant observer may not only wear an accepting look while listening to an informant, but may also be careful to wear the same look when observing the informant talking to others; observers of the observer will then not as easily discover where he actually stands. A specific illustration may be cited from Shetland Isle. When a neighbor dropped in to have a cup of tea, he would ordinarily wear at least a hint of an expectant warm smile as he passed through the door into the cottage. Since lack of physical obstructions outside the cottage and lack of light within it usually made it possible to observe the visitor unobserved as he

approached the house, islanders sometimes took pleasure in watching the visitor drop whatever expression he was manifesting and replace it with a sociable one just before reaching the door. However, some visitors, in appreciating that this examination was occurring, would blindly adopt a social face a long distance from the house, thus ensuring the projection of a constant image.

This kind of control upon the part of the individual reinstates the symmetry of the communication process, and sets the stage for a kind of information game—a potentially infinite cycle of concealment, discovery, false revelation, and rediscovery. It should be added that since the others are likely to be relatively unsuspicious of the presumably unguided aspects of the individual's conduct, he can gain much by controlling it. The others of course may sense that the individual is manipulating the presumably spontaneous aspects of his behavior, and seek in this very act of manipulation some shading of conduct that the individual has not managed to control. This again provides a check upon the individual's behavior, this time his presumably uncalculated behavior, thus re-establishing the asymmetry of the communication process. Here I would like only to add the suggestion that the arts of piercing an individual's effort at calculated unintentionality seem better developed than our capacity to manipulate our own behavior, so that regardless of how many steps have occurred in the information game, the witness is likely to have the advantage over the actor, and the initial asymmetry of the communication process is likely to be retained. . . .

In everyday life, of course, there is a clear understanding that first impressions are important. Thus, the work adjustment of those in service occupations will often hinge upon a capacity to seize and hold the initiative in the service relation, a capacity that will require subtle aggressiveness on the part of the server when he is of lower socioeconomic status than his client. W.F. Whyte suggests the waitress as an example:

> The first point that stands out is that the waitress who bears up under pressure does not simply respond to her customers. She acts with some skill to control their behavior. The first question to ask when we look at the customer relationship is, "Does the waitress get the jump on the customer, or does the customer get the jump on the waitress?" The skilled waitress realizes the crucial nature of this question. . . .
>
> The skilled waitress tackles the customer with confidence and without hesitation. For example, she may find that a new customer has seated himself before she could clear off the dirty dishes and change the cloth. He is now leaning on the table studying the menu. She greets him, says, "May I change the cover, please?" and, without waiting for an answer, takes his menu away from him so that he moves back from the table, and she goes about her work. The relationship is handled politely but firmly, and there is never any question as to who is in charge.[5]

When the interaction that is initiated by "first impressions" is itself merely the initial interaction in an extended series of interactions involving the same participants, we speak of "getting off on the right foot" and feel that it is crucial that we do so. Thus, one learns that some teachers take the following view:

> You can't ever let them get the upper hand on you or you're through. So I start out tough. The first day I get a new class in, I let them know who's boss. . . . You've got to start off tough, then you can ease up as you go along. If you start out easy-going, when you try to get tough, they'll just look at you and laugh.[6]

. . . In stressing the fact that the initial definition of the situation projected by an individual tends to provide a plan for the cooperative activity that follows—in stressing this action point of view—we must not overlook the crucial fact that any projected definition of the situation also has a distinctive moral character. It is this moral character of projections that will chiefly concern us in this report. Society is organized on the principle that any individual who possesses certain social characteristics has a moral right to expect that others will value and treat him in an appropriate way. Connected with this principle is a second, namely that an individual who implicitly or explicitly signifies that he has certain social characteristics ought in fact to be what he claims he is. In consequence, when an individual projects a definition of the situation and thereby makes an implicit or explicit claim to be a person of a particular kind, he automatically exerts a moral demand upon the others, obliging them to value and treat him in the manner that persons of his kind have a right to expect. He also implicitly foregoes all claims to be things he does not appear to be[7] and hence foregoes the treatment that would be appropriate for such individuals. The others find, then, that the individual has informed them as to what is and as to what they *ought* to see as the "is."

One cannot judge the importance of definitional disruptions by the frequency with which they occur, for apparently they would occur more frequently were not constant precautions taken. We find that preventive practices are constantly employed to avoid these embarrassments and that corrective practices are constantly employed to compensate for discrediting occurrences that have not been successfully avoided. When the individual employs these strategies and tactics to protect his own projections, we may refer to them as "defensive practices"; when a participant employs them to save the definition of the situation projected by another, we speak of "protective practices" or "tact." Together, defensive and protective practices comprise the techniques employed to safeguard the impression fostered by an individual during his presence before others. It should be added that while we may be ready to see that no fostered impression would survive if defensive practices were not employed, we are less ready perhaps to see that few impressions could survive if those who received the impression did not exert tact in their reception of it.

In addition to the fact that precautions are taken to prevent disruption of projected definitions, we may also note that an intense interest in these disruptions comes to play a significant role in the social life of the group. Practical jokes and social games are played in which embarrassments which are to be taken unseriously are purposely engineered.[8] Fantasies are created in which devastating exposures occur. Anecdotes from the past—real, embroidered, or fictitious—are told and retold, detailing disruptions which occurred, almost occurred, or occurred and were admirably resolved. There seems to be no grouping which does not have a ready supply of these games, reveries, and cautionary tales, to be used as a source of humor, a catharsis for anxieties, and a sanction for inducing individuals to be modest in their claims and reasonable in their projected expectations. The individual may tell himself through dreams of getting into impossible positions. Families tell of the time a guest got his dates mixed and arrived when neither the house nor anyone in it was ready for him. Journalists tell of times when an all-too-meaningful misprint occurred, and the paper's assumption of objectivity or decorum was humorously discredited. Public servants tell of times a client ridiculously misunderstood form instructions, giving answers which

implied an unanticipated and bizarre definition of the situation.[9] Seamen, whose home away from home is rigorously he-man, tell stories of coming back home and inadvertently asking mother to "pass the fucking butter."[10] Diplomats tell of the time a near-sighted queen asked a republican ambassador about the health of his king.[11]

To summarize, then, I assume that when an individual appears before others he will have many motives for trying to control the impression they receive of the situation.

Notes

1. Gustav Ichheiser, "Misunderstandings in Human Relations," supplement to *The American Journal of Sociology* 55 (Sept., 1949), 6–7.
2. Willard Waller, "The Rating and Dating Complex," *American Sociological Review* 2 (1937), 730.
3. William Sansom, *A Contest of Ladies* (London: Hogarth, 1956), pp. 230–32.
4. The widely read and rather sound writings of Stephen Potter are concerned in part with signs that can be engineered to give a shrewd observer the apparently incidental cues he needs to discover concealed virtues the gamesman does not in fact possess.
5. W. F. Whyte, "When Workers and Customers Meet," chap. 7, *Industry and Society*, ed. W. F. Whyte (New York: McGraw-Hill, 1946), pp. 132–33.
6. Teacher interview quoted by Howard S. Becker, "Social Class Variations in the Teacher-Pupil Relationship," *Journal of Educational Sociology* 25, p. 459.
7. This role of the witness in limiting what it is the individual can be has been stressed by Existentialists, who see it as a basic threat to individual freedom. See Jean-Paul Sartre, *Being and Nothingness*, trans. Hazel E. Barnes (New York: Philosophical Library, 1956), pp. 365ff.
8. Goffman, op. cit., pp. 319–27.
9. Peter Blau, "Dynamics of Bureaucracy" (Ph. D. dissertation, Department of Sociology, Columbia University, forthcoming, University of Chicago Press), pp. 127–29.

10. Walter M. Beattie, Jr., "The Merchant Seaman" (unpublished M.A. Report, Department of Sociology, University of Chicago, 1950), p. 35.
11. Sir Frederick Ponsonby, *Recollections of Three Reigns* (New York: Dutton, 1952), p. 46.

Selected Readings

Abel, Reuben. "Pragmatism and the Outlook of Modern Science," Philosophy and Phenomenological Research 27 (1966): 45–54.

Aboulafia, Mitchell. The Mediating Self: Mead, Sartre and self-determination. New Haven: Yale University, 1986.

Aboulafia, Mitchell. "Mead, Sartre: Self, Object and Reflection", Phil. Soc. (1986): 63–86.

Aboulafia, Mitchell. "Self-consciousness and the Quasi-epic of the Master", Philosophical Forum 18, (1987): 304–328.

Aboulafia, Mitchell (Ed). Philosophy, Social Theory and the thought of George Herbert Mead. Albany, NY: State University of New York Press (1991).

Aboulafia, Mitchell. "Mead, Sartre: Self, Object and Reflection", Philosophy and Social Criticism 11, (1986): 63-86.

Aboulafia, Mitchell. "Mead and the Social Self", in Robert W. Burt (ed), Frontiers in American Philosophy, Vol I. College Station, Texas: Texas A&M University Press (1992).

Aboulafia, Mitchell. "Was George Herbert Mead a Feminist?", Hypatia 8 (1993): 145–158.

Aboulafia, Mitchell. "Habermas and Mead: On Universality and Individuality", Constellations 2, (1995): 95–113.

Baert, Patrick J. N. "The Creation of an Invented Future: An Inquiry into G.H. Mead's Relatively-Open Future with Special Reference to Sociological Theory", Phil Quart. 29, (1980): 319–338.

Baert, Patrick J. "Social Evolution and Complexity", Paper presented at American Sociological Association (2000).

Baeten, Elizabeth M. "An American Naturalist Account of Culture", Metaphilosophy 27, (1996): 408–425.

Baldwin, John D. "George Herbert Mead and Modern Behaviorism", Pacific Sociological Review 24, (1981): 411–440.

Baldwin, John D. "Comment on Denzin's 'Note on Emotionality, Self, and Interaction'", American Journal of Sociology 90, (1984): 418–422.

Baldwin, John D. "Social Behaviorism on Emotions: Mead and Modern Behaviorism Compared", Symbolic Interaction 8, (1985): 263–289.

Callero, Peter L. "Putting the Social in Prosocial Behavior: An Interactionist Approach to Altruism", Humboldt Journal of Social Relations 13, (1986): 15–32.

Campbell, James. "George Herbert Mead on Intelligent Social Reconstruction", Symbolic Interaction 4, (1981): 191–205.

Campbell, James. "Review of 'American Sociology and Pragmatism: Mead, Chicago Sociology and Symbolic Interaction'", Transactions of the Ch. S. Peirce Society 18 (1982): 105–8.

Campbell, James. "Mead and Pragmatism", Symbolic Interaction 6, (1983): 383–92.

Campbell, James. "Politics and Conceptual Reconstruction," Philosophy and Rhetoric 17 (1984): 156-170.

Campbell, James. "George Herbert Mead: Philosophy and the Pragmatic Self", in Marcus Singer (ed) American Philosophy Cambridge: Cambridge University Press (1985).

Decesare, Richard A. A Comparative Evaluation of the Social Self in the Philosophies of George Herbert Mead and Gabriel Marcel. Doctoral Dissertation: 1968.

Deegan, Mary Jo. "Feminist pragmatism and the spirit of play: Jan Addams on Joy and Justice in the Democratic Society", paper presented at the Annual meeting of the American Sociological Association (1997).

Deegan, Mary Jo. "The world of Chicago Pragmatism", Paper presented at the Annual meeting of the American Sociological Association (1999).

Garnett, A.C. "Naturalism and the Concept of Obligation", Review of Metaphysics 2, (1949): 15–34.

Geier, "Der genius loci lipsiensis [The genius loci Lipsiensis]", Kultursoziologie (1996): 109-131.

Gier, Nicholas F. "Wittgenstein, intentionally and behaviorism", Metaphilosophy 13 (1982): 46–64.

Gillin, Charles T. "Freedom and the Limits of Social Behaviorism", Sociology 9 (1975): 29–47.

Gillogly, Robert Ross. Homo Socius—A Roycean Interpretation. Doctoral Dissertation. Claremont Graduate School, 1981. (see Appendix 1).

Glock, Hans-Johann. "Vygotsky and Mead on the Self, Meaning and Internalization", Stud. Soviet Tho. 31, (1986): 131–148.

Lee, Donald S. "The Pragmatic Origins of Concepts and Categories: Mead and Piaget", Southern Journal of Philosophy 21, (1983): 211–228.

Lee, Grace Chin. Social Individualism, A Systematic Treatment of the Metaphysics of George Herbert Mead. Doctoral Dissertation. Bryn Mawr College: 1940.

Lee, Grace Chin. George Herbert Mead: Philosopher of the Social Individual. New York: King's Crown Press, 1945.

Lee, Harold N., "Mead's Doctrine of the Past", Tulane Studies in Philosophy 12 (1963): 52–75.

Lee, Harold N. "Comment on David L. Miller's Paper 'George Herbert Mead's Conception of Creativity.'" Paper read at the meeting of the Society for Philosophy of Creativity at Cleveland, Ohio, May 1, 1969.

Lee, Harold N. "Pragmatism and a Behavioral Theory of Meaning," Journal of the History of Philosophy 14, (1976): 439–447.

Critical-Thinking Questions

1. What is symbolic interaction?

   _____

   _____

   _____

   _____

   _____

   _____

   _____

   _____

2. What are the three stages of development?

   _____

   _____

   _____

   _____

   _____

   _____

   _____

   _____

3. What is the I and Me?

   _____

   _____

   _____

   _____

   _____

   _____

   _____

CHAPTER VI

Functionalism and Conflict Views

Most of the sciences have several views or interpretations of the same phenomena. Quantum Physics for example has three views of the Universe. There is the "Big Bang Theory," "String Theory," and "Creationism." Albert Einstein, the foremost scientist in the twentieth century, once asked the question— Did God have choices in creating the universe? suggesting that some day he would understand the right choice of the law of nature, if God deems it so. In Astronomy there are several measurements for distance of space objects, there is the astronomical unit, light year, and parsec. Sociology as a science is no different. Although there are many views within sociology, two have become predominate because they are polar opposite understanding of social change in society—Functionalism developed by Talcott Parsons and Conflict View seen by Raf Dahrendorf.

Functionalism defined is that parts of society (family, education, the economy), and so on are structured to maintain social equilibrium. If a part of society is dysfunctional, it is not maintaining social balance. This dysfunctional part creates dysfunctionality among all other parts that it embraces. A dysfunctional family form for example affects the education of the children in that family, crime, and employment.

Talcott Parsons, by his own admission developed a theory of voluntaristic social action or Functionalism through a synthesis of Weber, Durkheim and Pareto's ideas.

Parsons' understanding of Durkheim's concepts of religion, philosophy, ideas, and morals all as products of the human social condition are expressed as social realities and are a society's conscience collective. Resulting in social cohesiveness of the group, assuring effect operation of that society is paramount for Parsons' Functionalism.

Although we have not looked at Pareto (an Italian sociologist), he deeply influenced Parsons because he was the first to use the term "social system" to describe the general state of human society. The chief task of sociology for Pareto is to investigate the nature and property of social systems, the transformations they undergo and the relationship between these elements, which produce social equilibrium.

Parsons uses Weber's concept of "Ideal Type" as another key sociological concept in the development of Functionalism. Weber and Parsons both saw society as having perfect or ideal standards by which members live. Very often we never achieve these ideal standards, but most actors are always making an effort. The American family form is an ideal type. The family is seen in the United States as consisting of four members. The parents (Mother/Father) and two children (one male, one female) are to replace the parents in society. Although there are no formal rules to this end, many of life's experience tacitly remind us of this form. A kitchen set always comes with four chairs, the toothbrush holder in the bathroom usually has only four spaces for the brushes and so on.

Parsons' sociological concept transforms these ideas into a set of analytical tools for interpretation and comparative study of systems known as "pattern variable", commonly referred to as the AGIL scheme. The AGIL scheme consists of adaptation, goal attainment, integration and latency.

The Adaptation cell contains those instrumental actions and capacities toward the means and selection and cognitive symbolization for adaptation and change. Intrinsic to this cell is the concept of homeostasis or harmony and balance within social systems, and most importantly harmonious social change. Parsons argued that the actor as a biological entity is always interacting and adapting to his/her environment. The Goal attainment cell contains consummatory needs, selection and expressive symbolization for action toward goal attainment. The Integration Cell contains affiliations, the ability for integration based on moral evaluations and responsible action. The Latency Cell contains normative commitment to the ideals of balanced social change.

The key to Parsons' sociology is the institutionalization and generalization of values and norms. This process occurs in the "I" cell of the AGIL scheme. Located in the "L" cell is the solidarity and system membership. Moreover, when social change occurs it occurs within the "L" cell, because it is this cell which allows for the inclusion of the outgroup or acceptancy of new conflicts.

If this idea was placed into an equation it would look like this: I cell = universality and generalization of values and norms - L cell = inclusion acceptancy = social change.

One should view this paradigm as a stew pot in which meat and vegetable are placed in separately and cook down into a stew. Likewise, people from the four corners of the world come to live in the United States of America and bring with them their culture. In American society their culture is assimilated into the American psyche reducing the gap between each of us.

This view is not limited to only social integration: indeed it can be applied to many forms of acceptance and inclusion. Technology over the last three-four years has had an important impact on our economy and social life. During the late 1990s only a third of Americans had a home computer. Today nearly 75 percent of the population has a computer in their homes and nearly 90 percent of the population has access to a computer. This piece of technology has had a profound influence on almost all segments of social life. In the AGIL scheme one can almost see this social change occurring before our eyes. In the A-cell the economy has gone through a change requiring most, if not all, to have a working knowledge of computers. We adapt to this requirement. In the G-cell member's behavior leads to gaining the necessary skills to operate a computer (formal or informal). In the I-cell the overall society suggests that we must learn computers through; and in the L-cell the official rules reflect this change. So one cannot graduate from college unless he/she is computer literate.

Raf Dahrendorf on the other hand argues that social systems are based in hierarchies of power or as Weber suggested "status groups"— people with shared common interests such as race, age, gender, and class, who are always in conflict and opposing one another for what they conceive to be "scarce resources" such as power, authority, wealth, health care, education employment and housing. Therefore, social conflict is ever present and can never be eliminated.

Conflict is progress and progress is conflict. This is because once a solution is uncovered from one set of conflicts and social change occurs, a series of new conflicts arise. Society, therefore, is always changing, and conflict is an ever-present feature.

One should view this paradigm as a tossed salad. If there are levels of vegetables placed one on top of each other, all you have are levels (or status groups) of vegetables. Someone must toss the vegetables in order to have a salad. Likewise, in social systems someone must do something to gain advancement, for example, as in a labor strike.

Functionalism views social change as occurring naturally and through interaction and adaptation to the social environment. A conflict view suggests that society is inherently antagonistic and requires an actor to create conflict in order for there to be change.

The Social Structure of Medicine

Talcott Parsons

Talcott Parsons, one of the most influential U.S. sociologists during the twentieth century, contributed greatly to the development of structural-functional analysis. In this selection, he examines the significance of health and illness within a social system, with particular attention to the social roles of physicians and patients.

A little reflection will show immediately that the problem of health is intimately involved in the functional prerequisites of the social system. . . . Certainly by almost any definition health is included in the functional needs of the individual member of the society so that from the point of view of functioning of the social system, too low a general level of health, too high an incidence of illness, is dysfunctional. This is in the first instance because illness incapacitates for the effective performance of social roles. It could of course be that this incidence was completely uncontrollable by social action, an independently given condition of social life. But insofar as it is controllable, through rational action or otherwise, it is clear that there is a functional interest of the society in its control, broadly in the minimization of illness. As one special aspect of this, attention may be called to premature death. From a variety of points of view, the birth and rearing of a child constitute a "cost" to the society, through pregnancy, child care, socialization, formal train-

ing, and many other channels. Premature death, before the individual has had the opportunity to play out his full quota of social roles, means that only a partial "return" for this cost has been received.

All this would be true were illness purely a "natural phenomenon" in the sense that, like the vagaries of the weather, it was not, to our knowledge, reciprocally involved in the motivated interactions of human beings. In this case illness would be something which merely "happened to" people, which involved consequences which had to be dealt with and conditions which might or might not be controllable but was in no way an expression of motivated behavior.

This is in fact the case for a very important part of illness, but it has become increasingly clear, by no means for all. In a variety of ways motivational factors accessible to analysis in action terms are involved in the etiology of many illnesses, and conversely, though without exact correspondence, many conditions are open to therapeutic influence through motivational channels. To take the simplest kind of case, differential exposure, to injuries or to infection, is certainly motivated, and the role of unconscious wishes to be injured or to fall ill in such cases has been clearly demonstrated. Then there is the whole range of "psychosomatic" illness about which knowledge has been rapidly accumulating in recent years. Finally, there is the field of "mental disease," the symptoms of which occur mainly on the behavioral level. . . .

Summing up, we may say that illness is a state of disturbance in the "normal" functioning of the total human individual, including both the state of the organism as a biological system and of his personal and social adjustments. It is thus partly biologically and partly socially defined. . . .

Medical practice . . . is a "mechanism" in the social system for coping with the illnesses of its members. It involves a set of institutionalized roles. . . . The immediately relevant social structures consist in the patterning of the role of the medical practitioner himself and, though to common sense it may seem superfluous to analyze it, that of the "sick person" himself. . . .

The role of the medical practitioner belongs to the general class of "professional" roles, a subclass of the larger group of occupational roles. Caring for the sick is thus not an incidental activity of other roles though, for example, mothers do a good deal of it—but has become functionally specialized as a full-time "job." This, of course, is by no means true of all societies. As an occupational role it is institutionalized about the technical content of the function which is given a high degree of primacy relative to other status-determinants. It is thus inevitable both that incumbency of the role should be achieved and that performance criteria by standards of technical competence should be prominent. Selection for it and the context of its performance are to a high degree segregated from other bases of social status and solidarities. . . . Unlike the role of the businessman, however, it is collectivity-oriented not self-oriented.

The importance of this patterning is, in one context, strongly emphasized by its relation to the cultural tradition. One basis for the division of labor is the specialization of technical competence. The role of physician is far along the continuum of increasingly high levels of technical competence required for performance. Because of the complexity and subtlety of the knowledge and skill required and the consequent length and intensity of training, it is difficult to see how the functions could, under modern conditions, be ascribed to people occupying a prior status as one of their activities in that status, following the pattern by which, to a degree, responsibility for the health of her children is ascribed to the mother-status. There is an intrinsic connection between achieved statuses and the requirements of high technical competence. . . .

High technical competence also implies specificity of function. Such intensive devotion to expertness in matters of health and disease precludes comparable expertness in other fields. The physician is not, by virtue of his modern role, a generalized "wise man" or sage—though there is considerable folklore to that effect—but a specialist whose superiority to his fellows is confined to the specific sphere of his technical training and experience. For example, one does not expect the physician as such to have better judgment about foreign policy or tax legislation than any other comparably intelligent and well-educated citizen. There are of course elaborate subdivisions of specialization within the profession. . . . The physician is [also] expected to treat an objective problem in objective, scientifically justifiable terms. For example, whether he likes or dislikes the particular patient as a person is supposed to be irrelevant, as indeed it is to most purely objective problems of how to handle a particular disease.

. . . The "ideology" of the profession lays great emphasis on the obligation of the physician to put the "welfare of the patient" above his personal interests, and regards "commercialism" as the most serious and insidious evil with which it has to contend. The line, therefore, is drawn primarily vis-à-vis "business." The "profit motive" is supposed to be drastically excluded from the medical world. This attitude is, of course, shared with the other professions, but it is perhaps more pronounced in the medical case than in any single one except perhaps the clergy. . . .

An increasing proportion of medical practice is now taking place in the context of organization. To a large extent this is necessitated by the technological development of medicine itself, above all the need for technical facilities beyond the reach of the individual practitioner, and the fact that treating the same case often involves the complex cooperation of several different kinds of physicians as well as of auxiliary personnel. This greatly alters the relation of the physician to the rest of the instrumental complex. He tends to be relieved of much responsibility and hence necessarily of freedom, in relation to his patients other than in his technical role. Even if a hospital executive is a physician himself, he is not in the usual sense engaged in the "practice of medicine" in performing his functions any more than the president of the Miners' Union is engaged in mining coal.

As was noted, for common sense there may be some question of whether "being sick" constitutes a social role at all—isn't it simply a state of fact, a "condition"? Things are not quite so simple as this. The test is the existence of a set of institutionalized expectations and the corresponding sentiments and sanctions.

There seem to be four aspects of the institutionalized expectation system relative to the sick role. First is the exemption from normal social role responsibilities, which of course is relative to the nature and severity of the illness. This exemption requires legitimation by and to the various alters involved and the physician often serving as court of appeal as well as a direct legitimizing agent. It is noteworthy that, like all institutionalized patterns, the legitimation of being enough to avoid obligations can not only be a right of the sick person but an obligation upon him. People are often resistant to admitting they are sick and it is not uncommon for others to tell them that they *ought* to stay in bed. The word generally has a moral connotation. It goes almost without saying that this legitimation has the social function of protection against "malingering."

The second closely related aspect is the instutionalized definition that the sick person cannot be expected by "pulling himself together" to get well by an act of decision or will. In this sense also he is exempted from responsibility—he is in a condition that must "be taken care of." His "condition" must be changed, not merely his "attitude." Of course the process of recovery may be spontaneous but while the illness lasts he cant "help it." This element in the definition of the state of illness is obviously crucial as a bridge to the acceptance of "help."

The third element is the definition of the state of being ill as itself undesirable with its obligation to want to "get well." The first two elements of legitimation of the sick role thus are conditional in a highly important sense. It is a relative legitimation so long as he is in this unfortunate state which both he and alter hope he can get out of as expeditiously as possible.

Finally, the fourth closely related element is the obligation—in proportion to the severity of the condition, of course—to seek *technical competent* help, namely, in the most usual case, that of a physician and to *cooperate* with him in the process of trying to get well. It is here, of course, that the role of the sick person as patient becomes articulated with that of the physician in a complementary role structure.

It is evident from the above that the role of motivational factors in illness immensely broadens the scope and increases the importance of the institutionalized role aspect of being sick. For then the problem of social control becomes much more than one of ascertaining facts and drawing lines. The privileges and exemptions of the sick role may become objects of a "secondary gain" which the patient is positively motivated, usually unconsciously, to secure or to retain. The problem, therefore, of the balance of motivations to recover becomes of first importance. In general motivational balances of great functional significance to the social system are institutionally controlled, and it should, therefore, not be surprising that this is no exception.

A few further points may be made about the specific patterning of the sick role and its relation to social structure. It is, in the first place, a "contingent" role into which anyone, regardless of his status in other respects, may come. It is, furthermore, in the type case temporary. One may say that it is in a certain sense a "negatively achieved" role, through failure to "keep well," though, of course, positive motivations also operate, which by that very token must be motivations to deviance. . . .

The orientation of the sick role vis-à-vis the physician is also defined as collectively-oriented. It is true that the patient has a very obvious self-interest in getting well in most cases, though this point may not always be so simple. But once he has called in a physician the attitude is clearly marked, that he has assumed the obligation to cooperate with that physician in what is regarded as a common task. The obverse of the physician's obligation to be guided by the welfare of the patient is the latter's obligation to "do his part" to the best of his ability. This point is clearly brought out, for example, in the attitudes of the profession toward what is called "shopping around." By that is meant the practice of a patient "checking" the advice of one physician against that of another without telling physician A that he intends to consult physician B, or if he comes back to A that he has done so or who B is. The medical view is that if the patient is not satisfied with the advice his physician gives him he may properly do one of two things. First he may request a consultation, even naming the physician he wishes called in, but in that case it is physician A not the patient who must call B in, the patient may not see B independently, and above all not without A's knowledge. The other proper recourse is to terminate the relation with A and become "B's patient." The notable fact here is that a pattern of behavior on the part not only of the physician but also of the patient, is expected which is in sharp contrast to perfectly legitimate behavior in a commercial relationship. If he is buying a car there is no objection to the customer going to a number of dealers before making up his mind, and there is no obligation for him to inform any one dealer what others he is consulting, to say nothing of approaching the Chevrolet dealer only through the Ford dealer.

The doctor-patient relationship is thus focused on these pattern elements. The patient has a need for technical services because he doesn't—nor do his lay associates, family members, etc.—"know" what is the matter or what to do about it, nor does he control the necessary facilities. The physician is a technical expert who by special training and experience, and by an institutionally validated status, is qualified to "help" the patient in a situation institutionally defined as legitimate in a relative sense but as needing help. . . .

Manifest and Latent Functions

Robert K. Merton

Robert Merton made a major contribution to structural-functional theory by pointing out that social patterns have both manifest and latent functions. Manifest functions are those consequences that are familiar, planned, and generally recognized. Latent functions, on the other hand, are unfamiliar, unplanned, and widely overlooked. For this reason, Merton argued, comprehending latent functions is a special responsibility of sociologists. Merton illustrates this process by offering observations about the pattern of conspicuous consumption.

. . . Armed with the concept of latent function, the sociologist extends his inquiry in those very directions which promise most for the theoretic development of the discipline. He examines the familiar (or planned) social practice to ascertain the latent, and hence generally unrecognized, functions (as well, of course, as the manifest functions). He considers, for example, the consequences of the new wage plan for, say, the trade union in which the workers are organized or the consequences of a propaganda program, not only for increasing its avowed purpose of stirring up patriotic fervor, but also for making large numbers of people reluctant to speak their minds when they differ with official policies, etc. In short, it is suggested that the *distinctive* intellectual contributions of the sociologist are found primarily in the study of unintended consequences (among which are latent functions) of social practices, as well as in the study of anticipated consequences (among which are manifest functions).

The Pattern of Conspicuous Consumption

The manifest purpose of buying consumption goods is, of course, the satisfaction of the needs for which these goods are explicitly designed. Thus, automobiles are obviously intended to provide a certain kind of transportation; candles, to provide light; choice articles of food to provide sustenance; rare art products to provide aesthetic pleasure. Since these products *do* have these uses, it was largely assumed that these encompass the range of socially significant functions. Veblen indeed suggests that this was ordinarily the prevailing view (in the pre-Veblenian era, of course): "The end of acquisition and accumulation is conventionally held to be the consumption of the goods accumulated. . . . This is at least felt to be the economically legitimate end of acquisition, *which alone it is incumbent on the theory to take account of.*

However, says Veblen in effect, as sociologists we must go on to consider the latent functions of acquisition, accumulation, and consumption, and these latent functions are remote indeed from the manifest functions. "But, it is only when taken in a sense of far removed from its naive meaning [i.e., manifest function] that the consumption of goods can be said to afford the incentive from which accumulation invariably proceeds." And among these latent functions, which help explain the persistence and the social location of the pattern of conspicuous consumption, is [the fact that] . . . it results in a *heightening or reaffirmation of social status.*

The Veblenian paradox is that people buy expensive goods not so much because they are superior but because they are expensive. For it is the latent equation ("costliness = mark of higher social status") which he singles out in his functional analysis, rather than the manifest equation ("costliness = excellence of the goods"). Not that he denies manifest functions *any* place in buttressing the pattern of conspicuous consumption. These, too, are operative. . . . *It is only that these direct, manifest functions do not fully account for the prevailing patterns of consumption. Otherwise put, if the latent functions of status-enhancement or status-reaffirmation were removed from the patterns of conspicuous consumption, these patterns would undergo severe changes of a sort which the "conventional" economist could not foresee.*

Note

1. Thorstein Veblen, *Theory of the Leisure Class* (1899) (New York: Vanguard Press, 1928), p. 25.

Selected Readings

The Social Theories of Talcott Parsons: A Critical Examination by Max Black; Prentice Hall, 1961

The Theory of Social and Economic Organization by A. M. Henderson, Talcott Parsons, Max Weber; Oxford University Press, 1947

Class and Class Conflict in Industrial Society by Dahrendorf Stanford University of California Press

The Chinese Family in the Communist Revolution Book by C. K. Yang, Talcott Parsons; Technology Press, Massachusetts Institute of Technology, 1959

Japan's Prospect Book by Edward A. Ackerman, William Henry Chamberlin, Merle Fainsod, Carl J. Friedrich, Douglas G. Haring, Talcott Parsons, G. Nye Steiger, Seiyei Wakukawa, Frederick M. Watkins; Harvard University Press, 1946

Subjects: Japan—Civilization, Japan—Economic Conditions—1945-, Japan—Politics And Government, Japan—History—Allied Occupation, 1945-1952

The Boundaries of Abortion Law: Systems Theory from Parsons to Luhmann and Habermas Journal article by Mathieu Deflem; Social Forces, Vol. 76, 1998

Structuralism Versus Individualism: Part 1, Shadowboxing in the Dark

Sociology and the Twilight of Man: Homocentrism and Discourse in Sociological Theory Charles C. Lemert; Southern Illinois University Press, 1979

On Theory and Verification in Sociology by Hans L. Zetterberg; The Bedminster Press, 1963 Subjects: Sociology—Methodology

The Sociology of Knowledge: An Essay in Aid of a Deeper Understanding of the History of Ideas W. Stark, Werner Stark; Routledge & Kegan Paul, 1958

Subjects: Sociology, Knowledge, Theory Of

The Sociology of Knowledge: An Essay in Aid of a Deeper Understanding of the History of Ideas W. Stark; Routledge & Paul, 1958

Contemporary Developments in Sociological Theory: Current Projects and Conditions of Possibility Journal article by Charles Camic, Neil Gross; Annual Review of Sociology, Vol. 24, 1998

Modernisation Theory, Income Evaluation, and the Transition in Eastern Europe Journal article by Wil Arts, Piet Hermkens, Peter Van Wijck; International Journal of Comparative Sociology, Vol. 40, 1999

Critical Realist Ethnography: The Case of Racism and Professionalism in a medical setting Journal article by Sam Porter; Sociology, Vol. 27, 1993, Subjects: Knowledge, Theory of—Analysis, Racism—Research, Ethnology—Philosophy, Frankfurt school of Social Movement Theory and the Sociology of Religion: Toward a New Synthesis Journal article by John A. Hannigan; SA. Sociological Analysis, Vol. 52, 1991

Parsons, Talcott Encyclopedia article; The Columbia Encyclopedia, Sixth Edition, 2000

Critical-Thinking Questions

1. How is social change seen by the Functionalists and the Conflict Sociologists?

_____

_____

_____

_____

_____

_____

_____

_____

_____

2. What is the process of social change for the Functionalists and Conflict Sociologist?

_____

_____

_____

_____

_____

_____

_____

_____

3. How are these views so different?

_____

_____

_____

_____

_____

_____

_____

_____

CHAPTER VII

Sociology of
Gender Roles

Gender roles are considered to be behavior patterns, which are expected of males and females in society. If a society has little or no flexibility in the types of behavior males and females display this society is considered high in gender typing. A society which has flexibility is considered low in gender typing. Gender typing is the degree to which a society accepts gender roles. The United States should be considered a low gender typed society for there is much flexibility in the types of behavior males and females display. Many cultures in the Middle East should be seen as a high gender typed society for there is little or no flexibility in the types of behavior males and females display. The male superiority role has had a connotation of aggression, dominance and independence. Female inferiority has been seen as a role of being passive, weak and dependent is seen as an historical and universal fact through time and cultures. However, upon closer look we do not see these roles as constant throughout time or in culture.

As was mentioned in Chapter 6, the two model interrelations of all social phenomena is the Conflict and Functionalist views, both being polar opposites of each other. Functionalist would interpret male superiority in terms of the more significant roles males play in meeting the needs of society and one's culture. The Conflict model suggests that male superiority arises and is related to the control of property by males.

Friedrich Engels in his book *The Origin of the Family, Private Property and the State* traces gender roles through the stages of economic development or the mode-of-production. He coins the concept known as the Resources Power Theory. This concept suggests that whoever has the most resources in a relationship has the most power. He identifies three stages of economic growth or mode of productions and suggests that every time there is a Mode-of-production change there is a direct change in the Resource Power Theory, which changes the status of males and females in society. Engels identifies three historical mode-of-production changes, which are hunting-and-gathering, agricultural, and industrial; today sociologists suggest that there is also a fourth—the Post-Industrial period.

According to Engels, in the hunting-and-gathering society property was communal and characterized by women holding high status because the biological fathers could not be identified in the communistic life form these people led. Also, the woman contributed equally to the survival of the group by providing food such as fruits, roots and nuts when the man did not bring back meat from hunting. No one held the Resource Power Theory, therefore both males and females were considered equal.

In the Agricultural stage females lost their status because they lacked the strength needed to do the labor. The domestication of animals was another factor which led to private property and monogamy.

Private property, marriage and reproduction all become linked during this stage. If one does a study of the inheritance patterns around the world, with the exception of the United States (which we will look at later), the oldest male child will inherit all the wealth, status, and power that the father has accumulated throughout his life, almost without exception. Engels suggested that this is so because of the patriarchal mindset found within the agricultural mode-of-production.

During the industrial mode-of-production females are still considered as inferior to males. Engels suggests that this is so because most factory workers during the late 1800s and 1900s were farmers, and therefore there is no change in the male/female mindset. During the first immigration to the United States in the earlier 1900's many immigrants entered with no skills or education except for farming. So two weeks ago in Eastern or South Europe they were farmers, two weeks later they are in New York

City as factory workers, their view of males and females does not change. This stage can be seen as a left over from the agricultural mode-of-production.

Today in the United States we find ourselves in a post-industrial mode-of-production. The growing need for educated skills will lead to females and males becoming more and more equal. Indeed, in the U.S.A. today there are more females than males in college. Although females still earn 75 cents for every dollar a male earns, much of that difference could be the so-called "glass ceiling" or the reproductive period for which most females go through during their careers reducing their total life earnings.

The functionalist view on the other hand sees gender roles as a function these roles perform in the maintenance of society's needs. Although Margaret Mead was an anthropologist and not a sociologist, her work on cross cultural variations in New Guinea in 1931 has been viewed as a classical case of how culture affects the roles males and females play in society.

In her work entitled *Sex and Temperament in Three Primitive Societies* laid the groundwork for much of the research and scholarship in the study of gender roles. This work suggested that cultural and not biological factors account for male and female behavior. Hence, there is no natural gender temperament or role associated with males and females which has been previously thought; rather culture defines who we are as males and females.

In her study, Mead identifies three tribes with three different "sex temperaments" or gender roles; they are the Arapesh, Mundugumore and the Tchamboli tribes.

The Arapesh Tribe were a mild mannered group with no notion of gender roles. They expected people to be gentle. Man and woman were seen as equal. This group believed in service to the weak, and man and woman equally contributed to child rearing, an important factor in the equality of women.

The Mundugumore Tribe were a fierce people with much hostility among the genders. Children were considered rivals to the parents, men exchanged sisters and daughters for younger wives. Fathers and sons had equal claim over females, and children receive minimal parent care.

By contrast, the Tchamboli Tribe were female controlled. Males exhibited "female like qualities, adorned themselves with colorful clothing and jewelry." The male also displayed labor pains when the female was giving birth to protect her status in that group. This type of behavior sociologist referred to a social safety value role.

Therefore, the functionalist suggest that individuals will always approximate the gender role patterns of their society because they have been socialized into that culture.

On the other hand, the Conflict paradigm suggests that the force behind role development throughout time is the changing economic conditions in society.

Sex and Temperament in Three Primitive Societies

Margaret Mead

The work of anthropologist Margaret Mead laid the foundation for much of our contemporary sociological research and debate on gender. Are "masculine" and "feminine" traits innate or learned? Do men and women differ because of nature (heredity) or nurture (socialization)? Based on her studies of three "primitive peoples" in New Guinea, Margaret Mead argues that cultural conditioning is more important than biology in shaping women's and men's behavior.

We have now considered in detail the approved personalities of each sex among three primitive peoples. We found the Arapesh—both men and women—displaying a personality that, out of our historically limited preoccupations, we would call maternal in its parental aspects, and feminine in its sexual aspects. We found men, as well as women, trained to be cooperative, unaggressive, responsive to the needs and demands of others. We found no idea that sex was a powerful driving force either for men or for women. In marked contrast to these attitudes, we found among the Mundugumor that both men and women developed as ruthless, aggressive, positively sexed individuals, with the maternal cherishing aspects of personality at a minimum. Both men and women approximated to a personality type that we in our culture would find only in an undisciplined and very violent male. Neither the Arapesh nor the Mundugumor profit by a contrast between the sexes; the Arapesh ideal is the mild, responsive man married to the mild, responsive woman; the Mundugumor ideal is the violent aggressive man married to the violent aggressive woman. In the third tribe, the Tchambuli, we found a genuine reversal of the sex attitudes of our own culture, with the woman the dominant, impersonal, managing partner, the man the less responsible and the emotionally dependent person. These three situations suggest, then, a very definite conclusion. If those temperamental attitudes which we have traditionally regarded as feminine—such as passivity, responsiveness, and a willingness to cherish children—can so easily be set up as the masculine pattern in one tribe, and in another be outlawed for the majority of women as well as for the majority of men, we no longer have any basis for regarding such aspects of behaviour as sex-linked. And this conclusion becomes even stronger when we consider the actual reversal in Tchambuli of the position of dominance of the two sexes, in spite of the existence of formal patrilineal institutions.

The material suggests that we may say that many, if not all, of the personality traits which we have called masculine or feminine are as lightly linked to sex as are the clothing, the manners, and the form of head-dress that a society at a given period assigns to either sex. When we consider the behaviour of the typical Arapesh man or woman as contrasted with the behaviour of the typical Mundugumor man or woman, the evidence is overwhelmingly in favour of the strength of social conditioning. In no other way can we account for the almost complete uniformity with which Arapesh children develop into contented, passive, secure persons, while Mundugumor children develop characteristically into violent, aggressive, insecure persons. Only to the impact of the whole of the integrated culture upon the growing child can we lay the formation of the contrasting types. There is no other explanation of race, or diet, or selection that can be adduced to explain them. We are forced to conclude that human nature is almost unbelievably malleable, responding accurately and contrastingly to contrasting cultural conditions. The differences between individuals who are members of different cultures, like the differences between individuals within a culture, are almost entirely to be laid to differences in conditioning, especially during early childhood, and the form of this conditioning is culturally determined. Standardized personality differences between the sexes are of this order, cultural creations to which each generation, male and female, is trained to conform. There remains, however, the problem of the origin of these socially standardized differences.

While the basic importance of social conditioning is still imperfectly recognized—not only in lay thought, but even by the scientist specifically concerned with such matters—to go beyond it and consider the possible influence of variations in hereditary equipment is a hazardous matter. The following pages will read very differently to one who has made a part of his thinking a recognition of the whole amazing mechanism of cultural conditioning—who has really accepted the fact that the same infant could be developed into a full participant in any one of these three cultures—than they will read to one who still believes that the minutiae of cultural behaviour are carried in the individual germ-plasm. If it is said, therefore, that when we have grasped the full significance of the malleability of the human organism and the preponderant importance of cultural conditioning, there are still further problems to solve, it must be remembered that these problems come *after* such a comprehension of the force of conditioning; they cannot precede it. The forces that make children born among the Arapesh grow up into typical Arapesh personalities are entirely social, and any discussion of the variations which do occur must be looked at against this social background.

With this warning firmly in mind, we can ask a further question. Granting the malleability of human nature, whence arise the differences between the standardized personalities that different cultures decree for all of their members, or which one culture decrees for the members of one sex as contrasted with the members of the opposite sex? If such differences are culturally created, as this material would most strongly suggest that they are, if the newborn child can be shaped with equal ease into an unaggressive Arapesh or an aggressive Mundugumor, why do these striking contrasts occur at all? If the clues to the different personalities decreed for men and women in Tchambuli do not lie in the physical constitution of the two sexes—an assumption that we must reject both for the Tchambuli and for our own society—where can we find the clues upon which the Tchambuli, the Arapesh, the Mundugumor, have built? Cultures are manmade, they are built of human materials; they are diverse but com-

parable structures within which human beings can attain full human stature. Upon
what have they built their diversities?

We recognize that a homogeneous culture
committed in all of its gravest institutions and
slightest usages to a cooperative, unaggressive
course can bend every child to that emphasis,
some to a perfect accord with it, the majority
to an easy acceptance, while only a few devi-
ants fail to receive the cultural imprint. To
consider such traits as aggressiveness or passivity to be sex-linked is not possible in the
light of the facts. Have such traits, then, as aggressiveness or passivity, pride or humility,
objectivity or a preoccupation with personal
relationships, an easy response to the needs of
the young and the weak or a hostility to the
young and the weak, a tendency to initiate
sex-relations or merely to respond to the dictates of a situation or another person's advances—have these traits any basis in temperament at all? Are they potentialities of all
human temperaments that can be developed
by different kinds of social conditioning and
which will not appear if the necessary conditioning is absent?

When we ask this question we shift our
emphasis. If we ask why an Arapesh man or
an Arapesh woman shows the kind of personality that we have considered in the first section of this book, the answer is: Because of
the Arapesh culture, because of the intricate,
elaborate, and unfailing fashion in which a
culture is able to shape each new-born child
to the cultural image. And if we ask the same
question about a Mundugumor man or
woman, or about a Tchambuli man as compared with a Tchambuli woman, the answer is
of the same kind. They display the personalities that are peculiar to the cultures in which
they were born and educated. Our attention
has been on the differences between Arapesh
men and women as a group and Mundugumor
men and women as a group. It is as if we had
represented the Arapesh personality by a soft

yellow, the Mundugumor by a deep red, while
the Tchambuli female personality was deep
orange, and that of the Tchambuli male, pale
green. But if we now ask whence came the
original direction in each culture, so that one
now shows yellow, another red, the third orange and green by sex, then we must peer
more closely. And leaning closer to the picture, it is as if behind the bright consistent
yellow of the Arapesh, and the deep equally
consistent red of the Mundugumor, behind the
orange and green that are Tchambuli, we
found in each case the delicate, just discernible outlines of the whole spectrum, differently
overlaid in each case by the monotone which
covers it. This spectrum is the range of individual differences which lie back of the so
much more conspicuous cultural emphases,
and it is to this that we must turn to find the
explanation of cultural inspiration, of the
source from which each culture has drawn.

There appears to be about the same range
of basic temperamental variation among the
Arapesh and among the Mundugumor, although the violent man is a misfit in the first
society and a leader in the second. If human
nature were completely homogeneous raw
material, lacking specific drives and characterized by no important constitutional differences between individuals, then individuals
who display personality traits so antithetical
to the social pressure should not reappear in
societies of such differing emphases. If the
variations between individuals were to be set
down to accidents in the genetic process, the
same accidents should not be repeated with
similar frequency in strikingly different cultures, with strongly contrasting methods of
education.

But because this same relative distribution
of individual differences does appear in culture after culture, in spite of the divergence
between the cultures, it seems pertinent to offer a hypothesis to explain upon what basis
the personalities of men and women have

been differently standardized so often in the history of the human race. This hypothesis is an extension of that advanced by Ruth Benedict in her *Patterns of Culture*. Let us assume that there are definite temperamental differences between human beings which if not entirely hereditary at least are established on a hereditary base very soon after birth. (Further than this we cannot at present narrow the matter.) These differences finally embodied in the character structure of adults, then, are the clues from which culture works, selecting one temperament, or a combination of related and congruent types, as desirable, and embodying this choice in every thread of the social fabric—in the care of the young child, the games the children play, the songs the people sing, the structure of political organization, the religious observance, the art and the philosophy.

Some primitive societies have had the time and the robustness to revamp all of their institutions to fit one extreme type, and to develop educational techniques which will ensure that the majority of each generation will show a personality congruent with this extreme emphasis. Other societies have pursued a less definitive course, selecting their models not from the most extreme, most highly differentiated individuals, but from the less marked types. In such societies the approved personality is less pronounced, and the culture often contains the types of inconsistencies that many human beings display also; one institution may be adjusted to the uses of pride, another to a casual humility that is congruent neither with pride nor with inverted pride. Such societies, which have taken the more usual and less sharply defined types as models, often show also a less definitely patterned social structure. The culture of such societies may be likened to a house the decoration of which has been informed by no definite and precise taste, no exclusive emphasis upon dignity or comfort or pretentiousness or beauty, but in which a little of each effect has been included.

Alternatively, a culture may take its clues not from one temperament, but from several temperaments. But instead of mixing together into an inconsistent hotchpotch the choices and emphases of different temperaments, or blending them together into a smooth but not particularly distinguished whole, it may isolate each type by making it the basis for the approved social personality for an age-group, a sex-group, a caste-group, or an occupational group. In this way society becomes not a monotone with a few discrepant patches of an intrusive colour, but a mosaic, with different groups displaying different personality traits. Such specializations as these may be based upon any facet of human endowment—different intellectual abilities, different artistic abilities, different emotional traits. So the Samoans decree that all young people must show the personality trait of unaggressiveness and punish with opprobrium the aggressive child who displays traits regarded as appropriate only in titled middle-aged men. In societies based upon elaborate ideas of rank, members of the aristocracy will be permitted, even compelled, to display a pride, a sensitivity to insult, that would be deprecated as inappropriate in members of the plebeian class. So also in professional groups or in religious sects some temperamental traits are selected and institutionalized, and taught to each new member who enters the profession or sect. Thus the physician learns the bedside manner, which is the natural behaviour of some temperaments and the standard behaviour of the general practitioner in the medical profession; the Quaker learns at least the outward behaviour and the rudiments of meditation, the capacity for which is not necessarily an innate characteristic of many of the members of the Society of Friends.

So it is with the social personalities of the two sexes. The traits that occur in some members of each sex are specially assigned to one sex, and disallowed in the other. The history of the social definition of sex-differences is filled with such arbitrary arrangements in the intellectual and artistic field, but because of the assumed congruence between physiological sex and emotional endowment we have been less able to recognize that a similar arbitrary selection is being made among emotional traits also. We have assumed that because it is convenient for a mother to wish to care for her child, this is a trait with which women have been more generously endowed by a carefully teleological process of evolution. We have assumed that because men have hunted, an activity requiring enterprise, bravery, and initiative, they have been endowed with these useful attitudes as part of their sex-temperament.

Societies have made these assumptions both overtly and implicitly. If a society insists that warfare is the major occupation for the male sex, it is therefore insisting that all male children display bravery and pugnacity. Even if the insistence upon the differential bravery of men and women is not made articulate, the difference in occupation makes this point implicitly. When, however, a society goes further and defines men as brave and women as timorous, when men are forbidden to show fear and women are indulged in the most flagrant display of fear, a more explicit element enters in. Bravery, hatred of any weakness, of flinching before pain or danger—this attitude which is so strong a component of *some human* temperaments has been selected as the key to masculine behaviour. The easy unashamed display of fear or suffering that is congenial to a different temperament has been made the key to feminine behaviour.

Originally two variations of human temperament, a hatred of fear or willingness to display fear, they have been socially translated into inalienable aspects of the personalities of the two sexes. And to that defined sex-personality every child will be educated, if a boy, to suppress fear, if a girl, to show it.

If there has been no social selection in regard to this trait, the proud temperament that is repelled by any betrayal of feeling will display itself, regardless of sex, by keeping a stiff upper lip. Without an express prohibition of such behaviour the expressive unashamed man or woman will weep, or comment upon fear or suffering. Such attitudes, strongly marked in certain temperaments, may by social selection be standardized for everyone, or outlawed for everyone, or ignored by society, or made the exclusive and approved behaviour of one sex only.

Neither the Arapesh nor the Mundugumor have made any attitude specific for one sex. All of the energies of the culture have gone towards the creation of a single human type, regardless of class, age, or sex. There is no division into age-classes for which different motives or different moral attitudes are regarded as suitable. There is no class of seers or mediums who stand apart drawing inspiration from psychological sources not available to the majority of the people. The Mundugumor have, it is true, made one arbitrary selection, in that they recognize artistic ability only among individuals born with the cord about their necks, and firmly deny the happy exercise of artistic ability to those less unusually born. The Arapesh boy with a tinea infection has been socially selected to be a disgruntled, antisocial individual, and the society forces upon sunny cooperative children cursed with this affliction a final approximation to the behaviour appropriate to a pariah. With these two exceptions no emotional role is forced upon an individual because of birth or accident. As there is no idea of rank which declares that some are of high estate and some of low, so there is no idea of sex-difference which declares that one sex must feel differently from the other. One possible imaginative social construct, the attribution of different personalities to different members of the community classified into sex-, age-, or caste-groups, is lacking.

When we turn however to the Tchambuli, we find a situation that while bizarre in one respect, seems nevertheless more intelligible in another. The Tchambuli have at least made the point of sex-difference; they have used the obvious fact of sex as an organizing point for the formation of social personality, even though they seem to us to have reversed the normal picture. While there is reason to believe that not every Tchambuli woman is born with a dominating, organizing, administrative temperament, actively sexed and willing to initiate sex-relations, possessive, definite, robust, practical and impersonal in outlook, still most Tchambuli girls grow up to display these traits. And while there is definite evidence to show that all Tchambuli men are not, by native endowment, the delicate responsive actors of a play staged for the women's benefit, still most Tchambuli boys manifest this coquettish play-acting personality most of the time. Because the Tchambuli formulation of sex-attitudes contradicts our usual premises, we can see clearly that Tchambuli culture has arbitrarily permitted certain human traits to women, and allotted others, equally arbitrarily, to men.

The Origin of the Family, Private Property and the State

Friedrich H. Engels

The Emergence of Monogamy and the Subjugation of Women

The pages in which Engels discusses early marriage forms are the most difficult in *Origin,* partly because kinship terminologies and practices are complicated and unfamiliar to the Western reader, and partly because confusions about biological and social forces obscure the significant parts of his discussion. However, Engels' fundamental theme is clear. He writes: "We . . . have three principal forms of marriage which correspond broadly to the three principal stages of human development: for the period of savagery, group marriage; for barbarism, pairing marriage; for civilization, monogamy. . . ." Monogamy arises from a transitional stage of polygyny, "when men have female slaves at their command;" coupled with male supremacy, it is "supplemented by adultery and prostitution," and is from the beginning monogamy for the women only. Marriage was frankly polygynous throughout classical times, and convertly so thereafter.

The significant characteristic of monogamous marriage was its transformation of the nuclear family into the basic economic unit of society, within which a woman and her children became dependent upon an individual man. Arising in conjunction with exploitative class relations, this transformation resulted in the oppression of women that has persisted to the present day. As corollary to, or symptomatic of this transformation, the reckoning of descent was changed from "mother right" (matrilineality) to "father right."

In the field of anthropology, it is the last proposition, that matrilineality was prior to patrilineality in the history of mankind, which has received most attention. The rest of Engels' discussion has been virtually ignored, and it is unfortunate testimony to the status of women both within and without the field that detailed studies of women's status and role in primitive societies are so rare. Nonetheless, there is sufficient evidence at hand to support in its broad outlines Engels' argument that the position of women relative to men deteriorated with the advent of class society, as well as data to fill in many particulars of his thesis. Above all, however, there is crying need for further analysis of existing materials and for the collection of new data.

Let us first examine the point that marriage is essentially different in hunting-gathering ("savage") and horticultural ("barbarian") societies on the one hand, and class society ("civilization") on the other, and that there is a further distinction between the freer "group marriage" of hunter-gatherers and its succes-

sor, "pairing marriage." The term "group marriage" unfortunately conjures up an unrealistic
image of mass weddings that are nowhere to
be found. In fact, however, Engels' actual
analysis of "group marriage" as it obtained in
Australia concurs with what has come to be
called "loose monogamy" in anthropological
writings. "All that the superficial observer sees
in group marriage," Engels pointed out, "is a
loose form of monogamous marriage, here
and there polygyny, and occasional infideli-
ties." Through the "mass marriage of an entire
section of men . . . with an equally widely distributed section of women . . . the Australian
aborigine, wandering hundreds of miles from
his home . . . often finds in every camp and
every tribe women who give themselves to
him without resistance and without resentment." On a day-to-day basis, marriage takes
the form of a "a loose pairing" among partners
whose marriageability is defined at birth by
their membership in one or another so-called
"marriage class."

The Australian "marriage classes" are today conceived to be part of a system whereby
various categories of kin are named so that a
person can readily define his relationships
within any group with whom he comes into
contact.[1] The system is far more elaborate
than anything found among other hunter-
gatherers, but nonetheless, all of them share
common features of family life. Divorce is
typically easy and at the desire of either partner, although it is not particularly common.
Death more frequently seems to break up the
marriage relationship; close and warm pairing
relationships are the rule. These are not based,
however, on any assumption of sexual exclusiveness for either partner among most hunter-

gatherers about whom we have information.
Perhaps it is because they were first contacted
by whalers instead of missionaries that we
have so much data on this point for the Eskimo. According to custom, it is hospitable for
an unattached Eskimo woman, or else the
host's wife, to sleep with a visitor. The practice
has at times been referred to as evidence of the
low status of women where it obtains—an
ethnocentric reading which presumes that a
woman does not (since she should not) enjoy
sex play with any but her "real" husband and
which refuses to recognize that variety in sex
relations is entertaining to women (where not
circumscribed by all manner of taboos) as well
as to men (a moralistic assumption from which
Engels himself was not wholly free).

"Pairing marriage" is more hedged around
with restrictions. Engels wrote: "the decisive
considerations are the new ties of kinship
which are to give the young pair a stronger
position in the gens and tribe." Parents take a
hand in the choice of marriage partners, and
marriages are cemented through an exchange
of goods—cattle, foods, or luxury items—between the relatives of the bride and those of
the groom. The kin of the young partners now
have a vested interest in the permanence of
the marriage. Engels wrote, that although "still
terminable at the desire of either partner . . .
among many tribes . . . public opinion has
gradually developed against such separations.
When differences arise between husband and
wife, the gens relatives of both partners act as
mediators, and only if these efforts prove fruitless does a separation take place."

There is no lack of data on what Morgan
called the "pairing family." It is intimately related to the clan organization of agricultural
peoples, whereby communal relations in the
production and distribution of goods are
maintained in what have become relatively
large and stable groups. Hunting-gathering
bands of some 25 to 40 or so people can operate almost anarchistically, but with the devel-

---

[1] A description of kinship among the Arunta of Australia can
be found in Service, 1963. These systems become unusually
elaborate in parts of Australia, although somewhat comparable elaborations are to be found in nearby Melanesian
tribes.

opment of agriculture more complex institutions are needed for ordering interpersonal relationships in villages of several hundred and more. Virtually everyone still stands in the same direct relation to production; at most a healer or priest-chief may receive gifts enough to release him or her from some agricultural and other labors. Therefore, economic, political, and social relations remain united; ties of kinship formalized as "gentes" or the term more commonly used today, "clans," form the framework of community life. With clan organization, kin are counted on one side only— you belong either to your mother's or your father's clan, not to both, and you marry "out" (clans are normally "exogamous"). The two practices, unilineality and exogamy, enable discrete groups to last over generations (which is difficult with "bilaterality" and overlapping lines of kinship), while at the same time the groups become linked through a network of marriage ties.[2]

The nuclear family of parents and children was embedded in the clan and village structures through a network of reciprocal relations.[3] Parties of relatives worked together in the fields and on the hunt, and exchanged foodstuffs and manufactured goods on the many occasions that called for festivity, such as at births, baptisms, puberty rites, marriages, deaths, and seasonal and religious ceremonies. The acceptance by the clan and village community, as formally represented by its respected elders, of the ultimate responsibility for the welfare of any member, was so totally taken for granted that it went unstated. On a day-to-day basis, however, it was the immediate lineage of grandparent, parent, and children, with spouses, that functioned as a working unit.

The significant point for women's status is that the household was communal and the division of labor between the sexes reciprocal; the economy did not involve the dependence of the wife and children on the husband. All major food supplies, large game and produce from the fields, were shared among a group of families. These families lived together in large dwellings among most village agriculturalists, and in hunting-gathering societies either shared large tepees or other such shelters in adverse climates, or might simply group together in separate wickiups or lean-tos in tropical or desert areas. The children in a real sense belonged to the group as a whole; an orphaned child suffered a personal loss, but was never without a family. Women did not have to put up with personal injuries from men in outbursts of violent anger for fear of economic privation for themselves or their children. By comparison with more "advanced" societies where wife-beating became accepted, even to the point of death, a mistreated wife could call on her relatives for re-

[2.] The social basis for incest taboos and exogamous marriage are discussed in White, 1949: Chapter 11; Slater, 1959; Aberle *et al.,* 1963; and in Washburn and Lancaster, "The Evolution of Hunting," in Lee and DeVore, 1968: especially 302. The ties of kinship and exogamous marriage were already practices in hunting-gathering societies, although they were more formally defined among the settled gatherers and fishermen than among nomadic hunters. This raises the question whether they were generally more well defined in early human society and lost under the harsh conditions endured by the Indians and Eskimo of the north and other hunters pushed into marginal areas. In any case, with agricultural society, they become highly defined and elaborated upon with endless variations from group to group. The Soviet anthropologist, Julia Averkieva, has suggested to me that in her view clan organization was primeval, and that its elaborate definition occurred when it was already beginning to decay. For further discussion of hunting-band organization, see Leacock, 1969.

[3.] These have seldom been described better than by one of the founders of the "functionalist" school of anthropology, Bronislaw Malinowski, in his writings on the Trobriand Islanders of Melanesia. Try, for example, his very readable *Crime and Custom in Savage Society,* 1926.

dress or leave if it was not forthcoming. Nor can "household management" be construed as it would be today. Whether a "public" industry or not, "managing the household" as the "task entrusted to the women" might be viewed dubiously as hardly very satisfactory. However, in primitive communal society, the distinction did not exist between a public world of men's work and a private world of women's household service. The large collective household *was* the community, and within it both sexes worked to produce the goods necessary for livelihood. Goods were as yet directly produced and consumed; they had not become transformed into "commodities" for exchange, the transformation upon which the exploitation of man by man, and the special oppression of women, was built.

In fact, women usually furnished a large share—often the major share—of the food. Many hunter-gatherers depended on the vegetable foods gathered by women as the staples to be augmented by meat (the Bushmen of the Kalahari Desert are a case in point), and in horticultural societies women, as the former gatherers of vegetable foods and in all likelihood, therefore, responsible for the domestication of crops, generally did most of the farming. Since in primitive communal society decisions were made by those who would be carrying them out, the participation of women in a major share of socially necessary labor did not reduce them to virtual slavery, as is the case in class society, but accorded them decision-making powers commensurate with their contribution.

There has been little understanding of this point in anthropological literature. Instead, the fact that men typically made decisions about hunting and warfare in primitive society is used to support the argument that they were the "rulers" in the Western sense. Men did indeed acquire power under the conditions of colonial rule within which the lifeways of hitherto primitive peoples have been recorded.

Nonetheless, the literature again and again reveals the autonomy of women and their role in decision-making; albeit such data are as often as not sloughed off with supposedly humorous innuendos about "henpecked husbands" or the like, rather than treated seriously as illustrative of social structure and dynamics.

Unfortunately, the debate over women's status in primitive society has largely ignored the actual role of women in primitive society in favor of an almost exclusive focus on descent systems. The growing body of literature on the world's cultures in the latter 19th century showed the clans of horticultural peoples to be commonly matrilineal, and that women often participated formally in the making of "political" decisions. Morgan had described the power the elder women among the Iroquois held in the nomination and possible deposition of the sachems, and the importance of "queen mothers" in Africa had been described. There, a woman and her brother (or son or nephew) often shared chiefly or royal responsibilities somewhat analogous to those of a Department of the Interior and Department of State respectively. And the magnificent army of perhaps 5,000 volunteer women soldiers of Dahomey were the legendary Amazons incarnate. All of this caught the imagination of theoreticians in so male-dominated and property-conscious a culture as was Victorian society,[4] and scholars spoke of patriarchal society as historically preceded by the "matriarchy," where rule by women was based

[4.] Although one cannot help but note that the very age was named after a woman. This fact points to the priority of class considerations over sex in the socialization of women when it came to royalty. Princesses were, first of all, potential rulers. Thus we have the anomaly that in the history of Europe the only public area in which individual women were in every way the equal of men, both to the general view and in their own behavior and abilities, was that associated most deeply with stereotypes of masculinity—the area of leadership, power, and decision-making.

on the indisputability of legitimacy reckoned in the female line.

It soon became clear that matriarchy, in the sense of power held by women over men comparable to that later held by men over women, had never existed. However, questions about the significance that matrilineal descent held for the status of women in primitive society remained. It is impossible to review here the twists and turns of subsequent argument over the universal priority of matrilineal descent. Suffice it to say that it is clear that matrilineal systems give way to patrilineal systems with the development of exploitative class relations. In many cases a patrilineal (or patrilocal) system can be shown to have been matrilineal (or matrilocal), but in other cases ethnohistorical data sufficient for definitive proof are lacking. Hence statistical studies of descent and its correlates have yielded conflicting interpretations.[5]

A standard contemporary formulation, at least in the United States, is that horticultural

societies were generally structured around matrilineally related groups since women were responsible for the major share of the farming, but that hunting societies were male-centered in their structure due to the importance of the men as hunters. The fact that the produce gathered by the women in many such societies was as important a source of food, or more so, than the produce of the hunt, led Service, in a recent formulation of this position (1966: 37–38) to point out that hunting required a close collaboration that is not important in most gathering activities. To Service, it was the need for the "delicate coordination of several people" that led to the practice whereby closely related men stayed together as the core of a hunting band while women married into other bands. The case is, however, that some hunter-gatherers are matrilineal, and others have been so in the recent past. My own field work among the Naskapi hunters of the Labrador Peninsula showed that patrilineal-patrilocal ties were strengthened at the expense of matrilineal-matrilocal ties after European contact, under the influence of missionaries, government agents, and especially the fur trade (Leacock, 1955, 1969). Despite the arduousness of hunting in the northern woods and tundra, there was no suggestion whatever that men had to grow up together to work well as a unit. Instead it was the norm for men in the past to marry away from the band of their youth.

In a recent study Martin also questions the "patrilocal band" as the primordial type of

[5.] An early study by Hobhouse et al. (1965) found the matrilineal-matrilocal principle to be more common among "lower hunters" than the patrilineal-patrilocal principle. A later study of Murdock's finds that "simpler cultures tend to be matrilineal, more advanced ones patrilineal," although "the patrilineate coexists too frequently with the absence of traits . . . (of more complex culture) and the matrilineate with their presence, to be consistent with the theory of universal matrilineal priority" (1937: 467). In a later work, Murdock writes: "While matrilineal societies appear, on the average, to be somewhat more archaic in culture than patrilineal societies the difference is relatively slight, the overlap is very great, and the disparity may well reflect principally the preponderant influence exerted throughout the world in recent centuries by the bilateral and patrilineal peoples of the Eurasiatic continent," (1949: 186). Using Murdock's figures, but without reference to Murdock's early study that involved a relatively sophisticated statistical analysis, Aberle comments on the greater patrilineality among hunter-gatherers than matrilineality, although bilaterality far exceeds them both (Schneider and Gough, 1961). Two distinctions between Murdock's figures and those of Hobhouse et al. must be noted. First, one of Murdock's criteria for selection

of his sample was that each major rule of descent should be represented for each culture area, a factor he took into account in his own analysis, but which does not seem to have been considered by Aberle. The second consideration involves the passage of time. For the people with whom I am most familiar, the Naskapi, Hobhouse et al. use a 17th century Jesuit account that showed them to be matrilineal-matrilocal in orientation; Murdock uses 20th century accounts that describe them as bilateral and bilocal with a paternal emphasis.

social organization. On the basis of reviewing descent and residence patterns, interband relations, and the recent histories of 33 predominantly matrilocal South American hunting-gathering peoples, she points out that there is greater cohesiveness with matrilocal rather than patrilocal organization. With matrilocal residence the men, who are responsible for defense and hence offense, are dispersed among related bands rather than forming localized clusters (1969: 256–57).

Works that deal directly with the role of women in primitive society are few and far between, and much of what has been done pertains to personality rather than socio-economic structure. Margaret Mead's early exposition of contrasting sex-role definitions in three primitive societies is a case in point (1950). Interestingly enough, Mead contradicts her own argument for the cultural definition of sex role by her later position which, in conformity with widely accepted Freudian thought, argues for a universal active-passive dichotomy differentiating male from female roles (1955). By contrast there is an early book by Mason, *Women's Share in Primitive Culture,* and the book, *The Mothers,* by Briffault, a surgeon, novelist, and amateur anthropologist. These draw together scattered ethnographic references to (1) women's role in decision-making and the administration of tribal affairs; (2) their importance as inventors of techniques for food production and the manufacture of baskets, leather goods, woven materials, etc.; and (3) their part in ritual and religious life. Impressive though the record of women's part in society appears, however, the data are lifted out of context and seem to be contradicted by the vast majority of extant ethnographic materials, for these seldom assess the impact of colonialism on the peoples described and generally focus on the activities and affairs of men. (This latter is not solely a problem of masculine bias, but also due to the greater ease of communicating with men who are far more commonly thrown into contact with Europeans and speak a European language.)

An unusually detailed study of women among a hunting-gathering people is afforded by Kaberry's work on the original inhabitants of Northwest Australia (1939). It is commonly stated that women's status is low among these people, as evidenced by their exclusion from the important ceremonies of the men and from participation in political affairs. Kaberry points out that the men in turn are kept out of the secret rituals held by the women; and that while warfare and the holding of formal meetings are the sole responsibility of the men, intragroup problems are handled by older women along with older men. Women are restricted as to whom they may marry; but so are men, and young people are free to have premarital affairs which either sex may initiate. In daily life, these Australian women emerge as autonomous participants in the affairs of their people, acting with assurance upon their rights and responsibilities, a view reinforced by a newly published study of Tiwi women by Jane Goodale (1971).

Similarly, biographical materials on Eskimo women contradict common assumptions about their subservient role, even in spite of its deterioration in recent times. The biography of Anauta (Washburne and Anauta, 1940), an Eskimo woman of Baffin Land who migrated to the United States with her children after the death of her husband, reveals her independence of action and strong sense of personal autonomy. Short biographies of Nunivak Island Eskimo women, one of them a shaman (a person who can communicate with the supernatural powers, usually for healing and/or divination), likewise indicate considerable freedom of choice and leeway for women to take the initiative in the running of their own lives (Lantis, 1960).

The position of women among the Naskapi hunting people of the Labrador Peninsula was stronger in the past than it is today. Seventeenth century Jesuit missionaries writing of their experiences state that "the women have great power here" and that "the choice of plans, of undertakings, of journeys, of winterings, lies in nearly every instance in the hands of the housewife" (Thwaites, 1906: Vol. V, 181; Vol. LXVIII, 93). A Jesuit scolds a man for not being "the master," telling him "in France women do not rule their husbands" (Vol. V, 181). To make the women obey their husbands became one of the concerns of the missionaries, particularly in relation to the sexual freedom that obtained: "I told him that it was not honorable for a woman to love anyone else except her husband, and that, this evil being among them (women's sexual freedom) he himself was not sure that his son, who was there present, was his son." The Naskapi's reply is telling: "Thou hast no sense. You French people love only your own children; but we love all the children of our tribe" (Vol. VI, 255).

Women are no longer shamans, as they could be in the past, nor do they commonly hunt, nor join the men in the sweat bath, nor hold their own formal councils in case of emergency (Vol. II, 77; Vol. VI, 191; Vol. VII, 61, 175; Vol. XIV, 183). However, traditions of individual autonomy, mutual support, and collective responsibility for the children still leave their mark on Naskapi life despite great changes. One of many incidents I observed must suffice to indicate what can lie behind the stereotyped ascription in monographic accounts of such people: the men hunt; the women gather berries and care for the children. For the greater part of one day a man sat patiently, lovingly crooning over his sickly and fretful infant but a few weeks old. His wife was busy. Though worried for the baby's health, he appeared in no way inept or harassed by his responsibility, nor did he call on another woman around the camp for help. His

unself-conscious assurance and patience set him quite apart from latter-day readers of Dr. Spock. This was his task while his wife tanned a caribou skin, a skilled and arduous job that demanded her complete attention. The men knew how to cook and tend the babies when called upon to do so, but did not really know how to tan leather.

There is a real need for studies that reconstruct from extant materials on primitive communal and transitional societies something of women's functioning before the development of the male dominance that accompanied European economic and colonial exploitation. For example, how were goods distributed in horticultural societies where garden produce still lay in the women's domain? How did older women function in the settling of disputes, a role often referred to but little documented? What were the paths of influence women held in relation to the men's sphere of war and the hunt? Conversely, what was the role of men in socializing young children? A recent analysis by Mintz (1971) of the entrepreneurial role played by Yoruba women traders exemplifies how published data can be used to begin answering such questions.

An interesting subject for reassessment is the mystique that surrounds the hunt and, in comparison, that surrounding childbirth. A common formulation of status among hunter-gatherers overlooks the latter and stresses the importance and excitement of the hunt. Albeit the primary staple foods may be the vegetable products supplied by the women, they afford no prestige, it is pointed out, so that while not precisely subservient women are still of lower status than men. However, women's power of child-bearing has been a focus for awe and even fear as long ago as the Upper Paleolithic, judging from the fertility figurines that date from that period. This point is easy to overlook, for the ability to bear children has led in our society not to respect but to women's oppressed status. Similarly, the mystique surrounding menstruation is underestimated. Attitudes of mystery and danger for men are interpreted in terms of our cultural judgment as "uncleanliness." Indeed, the semantic twists on this subject would be amusing to analyze. Women are spoken of as "isolated" in "menstrual huts" so that the men will not be contaminated. Where men's houses exist, however, they are written about respectfully; here the exclusion of women betokens men's high status. Doubtless this congeries of attitudes was first held by missionaries and traders, and from them subject peoples learned appropriate attitudes to express to whites.

However, a recent study by Hogbin (1970) on the religion of a New Guinea people reveals another side to the picture. Intriguingly titled "The Island of Menstruating Men," the study describes a practice also found among other peoples in this part of the world whereby the men simulate the phenomenon of menstruation. Blood is drawn from the penis (or some other part of the body among other groups) and men go through the ritual cycle of menstruation, retreating from the ordinary round of daily affairs, observing various taboos, then reentering, cleansed and renewed.

In some ways it is the ultimate alienation in our society that the ability to give birth has been transformed into a liability. The reason is not simply that, since women bear children, they are more limited in their movements and activities. As the foregoing discussion indicates, this was not a handicap even under the limited technology of hunting-gathering life; it certainly has no relevance today. Nor did women's low status simply follow their declining importance in food production when men moved into agriculture; nor automatically follow the growth in importance of domestic animals, the province of the men, although herding did relate to lowered status for women. However, what was basic was that these transitions occurred in the context of developing

exploitative relations whereby communal ownership was being undermined, the communal kin group broken up, and the individual family separated out as an isolated and vulnerable unit, economically responsible for the maintenance of its members and for the rearing of the new generation. The subjugation of the female sex was based on the transformation of their socially necessary labor into a private service through the separation of the family from the clan. It was in this context that women's domestic and other work came to be performed under conditions of virtual slavery.

The separation of the family from the clan and the institution of monogamous marriage were the social expressions of developing private property; so-called monogamy afforded the means through which property could be individually inherited. And private property for some meant no property for others, or the emerging of differing relations to production on the part of different social groups. The core of Engels' formulation lies in the intimate connection between the emergence of the family as an economic unit dominated by the male and this development of classes.

> The distinction of rich and poor appears beside that of freemen and slaves—with the new division of labor, a new cleavage of society into classes. . . . The transition to full private property is gradually accomplished, parallel with the transition of the pairing marriage into monogamy. The single family is becoming the economic unit of society.

Engels outlines for early Greece the way in which the division of labor and development of commodity production enabled new wealth in the form of slaves and herds to be accumulated by single individuals, thereby leading to a conflict between the family and the gens. Since men owned the "instruments of labor" (having largely displaced women in the fields, it is important to note, following the decline of hunting as an important activity), conflict between family and gens took the form of a conflict between the opposing principles of father right and mother right. "As wealth increased it made the man's position in the family more important than the woman's, and . . . created an impulse to exploit this strengthened position in order to overthrow, in favor of his children, the traditional order of inheritance" (119). Therefore, the formation of the family as the economic unit of society was affirmed by the overthrow of mother right, the *"world historical defeat of the female sex"* (italics Engels').

Far more empirical documentation than Engels offers is needed to clarify the process of women's subjugation, both in relation to the initial rise of class societies in the Old and New Worlds, and to the secondary diffusion of commodity production and class divisions that accompanied European expansion and colonial domination. Essentially Engels offers a paradigm, posing a sharp contrast between women's status in primitive communal society and in classical Greece and Rome. He then touches on Medieval Europe and jumps to industrialization. The many changes within the great span of history covered and the variations from place to place need analysis and, even more important, so do the variations in women's position in different classes: slave, free worker, peasant, serf, burgher, aristocrat.

Engels focuses on the emergence of the upper-class family as an instrument for the concentration of individual wealth. He does not clearly define the lower-class family as affording an important buttress for class society by making the individual acutely vulnerable to exploitation and control. The separation of the ordinary laborer from the communal security of the gens meant the worker was responsible as an individual not only for his own maintenance but also that of his wife and children. This to a large measure insured not only

his labor, but also his docility; it rendered him—as he is to this day—fearful of fighting against the extremities of exploitation as endangering not only himself but also his wife and his dependent children. With wonderful wit and satire, and warm sympathy, Engels deals with the conjugal relations produced by monogamy, but largely in relation to the bourgeois family. He writes of the proletarian wife who moves into public industry under conditions of great difficulty for herself and her children, but does not elaborate on the enormous ambivalence the individual family creates in the working-class man and his wife as a result of their isolation.

The dehumanization of conjugal relationships, caught as men and women are in a network of fear and confusion; the brutalization and petty dominance of the man; the anger and bitterness of the woman; the nature of marriage, all too often as a constant battle—all this is only too well known. Despite the fact that the pre-class societies which have been studied have already been undercut by European and American colonization, a quality of respectful ease, warmth, and assurance in interpersonal relations, including those between husband and wife, often persists as evidence that the tensions associated with conjugal relations in our society are based in our social structure, not in the natures of women and men.

Political Ramifications of Engels' Argument on Women's Subjugation

Engels writes, "the peculiar character of the supremacy of the husband over the wife in the modern family . . . will only be seen in the clear light of day when both possess legally complete equality of rights," although, in itself, legal equity affords no solution. Just as the legal equality of capitalist and proletarian makes visible "the specific character of the economic oppression burdening the proletariat," so also will legal equality reveal the fundamental change that is necessary for the liberation of women. Engels goes on to say: "Then it will be plain that the first condition for the liberation of the wife is to bring the whole female sex back into public industry, and that this in turn demands that the characteristic of the monogamous family as the economic unit of society be abolished."

Such a change is dependent on the abolition of private ownership. "With the transfer of the means of production into common ownership, the single family ceases to be the economic unit of society. Private housekeeping is transformed into a social industry. The care and education of the children becomes a public affair; society looks after all children alike." Only when this is accomplished will a new generation of women grow up, Engels writes, who have never known "what it is to give themselves to a man from any other considerations than real love or to refuse to give themselves to their lover from fear of the economic consequences." Then men and women "will care precious little what anybody today thinks they ought to do; they will make their own practice and their corresponding public opinion about the practice of each individual—and that will be the end of it." To which must be added today that the destruction of the family as an economic unit does not *automatically* follow with the establishment of socialism, but rather is one of the goals to be fought for as central to the transition to communism.

There has recently been much discussion about the extent to which women can achieve a measure of personal "liberation" by rejecting the sex-role definitions of the contemporary "monogamous" family, and about the relevance such rejection can have to the furthering of revolutionary aims and consciousness. There has also been considerable argument about the basis for women's inferior position, ranging from the extreme psychobiological view that it results from an innate masculine drive for domination and can be changed only through a single-minded "battle of the sexes," to the extreme economic determinist—and generally masculine—view that since all basic changes ultimately depend on the revolutionary restructuring of society, it is both illusory and diversionary to focus on ameliorating the special problems of women.

While there is still a great deal of abstract argument about the correct position on women's liberation, there is also a growing recognition that it is fruitless to debate the extent to which various parts of the women's movement can or cannot be linked with revolutionary goals, and there is a growing commitment to developing concrete tactics of program and organization around situations where women are in motion on basic issues. It might seem that Engels' discussion of family arrangements that have long ceased to exist in their pristine forms is somewhat esoteric and of little relevance today. However, it is crucial to the organization of women for their liberation to understand that it is the monogamous family as an economic unit, at the heart of class society, that is basic to their subjugation. Such understanding makes clear that child-bearing itself is not responsible for the low status of women, as has been the contention of some radical women's groups. And more important, it indicates the way in which working-class women, not only in their obviously basic fight on the job but also in their seemingly more conservative battles for their families around schools, housing and welfare, are actually posing a more basic challenge than that of the radicals. By demanding that society assume responsibility for their children, they are attacking the nature of the family as an economic unit, the basis of their own oppression and a central buttress of class exploitation. Therefore, while some of the activities of middle-class radical women's groups can be linked with the struggles of working-class women, such as the fight for free legalized abortion, others are so psychologically oriented as to be confusing and diversionary.

The self-declared women's movement in this country has historically been middle class and largely oriented toward a fight for the same options as middle-class men within the system, while the struggles of working-class women have not been conceived as fights for women's liberation as such. This has been true since the close of the Civil War, when the women's movement that had been closely concerned with the fight against slavery and for the rights of women factory workers broke away on its "feminist" course. Today there is more widespread awareness that all oppressive relations are interconnected and embedded in our system as a whole, and that only united effort can effect fundamental change. However, there has been little clear and consistent effort made to achieve such unity. For example, the committees formed by professional women to fight job discrimination are generally prepared to admit forth-rightly that their battle is ultimately inseparable from that of working-class and especially Black working-class women, but they have done virtually nothing to find ways of linking the two. And it is commonplace to point out that, despite basic differences between the oppression of women and the oppression of Blacks, there are marked parallels of both an economic and a social-psychological nature—not to mention the fact that half of Black people are women. But again, there has been no solid commitment to building organizational ties between the two movements around specific issues. The theoretical differentiation between the symptoms and the causes of women's oppression can help clarify the issues around which united organization must be built, and can help remove the blocks hampering the enor-

mous potential a women's movement could have for unifying sections of the middle and working classes and bridging some of the disastrous gap between white workers and Black, Puerto Rican, and Mexican American workers. However, in this effort it is important to be wary of a certain suspect quality of many white middle-class women (akin to that of their male counterparts) to be attracted and exhilarated by the assertiveness of the struggle for Black liberation, and to neglect their responsibility to find ways of also building an alliance with white working-class women and men.

Theoretical understanding is sorely needed to help combat the difficulties that will continue to beset the women's movement. Male supremacy, the enormous difficulty men have in facing up to their pathetic feelings of superiority and display of petty power over women, even when theoretically dedicated to revolutionary change, will continue to feed what is often a narrowly anti-men orientation among "movement women;" and the media will continue to exploit this as a gimmick that serves at the same time to sell cigarettes and shampoo, dissipate energies, and divide women from each other and from what should be allied struggles. As with the black-power movement, the sheer possibility of open confrontation will for some serve the need to express a great pent-up anger, and token victories will temporarily serve to give the illusion of some success. The overwhelming need is to keep this powerful anger from being dissipated—to find ways of building upon it through taking organizationally meaningful steps.

Selected Readings

International Handbook on Gender Roles by Leonore Loeb Adler, Nancy Felipe Russo.
Current Conceptions of Sex Roles and Sex Typing: Theory and Research by D. Bruce Carter.

Gender Roles: A Handbook of Tests and Measures by Carole A. Beere.

Sex Differences in Social Behavior: A Social-Role Interpretation by Alice H. Eagly.

Adolescent Sex Roles and Social Change by Lloyd B. Lueptow.

Sexual Rhetoric: Media Perspectives on Sexuality, Gender, and Identity by Meta G. Carstarphen, Susan C. Zavoina.

Job Queues, Gender Queues: Explaining Women's Inroads into Male Occupations by Barbara F. Reskin, Patricia A. Roos.

Gender Roles and Coping with Work Stress, in Sex Roles: A Journal of Research by Irene Gianakos.

Sexual Archetypes, East and West by Bina Gupta.

The Developmental Social Psychology of Gender by Thomas B. Eckes, Hanns M. Trautner.

Women and Men in Organizations: Sex and Gender Issues at Work by Jeanette N. Cleveland, Margaret Stockdale, Kevin R. Murphy.

A New Psychology of Men (includes "The Gender Role Strain Paradigm: An Update") by Ronald F. Levant, William S. Pollack.

Relationships and Well-Being over the Life Stages (includes "Gender Roles in the Family: Is the Older Family Different?" and "Gender-Role Attitudes, Characteristics of Employment, and Wellbeing of Single and Married Employed Mothers") by Pat M. Keith, Robert B. Schafer.

Gender Roles and Sexual Behavior among Young Women, in Sex Roles: A Journal of Research by Jayne C. Lucke.

Genesis and Gender: Biblical Myths of Sexuality and Their Cultural Impact by William E. Phipps.

Critical-Thinking Questions

1. What are gender roles?

_____

_____

_____

_____

_____

_____

_____

_____

2. How does the conflict paradigm see gender roles occurring?

_____

_____

_____

_____

_____

_____

_____

_____

2. How do the Functionalists see gender roles occurring?

_____

_____

_____

_____

_____

_____

_____

_____

CHAPTER VIII

Sociology of Education

The Civil War is the great watershed in American educational history because the mass public educational movement has its roots in the society that evolved after the Civil War. In 1820 seven out of ten Americans were farmers. During the 1870's, farmers comprised nearly half of the work force. Although there was a formal educational system, most schools were tuition-based college preparatory institutions. Indeed, since the Civil War, especially over the last 25 years, there has been rapid growth in the salaried middle class. Most recently there has been a rise in the technical class which requires formal educational credentials.

John Dewey was an educator and a social philosopher and is considered the father of the American educational system. He stressed the importance of learning cooperation in the classroom so that as adults we would cooperate with one another; open-mindedness should be a part of the educational system; the dignity of the individual should always be maintained; that teachers should keep democratic classrooms as often as possible; education must be a life-long experience; students should be taught self-expression for it is central to a political free system; and that the masses must be educated through a public school system.

He also insisted that the curriculum have included, the fine arts, English and literature, social sciences, mathematics, sciences, citizenship, abstract knowledge, and the importance of moral consensus and common values.

Employing much of Dewey's concepts the American Functionalist View has stressed that education is an important part of society which maintains stability. This view has emphasis that education provides skills necessary to put people to work in a complex society. According to this view, education has become a means by which there is the transmission of common values, such as attendance, study skills/work values, promptness, dress codes, language codes and treatment of others, which are all taught in schools but not tested on.

The functionalist view suggests that education has become a major vehicle for equal opportunity today and a triumph over all forms of ignorance, not just literacy, but also over prejudice and discrimination. Education also fosters tolerance of others.

Like all Functionalists, change within education must be self-regulating. Nothing can be more a poignant as Dr. Fernandez's tenure as Chancellor of the New York City's public school system during the early 1980s. Dr. Fernandez's goal was to formalize the "Rainbow Curriculum". This curriculum suggested that homosexual marriage and family life was equal to that of heterosexual marriage. Dr. Fernandez was asked to resign from this post because the people of New York City were not ready for this to be taught to their children. Functionalist would argue that if the time should come when the people of New York City sees this form of equal relationships to be adopted, than the curricula will reflect this social relationship, not before.

The Functionalist views education as Human Capital. Capital in the sense that education acts as an investment for the individual and society. The individual invests in knowledge by going to school and earns a return of increased earnings, better working conditions and so on. Society invests in education for a more productive individual. Evidence has been amassing which suggests that a quality education is critical for the sustained social and economic growth of nations and individuals (Benavot 1992, Brown et al. 1991, Cleland and Van-Ginneken 1988, Hadden and London 1996 and Sawyer 1997).

Moreover, education has become highly important in occupational payment in postmodern America. A number of studies have shown that the number of years of education is a strong determinant of occupational achievement in America with social origins constant (Sewell, W.H. and Shah, V.P., 1977 in Power and Ideology in Education).

This sociological concept holds that those skill requirements of jobs in post-modern society are constantly increased because of technological change. Two processes are involved: 1) the proportion of jobs requiring low skill have decreased and 2) the proportion requiring higher order skills have increase. Hence, formal education is necessary because it provides either the training in specific skills or in general capacity for the more highly skilled economy. Therefore, a larger proportion of the population is required to spend longer and longer periods of their lives in school. Although it is obvious that people will gain useful skills and knowledge during the course of their formal education, it is not obvious that these skills and knowledge may be seen as a form of capital—that is human capital. Human capital accounts for a substantial portion of the growth in western societies. Indeed, human capital has grown at a much faster rate than conventional capital.

The theory of human capital suggests that education in addition to being a form of consumption, is also a form of individually and socially productive investment. From this perspective the individual can consider him/herself capitalists in that the individual makes investments in the acquisition of knowledge and skill which has given him/her ownership of economically valuable capacities. Low earnings, reflect according to this theory, inadequate investments in education.

According to Schultz (1977), human capital theory further suggests that investment in education nationally facilitates economic growth in two ways: spurring technological innovation and increasing the productivity of labor. Throughout the last several decades human capital theory has served as a guideline and justification for rising educational expenditures both by government and individuals alike. Human capital theory also suggests that

those who do not acquire the proper dose of schooling are likely to occupy the low positions of the socioeconomic hierarchy.

Lastly, studies recently carried out in the field of human capital show that there is quite a close connection between the diffusion of education and economic development. Schultz, Harbison and Myers studied 75 countries at different levels of economic development. These data suggested that there was a significant correlation between the national income per capita and a series of indices concerning the levels of education among the labor force in each of these countries.

However with all this talk of human capital by the Functionalist, there is growing evidence that whether the sociological perspective is the influence of family background on school and occupation achievement (Status Attainment approach), or the mode of production in material life (Marxist approach), or the language-use at home and at school (socio-linguistic approach), or cultural socialization (cultural reproduction), or the changing needs and requirements of society's educational demands (Structural-Functionalist approach), students from working class, minority and low socio-economic backgrounds (SES), do poorly in school relative to the middle class.

Indeed, by any measurement they drop out more than their middle class contemporaries, score lower on standardized tests and achieve lower high school averages. When they do go to college, they achieve lower grade point averages, earn fewer credits, drop out more frequently and take longer to be graduated.

Almost without exception these poor educational outcomes can be traced to a number of long standing educational policies enacted in order to create a more efficient and allegedly humane manner of educating students with different learning styles. Two such touted educational policies are ability group assignments in the elementary schools and curriculum tracking in the comprehensive high schools. At first glance policies concerning the primary school and high schools seem independent of one another to the general public. However, in the educational continuum of the individual, especially for the individual assigned to the lower ability group (at the primary school level) and the non-college preparatory curriculum (within the high school), for whom working class, minority and low SES students are predominant, the educational effect for the individual is cumulative in nature. This is so because these educational career paths lead to student biographies and identities which crystallizes during the individuals' various educational life cycles (primary to secondary schools and beyond).

Furthermore, because of credential inflation the successful students upon graduation from high school are faced with two legitimate choices either try their chances at employment within the blue-collar industries of New York City, in which employment opportunities over the last two decades have been reduced seriously, or enter college.

Even with the increased need for higher order skills in New York City's post-industrial economy, less than seventy percent of New York City's high school graduates go on to college. Thus, the most recent data suggests that for a given one hundred New York City high school students, fifty will drop out and fifty will graduate. Of these survivors, approximately thirty-five will go to college. But, because of the knowledge gap created by low ability group placement, and non-college preparatory high school programs, sixty percent of such individuals generally find their only collegiate option the community college. Hence, of the thirty-five college-bound survivors mentioned earlier, twenty will enroll in a community college, where at worst the majority will stop out/drop out, and at best, the

minority can only expect to earn an AA/AAS degree.

The most recent research completed on degree requirements for white collar employment has shown that a Baccalaureate is the minimum qualification necessary for access into the managerial or professional ranks within New York City's post-industrial economy. This relegates those who have earned AA/AAS degrees to the bottom of the white collar career ladder where monetary rewards will be substantially less than their Baccalaureate counterparts (Blaug, 1972; Hauser and Swell 1986; Lavin and Crook, 1990; Leslie and Ramey 1996).

Then, to sum up, such factors as the ethno-cultural inheritance of a student, the socio-economic circumstances of the student's family and the cumulative educational deficit via ability grouping and non-college preparatory tracking can be equated to pieces of a puzzle, which when joined depict decreased educational achievement and life chances. Much of the research centering around the "self-fulfilling prophecy of failure" argues that ability-grouping practices at the primary school level are closely associated with economic impoverishment, class, culture, and race. The research also points to teacher expectations which tends to pace academic advancements, since teachers treat those they expect to be academically successful differently from students of whom they expect little.

Indeed, there is mounting evidence which suggests that high teacher expectation is a salient variable for student achievement. Felson and Bohrnstedt (1980), indicated that ability and effort were perceived by teachers as positively related. According to the authors, teachers may view students with high ability as more motivated than those with low ability. Bohrnstedt and Felson (1983) argued that teachers were providing what the authors described as the "halo effect" for their motivated students. Toughey and Villaney (1980) indicated that high-need achievers perceive their abilities as being high. In contrast, low-need achievers perceived their abilities as being low. Arkin and Baumgardner (1985) found that self-handicapping students doubted their academic abilities regardless of their performance. Levy and Baumgardner (1987) indicated that individuals who viewed themselves as having low ability were likely to be self-handicapping. Baumgardner and Levy (1987) found that individuals with high ability grouping perceived effort as validation of high ability, and low effort as an indicator of low ability. Furthermore, individuals perceive those with high ability as successful even when they are not.

Interconnected to these ideas are the policies of ability assignments, which help to create and advance inequalities among students. The body of research centered around ability assignments argues that students in low-ability groups may receive substantially less teaching time than students in high-ability groups in the same classroom (Eder, 1981; McDermott, 1977). Hence, perceptions of student performance become reality, not because a student may or may not have greater or lesser ability, but because students in different ability groups are taught differently.

The most frequently cited research supporting this hypothesis is Rosenthal and Jacobensen's (1968) work in a primary school in San Francisco. The main thrust of this research was to create different teacher expectations by providing misinformation about the ability of the students to teachers who were going to teach this group at the beginning of the academic year.

The policy of this school was (at the beginning of each school year) to test students in grades one through six using a nonverbal IQ test. The results of these tests were shared with the teachers. However, for a group of randomly selected students the teachers were told that these children were intellectually gifted.

The data suggested that the experimental group was treated differently from the control group and learned more.

Another example of the halo effect is Rist's studies of one all black elementary school, with an all black faculty in St. Louis. Rist found that: 1) teacher expectations and ability grouping were based on class perceived characteristics, 2) ability grouping is a somewhat permanent position, and 3) students were treated differently in each of the ability groups (Rist, 1970).

Hence, the teacher perception process unfolds during the flow of the classroom interaction when teachers judge the correctness and appropriateness of students' answers and behavior. The accumulation of such judgments results in the placement of students into ability groups. Thus, as the research has demonstrated teacher perceptions/expectations and ability grouping assignments have tangible results for the elementary school population.

There is good evidence that the teacher's initial impressions of student ability are centered around class. Hence, social class is an important indicator of cultural capital for the school setting (Bourdieu, 1977), since teachers demand a specific form of behavior which is believed to support learning. If this behavior is not located within the family's cultural resources, the child is likely not to comply with the expected school behavior.

Therefore, distinctive cultural knowledge is transmitted by families of each social class. Hence, children of the dominant class inherit substantially different cultural knowledge, skills, norms, styles of dress and linguistic abilities than do the children of those within subordinate classes. Consequently, schools reward students with the dominant class background by virtue of a certain cultural competency established through family socialization. Hence these students are provided with the means to succeed in schools, implicitly do so.

Schools similarly contribute to this reproduction process by designing and implementing curriculum that rewards the cultural capital of the dominant class, while systemically and continually devaluating, demeaning and debasing the cultural capital of subordinate classes.

Generally, it is common knowledge that the parents of working class and middle class children want them to succeed in schools. However, each class's social position leads them to employ different means to this end. The working class parents depend on the teacher and the school to educate their children because such parents are most often less educated than the teacher.

On the other hand, the middle class parent actively participates in the supervision and monitoring of his/her child's school achievements. Additionally, because the middle class parent's occupation and education may be equal, or greater than the teacher's, middle class parents will very often challenge the teacher and the school administrators, as well as assume that the school is at fault if problems arise for their children (Lamont and Lareau, 1988).

Lareau (1987) provides further support for the above mentioned idea by the observation of the parental involvement in schools located in a middle class and working class community. This research centered around the formal requests from teachers for parent participation. Lareau suggests that the parental response was much higher at the middle-class school than at the working class school. Additionally, the interaction between the working class parents and teachers was stiff, awkward, uncomfortable and the parent/teacher conversation usually centered around non-academic issues. On the other hand, the interaction between the middle class parents and teachers was natural, and the conversation most often centered around academic issues.

Lareau concludes that educational values of both parents did not differ. What did differ, however, was the manner in which they stressed academic success. The middle class parents viewed their child's education as a shared experience between teacher and parent. On the other hand the working class parents turned all responsibilities of their children's education to the teacher and school.

Furthermore, language comparisons of working and low SES families and middle class families suggest that there may be a differential between the language of the home and the language of the schools, especially among the working class and low SES background students (Cazden, 1986,; Delgado-Gaiton, 1987; Heath, 1982; and Philips, 1982).

Basil Bernstein's (1975) work on language, coding theory, curriculum and the transmission of knowledge is an important interpretation of class, family, school and the failure of Low SES students. Bernstein's concept of code is central to his analysis of the transmission of knowledge. Code refers to ideas which underlies various messages in curriculum and pedagogy. Curriculum, according to Bernstein, is valid knowledge. Pedagogy acts as the valid transmission of this knowledge, and evaluation is the realization of knowledge taught. Both the curriculum and the transmission of knowledge, for Bernstein, are based in language. According to Bernstein, language interpretation is by class, and thus a function of social differences. Furthermore, various functions of language in a given social context have a profound effect on children's social learning. Hence, Bernstein establishes a distinction between language usage of the working class or public language, and the language-use of the middle class labeled formal language.

Bernstein argues that formal language has greater complexity of possibilities, hence a relationship, which permits higher order processing. This form of language stresses the intensification and verbalization of separateness and differences. Furthermore, formal language stresses the significance of objects in the environment. Conversely, public language is structured around mediating personal qualifications and is limited in symbolic expression. It consists of words used as part of simple statements and questions in the description of tangible, concrete, and visual statements. Public language's emphasis is on emotion, rather than logical implications. The difference in these two language structures underlies the attitudes and values, which are compatible with formal education and thus increased life-chances.

The pulse of this theory is the mode of a language structure in which words and sentences are related. Bernstein cites a case in point concerning the transmission and modes of interpretation in the understanding of complex ideas. Bernstein argues that in the middle class family the mother may say to her child, "I'd rather you made less noise, darling." On the other hand, in a working class family the mother may say shut up! According to Bernstein, the operative words in the middle class scenario is "rather and less", because the child has learned to be sensitive to this form of sentence and the many possible sentences associated with these words. Hence, these words are understood when used in this case and are directly translatable cues for the immediate response and future responses. By comparison, the phase "shut up", does not have the same imperative cues for response as "rather and less" (Bernstein, 1975).

The importance of this example for Bernstein is that the middle class child understands both statements, that is "rather/less" and "shut up". However, the working class child has learned to respond to and discriminated only one—shut-up. The difference becomes problematic for the working class child in the school environment, because he/she has to translate and process the middle class language structure through a much simpler language structure, producing confusion and puzzlement.

Generally then, the use of public language is not a significant problem, except in the superior/inferior relationship of teacher and student. Within this relationship, because teachers and schools for the most part possess middle class codes, public language and its subsequent behavior may be interpreted as hostile, aggressive, and rude by the teacher, resulting in a perception that the individual is less intelligent. Moreover, this language/behavior continuum acts as a validation of the differences between the two codes.

Essentially then, the breakdown of communication between teacher and the working class child, results in a learning resistance and the failure of the child.

On the other hand, because the language mode of the middle class is that same mode used in schools, and because the child has been socialized to perceive work and play as weakly differential, the middle class child is usually successful in this form of environment.

Therefore, Bernstein concludes that the working class child attaches significance to an aspect of language because of his/her class socialization, which is different from that which is required by the learning situation of schools. I have cited Bernstein's thesis because I believe it can partially explain teacher perception and ability grouping based on class. Additionally, this hypothesis can also assist in explaining the self-fulfilling prophecy of failure, which has become associated with the socially and educationally disadvantaged.

Another factor is High School tracking because of its importance to the student's life-chances, has also created much controversy in the United States. Proponents of tracking argue that grouping students into homogeneous groupings in subject-ready areas provides instruction according to the individual's needs. Additionally, students have the opportunity to choose the subjects they are interested in, thus reducing the drop-out rate. On the other hand, critics argue that tracking practices reproduce educational inequalities because of a lower quality of instruction, as well as direction of path into vocational versus academic tracks.

There is much research, which points to the high school tracking system reproducing the values and attitudes characteristic of social class. Hence, the college preparatory track tends to reproduce middle class values by supporting the type of personality that reflects the possible demands of professional occupations. Conversely, the non-college preparatory track tends to reproduce values and attitudes which reflect the types of occupations associated with the working/blue collar class. Therefore, high schools provide a means of educating the working class in technical skills, but at the same time alienating these students from ideas which the dominant culture holds in high regard.

Moreover, high school tracking has all the trappings of ability grouping, in that it establishes different learning environments (Alexander and McDill, 1976). Tracking also creates peer association based on tracking assignments. Hence, individuals assigned to the college track curriculum have more high status friends who are planning college careers than do those assigned to the vocational track (Alexander, Cook and McDill, 1978), therefore creating a peer environment which establishes high academic achievement.

Research into the curriculum has shown that the social organization of the classroom and the power relationship between the student and teacher also contribute to class reproduction (Aggleton and Whitty, 1985; Anyon 1991). Additionally, there has been a large body of work which suggests that parental behavior toward school and participation in education promotes educational success (Berger, 1983; Seeley, 1984). There is also a body of literature which suggests that the unequal working class parental involvement in schools can be traced back to the schools which do not welcome, or just plainly discriminate against working and low SES parental involvement (Lightfoot, 1978; Ogbu, 1974).

Hence, the ideology concerning schooling in the United States revolves around the idea that schools provide a path out of poverty, is for many working class, minority and low SES students merely imaginary, because what humanity represents to itself in ideology is an imaginary relation to the real relations (Althusser, 1978). This imaginary relation (to the real relation) in which such students live, invokes the image of an easier, less alienated life, due them upon completion of their education. But the fact may be that such individuals are denied this satisfaction. This daily denial demonstrates that there is a better life, but that this better life is, for the most part, not within their grasp. This internal contradiction is perceived and understood as a distortion of the real relations in which such students live. Hence, individuals in such roles find it difficult to develop a commitment or an identification with the dominant school culture, when they believe that they are not a meaningful asset, thus rejecting the school and dominant culture. This rejection has been labeled Resistance Theory. A very good example of Resistance Theory is Willis' (1977) interviews with a group of disenfranchised white working class males in British secondary schools.

According to Willis the "lads" a group of high school students who have rejected the achievement ideology, school values, and the authority of the teachers, have these attitudes in part because the lads have insight into their disenfranchised economic and social position in England. Therefore, the lads equated manual labor with success and mental labor with failure, thus, creating a misrecognition and ignorance of the connection between education and social mobility, relegating the lads to manual labor and the active acceptance of their economic subordination.

MacLeod's (1987), ethnography examined two groups of high school students comprised of predominantly low income individuals, living in the same housing project and attending the same school. In this study MacLeod documents that the Hallway Hangers (a group of white males) rejected the achievement ideology, and the Brothers (a group of black males) conformed to the achievement ideology. MacLeod argues that the parents of the Brothers insisted that their children work toward professional careers and monitored their school progress. By contrast, the parents of the Hallway Hangers did not stress such career concerns with their children and did not monitor their children's school progress, or more accurately, their lack of progress.

Nonetheless, even with the diversity and variability of individuals in subjugated groups, students with such cultural capital as the lads and the hallway hangers possess the implicit and/or explicit understanding of their limited options in society, creating negative attitudes toward school, diminishing educational achievement and undoubtedly contributing to the appallingly high dropout rate among high school students in our nation's inner cities

As was mentioned earlier, for students who do stay in school and graduate from high school, employment opportunities in New York City are limited because of the rising floor of educational credentials needed for entry into desirable jobs in the New York City labor market. In effect, the value of the high school diploma has declined. This devaluation has led many high school graduates who normally would not seek a college education, to do so now.

Finally, the idea of a devaluation of the high school diploma is consistent with the Status Competition paradigm. There is evidence that high status groups seek to improve their status through increased levels of education for themselves and their children, setting into motion an upward movement of educational credentials (Bondon, 1974; Collins, 1979).

Collins (1979) argues that the dominant culture raises the educational "ante" in order to maintain their social distinction. There is evidence that the pool of college-educated workers began to exceed the number of jobs requiring college training after World War II. This view is supported by a number of studies: Young (1974) suggests that a substantial proportion of all college graduates were acquiring jobs that had no recognizable relationship to their major field study while in college. Berg and Freeman (1978) demonstrated a growing mismatch between the skills requirements of jobs and the education of workers. Knapp (1977) argued that most college graduates reported that on-the-job training contributed more than did college training to their mastery of work task.

Although college may be required in today's economy, individuals who enter the community colleges bring serious disadvantages with them as a result of ability grouping at the primary level and vocational tracking at the high school level. This disadvantage can be seen in the many New York City high school graduates who come to CUNY under prepared in the traditional academic skills such as reading, mathematics and writing.

Since the City University of New York (CUNY) initiated an Open Admissions policy in 1970, it has been faced with large numbers of freshmen from inner city schools in need of instruction in the basic skills. By the end of the 1970s, a Freshmen Skills Assessment Program was established on a University-wide basis to assess competencies in writing, mathematics and reading. These examinations are required for all incoming freshmen in order to identify skill deficiencies. Students so identified are placed in remedial courses to help them meet the university standards of competency prior to entering the upper-level courses.

The need for compensatory work is great; 84 percent of the CUNY community college entrants are required to take at least one remedial course. However, in most urban community colleges a little less than 90 percent are required to enroll in a remedial course (Bender and Chalfant-Thomas, 1987).

Remedial courses in and of themselves are educational hurdles because of the time necessary to successfully complete them. For students who had entered CUNY during the 1970s, each remedial course taken adds one-fifth of a year to the graduation date of that individual (Lavin & Crook, 1990).

Other obstacles, intrinsic to the social and academic context of the community college itself, may impede students' academic progress. A number of researchers have pointed to the community college curriculum tracking system (into academic transfer and terminal vocational tracks), the anti-academic orientation of a predominant working class student body, and institutional efforts to lower students' initially high educational aspirations, as factors that diminish ultimate educational attainment and hence, life chances (Alba & Lavin 1981; Anderson, 1981; Astin, 1972; Breneman & Nelson 1981; Brint & Karabel, 1989; London, 1978; Velez, 1985; Willis, 1981).

These social and academic processes in the community college are consistent with the conflict theory in sociology, which stresses that education merely transmits inequality from one generation to the next. Moreover, this same research suggests that low SES students may be steered away from occupations which traditionally require advanced levels of education because schools convince students that the selection of "talented" people is based on the Meritocratic process (Bowles and Gintis, 1976; Collins, 1979).

Advocates of the community college argue that they offer access to higher education to the educationally disadvantaged who normally are ill-prepared, and therefore are barred from the four-year colleges (Cohen and Brawer, 1982). Although the community college has increased the numbers of students from low SES backgrounds in college attendance, this access has not necessarily translated into increased education and life-chances. Since the 1960s the community college has offered an avenue to higher education for the masses by providing a vehicle for the first two years of a four-year higher education. However, during the 1920's the role of the two-year college was changed to include a vocational role, with curricula centered around technical skills. By the 1940s the two-year college was drawing on predominantly working class, low SES and educationally disadvantaged students because of its vocational focus.

Today, the community colleges enroll over 40 percent of all students college bound. But less than a quarter of these students transfer to a four-year college (*U.S. Department of Health, Education and Welfare*, 1977). This fact is further supported by a strong body of research which has emerged over the last two decades, which argues that even after relative differences in the initial social and academic status of two-year and four-year college students are taken into account, the educational attainment of community college students are less than the four-year students (Alba and Lavin 1981; Dougherty 1987; Velez, 1985). Students who initially enroll in a four-year college are 19 percent more likely to receive a bachelor's degree within seven years than those who enroll in a community college (Velez, 1985). Of those who enter an academic program at a two-year college, 51 percent transferred within seven years of high school graduation (Velez and Javalgi, 1987). Additionally, only a third of the community college students eventually received their associate's degree (Monk-Turner, 1983). For two groups of students that were roughly matched on high school performance and educational aspirations enrolled at the two-year and four-year colleges at the City University of New York, the community college students were 14 percent less likely to have received a Bachelor's degree in five years (Alba and Lavin, 1981). There is speculation that the lower eventual educational attainment of the community college students is related to the vocational curricula of the two-year colleges (Dougherty, 1987).

Therefore, over the last two decades the community college's educational effectiveness has been questioned. The main thrust of this criticism has been that the community college merely reproduces class (Karabel, 1972; Pincus, 1980).

Hence, there is growing evidence that the policy to rely on the community colleges as primary access to higher education for the working class, minority and low SES students may be imaginary. Even though there is evidence that the participation in higher education of students from working class and low SES/minority backgrounds has increased dramatically over the last two decades, there has been little change in their economic and class mobility. Minority, working class and low SES students now represent the greater concentration of entrants in the urban community college. The problem of disproportionate poor and minority students in the community college is largely due to serving inner cities. This fact has led many researchers to conclude that the community colleges are the anti-university colleges (Jencks and Riesman, 1968). Additionally, it has been argued that the community college may act not as alternative educational path to increasing life-chances, but as a safety valve that permits universities, and the labor market to pursue their priorities without criticism (Clark, 1960; Coleman and Hoffer 1965; Weiss, 1985).

To conclude this chapter, Bowles and Gintis have suggested that education has always had two objectives: one objective is social control through the emphasis on obedience which is taught to low SES students, and the other objective is social justice. These sociologists reject the complex society theory and skills required to function in this society, in favor of a view which suggests that some schools create docile future workers who internalize authority, that the Meritocratic system is a smokescreen to convince low SES individuals to fail, and finally that education fosters inequality. A case in point can be seen in a college where attendance MUST be taken every meeting, and still at others (in the same university system) here it is not a concern. This view would see the attendance Policy College as a force which containing individuals who internalize authority and thereby developing future followers or docile workers. The college that does not focus on attendance would educate future leaders. Of course the students enrolled at this college are those who are part of the privilege class promoting social justice. These concepts are seen as the hub of the current Conflict View within education.

Education and Inequality

Samuel Bowles and Herbert Gintis

Education has long been held to be a means to realizing U.S. ideals of equal opportunity. As Lester Ward notes at the beginning of this selection, the promise of education is to allow "natural" abilities to win out over the "artificial" inequalities of class, race, and sex. Samuel Bowles and Herbert Gintis claim that this has happened very little in the United States. Rather, they argue, schooling has more to do with maintaining existing social hierarchy.

Universal education is the power, which is destined to overthrow every species of hierarchy. It is destined to remove all artificial inequality and leave the natural inequalities to find their true level. With the artificial inequalities of caste, rank, title, blood, birth, race, color, sex, etc., will fall nearly all the oppression, abuse, prejudice, enmity, and injustice, that humanity is now subject to. (Lester Frank Ward, Education © 1872)

A review of educational history hardly supports the optimistic pronouncements of liberal educational theory. The politics of education are better understood in terms of the need for social control in an unequal and rapidly changing economic order. The founders of the modern U.S. school system understood that the capitalist economy produces great extremes of wealth and poverty, of social elevation and degradation. Horace Mann and other school reformers of the antebellum period knew well the seamy side of the burgeoning industrial and urban centers. "Here," wrote Henry Barnard, the first state superintendent of education in both Connecticut and Rhode Island, and later to become the first U.S. Commissioner of Education, "the wealth, enterprise and professional talent of the state are concentrated . . . but here also are poverty, ignorance, profligacy and irreligion, and a classification of society as broad and deep as ever divided the plebeian and patrician of ancient Rome."[1] They lived in a world in which, to use de Tocqueville's words, ". . . small aristocratic societies . . . are formed by some manufacturers in the midst of the immense democracy of our age [in which] . . . some men are opulent and a multitude . . . are wretchedly poor."[2] The rapid rise of the factory system, particularly in New England, was celebrated by the early school reformers; yet, the alarming transition from a relatively simple rural society to a highly stratified industrial economy could not be ignored. They shared the fears that de Tocqueville had expressed following his visit to the United States in 1831:

> *When a workman is unceasingly and exclusively engaged in the fabrication of one thing, he ultimately does his work with singular dexterity; but at the same time he loses the general faculty of applying his mind to the direction of the work. . . . [While] the science of manufacture lowers the class of workmen, it raises the class of masters. . . . [If] ever a permanent inequality of conditions . . . again penetrates into the world, it may be predicted that this is the gate by which they will enter.*[3]

While deeply committed to the emerging industrial order, the farsighted school reformers of the mid-nineteenth century understood the explosive potential of the glaring inequalities of factory life. Deploring the widening of social divisions and fearing increasing unrest, Mann, Barnard, and others proposed educational expansion and reform. In his Fifth Report as Secretary of the Massachusetts Board of Education, Horace Mann wrote:

> *Education, then, beyond all other devices of human origin, is the great equalizer of the conditions of men—the balance wheel of the social machinery. . . . It does better than to disarm the poor of their hostility toward the rich; it prevents being poor.*[4]

Mann and his followers appeared to be at least as interested in disarming the poor as in preventing poverty. They saw in the spread of universal and free education a means of alleviating social distress without redistributing wealth and power or altering the broad outlines of the economic system. Education, it seems, had almost magical powers:

> *The main idea set forth in the creeds of some political reformers, or revolutionizers, is that some people are poor because others are rich. This idea supposed a fixed amount of property in the community . . . and the problem presented for solution is how to transfer a portion of this property from those who are supposed to have too much to those who feel and know that they have too little. At this point, both their theory and their expectation of reform stop. But the beneficent power of education would not be exhausted, even though it should peaceably abolish all the miseries that spring from the coexistence, side by side, of enormous wealth and squalid want. It has a higher function. Beyond the power of diffusing old wealth, it has the prerogative of creating new.*[5]

The early educators viewed the poor as the foreign element that they were. Mill hands were recruited throughout New England, often disrupting the small towns in which textile and other rapidly growing industries had located. Following the Irish potato famine of the 1840s, thousands of Irish workers settled in the cities and towns of the northeastern United States. Schooling was seen as a means of integrating this "uncouth and dangerous" element into the social fabric of American life. The inferiority of the foreigner was taken for granted. The editors of the influential *Massachusetts Teacher*, a leader in the educational reform movement, writing in 1851, saw ". . . the increasing influx of foreigners . . ." as a moral and social problem:

> *Will it, like the muddy Missouri, as it pours its waters into the clear Mississippi and contaminates the whole united mass, spread ignorance and vice, crime and disease, through our native population?*

If . . . we can by any means purify this foreign people, enlighten their ignorance and bring them up to our level, we shall perform a work of true and perfect charity, blessing the giver and receiver in equal measure. . . .

With the old not much can be done; but with their children, the great remedy is education. *The rising generation must be taught as our own children are taught. We say* must be *because in many cases this can only be accomplished by coercion.*[6]

Since the mid-nineteenth century the dual objectives of educational reformers—equality of opportunity and social control—have been intermingled, the merger of these two threads sometimes so nearly complete that it becomes impossible to distinguish between the two. Schooling has been at once something done for the poor and to the poor.

The basic assumptions which underlay this commingling help explain the educational reform movement's social legacy. First, educational reformers did not question the fundamental economic institutions of capitalism: Capitalist ownership and control of the means of production and dependent wage labor were taken for granted. In fact, education was to help preserve and extend the capitalist order. The function of the school system was to accommodate workers to its most rapid possible development. Second, it was assumed that people (often classes of people or "races") are differentially equipped by nature or social origins to occupy the varied economic and social levels in the class structure. By providing equal opportunity, the school system was to elevate the masses, guiding them sensibly and fairly to the manifold political, social, and economic roles of adult life.

Jefferson's educational thought strikingly illustrates this perspective. In 1779, he proposed a two-track educational system which would prepare individuals for adulthood in one of the two classes of society: the "laboring and the learned."[7] Even children of the laboring class would qualify for leadership. Scholarships would allow ". . . those persons whom nature hath endowed with genius and virtue . . ." to ". . . be rendered by liberal education worthy to receive and able to guard the sacred deposit of the rights and liberties of their fellow citizens."[8] Such a system, Jefferson asserted, would succeed in ". . . raking a few geniuses from the rubbish."[9] Jefferson's two-tiered educational plan presents in stark relief the outlines and motivation for the stratified structure of U.S. education which has endured up to the present. At the top, there is the highly selective aristocratic tradition, the elite university training future leaders. At the base is mass education for all, dedicated to uplift and control. The two traditions have always coexisted although their meeting point has drifted upward over the years, as mass education has spread upward from elementary school through high school, and now up to the post-high-school level.

Though schooling was consciously molded to reflect the class structure, education was seen as a means of enhancing wealth and morality, which would work to the advantage of all. Horace Mann, in his 1842 report to the State Board of Education, reproduced this comment by a Massachusetts industrialist:

The great majority always have been and probably always will be comparatively poor, while a few will possess the greatest share of this world's goods. And it is a wise provision of Providence which connects so intimately, and as I think so indissolubly, the greatest good of the many with the highest interests in the few.[10]

Much of the content of education over the past century and a half can only be construed as an unvarnished attempt to persuade the "many" to make the best of the inevitable.

The unequal contest between social control and social justice is evident in the total functioning of U.S. education. The system as it stands today provides eloquent testimony to the ability of the well-to-do to perpetuate in the name of equality of opportunity an arrangement which consistently yields to themselves disproportional advantages, while thwarting the aspirations and needs of the working people of the United States. However grating this judgment may sound to the ears of the undaunted optimist, it is by no means excessive in light of the massive statistical data on inequality in the United States. Let us look at the contemporary evidence.

We may begin with the basic issue of inequalities in the years of schooling. As can be seen in the number of years of schooling attained by an individual is strongly associated with parental socioeconomic status. This figure presents the estimated distribution of years of schooling attained by individuals of varying socioeconomic backgrounds. If we define socioeconomic background by a weighted sum of income, occupation, and educational level of the parents, a child from the ninetieth percentile may expect, on the average, five more years of schooling than a child in the tenth percentile.[11]

. . . We have chosen a sample of white males because the most complete statistics are available for this group. Moreover, if inequality for white males can be documented, the proposition is merely strengthened when sexual and racial differences are taken into account.

Additional census data dramatize one aspect of educational inequalities: the relationship between family income and college attendance. Even among those who had graduated from high school in the early 1960s, children of families earning less than $3,000 per year were over six times as likely *not* to attend college as were the children of families earning over $15,000.[12] Moreover, children from less well-off families are *both* less likely to have graduated from high school and more likely to attend inexpensive, two-year community colleges rather than a four-year B.A. program if they do make it to college.[13]

Not surprisingly, the results of schooling differ greatly for children of different social backgrounds. Most easily measured, but of limited importance, are differences in scholastic achievement. If we measure the output of schooling by scores on nationally standardized achievement tests, children whose parents were themselves highly educated outperform the children of parents with less education by a wide margin. Data collected for the U.S. Office of Education Survey of Educational Opportunity reveal, for example, that among white high-school seniors, those whose parents were in the top education decile were, on the average, well over three grade levels in measured scholastic achievement ahead of those whose parents were in the bottom decile.[14]

Given these differences in scholastic achievement, inequalities in years of schooling among individuals of different social backgrounds are to be expected. Thus one might be tempted to argue that the close dependence of years of schooling attained on background displayed in the left-hand bars of [Figure 1] is simply a reflection of unequal intellectual abilities, or that inequalities in college attendance are the consequences of differing levels of scholastic achievement in high school and do not reflect any additional social class inequalities peculiar to the process of college admission.

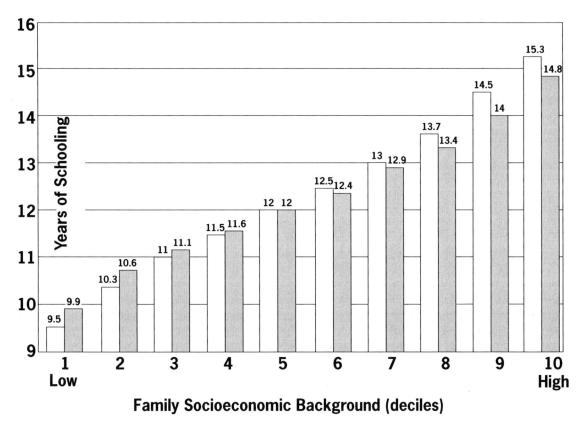

Figure 1 Educational Attainments Are Strongly Dependent on Social Background Even for People of Similar Childhood IQs

Notes: For each socioeconomic group, the left-hand bar indicates the estimated average number of years of schooling attained by all men from that group. The right-hand bar indicates the estimated average number of years of schooling attained by men with IQ scores equal to the average for the entire sample. The sample refers to "non-Negro" men of "nonfarm" backgrounds, aged 35–44 years in 1962. Source: Samuel Bowles and Valerie Nelson, "The 'Inheritance of IQ' and the Intergenerational Transmission of Economic Inequality," *The Review of Economics and Statistics,* vol. LVI, no. 1 (Feb. 1974).

This view, so comforting to the admissions personnel in our elite universities, is unsupported by the data, some of which is presented in [the figure]. The right-hand bars of [the figure] indicate that even among children with identical IQ test scores at ages six and eight, those with rich, well-educated, high-status parents could expect a much higher level of schooling than those with less-favored origins. Indeed, the closeness of the left-hand and right-hand bars in [the figure] shows that only a small portion of the observed social class differences in educational attainment is re-

lated to IQ differences across social classes.[15] The dependence of education attained on background is almost as strong for individuals with the same IQ as for all individuals. Thus, while [the figure] indicates that an individual in the ninetieth percentile in social class background is likely to receive five more years of education than an individual in the tenth percentile, it also indicated that he is likely to receive 4.25 more years schooling than an individual from the tenth percentile with the same IQ. Similar results are obtained when we look specifically at access to college education for students with the same measured IQ. Project Talent data indicates that for "high ability" students (top 25 percent as measured by a composite of tests of "general aptitude"), those of high socioeconomic background (top 25 percent as measured by a composite of family income, parents' education, and occupation) are nearly twice as likely to attend college than students of low socioeconomic background (bottom 25 percent). For "low ability" students (bottom 25 percent), those of high-social background are more than four times as likely to attend college as are their low-social background counterparts.[16]

Inequality in years of schooling is, of course, only symptomatic of broader inequalities in the educational system. Not only do less well-off children go to school for fewer years, they are treated with less attention (or more precisely, less benevolent attention) when they are there. These broader inequalities are not easily measured. Some show up in statistics on the different levels of expenditure for the education of children of different socioeconomic backgrounds. Taking account of the inequality in financial resources for each year in school and the inequality in years of schooling obtained, Jencks estimated that a child whose parents were in the top fifth of the income distribution receives roughly twice the educational resources in dollar terms as does a child whose parents are in the bottom fifth.[17]

The social class inequalities in our school system, then, are too evident to be denied. Defenders of the educational system are forced back on the assertion that things are getting better; the inequalities of the past were far worse. And, indeed, there can be no doubt that some of the inequalities of the past have been mitigated. Yet new inequalities have apparently developed to take their place, for the available historical evidence lends little support to the idea that our schools are on the road to equality of educational opportunity.

For example, data from a recent U.S. Census survey reported in Spady indicate that graduation from college has become no less dependent on one's social background. This is true despite the fact that high-school graduation is becoming increasingly equal across social classes.[18] Additional data confirm this impression. The statistical association (coefficient of correlation) between parents' social status and years of education attained by individuals who completed their schooling three or four decades ago is virtually identical to the same correlation for individuals who terminated their schooling in recent years.[19] On balance, the available data suggests that the number of years of school attained by a child depends upon family background as much in the recent period as it did fifty years ago.

Thus, we have empirical reasons for doubting the egalitarian impact of schooling. . . . We conclude that U.S. education is highly unequal, the chances of attaining much or little schooling being substantially dependent on one's race and parents' economic level. Moreover, where there is a discernible trend toward a more equal educational system—as in the narrowing of the black education deficit, for example—the impact on the structure of economic opportunity is minimal at best.

Notes

1. H. Barnard, *Papers for the Teacher: 2nd Series* (New York: F. C. Brownell, 1866), pp. 293–310.
2. A. de Tocqueville, as quoted in Jeremy Brecher, *Strike!* (San Francisco: Straight Arrow Books, 1972), pp. xi, xii.
3. Ibid., p. 172.
4. Horace Mann as quoted in Michael Katz, ed., *School Reform Past and Present* (Boston: Little, Brown, 1971), p. 141.
5. Ibid., p. 145.
6. *The Massachusetts Teacher* (Oct., 1851), quoted in Katz, pp. 169–70.
7. D. Tyack, *Turning Points in American Edu-*

cational History (Waltham, Mass.: Blaisdell, 1967), p. 89.

8. Ibid., p. 10.

9. Ibid., p. 89.

10. Mann, quoted in Katz, p. 147.

11. This calculation is based on data reported in full in Samuel Bowles and Valerie Nelson, "The 'Inheritance of IQ' and the Intergenerational Transmission of Economic Inequality," *The Review of Economics and Statistics,* 56, 1 (Feb., 1974). It refers to non-Negro males from nonfarm backgrounds, aged 35–44 years. The zero-order correlation coefficient between socioeconomic background and years of schooling was estimated at 0.646. The estimated standard deviation of years of schooling was 3.02. The results for other age groups are similar.

12. These figures refer to individuals who were high-school seniors in October 1965, and who subsequently graduated from high school. College attendance refers to both two- and four-year institutions. Family income is for the twelve months preceding October 1965. Data is drawn from U.S. Bureau of the Census, *Current Population Reports,* Series P-60, No. 183 (May, 1969).

13. For further evidence, see ibid.; and Jerome Karabel, "Community Colleges and Social Stratification," *Harvard Educational Review,* 424, 42 (Nov., 1972).

14. Calculation based on data in James S. Coleman et al., *Equality of Educational Opportunity* (Washington, D.C.: U.S. Government Printing Office, 1966), and the authors.

15. The data relating to IQ is from a 1966 survey of veterans by the National Opinion Research Center; and from N. Bayley and E. S. Schaefer, "Correlations of Maternal and Child Behaviors with the Development of Mental Ability: Data from the Berkeley Growth Study," *Monographs of Social Research in Child Development,* 29, 6 (1964).

16. Based on a large sample of U.S. high-school students as reported in John C. Flannagan and William W. Cooley, *Project Talent, One Year Follow-up Study,* Cooperative Research Project, No. 2333 (Pittsburgh: University of Pittsburgh, School of Education, 1966).

17. C. Jencks et al., *Inequality: A Reassessment of the Effects of Family and Schooling in America* (New York: Basic Books, 1972), p. 48.

18. W. L. Spady, "Educational Mobility and Access: Growth and Paradoxes," in *American Journal of Sociology,* 73, 3 (Nov. 1967); and Peter Blau and Otis D. Duncan, *The American Occupational Structure* (New York: John Wiley, 1967). More recent data support the evidence of no trend toward equality. See U.S. Bureau of Census, op. cit.

19. Ibid., Blau and Duncan.

Academic Achievement in Southeast Asian Refugee Families

Nathan Caplan, Marcella H. Choy, and John K. Whitmore

Many analysts pronounce the U.S. educational system in crisis. But are schools to blame for the modest achievement of some children? In this selection, the authors argue that socialization has a greater impact on academic performance than the quality of our schools. Even though most of the Southeast Asian boat people are poor, have had limited exposure to Western culture, know virtually no English, and live in low-income metropolitan areas, their children are excelling in the U.S. school system.

The scholastic success of Asian children is well recognized. Their stunning performance—particularly in the realm of science and mathematics—has prompted American educators to visit Japanese and Taiwanese schools in an effort to unearth the foundations of these achievements. Experts recommend that American schools adopt aspects of their Asian counterparts, such as a longer school year or more rigorous tasks, in order to raise the scholastic level of U.S. students.

Yet there is no need to go abroad to understand why these children do so well. The achievement of Asian-American students indicates that much may be learned about the origins of their triumph within the American school system itself. More specifically, during the late 1970s and early 1980s, devastating political and economic circumstances forced many Vietnamese, Lao and Chinese-Vietnamese families to seek a new life in the United States. This reset-tlement boat people from Indochina offered a rare opportunity to examine the academic achievement of their children.

These young refugees had lost months, even years of formal schooling while living in relocation camps. Like their parents, they suffered disruption and trauma as they escaped from Southeast Asia. Despite their hardships and with little knowledge of English, the children quickly adapted to their new schools and began to excel.

In researching the economic and scholastic accomplishments of 1,400 refugee households in the early 1980s, our group at the University of Michigan studied the forces that shaped the performance of these children. Some of the standard explanations for educational excellence—parental encouragement and dedication to learning—applied to the young students, but other theories proved inadequate.

Although some of our findings are culturally specific, others point overwhelmingly to the pivotal role of the family in the children's academic success. Because this characteristic extends beyond culture, it has implications for educators, social scientists and policymakers as well as for the refugees themselves. It is clear that the U.S. educational system can work—if the requisite familial and social supports are provided for the students outside school.

Our study encompassed many features of resettlement. We gathered survey and other data on 6,750 persons in five urban areas—Orange County, Calif., Seattle, Houston, Chicago, and Boston—and obtained information about their background and home life as well as economic and demographic facts. We discovered that with regard to educational and social status, the refugees proved to be more ordinary than their predecessors who fled Vietnam in 1975 during the fall of Saigon. These newer displaced persons had had limited exposure to Western culture and knew virtually no English when they arrived. Often they came with nothing more than the clothes they wore.

From this larger group, we chose a random sample of 200 nuclear families and their 536 school-age children. Twenty-seven percent of the families had four or more children. At the time of the study, these young refugees had been in the United States for an average of three and a half years. We collected information on parents and their children during interviews conducted in their native tongues; we also gained access to school transcripts and other related documents.

All the children attended schools in low-income, metropolitan areas—environs not known for outstanding academic records. The refugees were fairly evenly distributed throughout the school levels: Grades one through eleven each contained about 8 percent of the children in the study; kindergarten and twelfth

grade each contained about 5 percent. We converted the students' letter grades into a numerical grade point average (GPA): An A became a four; a D became a one. After calculations, we found that the children's mean GPA was 3.05, or a B average. Twenty-seven percent had an overall GPA in the A range, 52 percent in the B range and 17 percent in the C range. Only 4 percent had a GPA below a C grade.

Even more striking than the overall GPAs were the students' math scores. Almost half of the children earned As in math; another third earned Bs. Thus, four out of five students received either As or Bs. It is not surprising that they would do better in this subject. Their minds could most easily grasp disciplines in which English was not so crucial: math, physics, chemistry and science. As expected, their grades in the liberal arts were lower: In areas where extensive language skills were required, such as English, history or social studies, the combined GPA was 2.64.

To place our local findings in a national context, we turned to standardized achievement test scores, in particular, the California Achievement Test (CAT) results. In this arena as well, we found that the performance of the newly arrived students was exceptional. Their mean overall score on the CAT was in the 54th percentile; that is, they outperformed 54 percent of those taking the test—placing them just above the national average. Interestingly, their scores tended to cluster toward the middle ranges: They showed a more restricted scope of individual differences.

The national tests also reflected an above-average ability in math when the Indochinese children were compared with children taking the exam at equivalent levels. Half of the children studied obtained scores in the top quartile. Even more spectacularly, 27 percent of them scored in the 10th decile—better than 90 percent of the students across the country and almost three times higher than the national norm. The CAT math scores confirmed that the GPAs of these children were not products of local bias but of true mathematical competence.

Again, the lowest scores were found in the language and reading tests. In this case, the mean score was slightly below the national average. For reasons discussed earlier, this finding was expected. It remains remarkable, however, that the students' scores are so close to the national average in language skills.

The GPA and CAT scores show that the refugee children did very well, particularly in light of their background. A history marked by significant physical and emotional trauma as well as a lack of formal education would not seem to predispose them to an easy transition into U.S. schools. Yet even though they had not forgotten their difficult experiences, the children were able to focus on the present and to work toward the future. In so doing, they made striking scholastic progress. Moreover, their achievements held true for the majority, not for just a few whiz kids.

Clearly, these accomplishments are fueled by influences powerful enough to override the impact of a host of geographic and demographic factors. Using various statistical approaches, we sought to understand the forces responsible for this performance. In the process, a unique finding caught our attention, namely, a positive relation between the number of siblings and the children's GPA.

Family size has long been regarded as one of the most reliable predictors of poor achievement. Virtually all studies on the topic show an inverse relation: The greater the number of children in the family, the lower the mean GPA and other measures associated with scholastic performance. Typically, these reports document a 15 percent decline in GPA and other achievement-related scores with the addition of each child to the family. The interpretation of this finding has been subject to

disagreement, but there is no conflict about its relation to achievement.

For the Indochinese students, this apparent disadvantage was somehow neutralized or turned into an advantage. We took this finding to be an important clue in elucidating the role of the family in academic performance. We assumed that distinctive family characteristics would explain how these achievements took place so early in resettlement as well as how these children and their parents managed to overcome such adversities as poor English skills, poverty and the often disruptive environment of urban schools.

Because they were newcomers in a strange land, it was reasonable to expect that at least some of the reasons for the children's success rested on their cultural background. While not ignoring the structural forces present here in the United States—among them the opportunity for education and advancement—we believed that the values and traditions permeating the lives of these children in Southeast Asia would guide their lives in this country.

Knowledge of one's culture does not occur in a vacuum; it is transmitted through the family. Children often acquire a sense of their heritage as a result of deliberate and concentrated parental effort in the context of family life. This inculcation of values from one generation to another is a universal feature of the conservation of culture.

We sought to determine which values were important to the parents, how well those values had been transmitted to the children and what role values played in promoting their educational achievement. In our interviews we included twenty-six questions about values that were derived from a search of Asian literature and from social science research. Respondents were asked to rate the perceived importance of these values.

We found that parents and children rated the perceived values in a similar fashion, providing empirical testimony that these parents had served their stewardship well. For the most part, the perspectives and values embedded in the cultural heritage of the Indochinese had been carried with them to the United States. We also determined that cultural values played an important role in the educational achievement of the children. Conserved values constituted a source of motivation and direction as the families dealt with contemporary problems set in a country vastly different from their homeland. The values formed a set of cultural givens with deep roots in the Confucian and Buddhist traditions of East and Southeast Asia.

The family is the central institution in these traditions, within which and through which achievement and knowledge are accomplished. We used factor analyses and other statistical procedures to determine value groupings and their relation to achievement. These analyses showed that parents and children honor mutual, collective obligation to one another and to their relatives. They strive to attain respect, cooperation and harmony within the family.

Nowhere is the family's commitment to accomplishment and education more evident than in time spent on homework. During high school, Indochinese students spend an average of three hours and ten minutes per day; in junior high, an average of two and a half hours; and in grade school, an average of two hours and five minutes. Research in the United States shows that American students study about one and a half hours per day at the junior and senior high school levels.

Among the refugee families, then, homework clearly dominates household activities during weeknights. Although the parents' lack of education and facility with English often prevents them from engaging in the content of the exercise, they set standards and goals for the evening and facilitate their children's studies by assuming responsibility for chores and other practical considerations.

After dinner, the table is cleared, and homework begins. The older children, both male and female, help their younger siblings. Indeed, they seem to learn as much from teaching as from being taught. It is reasonable to suppose that a great amount of learning goes on at these times—in terms of skills, habits, attitudes and expectations as well as the content of a subject. The younger children, in particular, are taught not only subject matter but how to learn. Such sibling involvement demonstrates how a large family can encourage and enhance academic success. The familial setting appears to make the children feel at home in school and, consequently, perform well there.

Parental engagement included reading regularly to young children—an activity routinely correlated to academic performance. Almost one half (45 percent) of the parents reported reading aloud. In those families, the children's mean GPA was 3.14 as opposed to 2.97 in households where the parents did not read aloud. (This difference, and all others to follow in which GPAs are compared, is statistically reliable.) It is important to note that the effects of being read to held up statistically whether the children were read to in English or in their native language.

This finding suggests that parental English literacy skills may not play a vital role in determining school performance. Rather, other aspects of the experience—emotional ties between parent and child, cultural validation and wisdom shared in stories read in the child's native language, or value placed on reading and learning—extend to schoolwork. Reading at home obscures the boundary between home and school. In this context, learning is perceived as normal, valuable and fun.

Egalitarianism and role sharing were also found to be associated with high academic performance. In fact, relative equality between the sexes was one of the strongest predictors of GPA. In those homes where the respondents disagreed that a "wife should always do as her husband wishes," the children earned average GPAs of 3.16. But children from homes whose parents agreed with the statement had an average GPA of 2.64. In households where the husband helped with the dishes and laundry, the mean GPA was 3.21; when husbands did not participate in the chores, the mean GPA was 2.79.

This sense of equality was not confined to the parents—it extended to the children, especially in terms of sex-role expectations and school performance. GPAs were higher in households where parents expected both boys and girls to help with chores. Families rejecting the idea that a college education is more important for boys than for girls had children whose average GPA was 3.14; children from families exhibiting a pro-male bias had a mean GPA of 2.83.

Beyond the support and guidance provided by the family, culturally based attributions proved to be important to refugees in their view of scholastic motivation. The "love of learning" category was rated most often by both parents and students as the factor accounting for their academic success. There appeared to be two parts to this sentiment. First, the children experienced intrinsic gratification when they correctly worked a problem through to completion. The pleasure of intellectual growth, based on new knowledge and ideas and combined with increased competence and mastery, was considered highly satisfying. Second, refugee children felt a sense of accomplishment on seeing their younger siblings learn from their own efforts at teaching. Both learning and imparting knowledge were perceived as pleasurable experiences rather than as drudgery.

The gratification accompanying accomplishment was, in turn, founded on a sense of the importance of effort as opposed to ability. The refugees did not trust fate or luck as the determinant of educational outcome; they be-

lieved in their potential to master the factors that could influence their destiny. And their culture encompasses a practical approach to accomplishment: setting realistic goals. Without the setting of priorities and standards for work, goals would remain elusive. But anyone endorsing the values of working in a disciplined manner and taking a long-term view could establish priorities and pursue them.

Belief in one's own ability to effect change or attain goals has long been held to be a critical component of achievement and motivation—and our findings support this conclusion. Parents were asked a series of questions relating to their perceived ability to control external events influencing their lives. Those who had a clear sense of personal efficacy had children who attained higher GPAs.

We had some difficulty, however, interpreting the perception of efficacy as an idea generated solely by the individual. Despite a vast social science literature asserting the contrary, we believe that these refugees' sense of control over their lives could be traced to family identity. It seemed to us that the sense of familial efficacy proved critical, as opposed to the more Western concept of personal efficacy.

Other cultural values show us that the refugee family is firmly linked not only to its past and traditions but to the realities of the present and to future possibilities. This aptitude for integrating the past, present and future appears to have imparted a sense of continuity and direction to the lives of these people.

Education was central to this integration and to reestablishment in the United States. It was and still is the main avenue for refugees in American society to succeed and survive. In contrast, education in Indochina was a restricted privilege. The future of the refugee children, and of their families, is thus inextricably linked to schools and to their own children's performances within them. The emphasis on education as the key to social acceptance and economic success helps us understand why academic achievement is reinforced by such strong parental commitment.

Outside school, the same sense of drive and achievement can be seen in the parents. Having a job and being able to provide for the family is integral to family pride. Shame is felt by Asian families on welfare. Reflecting the same determination and energy that their children manifest in school, Indochinese parents have found employment and climbed out of economic dependency and poverty with dispatch.

Two of the twenty-six values included as a measure of cultural adaptation entailed integration and the acceptance of certain American ways of life: the importance of "seeking fun and excitement" and of "material possessions." These ideas are of particular concern because they address the future of refugee families and mark the potential power and consequence of American life on the refugees and subsequent generations. Not surprisingly, when our subjects were asked to indicate which values best characterized their nonrefugee neighbors, these two items were most frequently cited.

More interesting, however, was our finding that these same two values were correlated with a lower GPA. We found that parents who attributed greater importance to fun and excitement had children who achieved lower GPAs: 2.90 as opposed to 3.14. The results for material possessions were similar: GPAs were 2.66 versus 3.19.

It is not clear why these negative associations exist. Do they reflect less strict parents or families who have integrated so quickly that cultural stability has been lost? We believe it is the latter explanation. Refugees who held that "the past is as important as the future" had children whose GPAs averaged 3.14. Children of those who did not rate the preservation of the past as highly had an average GPA of 2.66.

This item was one of the most powerful independent predictors of academic performance. Our findings run contrary to expectations. Rather than adopting American ways and assimilating into the melting pot, the most successful Indochinese families appear to retain their own traditions and values. By this statement we are in no way devaluing the American system. The openness and opportunity it offers have enabled the Indochinese to succeed in the United States even while maintaining their own cultural traditions.

Although different in origins, both traditional Indochinese and middle-class American values emphasize education, achievement, hard work, autonomy, perseverance and pride. The difference between the two value systems is one of orientation to achievement. American mores encourage independence and individual achievement, whereas Indochinese values foster interdependence and a family-based orientation to achievement. And in view of the position of these refugees in society during the early phase of resettlement in this country, this approach appears to have worked well as the best long-term investment. It appears to be the reason why these children are highly responsive to American schools.

The lack of emphasis on fun and excitement also does not indicate misery on the part of these refugee children. Despite evidence that the suicide rate is growing among some Asian-American children, we found that those in our sample were well adjusted. Our interviews revealed no damaging manipulation of their lives by their parents; moreover, their love of learning sustained their academic pursuits.

The Indochinese values that encourage academic rigor and excellence are not culturally unique: earlier studies of other groups have found similar results. The children of Jewish immigrants from Eastern Europe, for example, excelled in the U.S. school system.

In 1961 Judith R. Kramer of Brooklyn College and Seymour Leventman of the University of Pennsylvania reported that nearly 90 percent of the third generation attended college, despite the fact that the first generation had little or no education when they arrived in the United States. Their emphasis on family and culture was held to be instrumental in this success.

In 1948 William Caudill and George De-Vos of the University of California at Berkeley found that Japanese students overcame prejudice in U.S. schools immediately after World War II and thrived academically. Their success was attributed to cultural values and to parental involvement. More recently, a study by Reginald Clark of the Claremont Graduate School documented the outstanding achievement of low-income African American students in Chicago whose parents supported the school and teachers and structured their children's learning environment at home.

These findings, as well as our own, have significance for the current national debate on education. It is clear that the American school system—despite widespread criticism—has retained its capacity to teach, as it has shown with these refugees. We believe that the view of our schools as failing to educate stems from the unrealistic demand that the educational system deal with urgent social service needs. Citizens and politicians expect teachers and schools to keep children off the streets and away from drugs, deal with teenage pregnancy, prevent violence in the schools, promote safe sex and perform myriad other tasks and responsibilities in addition to teaching traditional academic subjects.

As the social needs of our students have moved into the classroom, they have consumed the scarce resources allocated to education and have compromised the schools' academic function. The primary role of teachers has become that of parent by proxy; they are expected to transform the attitude and behavior of children, many of whom come to school ill prepared to learn.

If we are to deal effectively with the crisis in American education, we must start with an accurate definition of the problem. We must separate teaching and its academic purpose from in-school social services. Only then can we assess the true ability of schools to accomplish these two, sometimes opposing, functions—or we can identify and delegate these nonacademic concerns to other institutions.

Throughout this article we have examined the role of the family in the academic performance of Indochinese refugees. We firmly believe that for American schools to succeed, parents and families must become more committed to the education of their children. They must instill a respect for education and create within the home an environment conducive to learning. They must also participate in the process so that their children feel comfortable learning and go to school willing and prepared to study.

Yet we cannot expect the family to provide such support alone. Schools must reach out to families and engage them meaningfully in the education of their children. This involvement must go beyond annual teacher-parent meetings and must include, among other things, the identification of cultural elements that promote achievement.

Similarly, we cannot adopt the complete perspective of an Indochinese or any other culture. It would be ludicrous to impose cultural beliefs and practices on American children, especially on those whose progress in this country has been fraught with blocked access.

We can, however, work to ensure that families believe in the value of an education and, like the refugees, have rational expectations of future rewards for their efforts. Moreover, we can integrate components of the refugees' experience regarding the family's role in education. It is possible to identify culturally compatible values, behaviors and strategies for success that might enhance scholastic achievement. It is in this regard that the example of the Indochinese refugees—as well as the Japanese and Jewish immigrants before them—can shape our priorities and our policies.

Selected Readings

Anderson, K. 1981. "Post-High School Experiences and College Attrition". Sociology of Education, 54, 1–15.

Astin, A.W. 1992. "Minorities in American higher education: Recent trends, current prospects, and recommendations". San Francisco: Jossey-Boss.

Bailey, R. N. 1998. Minority Admissions. Lexington, Mass.: Heath. Berint, S. and Karabel, J. 1989. The Diverted Dream: Community Colleges and the Promise of Education Opportunity in America, 1900-1985. New York:Oxford University Press.

Bourdieu, P. 1977. Cultural Reproduction and Social Reproduction. in Power and Ideology in Education. edited by Karabel and Halsey. New York: Oxford University Press.

Bohrnstedt, G. & Felson, R. 1993, "Explaining relations among children's actual and perceived performance." Social Psychology Quarterly 45, 43–56.

Brookover, W., Thomas, S., & Paterson, A. 1964. "Self-concept and school achievement". Sociology of Education, 17, 271–283.

Brookover, W. & Passalacqua, J. 1982. "Comparison of Aggregate Self-concept for Populations with Different Reference Groups". Self-concept: Advances in Theory and Practice. (Pg. 216–221)

Byrne, B.M., & Shavelson, R.J. 1987. "Adolescent self-concept: Testing the assumptions of equivalent students across gender". American Educational Research Journal, 24, 365–385.

Deutsch, M. & Gerard, H.G. 1955. "A Study of normative and informational influence upon individual judgment". Journal of Abnormal and Social Psychology, 55. 629–636

DiCesare, A., 1992. "Non-intellectual correlates of black student attrition". Journal of College Student Personnel, 13, 319–24.

Educational Testing Service. 1978. Guide to the Use of the Descriptive Test of Basic Skills. Princeton: NJ

Felson, R.B., & Bohrnstedt, G.W. 1990. "Attributions of Ability and Motivation in a Natural Setting". Journal of Personality and Social Psychology, 39, 799–805.

Griffore, R.J., & Samuels, D.D. 1979. "Self-concept of ability and college students academic achievement". Psychology Reports, 43, 38–43.

Gurin, P., Miller, A.H., & Gurin, G. 1980. "Stratum identification and consciousness". Social Psychology Quarterly, 43, 30–47.

Hansford, B.C. & Hattie, J. A 1982. "The relationship between self and achievement-performance". Psychology Reports, 52, 123–129.

Horowitz, J.L., Sedlacek, W.E., & Brooks G.C. 1992. "Correlations of black and white university student grades beyond the freshman year". Cultural Study Center Research Report No. 7–12. College Park, University of Maryland.

Jencks, C. & Riesman, D. 1968. The American Education Revolution. New York: Doubleday.

Jussim, Coleman & Nassau, 1987.The Influence of Self-esteem on Perceptions of performance and Feedback. Social Psychology Quarterly, 50, 95–99.

Lavin, D.E., Alba R.D. & Silberstein, R.A. 1981. Right Versus Privilege: The Open Admissions Experiment at The City University of New York. The Free Press: London.

Lavin, D.E. 1965. The Predication of Academic Performance. New York: Russell Sage Foundation.

Robinson, D.A.O., & Copper, S.E. 1984. "The influence of self-concept on academic success in the technological careers". Journal of College Student Personnel, 25, 145–149.

Sedlacek, W.F. 1977. "Should higher education students readmitted differentially by race and sex? The evidence". Journal of the National Association of College Admissions Counselors, 22, 22–24.

Sedlacek, W.F. & Brooks, G.C. 1996. "Predictors of academic success for university students in special programs". Cultural Study Research Report No. 4-72. College Park: University of Maryland.

Shavelson, R.J., Hubner, J.T., & Stanton, G.C. 1976. "Self-concept validation of construct interpretation". Review of Educational Research, 46, 407–41.

Velez, W. 1985. Questioning the Community College Role. San Francisco: Jossey-Bass.

Weis, L. 1985. Between Two Worlds: Black Students in an Urban Community College. Boston: Routledge and Kegan.

Wells, E. & Sweeney, P. 1996. A Test of Three Models of Self-assessment. Social Psychology, 49, 1–10.

Self-Concept of Ability as a Predictor of Academic Success among Urban Technical College Students

Steven Gerardi

Abstract

Academic self-concept, rather than the traditional cognitive skills was a signifi-cant predictor of academic performance among minority and low-income stu-dents in an urban technical college. © 2005 Published by Elsevier Inc.

1. Context and Overview of Research

The connection between positive self-con-cept and academic performance has long been perceived as an important linkage by Sociologists and educators alike in assessing academic performance. Self-concept is formed based upon past judgments, perceptions and feedback of the generalized and significant others, and a "person's conception of his/her own ability to learn the accepted types of aca-demic behavior . . . and performance in terms of school achievement" (Brookover, Thomas, & Paterson, 1964, p. 271).

The research in this area suggests that in-dividuals interpret and judge their achieve-ments and abilities in ways congruent with prior self-conceptions, actively seeking self-confirming feedback and resisting that which is inconsistent with past self-perceptions (Jus-sim, Coleman, & Nassau, 1987). Wells and Sweeney (1996), demonstrated that students with high academic self-concept continually overestimate their academic performance. Furthermore, self-concept may be partially self-maintaining. Specifically, this interpretive process may lead students to believe they suc-ceed more and fail less, even when actual performances are similar (Jussim et al., 1987).

There is mounting evidence that teacher expectations of student performance tends to pace academic advancements, since teachers treat those they expect to be academically suc-cessful differently than students of whom they expect little. Indeed, the evidence suggests that high teacher expectation is a salient vari-able for student achievement. Felson and Bohrnstedt (1990), indicated that ability and effort were perceived by teachers as positively related. According to the authors, teachers may view students with high ability as more motivated than those with low ability. Bohrn-stedt and Felson (1993), argued that teachers were providing what the authors described as the "halo effect" for their motivated students.

Astin (1992) found that individuals with high academic self-concept of ability (ASC) perceived their efforts as validation of positive academic achievement, and low effort as an indicator of low achievement. Furthermore, individuals perceive those with high self-concept of ability as successful even when they are not.

This evidence is consistent with a long body of research which suggests that the self-remains comparatively resolute as a result of long-term stable social relationships. On the other hand, Brookover et al. (1964), report having observed that self-concept changes, as the generalized and significant others change, and over time and social event.

Brookover and Passalacqua (1982) have reported that black students within predominantly black schools consistently rate their self-academic ability higher than white students within predominantly white schools. The authors argue that this reported high self-assessment may be related to estimating themselves within their reference group, and if placed within a heterogeneous group, these relatively high assessments may spiral downward.

Furthermore, there is mounting evidence that ASC is highly correlated with academic success, especially, among minority and low socio-economic status (SES) students (Astin, 1992; Bailey, 1998; DiCesare, 1992; Gurin, Miller, & Gurin, 1980; Horowitz, Sedlacek, & Brooks, 1992; Sedlacek, 1977).

Sedlacek and Brooks (1996), demonstrated that minority students who have achieved academic success at the college level have strong positive self-concept. The authors indicated that black high school students who overcome many of these academic setbacks are positive they will earn a college degree. This research also found that black students with high self-concept had greater academic success than those with low self-concept.

Although research has shown that academic self-concept factors have been good predictors of academic performance on the college level, academic performance measurements such as the SAT, academic placement tests and high school background generally, have been better predictors of college grades than the self-concept (Bailey, 1998; Griffore & Samuels, 1979; Lavin, 1965; Robinson & Copper, 1984).

Given these paradoxical findings, this research raises the following question: Is self-concept of ability an important and significant predictor of positive academic outcomes among minority and low socio-economic college students?

2. Types of Data/Research Procedure

2.1. Types of Data

This study employs four categories of data in analyzing the above question. The categories of data are: (1) *educational background* including the number of college preparatory courses taken in high school, high school average, and high school average in mathematics. (2) *Scores on City University of New York's (CUNY) standardized assessment examinations*: The CUNY standardized examinations have three components: (a) *The CUNY Mathematics Skills Assessment Test* is a 40-item math and algebra test designed to identify students with math deficiencies. The test is locally constructed with no national norms. This exam measures basic mathematical skills in whole numbers, fractions, decimals, percent, ratio and proportion, signed numbers, equations, Pythagorean Theorem, word problems and all forms of algebraic representations; (b) *CUNY Freshmen Skills Assessment Test* in reading is a 45-item reading comprehension subject of the Descriptive

Tests of Language Skills (DTLS) (Educational Testing Service, 1978). The DTLS was specifically designed to identify students who may need special assistance in particular aspects of reading and language use before undertaking standard college level work and (c) the *CUNY Writing Skills Assessment Test* is a choice of three out of five essay type test designed to identify students with deficiencies in writing. This examination was also locally constructed with no national norms. (3) *Measures of college performance* including the respondent's Grade Point Average (GPA) over the eight semester period and (4) *self-concept of ability* as measured by the Brookover Self-concept of Ability Scale.

Over the last two decades the Brookover Self-concept of Ability Scale has been a reliable and valid instrument for assessing academic self-concept and has been cited in over 175 publications. The scale consists of eight Guttman scale items selected to differentiate students on perception of academic ability. The eight items are divided into two conceptual dimensions each composed of two logical subjects: (a) future-oriented (questions concerned with future educational goals and their ability to realize them) and present-oriented items (questions concerned with one's ability to do college work), and (b) comparative and absolute evaluations of self-concept of ability. Brookover et al. (1964) reported test-retest coefficients for their normalization sample of .95 for males and .96 for females. They also reported internal reliability coefficients of .82 for males and .77 for females. Shavelson, Hubner, and Stanton (1976) reported predictive validity coefficients for the ASC and various subject area achievement tests ranging from .63 to .88 for males, and .52 to .68 for females. In meta analysis of the relationship between self and achievement performance measures, Hansford and Hattie (1982) found the ASC correlated best to academic performance measures ($M = 0.43$ in 18 studies analyzed) among a group of nine self-concept scales. Byrne and Shavelson (1987) found the ASC significantly and consistently correlated with various English self-concept scales, as well as grades in English and mathematics.

Data on educational background, CUNY assessment examinations and academic performance have been extracted from the official records of a technical college within the City University of New York.

This technical college graduates 25% of the minority and low-SES background professionals in areas of engineering and health fields in New York State and 10% nationally.

Information on self-concept of ability were assessed from a questionnaire randomly administered to 307 Freshmen the first day of classes. This random sample represents approximately 10% of the entering Freshmen class of this CUNY technical college. This sample was followed through eight college semesters (from September of 1994 through June 1998) of study.

This research calls upon a set of widely used traditional independent variables such as: (1) academic educational background and (2) self-concept of ability. This study also calls upon a critical indicator (dependent variables) which will help assess the academic performance of this sample based upon the quality of college work as indicated by the cumulative grade point average after eight semesters of study.

A four stage regression analysis was undertaken using the above mentioned dependent and the independent variables. Generally, only significant coefficients are discussed. The substantive discussion relates only to the last stage of the regression analysis (stage 4).

3. Results

Over the last three decades social scientists have examined self-concept's place in human growth and development. Many congruent principles have emerged as a result of these inquires: (1) self-concept has a central place in guiding human behavior; (2) self-concept seeks consistency and stability; (3) self-concept is based on roles people play; (4) self-concept is a product of the social context and the feedback of others and (5) a positive self-concept is correlated with academic achievement and success.

Table 1 suggests that self-concept of ability (Brookover Self-concept of Ability Scale) was a strong predictor of *Grade Point Average*. Consistent with this research tradition, these data suggested that GPA was strongly influenced by ASC. Table 1 indicates that for every 5-point difference in high school average over the mean of 72 for this sample, there is a 10th of a letter grade increase in GPA. Furthermore, for every three additional college preparatory course difference taken in high school over the mean of 9 units for this sample, creates a 10th of a letter grade increase in GPA. Every 6-point difference in high school average in mathematics over the mean of 70, produces an increase of a 10th of a letter grade in GPA. Additionally, for every 7-point difference on CUNY Reading Examination over the mean of 27, there is also a 10th of a letter grade increase in GPA. Every 6-point difference on the CUNY Mathematics Assessment Examination over the mean of 26, there is a 10th of a letter grade difference in GPA.

By contrast, for every 3-point increase in the Brookover Self-concept of Academic Ability Scale over the mean of 40, there is a three-tenths of a letter grade increase in GPA. Suggesting that ASC was a more powerful predictor of academic outcomes than the traditional measurements of college performance.

4. Conclusion

Two decades of research within the sociology of education has suggested that the typical urban college student is predominantly from low socio-economic status (SES) and minority group origins (Berint & Karabel, 1989). Historically, such groups have had limited exposure to a college preparatory high school track and are usually students who have achieved a minimum satisfactory high school average and performed poorly on standardized examinations. Indeed, such an educational background acts as an obstacle to college success.

Whether such students survive in college may depend on the individual possessing a high self-concept of ability. There is a long tradition within the sociology of education which suggest that a positive self-concept of ability has an important influence on the student's academic success, especially among minority and low SES individuals. Though research repeatedly has shown that academic performance

TABLE 8.1

Grade Point Average as a Function of Academic Self-Concept

N = 307	Means	S.D.	b	Beta
High school average	72	5	.008	.004
Math high school average	70	6	.002	.130
High school college preparatory courses	9	3	.003	.097
CUNY reading	27	7	.015	.116
CUNY math	26	6	.020	.115
CUNY writing	—	—	—	—
ASC	40	3	.015	.048

measurement such as the SAT, academic placement examinations and high school average have been better predictors of college success, this research suggests that ASC may be a positive force in overcoming past disadvantages. In fact, ASC proved to be more influential in predicting GPA than the traditional academic performance measurements.

Finally, the respondents in this study were typically not proficient in reading, writing and mathematics when measured by the CUNY Assessment Examinations and had earned the minimum high school graduation average. Indeed, these students had been classified as academic high risks because of their poor academic performance. However, these data may suggest that a positive student ASC may act as a counter veiling force in combating the compounding socio-economic disabilities associated with the inner-city environment.

References

Astin, A. W. (1992). *Minorities in American higher education: Recent trends, current prospects, and recommendations.* San Francisco: Jossey-Boss.

Bailey, R. N. (1998). *Minority admissions.* Lexington, Mass: Heath.

Berint, S., & Karabel, J. (1989). *The diverted dream: Community colleges and the promise of educational opportunity in America, 1900–1985.* New York: Oxford University Press.

Bohrnstedt, G., & Felson, R. (1993). Explaining relations among children's actual and perceived performance. *Social Psychology Quarterly, 45,* 43–56.

Brookover, W., & Passalacqua, J. (1982). Comparison of aggregate self-concept for populations with different reference groups. *Self-concept: Advances in Theory and Practice,* 216–221.

Brookover, W., Thomas, S., & Paterson, A. (1964). Self-concept and school achievement. *Sociology of Education, 17,* 271–283.

Byrne, B. M., & Shavelson, R. J. (1987). Adolescent self-concept: Testing the assumptions of equivalent students across gender. *American Educational Research Journal, 24,* 365–385.

DiCesare, A. (1992). Non-intellectual correlates of black student attrition. *Journal of College Student Personnel, 13,* 319–324.

Educational Testing Service. (1978). *Guide to the use of the descriptive test of basic skills.* Princeton: NJ.

Felson, R. B., & Bohrnstedt, G. W. (1990). Attributions of ability and motivation in a natural setting. *Journal of Personality and Social Psychology, 39,* 799–805.

Griffore, R. J., & Samuels, D. D. (1979). Self-concept of ability and college students academic achievement. *Psychology Reports, 43,* 38–43.

Gurin, P., Miller, A. H., & Gurin, G. (1980). Stratum identification and consciousness. *Social Psychology Quarterly, 43,* 30–47.

Hansford, B. C., & Hattie, J. A. (1982). The relationship between self and achievement-performance. *Psychology Reports, 52,* 123–129.

Horowitz, J. L., Sedlacek, W. E., & Brooks G. C. (1992). *Correlations of black and white university student grades beyond the freshman year* (Cultural Study Center Research Report No. 7–12). College Park: University of Maryland.

Jussim, Coleman, & Nassau. (1987). The influence of self-esteem on perceptions of performance and feedback. *Social Psychology Quarterly, 50,* 95–99.

Lavin, D. E. (1965). *The predication of academic performance.* New York: Russell Sage Foundation.

Robinson, D. A. O., & Copper, S. E. (1984). The influence of self-concept on academic success in the technological careers. *Journal of College Student Personnel, 25,* 145–149.

Sedlacek, W. F. (1977). Should higher education students readmitted differentially by race and sex? The evidence. *Journal of the National Association of College Admissions Counselors, 22,* 22–24.

Sedlacek, W. F., & Brooks, G. C. (1996). *Predictors of academic success for university students in special programs* (Cultural

Study Research Report No. 4–72). College Park: University of Maryland.

Shavelson, R. J., Hubner, J. T., & Stanton, G. C. (1976). Self-concept validation of construct interpretation. *Review of Educational Research, 46,* 407–441.

Wells, E., & Sweeney, P. (1996). A test of three models of self-assessment. *Social Psychology, 49,* 1–10.

Positive College Attitudes among Minority and Low-Income Students as an Indicator of Academic Success

Steven Gerardi

Abstract

Positive student attitudes among minority and low SES students toward the effectiveness of their college may be seen as a function of college success. These data suggest that students with positive attitudes toward their college experience had greater academic achievements than those who had negative attitudes. © 2005 Elsevier Inc. All rights reserved.

1. Context and Overview of the Research

Since the City University of New York's (CUNY) initiation of an Open Admissions policy in 1970, New York City's (NYC) economy and work force has gone through an evolution. Although, unlike most urban centers New York City has been growing, the late-1970s through the mid-1980s there was a large exodus of native New Yorkers to the suburbs. In the late-1980s, this loss was more than offset by a huge influx of the so called "2nd wave immigrant" (SWI) (many were/are of Hispanic descent). Today, the SWI makes up at least 30% of the City's population, and their children are now college age.

However, during this same period important changes occurred in the structure of NYC labor market leading to the contraction of the number of blue-collar and semiskilled jobs, and an increase in the technical and white-collar opportunities. As a result, the blue-collar job market that was so rich in the early-1940s to the mid-1960s, and one on which many of the 1st wave of immigrants traditionally dependent on as a source of employment, has dwindled to approximately half of itself today. These market changes have coincided with the arrival of the SWI who tend not to speak English and/or tend to have weak academic backgrounds, even in their native country.

Another factor occurring simultaneously with the structural changes in labor has been the rising floor of educational credentials needed for entry into the postmodern labor market.

Essentially, credential inflation in conjunction with the loss of the blue-collar labor market has led many of the SWI who normally would not seek a college education, to do so now in ever increasing numbers.

CUNY since its inception has played a large role in the education of the children and grandchildren of the historically earlier immigrant populations (1st wave) of NYC. This tradition dates back 143 years. It is a tradition which has been instrumental in assisting hundreds of thousands of CUNY graduates out of the grip of poverty by creating upward mobility (Lavin, Alba, & Silberstein, 1981).

Since CUNY draws most of its students from New York City, the changes in the demographic make-up of the City has become a reflection of the CUNY student body. A case in point is the CUNY 1992 Freshmen cohort. When asked what their country of birth was, 3.3% reported Africa, 8.8% Asia, 25.6% the Caribbean, 10.1% the Dominican Republic, 4.9% Eastern Europe, 1.6% the Middle East, 11.2% South/Central America, 14.8% Western Europe, 13.7% Puerto Rico, and 6.1% reported other (Immigration/Migration and the CUNY Student of the Future, Winter, 1995). It has been further suggested that there are 110 different language dialects spoken in NYC, adding to CUNY's overriding pedagogical challenge.

Even with the increased need for higher order skills in New York City's postindustrial economy, less than 70% of New York City's high school graduates go on to college. Thus, the most recent data suggest that for a given 100 New York City high school students, 50 will dropout and 50 will graduate. Of these survivors, approximately 35 will go to college. But, because of the knowledge gap created by the cultural background of the SWI, 60% of such individuals generally find their only collegiate option the Associate Degree College. Hence, of the 35 college-bound survivors mentioned earlier, 20 will enroll in an Associate Degree College, where at best they can only expect to earn an AA/AAS degree.

As a result, the overriding pedagogical challenge CUNY has become faced with is the integration of the SWI student into the mainstream curricula. This challenge has been met with programs which create strategies for the effective acculturation of those from non-English speaking cultures into the American system of higher education. But there is a long sociological tradition which suggests that non-English speaking immigrates require at least three generations to become fully enculturated into the American educational mainstream. A case in point is that during the 2002 school year in NYC public schools, 60% of the 4th grade students were not at the grade level in Reading and Mathematics.

Furthermore, those who enter the AA/AAS Degree colleges within CUNY tend to be under-prepared in the traditional academic skills such as English, Mathematics, and Writing. Therefore, the need for compensatory work is great; 84% of the CUNY AA/AAS Degree College entrants are required to take at least one remedial course. However, in most urban Associate Degree colleges a little less than 90% are required to enroll in a remedial course (Cohen & Brawer, 1992). But for each remedial course taken at CUNY adds one-fifth of a year to the graduation date of that individual (Lavin & Crook, 1993).

The AA/AAS Degree College for which these data were collected for this study is one of twenty units within the CUNY system. This college has 11,500 students in which 65% were not proficient in Math, 53% in Reading, and 67% in Writing, and were placed into remediation.

Whether this background student survives college may depend on the individual's attitude and opinion of how successful their college was in shaping intellectual growth. According to the Sociological literature, attitudes and opinions of individuals toward social events are seen as helping to organize and categorize the world in a meaningful and consistent fashion. Attitudes and opinions from this research suggests: (1) provides order; (2) maximize rewards; (3) minimize punishments; and (4) generally acts to clarify the individual's frame of reference.

Student satisfaction with their college experience is important because it may determine the students' persistence and academic performance. The dissatisfied student is likely to stop-out or drop-out and perform poorly academically. Indeed, research suggests that the degree of satisfaction, measured by mid-year, differentiated between students who re-enrolled or dropped-out and have positive or negative academic outcomes the following year.

Furthermore, Mickelson (2000) argued that there are two forms of educational attitudes—abstract and concrete.

Abstract attitudes are based upon ideologies about education and opportunity. These attitudes are associated with the American merit system and education. Concrete attitudes are indicators of realized benefits of social mobility and education.

Those with low abstract and concrete attitudes are likely to perform poorly academically. However, those with high abstract and concrete attitudes are expected to have positive academic performance.

Therefore, this research asked the following question: Is there a relationship between positive college student attitudes and academic outcomes?

2. Types of Data and Research Procedure

This study was a longitudinal project covering three academic years which employed two categories of data in analyzing the main question posed within this research. The categories of data are:

(1) *STUDENT ATTITUDES TOWARD THEIR COLLEGE CAREER* assessed by a commercially prepared questionnaire by A. C.T. entitled "College Outcomes Survey" which was randomly administered to 300 students enrolled at a college of technology in New York City during the Fall, 1998 semester. This college of technology has a large minority 72%, and low-income population reported mean yearly income is $12,500.00. This college graduates 60% of the minority technicians in the health and computer science areas in New York State, and 10% of the minority technicians nationally equality.

Approximately 121 questionnaires were returned completed. This sample represents approximately 10% of the students within the Freshman Class.

The questionnaire is a Guttman type survey which asked the respondent to rate the effectiveness of the college in developing important intellectual abilities. The responses ranged from very great, great, moderate, little to none. This survey has a 95% confidence level with a ±.01 error range based upon a 10% random sample.

(2) *MEASURES OF COLLEGE PERFORMANCE* including the respondent's Grade Point Average (GPA), the number of college credits earned, and graduation status after three academic years. These data were taken from this college's official student records.

A three-stage regression analysis was undertaken using the above mentioned dependent and the independent variables. The first stage of the Multiple regression will include the GPA of the student after three years of study. Stage 2 will include Stage 1 and credits earned over the period and Stage 3 will include stages 1, 2 the graduation rate. The substantive discussion relates only to the last stage of the regression analysis (Stage 3). Generally, only the significant coefficients are discussed.

3. Results

As was indicated earlier, student satisfaction with their college experience is important because it may determine the students' persistence and performance. The Sociological literature suggests that the dissatisfied student is likely not to progress academically as readily as the student with positive attitudes. Indeed, this research suggests that the degree of satisfaction differentiated between students who were academically successful or not during this three-year period. For purpose of reporting, (although Table 1 has the actual percentages) the very great and the great responses were combined.

These data suggest that a positive attitude toward the college experience was an important indicator of academic performance.

As a case in point is GPA. Those students who have earned a GPA of 0–1.99, 50% indicated during their college experience effected their intellectual growth, and 11% responded that it had little influence on their intellectual growth.

Students who have earned a GPA of 2.00–2.99, 73% indicated that their intellectual growth was effected, and only 4% responded that the college had little influence on their intellectual growth.

Of those students who have earned a GPA of 3.00–4.00, 57% indicated that their intellectual growth was affected, and 10% responded that the college had little influence on their intellectual growth.

Another academic outcome this study looked at was credits earned over the time in question. These data suggest that students who have earned 0–29 credits, 70% indicated that their intellectual growth was effected, and 11% responded that the college had little influence on their intellectual growth.

Of those students who have earned 30–49 credits, 82% indicated that their intellectual growth was affected, and 11% responded that the college had little influence on their intellectual growth.

Students who have earned 50–69 credits, 50% indicated that their intellectual growth was affected, and 5% responded that the college had little influence on their intellectual growth.

Of those students who have earned 70 or more credits, 71% indicated that their intellectual growth was affected, and no one responded that the college had little influence on their intellectual growth.

The final academic outcome this study investigated was graduation after three academic years of study. These data suggest that

TABLE 8.1

Mean Analysis of Attitudinal Response N = 121

	Very great (%)	Great (%)	Moderate (%)	Little effect (%)	None
GPA					
0–1.99	30	20	39	11	—
2.00–2.99	40	33	23	4	—
3.00–4.00	37	20	33	10	—
Credits					
0–29	40	30	19	11	—
30–49	50	22	7	11	—
50–69	40	17	38	5	—
70>	41	30	29	0	—
Graduated	27	23	50	0	—

$X = 3.7$.

TABLE 8.2 TABLE 8.2 TABLE 8.2 TABLE 8.2 TABLE 8.2 TABLE 8.2 **TABLE 8.2**

Positive College Attitudes as a Function of Academic Performance: Regression Analysis N = 121

Independent variable	Dependent variables					
	GPA		Credits		Graduation	
	b	beta	*b*	beta	*b*	beta
Positive college attitude	.168	.133	N/S		.029	.123

$R^2 = .2155$; N/S = not significant.

students who have been graduated, 50% indicated that their intellectual growth was affected, and no one responded that the college had little influence on their intellectual growth.

It should be noted that no one suggested that this college had no influence on their intellectual growth.

After a regression analysis these data suggest that for every one point positive increase in student attitude over the mean in their attitude toward intellectual growth, there is about a one-sixth letter grade increase in GPA.

Additionally, these data suggest that for every one increased difference in positive student attitude produces a gap of about 3% likelihood that the student will be graduated in three academic years (Table 2).

4. Conclusion

As was indicated earlier, student satisfaction with the college experience is important because it may determine the students' persistence and performance. This research suggests that the degree of satisfaction the student had with the college's ability to influence their intellectual growth differentiated between students who had positive or negative academic outcomes over the study period.

These data suggest that students with the highest level of dissatisfaction with their college, were more likely to have achieved a GPA of between 0 and 1.99, earn 0–29 credits and did not graduate over the three-year study period.

By contrast, those with the highest level of satisfaction were more likely to have been graduated, earned greater credits and have achieved GPA's of between 2.00 and 4.00.

Overall, these data suggest that those who were satisfied with the college's influence over their intellectual growth, had on average, positive academic outcomes.

To illustrate the implications of the regression analysis, consider two hypothetical students entering this college for their first semester of study. The first student enters this college with the mean on this attitude survey, and the second achieves one point greater. These data suggest that the first student is likely to earn a GPA of 2.00 or under and not graduate. The second student is likely to earn a GPA of 2.15 or greater and has a 3% chance of graduating from this college over the first hypothetical student.

Perhaps, students who have a strong abstract and concrete attitude toward the college's ability to educate them can translate that into positive academic performance. These results could have particular significance for: (a) retention, (b) the economic growth, and (c) produce educational of minority and low-income students.

References

Cohen, A., & Brawer, F. (1992). *The American Community College*. San Francisco: Jossey-Bass.

Lavin, D. E., Alba, R. D., & Silberstein, R. A. (1981). *Right versus privilege: The open admissions experiment at the City University of New York*. London: The free Press.

Lavin, D., & Cook, D. (1993). Open admissions and its outcomes: Ethnic differences in long term educational attainment. *American Journal of Education, 98*, 389–425.

Mickelson, R. A. (2000). Race, class and differences in adolescents' academic achievement attitudes and behavior. *Sociology of Education, 62*, 47–63.

Critical-Thinking Questions

1. What is the Functionalist view of education?

    _____

    _____

    _____

    _____

    _____

    _____

    _____

    _____

2. What are the two historical educational objectives referred to by the conflict view?

    _____

    _____

    _____

    _____

    _____

    _____

    _____

    _____

3. What has the American Community College accomplished?

    _____

    _____

    _____

    _____

    _____

    _____

    _____

CHAPTER IX

Mass Society and Culture

A Mass Society is a population of people not limited to social origins such as race, ethnicity, class, education and so on. A mass society is characterized by the population as wishing anonymity or a sense of remaining nameless or unknown. Isolation or a willingness to set apart from others in a social setting. Apathy or a feeling of little or no emotion almost removed not interested in our social environment, and passivity a behavior which renders us inactive or offering no opposition to much of the social conditions.

These characteristics are amplified in the so-called "Kitty Genovese Case". In the 1970s Ms. Genovese was murdered in Queens, New York, in plain sight of onlookers during the daytime hours, and no one got involved or even called the police.

Sociologists suggest that the causes of a Mass Society are: 1) the Nature of Technology, 2) Bureaucratic Order, 3) Population Size, and 4) Urbanization. The movement of technology has created a human relationship of distance. We spend most of our awakened hours in front of some form of technology which restricts our human contact. As we saw Weber viewed bureaucratic as creating needed order in society but it also led to disenchantment— or a human behavior rooted in objective and an impersonal behavior. The greater the size of the population the more alienated we become mainly because we believe we have nothing in common, and the urbanized our environment which condenses our living conditions and violates our personal space. These conditions lead to self-restrictions limiting our social interaction.

A mass society requires a well developed Mass Communication/Mass Media system for the mass population to have: 1) information—even the most mundane such as the weather conditions, 2) entertainment which includes sports which has become a multi-billion dollar industry in United States of America, and 3) education there are probably as many educational channels on pay TV as there is entertainment.

The larger the size of the mass society the greater the use of Mass Media. The basic rule which the mass media relies on, is that the larger the public/audience the more simplistic the symbolic content of the material. This is so because the information must reach everyone in that mass society from all backgrounds. By contrast the smaller the public/audience the more complex the symbolic content.

However, as a result of simplistic message content, a mass culture arises which is a communication technique that lacks significant substance and has little or no aesthetical judgment. Many conflict sociologists who study the mass culture suggest that this simplistic content may dumb the population down, in that we do not have to think about the symbolic content of the message. So then, why can't Jane or John read or do mathematics? In the New York City public schools during the 2000s, 60 percent of the third graders could not read or do math at their grade level. This educational problem could be argued as the result of the mass cultural, in that students might have difficulty applying themselves to reading or mathematics because they do not have to use their intellectual capacity. The brain is akin to a muscle—use it or lose it!

Conflict sociologists would even take this concept one step further by suggesting that exposure to mass culture is unavoidable and inescapable. Heavy consumption of mass culture, and it is assumed that we are all consuming mass culture in ever increasing amounts, makes a person unfit to accept and understand complex symbolization.

Bernard Rosenberg suggested that as a result of the mass culture, a passive receivership occurs, or receiving will/truth of another, which creates a non-critical thought process. We have seen over the last decades that young black males are followed in department stores. This stereotype suggests that these young men are all shoplifters regardless of the truth. This may be because the Mass Media portrays this group as criminals. Under the concept of Passive Receivership we simply accept the truth/will of another.

Additionally, if one views the "Godfather" movies or HBO's series the "Sopranos" one begins to see all Italian-American males as members of the Italian Mafia.

Another negative effect of Passive Receivership is that in a democracy it is an anti-democratic force. Following the will of another can lead to a loss of democratic principles. During the Presidential election of 2000, only 51 percent of Americans voted. Of that 51 percent, 25 percent voted for Al Gore, and 26 percent of the American public voted for George W. Bush. Theoretically then, only one-fourth of the American public voted for the most powerful man on earth. This paradigm would view this as troublesome and anti-democratic.

On the other hand, David Manning White suggests that there are substantial amounts of higher order symbols which can be found within the mass culture. We chose what to expose ourselves to, and that is our constructional right—that of free choice. There are nearly as many "highbrow" mass media events as there are "lowbrow". However, most of the public wishes to access the "lowbrow" event, but the "highbrow" event is available.

Furthermore, the effects of Mass Culture are overstated and not proven. For every study that suggests that the mass culture affects behavior, there is another, which suggest that it does not. During September of 2003, a study suggested that violent video games actually channels violent behavior, and it can be almost therapeutic in controlling violent behavior. President Clinton blamed Marilyn Manson's music for the Columbine massacre. Surely, the lack of parental involvement has to take some part!

The mass culture may actually have many benefits. For the first time in human history the average person has access to information and high culture that he/she would never have had just six decades ago. This is an important factor in a democracy for all would be informed. The functionalists would suggest that a mass culture is a democratic force based upon the free-market system. To eliminate a topic from the mass culture, all one simply has to do is not to access the topic, and it would go away. On the topic of violence—to eliminate this from our mass media system, simply do not watch, read or listen to it, and the free-market system would remove this topic. As a free society, we do not need censorship. We do not need people dictating to the general public their values, norms, and beliefs.

Mass Culture Revisited

Bernard Rosenberg

"If . . . *Othello* is absolutely better than *Bonanza,* then the Nielsen ratings are not so much a justification as an indictment. . . ."

Is mass culture an abomination, a harmless anodyne, a blessing? These are the real, if too often merely implicit, questions in an interminable and ferocious debate. No one yields. (Like travel, disputation very often narrows one—causing a man to confirm his old biases.) Even now, when most of us are sick of each other's polemics, the issue will not go away. And why should it? Could anything matter more than our manhood, and is anything less than that at stake?

Protagonists lambaste antagonists—who clobber neutralists—in an arena littered with faulty logic, shopworn analogies, dubious data and, over all, the unappetizing remains of a stale argument. I was once chided by an eminent art critic for sullying myself with this subject matter. He said to me and people of my captious disposition, as though addressing himself to sex censors who privately revel in the pornography they publicly condemn, "If you don't like the goods, stop handling them." (Days after his printed attack, we met by chance at Amos Vogel's Cinema 16 where he and I had gone, for our delectation, to view *Gold Diggers of 1936.*) Of course you can stop handling the stuff, but it won't stop handling you. Or has someone discovered a way not to hear Muzak, not to see billboards, not to be touched by propaganda? We are all deeply and equally implicated in a phenomenon which continues to revolt some of us as much as it pleases others. Many, like Marshall McLuhan and his followers, have managed to swallow the nausea they once felt. At peace in the electric wonderland, they celebrate what used to sicken them. After years of courtship, and growing but unrequited love, McLuhan married the Mechanical Bride whose every gesture used to repel him. He moves and anachronistically writes in a psychedelic delirium comparable only to that of Timothy Leary. (Will they collide and embrace as inner and outer space converge?) Whole pages from that dated medium of Gutenberg's by which they so often go on expressing themselves, could be transposed from one author's work to the other's.

Here then we confront the champions of two debilitating and medically hazardous drugs: TV and LSD. TV, which probably does much to derange the nervous system through constant interruption and certainly hastens the onset of glaucoma, also turns out to be radioactive (and not just from cultural fallout). Color adds to the danger, and color sets multiply like cancer cells. LSD in good solid cubes can induce psychosis. Each is hallucinogenic in its own way. These are the media we are asked to exalt, complete with their appalling "massage" that "works us all over."

To what end? To the end that we should have a transcendental experience hitherto denied the species, to the end that we should explore previously unknown realms—and find God. Can anyone in possession of his senses, a human being who despite Leary's advice has not fully "blown his mind," help squirming and resisting when the Ad Alley physiotherapists lay their hands on him?

So, although I hesitate a split second on account of Harold Rosenberg's admonition (maybe I unconsciously love the thing I profess to hate, but if so, then like Oscar Wilde, I wish to kill that thing), allow me to reenter the fray. Back we go, and damn the opposition. Above all, damn that part of the opposition according to which mass or so-called popular culture does not even constitute a problem. My strongest criticism I therefore reserve for a friend and fellow sociologist, Herbert J. Gans—but solely in his role as culture critic. Gans does excellent community studies, and only now and then, but always disastrously, ventures outside his field.

It is a little thing if in California he lectures Hollywood screenwriters by telling them that they never had it so good. Such talk simply makes his auditors marvel at the staggering naïveté of an apparently sophisticated man, Gans, however, does a bigger and sillier thing when he covers popular culture in prose. His lengthy contribution to a widely disseminated textbook called *Social Problems* bears a subtitle which asks a nearly unintelligible question: "Popular Culture in America: Social Problem in a Mass Society or Social Asset in a Pluralist Society?" Reams of prose follow, all designed to answer that rhetorical question by insisting that his chosen social problem is really not a problem. One can only tell him, "All right, already. If you like the goods so much, go on handling them, but do not trouble your

mind with Social Assets. Let the White House compute them. Find Liabilities, possibly a few lying around in some neglected community, uncounted, unweighed. Study them. If not, cease and desist."

Typical of those who attempt to dispose of the problem either by denying it or embracing it is the pose of objectivity. Rational discourse cannot take place when one group of passionate defenders claims scientific detachment for itself and dismisses every detractor as hopelessly subjective and emotional. Facts must be gathered and analyzed, but every one of us is, at bottom, engaged in a battle over values. Literary intellectuals are licensed to express their preferences; social scientists, if governed by positivist dogma, must remain disinterested. Whether there are more television sets than bathtubs in the land (there are) can be statistically determined. Whether this ratio is desirable or not is a question social science can neither answer nor evade. Moral judgment comes into play, always and necessarily, and certainly not as the exclusive concern of sociologists.

Auguste Comte, that brilliant neologist, coined two durable terms, and unnaturally conjoined one to the other. They are: sociology and positivism. Comte's first publication was *A Program of Scientific Work Required for the Reorganization of Society*. The founder of sociology saw a world out of kilter, and quixotically proposed to set it aright. Here and abroad, Comte's successors have followed in his footsteps. Social scientists, hip-deep in the values they ritually forswear, a majority of them genuinely concerned about the malaise of modern man, cannot help being "problem centered." Given something like race prejudice, overpopulation, suicide, international tension, or juvenile delinquency, they commit themselves to studying the problem in hand, with a view to ameliorating or abolishing it. Many practitioners apply the pretense of utter detachment to mass communications but surely, on this topic, everyone is prejudiced.

We had better own up to that simple truth: you tend to be for mass culture or against it *tout court*. If not, you have mixed feelings, strong or bland, but in neither case are they to be confounded with Olympian indifference. Dwight Macdonald, say, or Ernest van den Haag and I, for rather different reasons, abhor the whole business. Do evidence and reason support our revulsion? The question is discussable, and it might even be answerable. By the same token, when Gilbert Seldes or David Manning White or Frank Stanton is in the mood to offer qualified, reasoned praise for mass culture, one can come to grips with their case. But apparitions are not so easy to combat. Beware therefore the disguised apologist who hides his ghostly "objective" presence behind a smoke screen of jargon and gibberish. In other words, gentlemen, come on out and fight.

If sham objectivity is inadmissible, so is the contention that critics of mass culture are ipso facto critics of "the masses." Some are, and they speak from an aristocratic point of view best elucidated over a century ago by Alexis de Tocqueville. But there are other bases for criticism. I side with that earlier Macdonald who saw the masses (which is to say, everybody) as victims of a merciless technological invasion that threatened to destroy their humanity.

To reject "mass-cult" and "mid-cult" is to espouse high culture—and to do that is to be put down in certain circles as a snob. Very well, there are worse epithets. Shakespeare really does seem to me to be a better playwright than Arthur Miller and a better writer than Mickey Spillane. That they—and Homer and Faith Baldwin—are all popular is as incontrovertible as it is irrelevant. Such enormous qualitative differences separate them that no common frame of reference is broad enough to encompass their works. If to hold such a view is proof of snobbery, so be it.

But there is an attitude far more vicious than snobbery which converts the term "masses" into "slobs." Mad Avenue chefs "know" that finer fare, which they themselves prefer, should not be wasted on ordinary men and women. The communications industry drips with this contempt. Tough executives crudely and brutally assert the complete disdain they feel for their audiences. When a Dr. Frank Stanton or a Dr. Leo Rosten phrases these feelings with elegance, we are only slightly shocked. Intellectuals inside the business world may even deserve a measure of compassion: the late Gilbert Seldes of CBS had to walk more softly than Professor Gilbert Seldes of the academic world. But it is really distressing that so many philosophers, historians, psychologists, and other academics should also be irremediably contemptuous of the people at large. They form a sonorous and gratuitous echo of the noises made for money by manipulators and managers who at least have the goodness to hate themselves for bamboozling the rest of us.

All this talk of culture snobbery and bamboozling brings us at last to that central, unavoidable question that makes the cynical purveyors of and apologists for mass-cult so uneasy. It is a question, incidentally, that also makes Millsian democrats and utilitarians uneasy and probably should make all the rest of us uneasy as well. Quite simply, it is: by what right do we call high culture "high"?

If, as Jeremy Bentham insisted, pushpin (that is, pinball) brings greater happiness to a greater number of people than does poetry, and if there is no other way to compare poetry and pushpin, it follows that the slaves of the Nielsen ratings are home free. Then by any objective standard *The Beverly Hillbillies* are as good as—in fact, demonstrably better than—Mr. Leinsdorf and the Boston Symphony. To prefer Shakespeare to Spillane becomes mere eccentricity, and to publish *Valley of the Dolls* in contravention of one's own better taste becomes a sort of philanthropy—a little self-interested, perhaps, but plainly benign.

If, on the other hand, *Othello* is asolutely better than *Bonanza,* then the Nielsen ratings are not so much a justification as an indictment, and it makes no difference how many people at any given moment think otherwise. In that case there have to be persuasive arguments for describing *The Beverly Hillbillies*—without apology—as cultural garbage and the people who present the *Hillbillies,* as cultural garbagemen.

Does this sound offensively absolutist—a matter of elevating the prejudices of a minority to the level of categorical imperatives? Are cultural standards really exempt from that most cherished American method of extracting decisions from imponderables: majority rule?

Certainly standards of cultural excellence are created by people, and certainly, in the end, they are products of a consensus. But the important thing to remember is that the process has meaning only in a dimension of time. The judgment of one generation is merely a fragment of the consensus of many generations, one vote in the parliament of history. And about some cultural matters, the verdict of history seems reasonably clear. For example, it seems reasonably clear that for human beings everywhere art has always been a fairly serious and central preoccupation and that the most affecting and enduring art has related most closely to what is essential in the human condition. Conrad once summed up the elementary stuff of the novel by saying simply, "Men were born, they suffered, they died." There is more to it than that, of course—men also enjoy, love, wonder about their place in the universe—but Conrad was talking about priorities, and his point was that all these matters are high-priority concerns of art. Pre-

sumably he would have felt that showing for the ten-thousandth time what an amiable boob dear old Dad is would rate fairly low in the aesthetic sweepstakes.

Hardly anyone is unaware—at least viscerally—that ninety-nine percent of the material conveyed to us by the mass communications media is aesthetically and intellectually trivial. Why, then, do we put up with it? Worse, why do we vote for it, paying good money for kitsch magazines, elevating worthless books to best-sellerdom, and endorsing television imbecilities via the rating polls? It is not—as too many of my colleagues and all mass communicators insist—that the average man is no better than what he votes for. To a truly shocking degree, his vote is the product of communications-induced anesthesia. He is a victim, and his victimized voting tells us nothing about the thing in him on which the future of our culture and, no doubt, our democratic system absolutely depends. I am talking about his *potential.*

I mean to come back to this, for it is the core of my argument. But first I want to say a little more about the ways that mass communications can and do anesthetize us.

Do you doubt that they are capable of anesthetizing us? Competitive, if basically indistinguishable products—like variously packaged and skillfully projected political candidates—are said to be bought on the basis of personal influence. Those who propound this theory, when they are not subverting it (the same distinguished social scientist who acts as prime consultant to the ad racket is capable of writing a book which purports to demonstrate that ads have no appreciable effect whatsoever)—those who propound this theory believe that direct face-to-face confrontation is really decisive: parishioners look to their priests, wives to their husbands, an army of susceptible followers respond to the "influentials" in their midst. Only small children and total amnesiacs could mistake this grotesque picture for reality, but it is not, therefore, a total falsehood.[1]

Let us not overtax our memories. You will recall in the year 1942 Japanese-American citizens and noncitizens were herded into concentration camps, their rights ruthlessly abrogated by an executive order straight from President Franklin D. Roosevelt. Why? Because the only good Jap was a dead one. China was, meanwhile, our noble Far Eastern ally. Now the only good Chinaman (unless resident on the island of Formosa) is a dead one, and Japan is our noble Far Eastern ally. Suppose the year is 1938: Stalin is a butcher, the USSR is a police state, its people are slaves. By 1943, "Uncle Joe" was an amiable autocrat and the USSR was economically democratic and get-

ting to be politically democratic. By 1948 it was okay, or rather, it was mandatory to repeat what had been said in 1938. Later, as President Eisenhower made a move toward rapprochement with Russia soon after settling the Korean War, it looked for a moment as if the infinitely flexible media would be mobilized yet again.

We have learned as well as any people on earth that vice and virtue are interchangeable terms. Pollsters recently discovered that twenty-five percent of the American public believe Chiang Kai-shek still holds sway over mainland China. Thirty million Americans represent a large reservoir of superfluous goodwill: Red China could as easily be glorified tomorrow as it is reviled today. The trick consists of turning on the faucets of influence, of mobilizing the media.

Tyranny plus technology is the formula for totalitarianism. In this context, technology usually refers to modern mechanical means of production, but it should also refer to modern mechanical means of communication. I do not mean to divagate further into the relationship between mass communications and political tyranny. Suffice it to say that mass communications have demonstrated such a distressing ability to promote tyranny in the cultural realm that we can only tremble at the implications of their political misuse. Tremble, and fortify ourselves.

How? I think the answer, simply, is to take a more respectful attitude toward our fellow man. My position is that the antidote to mass culture is high culture, that high culture means art and learning and that these goods are potentially accessible to every person not suffering from severe brain damage.

I have never heard the disrespectful attitude more offensively presented than at a conference, some years ago, on mass culture, to which a wide assortment of scholars and artists were invited. A truncated version of what they said may be found in a back issue of

---

[1] A friendly critic objects that I have been less than fair in presenting Paul Lazarsfeld's famous thesis. But no one protested in 1963 when Joseph Bensman and I put the matter as follows: "The public is unequally exposed to mass communications, and quite often, as the sociologist Paul Lazarsfeld has shown, those more exposed influence others who have trouble deciding between candidates and commodities. A personal element is present in what Lazarsfeld and Elihu Katz call 'the two-step flow' of mass communications. A heavy consumer of mass culture watches Ben Casey, listens to Chet Huntley, or vibrates via old movies to Clark Gable, and perhaps influences others to smoke Camels, buy EverReady Batteries, prize dimpled masculinity and abandon the undershirt. That messages originating in television, radio and films circulate this way—in a kind of aquatic mazurka, taking two steps instead of one—has misled some students into believing that personal influence is more powerful than the mass media. Yet, on the evidence so far adduced, opinion leaders who learn what to think from *Time* magazine, from *The Defenders,* from David Brinkley, merely magnify the power of these institutions by incorporating and transmitting their judgments to a still wider circle. I may buy Richard Nixon as my candidate at your suggestion, but if your suggestion comes from the firm of Batten, Barton, Durstine and Osborne, the advertising agency for the Republican National Committee, *there,* and not in your persuasive skill, lies the locus of power."

the magazine *Daedalus* (Spring, 1960) and in a book called *Culture for the Millions*. The conference was rigged in favor of intellectuals who support mass culture. Its centerpiece was a paper by Edward W. Shils who had long contended that "brutal culture" perfectly suited the masses. He repeated his thesis with the utmost gentility, thereafter lapsing into merciful silence. Others took up the cudgels; but as a peripheral participant, I had no opportunity to deal with Shils' peculiar system of classifying his opponents. As an anti-anti-mass-culturalist, Shils had some while before explained that writers upset about mass culture are mostly disillusioned Marxists, angry at the masses they foolishly idealized in the thirties. Now I realize there are many more ex-Trotskyites than there ever were Trotskyites; but as a case in point I, who beginning with my first "scholarly" article in 1948 have consistently found fault with Karl Marx's thought, really did not then, or ever, belong to a school of German sociologists into which Mr. Shils squeezed me. Anyhow, my target—like that of most anti-mass-cultists—was not the masses, but those who gull and dehumanize them.

To the fore of the conference stepped Arthur Schlesinger, Jr. He pointed out—with no mention of their notorious inadequacies—that IQ tests show an unequal distribution of intelligence in the population. Additionally, he suggested the existence of an AQ, or aesthetic quotient. Some few people are naturally responsive to art; the masses are not; everyone gets exactly what he is capable of absorbing. Neat, equitable, democratic—provided only that most people are natural inhabitants of Slobbovia. Are they? I would suggest several lines of evidence which indicate that they are not.

Almost all introductions to sociology contain a brief list of "universals," or institutions found everywhere. Religion and the family nearly exhaust the list. Anthropologists are likely to add art. From Frazer to Kroeber and beyond, anthropologists have been fascinated with primitive art. Few sociologists are expert in primitive art, and even fewer display interest in its civilized manifestation. Nevertheless, art is universal. No human society, however oppressive its circumstances, is devoid of art. This singular datum merits some sociological consideration. At present, it receives hardly any.

Since art is universal, the aesthetic impulse may be an integral part of human nature. I have argued elsewhere that it is. The individual needs food and shelter simply to survive; I would contend that he needs art about as much as he needs sex. Either drive can be extinguished, and he will go on living, but not without paying a heavy price in the diminution of his being. Small children in the United States spontaneously express themselves with whatever art materials they find. Youngsters react to pictures and to music with a measure of authenticity rarely attainable later on in their lives. What happens? It is like what happens to American taste buds. Frozen and packaged foods, above all bread (the staff of life—that compost of air and glue), those oats which only horses ate until Mr. Kellogg sold them as dry cereal: a diet like this from infancy onward can deaden anybody's palate. With gruel today and gruel tomorrow, who can savor gourmet meals? Similarly, extended pseudosexual behavior produces fixation at that level, virtually barring "the real thing," true sexual fulfillment. In precisely the same way, kitsch and instant education, if ingested for long enough, lead to cultural and intellectual dyspepsia or anesthesia.

In *The Theater of the Absurd*, Martin Esslin describes an unusual presentation of *Waiting for Godot*, a play that flopped on Broadway after the daily reviewers declared it to be excessively obscure. The production mentioned by Esslin took place in a maximum-security prison before a truly captive audience—which was enthralled by a play it found perfectly intelligible. The Freedom Southern Theater does vanguard drama successfully before rural Negroes who dig the message that a meaningful contemporary play somehow cannot convey to jaded middle-class theater-goers seeking expensive entertainment. The Théâtre Nationale Populaire performs in tents outside Paris; proletarian theatrical enterprises have been revived in England; Shakespeare clicks in the park or on the street. What does this enthusiasm signify if not the capacity of common men to surmount the trash that is heaped upon them? They too are able to have aesthetic experiences. One percent of the public views living drama with any regularity on the stages of North America. An ambitious, and no doubt unrealizable, goal is to double that number, all the way to two percent. Those who go are homogeneous: overwhelmingly upper middle class, professional, disproportionately Jewish. Blue-collar workers shun theaters and bookstores all over the Western world—which does not prove that they are constitutionally unresponsive to the drama or incapable of reading good books. Workers in Buenos Aires buy Argentine classics (deliberately priced low on an experimental basis) at kiosks instead of bookstores, which they would never dream of entering. A change of locus—for instance, theater in union halls and not in ever more lavish "cultural centers"—is frequently all that we need to reanimate the aesthetic impulse which lies dormant in every man.

Dedicated artists and teachers realize all this. The custodians of mass culture and their academic satraps do not. By their gross underestimation of human potentialities, they drug us beyond any hope of redemption. We must continue to do battle with them or become willing accomplices in the creation of "joyous serfdom." For, to withdraw from that battle out of fatigue, boredom, or despair, is in large measure to be morally accountable for losing it.

If Godard can do three or four low-budget films a year and make money producing art, albeit not necessarily great art; if Pacifica can operate a network of FM stations, broadcasting views that may be politically repugnant, but are usually dissident and provocative, and all this on a shoestring; if even Hollywood, after destroying much of its best talent (Welles and Huston in our time, Griffith, Von Stroheim, and Keaton long ago), can offer directors enough leeway to be creative without forcing them into exile or into obsequious submission, and Warsaw or Budapest can do the same; if little magazines with limited circulation can survive; and if subscription TV finally emerges as something less than a disaster—then, the direction in which we must try to move is clear.

Art does not have to be swamped by machines—provided the machines are used to foster pluralism, diversity, and decentralization. However Sisyphean a job it may be, the present process which involves depersonalization, concentration, and deracination must be reversed, and as rapidly as possible. For, just as only the young can effortlessly learn a second language, so there is a chronological point after which generations bred on TV cannot assimilate the best that has been written and said. Sub-art systematically unfits a person for art, and vice versa. They really are incompatible. Not mere dabbling, but heavy consumption of one eventually obviates the other. You cannot have a lot of both.

If art is long, sub-art is longer and life remains incredibly short. I would rather miss a flower in the jungle of mass culture (possibly the Beatles are such a flower) than lose myself in that jungle. "Liberalized" totalitarianism isn't good enough for most of us who still reject any oppressive system. Similarly, a thaw in the arts, here or elsewhere, does not produce that rich and wonderfully varied garden we have every right to demand.

The artist is basically an anarchist who should have as much solitude and tranquillity and as much withdrawal from commercial or political clamor as society can provide. He and we desperately need his creations. The human spirit will perish without them. As things stand, I can only agree with Herbert Read that Shelley chose his epithet well in calling poets *unacknowledged* legislators of the world. Read goes on, "The catalyst is unchanged, unabsorbed; its activity therefore not acknowledged. It is peculiarly difficult for the artist in society to accept this thankless task: to stand apart, and yet to mediate, to communicate something to society as essential as bread and water, and yet to be able to do so from a position of insulation, of disaffection. Society will never understand or love the artist because it will never appreciate his indifference, his so-called objectivity. But the artist must learn to love and understand the society that renounces him. He must accept the contrary experience, and drink, with Socrates, the deadly cup." Perhaps not forever. Surely now.

Critical-Thinking Questions

1. What is a Mass Society?

   _____

   _____

   _____

   _____

   _____

   _____

   _____

   _____

2. What is a mass culture?

   _____

   _____

   _____

   _____

   _____

   _____

   _____

   _____

3. What are the two views of mass culture and their differences?

   _____

   _____

   _____

   _____

   _____

   _____

   _____

   _____

CHAPTER X

Urban Ecological Theory

Ernest Burgess and Robert Park, urban sociologists from the Chicago School suggested an urban development pattern which was viewed as a branch of the natural sciences, mainly biological science.

They suggested that humans are adapting to their surrounding environment or the urban landscape. This view should be seen as the human species, always creating a niche for itself. Like the natural environment, cities spontaneously develop without planning. As in biological fashion, the city will grow in a predictable manner, with specific features.

Also urban centers evolve based upon the competitive process with established groups for resources. This concept is akin to plant community in which a dominant group imposes order over other plants. One can notice that yellow daisies are never found with brown colored of the species. The scientific reasoning is that yellow daisies are light in color and therefore reflects the sunlight and the heat. On the other hand, the brown daisy absorbs the sunlight and the heat, so the brown daisy environment is much warmer than the yellow. The yellow daisy cannot live in the brown environment, so you will not see brown living with the yellow daisy.

In the urban human ecology, humanity, according to this view is always competing for social access much like the daisy is competing for light. This social access competition is for desirable housing, employment, education, careers, health facilities and so on.

As a result of this competition, groups who dominate will impose their control over urban centers. The result is the Chicago Concentric Model of cities, which are ever widening zones of development around the central business district or the core of the city. When the "newcomers" encroach on established groups it is referred to as INVASION. If and when the newcomers replace the established groups it is referred to as SUCCESSION.

The Concentric Zone Model suggests that zone one is the central business district where there are retail shops, department stores, theaters, banks, federal, state and local government; and the residence of upper socio-economic class. In zone two the outer fringes of the central business district or what is called the transition area, here one finds tenement homes, older factories, inexpensive housing and immigrant's residence.

The third zone is the so-called working class zone in which there are second-generation immigrant families, and two and three family housing. The residents are blue-collar workers and their children plan to move out of this zone.

The fourth zone is the middle-class zone with more expensive one-family homes, and the residents are professional, white-collar and small business owners.

The fifth zone is the so-called commuter or suburban zone with upper-middle class influence. This zone requires railroads and cars.

As one can imagine there can be much criticism of this view because of the reliance on competition as a form of human organization, and because it excludes cultural patterns. People may wish to live with members of their own culture.

Moreover, it excludes many other forces such as technological advancements. Therefore, this concept was modified to exclude competition for technological innovation and ethnic homogeneity.

The Contemporary Ecological view is based upon Max Weber's principle of Rationality in that urban centers are seen as development along corridors adjacent to rapid transit.

During the 19th and 20th century most urban transportation systems moved from horse drawn streetcars to electric trolley and electric rail systems. As a result, the horse streetcars moved at a rate of 5 miles an hour.

The electric trolley at 10 miles an hour and the electric rail 20 miles an hour.

As automobiles became popular they moved residents at 55 miles an hour, and the automobile overcame the corridor to include the suburban areas. The truck to haul industrial freight outside the corridors and the automobile created a mobile society to "push factors such as taxes, expensive land, the job market and other economic market forces." The commuter rail moved people at 80 miles an hour, during the 1970s 70 percent of the population lived in the cities, while today 40 percent of the population lives in the city. Therefore, the city as a social ecosystem should be seen as growth and expansion based upon the cumulating process of technological change. The accumulation of advances in technology and scientific knowledge has made it possible for new uses of environment, land and resources.

The critical factor for the Conflict Sociologists as it relates to urban development and the social problems in the city, is capital accumulation. These sociologists suggest that capital accumulation, NOT technology or social evolution shape urban America. Indeed, history suggests that cities have played a central role in the development of surplus value, in the change of the mode-of-production from commercial to industrial to the factory.

There are three major aspects of capital accumulation, which has led to urban centers. They are the production of goods and services, surplus value, and the commodities market.

The Conflict View combines all three areas into the so-called "putting out system" (1830s). It is suggested that most urban centers begin as "commercial cities" in which there is the exchange of agricultural commodities. The buying and selling by the merchant capitalist of these grown commodities such as cotton, wheat and so on developed large finance centers in the cities. Today we still find this center which is known as the

Commodities Exchange on Wall Street in New York City. This investment class generated large surplus value, which needed to be reinvested. This reinvestment found itself in the distribution of raw materials to the so-called Handicraft Shops found in many cities during the late 1880s. The merchant class through investments in raw materials for the Handicraft Shops took control of the collection and selling of the products these Handicraft Shops produced, eliminating this mode-of-production.

During the turn of the 20th century this putting-out system converted to industrialism, which concentrated workers in a central production area known as factories.

The factory becomes, according to the Conflict View, the nucleus of the city or zone one. The so-called "slums" where the workers of the factory resided became zone two, and all other "better" residential areas become segregated from zone two. This change in the mode-of-production underscored changes in occupational structure and patterns of residential areas. The more affluent individuals became, the more they withdrew from areas of the city leading to growth.

The next phase, according to the Conflict View, is the growth of labor unrest in which factories moved to the suburban areas to escape unionism. Once in the suburbs the automobile was an important means of transportation. As a result, large economic interests gathered around the manufacturing of the automobile such as the rubber industry, oil companies and the development of highway construction projects leading to the dependency of the automobile by the suburbanite. Today one cannot live in the suburban areas in the United States without an automobile. These sociologists suggest that there was powerful interests found in the automobile industry which destroyed all possibilities of mass transit system developing in the suburbs.

Finally, there is a school of thought, which views four intergovernmental relationships as shaping the urban centers. The first Dual Federalism in which governments are decentralized as independent states with separation of powers. However, in 1913 with the advent of the Federal income tax, there was several federal projects such as highway, forestry, education, and some cash grants to states. This produced some growth.

The next phase is Cooperative Federalism in which government shared responsibility. As a result of the economic crisis of 1929 depression, industry and the economy was set to collapse. States and cities faced bankruptcy. These factors led Franklin Roosevelt to create the New Deal Program, which acted as a turning point for urban development. It created jobs in public works, made mortgage money available, lead to construction of major bridges, dams, tunnels and highways.

In 1934 the Federal Housing Administration played a major role in construction of private housing. Federal monies became at the disposal of banks, insurance, and savings and loan companies. Interest rates went down from 10 percent to 5 percent, and increased maturity dates of mortgages from 10 years to 30 years. The National Industrial Recovery Act cleared slums and created low rent housing.

In 1942 as a result of World War II, the Defense Policy increased war production some 60 percent. The need for unused space was important for the production of large war equipment leading to the suburban areas.

During the 1960s federal involvement grew, creating the next phase Creative Federalism. The so-called Model Cities Program made an effort at the redevelopment of poverty areas, this rehabilitation was based upon massive physical symbolic social change. Federal government bypassing state and local Governments to deal with social and urban problems all mark this period.

The last and final stage began during the 1980s with the concentration and dismantling of War on Poverty and consolidating 100 federal programs into 6 large block grants. This stage is referred to as New Federalism. The growth of a federal partnership with business, and the reduction of federal taxation.

Spending on defense system, and the reliance on private sector for urban growth increased. These four stages created the expansion and contraction of urban centers.

When Work Disappears

William Julius Wilson

Many inner-city areas of the United States are facing catastrophic levels of poverty. Why? In this excerpt from a recent book, William Julius Wilson offers his assessment of the causes of urban decline and makes practical suggestions about how we can solve this pressing problem.

The disappearance of work in the ghetto cannot be ignored, isolated or played down. Employment in America is up. The economy has churned out tens of millions of new jobs in the last two decades. In that same period, joblessness among inner-city blacks has reached catastrophic proportions. Yet in this Presidential election year, the disappearance of work in the ghetto is not on either the Democratic or the Republican agenda. There is harsh talk about work instead of welfare but no talk of where to find it.

The current employment woes in the inner city continue to be narrowly defined in terms of race or lack of individual initiative. It is argued that jobs are widely available, that the extent of inner-city poverty is exaggerated. Optimistic policy analysts—and many African Americans—would prefer that more attention be devoted to the successes and struggles of the black working class and the expanding black middle class. This is understandable. These two groups, many of whom have recently escaped from the ghetto, represent a majority of the African American population. But ghetto joblessness still afflicts a substantial—and increasing—minority: It's a problem that won't go away on its own. If it is not addressed, it will have lasting and harmful consequences for the quality of life in the cities and, eventually, for the lives of all Americans. Solutions will have to be found—and those solutions are at hand.

For the first time in the twentieth century, a significant majority of adults in many inner-city neighborhoods are not working in a typical week. Inner cities have always featured high levels of poverty, but the current levels of joblessness in some neighborhoods are unprecedented. For example, in the famous black-belt neighborhood of Washington Park on Chicago's South Side, a majority of adults had jobs in 1950; by 1990, only one in three worked in a typical week. High neighborhood joblessness has a far more devastating effect than high neighborhood poverty. A neighborhood in which people are poor but employed is different from a neighborhood in which people are poor and jobless. Many of today's problems in the inner-city neighborhoods—crime, family dissolution, welfare—are fundamentally a consequence of the disappearance of work.

What causes the disappearance of work? There are several factors, including changes in the distribution and location of jobs, and in the level of training and education required to obtain employment. Nor should we overlook the legacy of historic racial segregation. However, the public debate around this question is not productive because it seeks to assign blame rather than recognizing and dealing with the complex realities that have led to economic distress for many Americans. Explanations and proposed solutions to the problem are often ideologically driven.

Conservatives tend to stress the importance of values, attitudes, habits, and styles. In this view, group differences are reflected in the culture. The truth is, cultural factors do play a role; but other, more important variables also have to be taken into account. Although race is clearly a significant variable in the social outcomes of inner-city blacks, it's not the *only* factor. The emphasis on racial differences has obscured the fact that African Americans, whites, and other ethnic groups have many common values, aspirations, and hopes.

An elderly woman who has lived in one inner-city neighborhood on the South Side of Chicago for more than forty years reflects: "I've been here since March 11, 1953. When I moved in, the neighborhood was intact. It was intact with homes, beautiful homes, minimansions, with stores, Laundromats, with Chinese cleaners. We had drugstores. We had hotels. We had doctors over on 39th street. We had doctors' offices in the neighborhood. We had the middle class and upper middle class. It has gone from affluent to where it is today. And I would like to see it come back, that we can have some of the things we had. Since I came in young, and I'm a senior citizen now, I would like to see some of the things come back so I can enjoy them like we did when we first came in."

In the neighborhood of Woodlawn, on the South Side of Chicago, there were more than 800 commercial and industrial establishments in 1950. Today, it is estimated that only about 100 are left. In the words of Loïc Wacquant, a member of one of the research teams that worked with me over the last eight years: "The

once-lively streets—residents remember a time, not so long ago, when crowds were so dense at rush hour that one had to elbow one's way to the train station—now have the appearance of an empty, bombed-out war zone. The commercial strip has been reduced to a long tunnel of charred stores, vacant lots littered with broken glass and garbage, and dilapidated buildings left to rot in the shadow of the elevated train line. At the corner of 63d Street and Cottage Grove Avenue, the handful of remaining establishments that struggle to survive are huddled behind wrought-iron bars. . . . The only enterprises that seem to be thriving are liquor stores and currency exchanges, those 'banks of the poor' where one can cash checks, pay bills and buy money orders for a fee."

The state of the inner-city public schools was another major concern expressed by our urban-poverty study respondents. The complaints ranged from overcrowded conditions to unqualified and uncaring teachers. Sharply voicing her views on these subjects, a twenty-five-year-old married mother of two children from a South Side census tract that just recently became poor stated: "My daughter ain't going to school here. She was going to a nursery school where I paid and of course they took the time and spent it with her, because they was getting the money. But the public schools, no! They are overcrowded and the teachers don't care."

A resident of Woodlawn who had left the neighborhood as a child described how she felt upon her return about the changes that had occurred: "I was really appalled. When I walked down 63d Street when I was younger, everything you wanted was there. But now, coming back as an adult with my child, those resources are just gone, completely. . . . And housing, everybody has moved, there are vacant lots everywhere."

Neighborhoods plagued by high levels of joblessness are more likely to experience low levels of social organization: The two go hand in hand. High rates of joblessness trigger other neighborhood problems that undermine social organization, ranging from crime, gang violence, and drug trafficking to family breakups. And as these controls weaken, the social processes that regulate behavior change.

Industrial restructuring has further accelerated the deterioration of many inner-city neighborhoods. Consider the fate of the West Side black community of North Lawndale in Chicago: Since 1960, nearly half of its housing stock has disappeared; the remaining units are mostly run-down or dilapidated. Two large factories anchored the economy of this neighborhood in its good days—the Hawthorne plant of Western Electric, which employed more than 43,000 workers, and an International Harvester plant with 14,000 workers. But conditions rapidly changed. Harvester closed its doors in the late 1960's. Sears moved most of its offices to the Loop in downtown Chicago in 1973. The Hawthorne plant gradually phased out its operations and finally shut down in 1984.

"Jobs were plentiful in the past," attested a twenty-nine-year-old unemployed black man who lives in one of the poorest neighborhoods on the South Side. "You could walk out of the house and get a job. Maybe not what you want, but you could get a job. Now, you can't find anything. A lot of people in this neighborhood, they want to work but they can't get work. A few, but a very few, they just don't want to work."

The more rapid the neighborhood deterioration, the greater the institutional disinvestment. In the 1960s and 1970s, neighborhoods plagued by heavy abandonment were frequently redlined (identified as areas that should not receive or be recommended for mortgage loans or insurance); this paralyzed the housing market, lowered property values and encouraged landlord abandonment.

As the neighborhood disintegrates, those who are able to leave depart in increasing numbers; among these are many working- and middle-class families. The lower population density in turn creates additional problems. Abandoned buildings increase and often serve as havens for crack use and other illegal enterprises that give criminals—mostly young blacks who are unemployed—footholds in the community. Precipitous declines in density also make it even more difficult to sustain or develop a sense of community. The feeling of safety in numbers is completely lacking in such neighborhoods.

Problems in the new poverty or high-jobless neighborhoods have also created racial antagonism among some of the high-income groups in the city. The high joblessness in ghetto neighborhoods has sapped the vitality of local businesses and other institutions and has led to fewer and shabbier movie theaters, bowling alleys, restaurants, public parks and playgrounds and other recreational facilities. When residents of inner-city neighborhoods venture out to other areas of the city in search of entertainment, they come into brief contact with citizens of markedly different racial or class backgrounds. Sharp differences in cultural style often lead to clashes.

Some behavior on the part of residents from socially isolated ghetto neighborhoods—for instance, the tendency to enjoy a movie in a communal spirit by carrying on a running conversation with friends and relatives or reacting in an unrestrained manner to what they see on the screen—is considered offensive by other groups, particularly black and white members of the middle class. Expressions of disapproval, either overt or with subtle hostile glances, tend to trigger belligerent responses from the ghetto residents, who then purposely intensify the behavior that is the source of irritation. The white and even the black middle-class moviegoers then exercise their option and exit, expressing resentment and experiencing intensified feelings of racial or class antagonism as they depart.

The areas surrendered in such a manner become the domain of the inner-city residents. Upscale businesses are replaced by fast-food chains and other local businesses that cater to the new clientele. White and black middle-class citizens complain bitterly about how certain areas of the central city have changed— and thus become "off-limits"—following the influx of ghetto residents.

The negative consequences are clear: Where jobs are scarce, many people eventually lose their feeling of connectedness to work in the formal economy; they no longer expect work to be a regular, and regulating, force in their lives. In the case of young people, they may grow up in an environment that lacks the idea of work as a central experience of adult life—they have little or no labor-force attachment. These circumstances also increase the likelihood that the residents will rely on illegitimate sources of income, thereby further weakening their attachment to the legitimate labor market.

A twenty-five-year-old West Side father of two who works two jobs to make ends meet condemned the attitude toward work of some inner-city black males:

> *They try to find easier routes and had been conditioned over a period of time to just be lazy, so to speak. Motivation nonexistent, you know, and the society that they're affiliated with really don't advocate hard work and struggle to meet your goals such as education and stuff like that. And they see who's around them and they follow that same pattern, you know. . . . They don't see nobody getting up early in the morning, going to work or going to school all the time. The guys they be with don't do that . . . because that's the crowd that you choose— well, that's been presented to you by your neighborhood.*

Work is not simply a way to make a living and support one's family. It also constitutes a framework for daily behavior because it imposes discipline. Regular employment determines where you are going to be and when you are going to be there. In the absence of regular employment, life, including family life, becomes less coherent. Persistent unemployment and irregular employment hinder rational planning in daily life, the necessary condition of adaptation to an industrial economy.

It's a myth that people who don't work don't want to work. One mother in a new poverty neighborhood on the South Side explained her decision to remain on welfare even though she would like to get a job:

> *I was working and then I had two kids. And I'm struggling. I was making, like, close to $7 an hour. . . . I had to pay a baby-sitter. Then I had to deal with my kids when I got home. And I couldn't even afford medical insurance. . . . I was so scared, when my kids were sick or something, because I have been turned away from a hospital because I did not have a medical card. I don't like being on public aid and stuff right now. But what do I do with my kids when the kids get sick?*

Working mothers with comparable incomes face, in many cases, even greater difficulty. Why? Simply because many low-wage jobs do not provide health-care benefits, and most working mothers have to pay for transportation and spend more for child care. Working mothers also have to spend more for housing because it is more difficult for them to qualify for housing subsidies. It is not surprising, therefore, that many welfare-reliant mothers choose not to enter the formal labor market. It would not be in their best economic interest to do so. Given the economic realities, it is also not surprising that many who are working in these low-wage jobs decide to rely on or return to welfare, even though it's not a desirable alternative for many of the black single mothers. As one twenty-seven-year-old welfare mother of three children from an impoverished West Side neighborhood put it: "I want to work. I do not work but I want to work. I don't want to just be on public aid."

As the disappearance of work has become a characteristic feature of the inner-city ghetto, so too has the disappearance of the traditional married-couple family. Only one-quarter of the black families whose children live with them in inner-city neighborhoods in Chicago are husband-wife families today, compared with three-quarters of the inner-city Mexican families, more than one-half of the white families and nearly one-half of the Puerto Rican families. And in census tracts with poverty rates of at least 40 percent, only 16.5 percent of the black families with children in the household are husband-wife families.

There are many factors involved in the precipitous decline in marriage rates and the sharp rise in single-parent families. The explanation most often heard in the public debate associates the increase of out-of-wedlock births and single-parent families with welfare. Indeed, it is widely assumed among the general public and reflected in the recent welfare reform that a direct connection exists between the level of welfare benefits and the likelihood that a young woman will bear a child outside marriage.

However, there is little evidence to support the claim that Aid to Families With Dependent Children plays a significant role in promoting out-of-wedlock births. Research examining the association between the generosity of welfare benefits and out-of-wedlock childbearing and teen-age pregnancy indicates that benefit levels have no significant effect on the likelihood that African American girls and women will have children outside marriage.

Likewise, welfare rates have either no significant effect or only a small effect on the odds that whites will have children outside marriage. The rate of out-of-wedlock teen-age childbearing has nearly doubled since 1975—during years when the value of A.F.D.C., food stamps, and Medicaid fell, after adjusting for inflation. And the smallest increases in the number of out-of-wedlock births have not occurred in states that have had the largest declines in the inflation-adjusted value of A.F.D.C. benefits. Indeed, while the real value of cash welfare benefits has plummeted over the past twenty years, out-of-wedlock childbearing has increased, and postpartum marriages (marriages following the birth of a couple's child) have decreased as well.

It's instructive to consider the social differences between inner-city blacks and other groups, especially Mexicans. Mexicans come to the United States with a clear conception of a traditional family unit that features men as breadwinners. Although extramarital affairs by men are tolerated, unmarried pregnant women are "a source of opprobrium, anguish or great concern," as Richard P. Taub, a member of one of our research terms, put it. Pressure is applied by the kin of both parents to enter into marriage.

The family norms and behavior in inner-city black neighborhoods stand in sharp contrast. The relationships between inner-city black men and women, whether in a marital or nonmarital situation, are often fractious and antagonistic. Inner-city black women routinely say that black men are hopeless as either husbands or fathers and that more of their time is spent on the streets than at home.

The men in the inner city generally feel that it is much better for all parties to remain in a nonmarital relationship until the relationship dissolves rather than to get married and then have to get a divorce. A twenty-five-year-old unmarried West Side resident, the father of one child expressed this view:

> *Well, most black men feel now, why get married when you got six to seven women to one guy, really. You know, because there's more women out here mostly than men. Because most dudes around here are killing each other like fools over drugs or all this other stuff.*

The fact that blacks reside in neighborhoods and are engaged in social networks and households that are less conducive to employment than those of other ethnic and racial groups in the inner city clearly has a negative effect on their search for work. In the eyes of employers in metropolitan Chicago, these differences render inner-city blacks less desirable as workers, and therefore are reluctant to hire them. The white chairman of a car transport company, when asked if there were differences in the work ethic of whites, blacks and Hispanics, responded with great certainty:

> *Definitely! I don't think, I know: I've seen it over a period of thirty years. Basically, the Oriental is much more aggressive and intelligent and studious than the Hispanic. The Hispanics, except Cubans of course, they have the work ethnic [sic]. The Hispanics are* mañana, mañana, mañana—*tomorrow, tomorrow, tomorrow. As for native-born blacks, they were deemed "the laziest of the bunch."*

If some employers view the work ethic of inner-city poor blacks as problematic, many also express concerns about their honesty, cultural attitudes and dependability—traits that are frequently associated with the neighborhoods in which they live. A white suburban retail drugstore manager expressed his reluctance to hire someone from a poor inner-city neighborhood. "You'd be afraid they're going to steal from you," he stated. "They grow up that way. They grow up dishonest and I guess you'd feel like, geez, how are they going to be honest here?"

In addition to qualms about the work ethic, character, family influences, cultural predispositions and the neighborhood milieu of ghetto residents, the employers frequently mentioned concerns about applicants' language skills and educational training. They "just don't have the language skills," stated a suburban employer. The president of an inner-city advertising agency highlighted the problem of spelling:

> *I needed a temporary a couple months ago, and they sent me a black man. And I dictated a letter to him. He took shorthand, which was good. Something like 'Dear Mr. So-and-So, I am writing to ask about how your business is doing.' And then he typed the letter, and I read the letter, and it's 'I am writing to ax about your business.' Now you hear them speaking a different language and all that, and they say 'ax' for 'ask.' Well, I don't care about that, but I didn't say 'ax.' I said 'ask.'*

Many inner-city residents have a strong sense of the negative attitudes that employers tend to have toward them. A thirty-three-year-old employed janitor from a poor South Side neighborhood had this observation: "I went to a couple jobs where a couple of the receptionists told me in confidence: 'You know what they do with these applications from blacks as soon as the day is over?' They say, 'We rip them and throw them in the garbage.'" In addition to concerns about being rejected because of race, the fears that some inner-city residents have of being denied employment simply because of their inner-city address or neighborhood are not unfounded. A welfare mother who lives in a large public housing project put it this way:

> Honestly, I believe they look at the address and the—your attitudes, your address, your surround—you know, your environment has a lot to do with your employment status. The people with the best addresses have the best chances. I feel so, I feel so.

It is instructive to study the fate of the disadvantaged in Europe. There, too, poverty and joblessness are on the increase; but individual deficiencies and behavior are not put forward as the culprits. Furthermore, welfare programs that benefit wide segments of the population like child care, children's allowances (an annual benefit per child), housing subsidies, education, medical care and unemployment insurance have been firmly institutionalized in many Western European democracies. Efforts to cut back on these programs in the face of growing joblessness have met firm resistance from working- and middle-class citizens.

My own belief is that the growing assault on welfare mothers is part of a larger reaction to the mounting problems in our nation's inner cities. When many people think of welfare they think of young, unmarried black mothers having babies. This image persists even though roughly equal numbers of black and white families received A.F.D.C. in 1994, and there were also a good many Hispanics on the welfare rolls. Nevertheless, the rise of black A.F.D.C. recipients was said to be symptomatic of such larger problems as the decline in family values and the dissolution of the family. In an article published in *Esquire*, Pete Hamill wrote:

> The heart of the matter is the continued existence and expansion of what has come to be called the Underclass. . . . trapped in cycles of welfare dependency, drugs, alcohol, crime, illiteracy and disease, living in anarchic and murderous isolation in some of the richest cities on the earth. As a reporter, I've covered their miseries for more than a quarter of a century. . . . And in the last decade, I've watched this group of American citizens harden and condense, moving even further away from the basic requirements of a human life: work, family, safety, the law.

One has the urge to shout, "Enough is enough!"

What can be done? I believe that steps must be taken to galvanize Americans from all walks of life who are concerned about human suffering and the public policy direction in which we are now moving. We need to generate a public-private partnership to fight social inequality. The following policy frameworks provide a basis for further discussion and debate. Given the current political climate, these proposals might be dismissed as unrealistic. Nor am I suggesting that we can or should simply import the social policies of the Japanese, the Germans, or other Western Europeans. The question is how we Americans can address the problems of social inequality, including record levels of joblessness in the inner city, that threaten the very fabric of our society.

Create Standards for Schools

Ray Marshall, former Secretary of Labor, points out that Japan and Germany have developed policies designed to increase the number of workers with "higher-order thinking skills." These policies require young people to meet high performance standards before they can graduate from secondary schools, and they hold each school responsible for meeting these standards.

Students who meet high standards are not only prepared for work but they are also ready for technical training and other kinds of post-secondary education. Currently, there are no mandatory academic standards for secondary schools in the United States. Accordingly, students who are not in college-preparatory courses have severely limited options with respect to pursuing work after high school. A commitment to a system of performance standards for every public school in the United States would be an important first step in addressing the huge gap in educational performance between the schools in advantaged and disadvantaged neighborhoods.

A system of at least local performance standards should include the kind of support that would enable schools in disadvantaged neighborhoods to meet the standards that are set. State governments, with federal support, not only would have to create equity in local school financing (through loans and scholarships to attract more high-quality teachers, increased support for teacher training and reforms in teacher certification) but would also have to insure that highly qualified teachers are more equitably distributed in local school districts.

Targeting education would be part of a national effort to raise the performance standards of all public schools in the United States to a desirable level, including schools in the inner city. The support of the private sector should be enlisted in this national effort. Corporations, local businesses, civic clubs, community centers and churches should be encouraged to work with the schools to improve computer-competency training.

Improve Child Care

The French system of child welfare stands in sharp contrast to the American system. In France, children are supported by three inter-related government programs, as noted by Barbara R. Bergmann, a professor of economics at American University: child care, income support, and medical care. The child-care program includes establishments for infant care, high-quality nursery schools (*écoles maternelles*), and paid leave for parents of newborns. The income-support program includes child-support enforcement (so that the absent parent continues to contribute financially to his or her child's welfare), children's allowances, and welfare payments for low-income single mothers. Finally, medical care is provided through a universal system of national health care financed by social security, a preventive-care system for children, and a group of public-health nurses who specialize in child welfare.

Establish City-Suburban Partnerships

If the other industrial democracies offer lessons for a long-term solution to the jobs problem involving relationships between employment, education, and family-support systems, they also offer another lesson: the importance of city-suburban integration and cooperation. None of the other industrialized democracies have allowed their city centers to deteriorate as has the United States.

It will be difficult to address growing racial tensions in American cities unless we tackle the problems of shrinking revenue and inadequate social services and the gradual disappearance of work in certain neighborhoods. The city has become a less desirable place in which to live, and the economic and social gap between the cities and suburbs is growing. The groups left behind compete, often along racial lines, for declining resources, including the remaining decent schools, housing, and neighborhoods. The rise of the new urban poverty neighborhoods has worsened these problems. Their high rates of joblessness and social disorganization have created problems that often spill over into other parts of the city. All of these factors aggravate race relations and elevate racial tensions.

Ideally, we would restore the federal contribution to city revenues that existed in 1980 and sharply increase the employment base. Regardless of changes in federal urban policy, however, the fiscal crises in the cities would be significantly eased if the employment base could be substantially increased. Indeed, the social dislocations caused by the steady disappearance of work have led to a wide range of urban social problems, including racial tensions. Increased employment would help stabilize the new poverty neighborhoods, halt the precipitous decline in density, and ultimately enhance the quality of race relations in urban areas.

Reforms put forward to achieve the objective of city-suburban cooperation range from proposals to create metropolitan governments to proposals for metropolitan tax-base sharing (currently in effect in Minneapolis-St. Paul), collaborative metropolitan planning, and the creation of regional authorities to develop solutions to common problems if communities fail to reach agreement. Among the problems shared by many metropolises is a weak public transit system. A commitment to address this problem through a form of city-suburban collaboration would benefit residents of both the city and the suburbs.

The mismatch between residence and the location of jobs is a problem for some workers in America because, unlike the system in Europe, public transportation is weak and expensive. It's a particular problem for inner-city blacks because they have less access to private automobiles and, unlike Mexicans, do not have a network system that supports organized car pools. Accordingly, they depend heavily on public transportation and therefore have difficulty getting to the suburbs, where jobs are

more plentiful. Until public transit systems are improved in metropolitan areas, the creation of privately subsidized car-pool and vanpool networks to carry inner-city residents to the areas of employment, especially suburban areas, would be a relatively inexpensive way to increase work opportunities.

The creation of for-profit information and placement centers in various parts of the inner city not only could significantly improve awareness of the availability of employment in the metropolitan area but could also serve to refer workers to employers. These centers would recruit or accept inner-city workers and try to place them in jobs. One of their main purposes would be to make persons who have been persistently unemployed or out of the labor force "job ready."

Reintroduce the W.P.A.

The final proposal under consideration here was advanced by the perceptive journalist Mickey Kaus of *The New Republic*, who has long been concerned about the growth in the number of welfare recipients. Kaus's proposal is modeled on the Works Progress Administration (W.P.A.), the large public-works program initiated in 1935 by President Franklin D. Roosevelt. The public-works jobs that Roosevelt had in mind included highway construction, slum clearance, housing construction, and rural electrification. As Kaus points out:

> *In its eight-year existence, according to official records, the W.P.A. built or improved 651,000 miles of roads, 953 airports, 124,000 bridges and viaducts, 1,178,000 culverts, 8,000 parks, 18,000 playgrounds and athletic fields, and 2,000 swimming pools. It constructed 40,000 buildings (including 8,000 schools) and repaired 85,000 more. Much of New York City—including La Guar-*

dia Airport, F.D.R. Drive, plus hundreds of parks and libraries—was built by the W.P.A.

A neo-W.P.A. program of employment, for every American citizen over eighteen who wants it, would provide useful public jobs at wages slightly below the minimum wage. Like the work relief under Roosevelt's W.P.A., it would not carry the stigma of a cash dole. People would be earning their money. Although some workers in the W.P.A.-style jobs "could be promoted to higher-paying public service positions," says Kaus, most of them would advance occupationally by moving to the private sector. "If you have to work anyway," he says, "why do it for $4 an hour?"

Under Kaus's proposal, after a certain date, able-bodied recipients on welfare would no longer receive cash payments. However, unlike the welfare-reform bill that Clinton has agreed to sign, Kaus's plan would make public jobs available to those who move off welfare. Also, Kaus argues that to allow poor mothers to work, government-financed day care must be provided for their children if needed. But this service has to be integrated into the larger system of child care for other families in the United States to avoid creating a "day-care ghetto" for low-income children.

A W.P.A.-style jobs program will not be cheap. In the short run, it is considerably cheaper to give people cash welfare than it is to create public jobs. Including the costs of supervisors and materials, each subminimum-wage W.P.A.-style job would cost an estimated $12,000, more than the public cost of staying on welfare. That would represent $12 billion for every 1 million jobs created.

The solutions I have outlined were developed with the idea of providing a policy framework that could be easily adopted by a reform coalition. A broad range of groups would support the long-term solutions—the development of a system of national performance standards in public schools, family policies to reinforce the learning system in the schools, a national system of school-to-work transition, and the promotion of city-suburban integration and cooperation. The short-term solutions, which range from job information and placement centers to the creation of W.P.A.-style jobs, are more relevant to low-income people, but they are the kinds of opportunity-enhancing programs that Americans of all racial and class backgrounds tend to support.

Although my policy framework is designed to appeal to broad segments of the population, I firmly believe that if adopted, it would alleviate a good deal of the economic and social distress currently plaguing the inner cities. The immediate problem of the disappearance of work in many inner-city neighborhoods would be confronted. The employment base in these neighborhoods would be increased immediately by the newly created jobs, and income levels would rise because of the expansion of the earned-income tax credit. Programs like universal health care and day care would increase the attractiveness of low-wage jobs and "make work pay."

Increasing the employment base would have an enormous positive impact on the social organization of ghetto neighborhoods. As more people become employed, crime and drug use would subside; families would be strengthened and welfare receipt would decline significantly; ghetto-related culture and behavior, no longer sustained and nourished by persistent joblessness, would gradually fade. As more people became employed and gained work experience, they would have a better chance of finding jobs in the private sector when they became available. The attitudes of employers toward inner-city workers would change, partly because the employers would be dealing with job applicants who had steady work experience and would furnish references from their previous supervisors.

This is not to suggest that all the jobless individuals from the inner-city ghetto would take advantage of these employment opportunities. Some have responded to persistent joblessness by abusing alcohol and drugs, and these handicaps will affect their overall job performance, including showing up for work on time or on a consistent basis. But such people represent only a small proportion of inner-city workers. Most of them are ready, willing, able and anxious to hold a steady job.

The long-term solutions that I have advanced would reduce the likelihood that a new generation of jobless workers will be produced from the youngsters now in school and preschool. We must break the cycle of joblessness and improve the youngsters' preparation for the new labor market in the global economy.

My framework for long-term and immediate solutions is based on the notion that the problems of jobless ghettos cannot be separated from those of the rest of the nation. Although these solutions have wide-ranging application and would alleviate the economic distress of many Americans, their impact on jobless ghettos would be profound. Their most important contribution would be their effect on the children of the ghetto, who would be able to anticipate a future of economic mobility and harbor the hopes and aspirations that for so many of their fellow citizens help define the American way of life.

The Urban Real Estate Game: Traditional and Critical Perspectives

Joe R. Feagin and Robert Parker

Feagin and Parker argue that traditional urban sociology has emphasized demographic and technological dimensions of city growth, while accepting the validity of classical economics' market model. Traditionalists explain the growth and change of cities in terms of various demands made by countless urban consumers. A newer, critical perspective sees the process of urban development as dominated by powerful economic interests—industrial executives, developers, and politicians sympathetic to their aims. The authors condemn the traditional model and argue the virtues of the critical approach.

Introduction

Locating new factories. Relocating offices. Buying hotels. Building office towers. Mortgaging whole streets of houses. Buying and selling utility companies. Bulldozing apartment buildings for office construction. Purchasing large blocks of urban land to secure a land monopoly. Going bankrupt because of overextension in real estate. These actions are part of the real estate game played in every American city. The only place most Americans are able to play anything analogous to this is on the *Monopoly* game board in living-room encounters with their friends. The board game mimics the real world of real estate buying, selling, and development, but the parallels between playing *Monopoly* on the board and playing the real estate game in cities are limited, for in the everyday world of urban development and decline there are real winners and real losers.

In U.S. cities the powerful elites controlling much development—the industrial executives, developers, bankers, and their political allies—have built major development projects, not just the hotels and houses of the *Monopoly* game, but also shopping malls, office towers, and the like. They typically build with little input from local community residents. Executives heading industrial firms and real estate developers have frequently been able to win a string of favorable concessions from city officials: cheap land, industrial parks, tax decreases, and utility services subsidized by rank-and-file taxpayers. In many cities these industrial executives and developers threaten to go elsewhere if these governmental subsidies are not provided. Yet in the 1970s and 1980s some citizen groups . . . tried to change this way of doing city business. Periodically, the voters in cities, from Santa Monica and Berkeley on the West Coast, to Cleveland in the Midwest, to Burlington and Hartford on the East Coast, voted out pro-development political officials in favor of candidates more tuned to slow growth and enhancing the local quality of life. For instance, in the 1980s the residents of Santa Monica, California, voted out a city council allied with landlords, developers, and bankers. They elected in their place a progressive council determined to break with the developer-oriented dominance of city politics. The new council has rejected policies favoring developers and has used a policy called "linked development" to force those developers building new office complexes and shopping centers to take action to meet important local needs. One Santa Monica city council agreement with a developer building a million-square-foot hotel-office complex specified that he must include landscaped park areas, a day-care center, energy conservation measures, and a positive plan for hiring minority workers.[1]

Who Decides on Development?

Some powerful developers, bankers, and other development decision makers are becoming known to the public. There is, for example, Gerald D. Hines, a Houston mechanical engineer whose $200 million estimated net worth was just under the amount necessary to be listed among the nation's 400 richest people by *Forbes* in 1987.[2] Still, Gerald D. Hines Interests of Houston, one of the largest U.S. development firms, controlled buildings worth more than $4.5 billion. In the early 1980s Hines celebrated the laying of the foundation of a Republic Bank office complex in Houston with a lavish $35,000

reception for top business and government leaders; it included a brass ensemble playing fanfares, fine wine and cheeses, and other culinary delights. The massive building itself, red granite in a neo-Gothic style, is just one of more than 360 such office buildings, shopping malls, and other urban projects that have been built by Hines' company in cities from New York to San Francisco.

Residential developers have also shaped U.S. cities in fundamental ways. The famous firm Levitt and Sons is among the 2 percent of developer-builders that have constructed the lion's share of U.S. residential housing since World War II. Using nonunion labor, Levitt and Sons pulled together in one corporation the various aspects of the house manufacturing and marketing process, from controlling the source of nails and lumber to marketing the finished houses. After World War II, Levittowns—names now synonymous with suburbs—were built in cities on the East Coast. One subdivision, Levittown, New Jersey, was carefully planned so that the acreage was within one political jurisdiction. According to Herbert Gans, the company executives had the boundaries of a nearby township changed so that it was not part of the area in which this Levittown would be built, thus giving Levitt and Sons more political control. William Levitt was the key figure in this development firm for decades, and he reportedly built his suburbs with little concern for the expressed tastes of his potential customers; Levitt was not especially "concerned about how to satisfy buyers and meet their aspirations. As the most successful builder in the East . . . he felt he knew what they wanted."[3] Profitability was the basic standard; community-oriented features were accepted when they enhanced profit. No surveys of potential buyers were made to determine consumer preferences, but a great deal of attention was given to advertising, marketing, and selling the houses to consumers. Friendly salespeople were selected and trained by a professional speech teacher. Buyers who were viewed as "disreputable" were excluded; and blacks were excluded until the state government began to enforce a desegregation law.[4]

Developers such as Hines and Levitt and Sons have been a major force in making and remaking the face of American cities. They are key figures in shaping city diversity and decentralization. Since World War II, U.S. cities have exploded horizontally and vertically with thousands of large-scale developments—shopping centers, office towers, business parks, multiple-use projects, convention centers, and residential subdivisions. The "built environments" of our cities have expanded to the point that their growing, and dying, pains have become serious national problems. Trillions of dollars have been invested in tearing down, constructing, and servicing the many and diverse physical structures scattered across hundreds of urban landscapes. For large development projects to be completed in downtown or outlying areas of cities, older buildings are often leveled even when local citizens oppose such development. The major U.S. developers often see their projects as the "cutting-edge of western civilization." Yet these massive expenditures of capital for large-scale urban development, for lavish towers and the parties celebrating them, are made in cities with severe urban problems—extreme poverty, housing shortages, severe pollution—for whose solution little money allegedly can be found.[5]

Cities are not chance creations; rather, they are human developments. They reflect human choices and decisions. But exactly who decides that our cities should be developed the way they are? Who chooses corporate locations? Who calculates that sprawling suburbs are the best way to house urbanites? Who decides to put workers in glassed-in office towers? Who determines that shopping is best done in centralized shopping centers? Who creates the complex mazes of buildings, high-

ways, and open spaces? There is an old saying that "God made the country, but man made the town." Cities are indeed human-engineered environments. But which men and women made the cities? And what determines how they shape our cities?

Growth and Decline of Cities: Traditional Social Science Perspectives

THE TRADITIONAL APPROACH: THE MARKET KNOWS BEST

Examination of urban development and decline has been dominated by a conflict between the market-centered approaches of traditional social scientists and the newer critical analyses developed in recent decades. Traditional social scientists have dominated research and writing about American cities. Beginning in the 1920s and 1930s, there was a major spurt of activity in urban sociology and ecology at the University of Chicago, where researchers such as Robert Park and Ernest W. Burgess drew on the nineteenth-century social philosopher Herbert Spencer to develop their concept of city life, organization, and development; they viewed the individual and group competition in markets in metropolitan areas as resulting in "natural" regularities in land-use patterns and population distributions—and thus in an urban ecological or geographical map of concentric zones of land use, moving out from a central business district zone, with its office buildings, to an outlying commuter zone, with residential subdivisions.[6]

Much urban research between the 1940s and the 1970s established the dominance of the traditional market-centered paradigm in urban sociology, geography, economics, political science, and other social science disciplines. Largely abandoning the concern of the earlier social scientists with urban space and land-use zones, sociological, economic, and geographical researchers have for the most part accented demographic analysis and have typically focused on population trends such as migration flows, suburbanization, and other deconcentration, and on statistical distributions of urban and rural populations in examining modern urban development. Writing in the *Handbook of Sociology,* the urban analysts Kasarda and Frisbie review mainstream research and a small portion of the newer critical research, but they explicitly regard the ecological approach in sociology, geography, and economics as the "dominant (and arguably, the only) general theory of urban form" that has been tested by empirical verification.[7] Books such as Berry and Kasarda's *Contemporary Urban Ecology,* Micklin and Choldin's *Sociological Human Ecology,* and textbooks like Choldin's *Cities and Suburbs* have been influential in establishing a conventional perspective accenting the role of a competitive market in urban development and emphasizing market-centered city growth as beneficial to all urban interest groups. The political scientists in this tradition have also given attention to capitalism-generated growth and the role of the market in city development; they alone have given much attention to the importance of government in urban development. However, their view of government typically accents a pluralism of competing interest groups and an array of government officials acting for the general welfare, a perspective that, as we will discuss, is rather limited.[8]

CONSUMERS AND WORKERS AS DOMINANT

Conventional social scientists have accepted uncritically the workings of the dominant market and the processes of capital accumulation. This perspective on competitive urban markets is grounded in neoclassical economic theory; it sees urban society as the "algebraic sum of the individuals . . . the sum of the interests of individuals."[9] In this view, given a "freemarket" system, urban consumers and business firms will freely buy and sell. "If consumers want certain goods they will demand them. Businessmen will sense this demand through the marketplace and seek to satisfy the consumers' wishes. Everyone is happy."[10] Urban sociologist John Kasarda has written of profit-seeking entrepreneurs operating in self-regulating markets as a wise guiding force in city development.[11] Similarly, economists Bradbury, Downs, and Small, reviewing problems of city decline, argue that "market forces are extremely powerful; so it would be folly to try [governmental] policies that ignored their constructive roles in guiding the form and structure of economic change."[12] From this perspective capitalists follow the profit logic of capital investments that seeks out "good business climates" (low taxes and pro-business governments) in certain cities, such as those in the South. This conventional view implies that whatever exists as the economics and geography of the urban landscape today is fundamentally good for all concerned, if it has resulted from competitive market activity. The rather utopian competitive market idea, Lewis Mumford has suggested, was taken over from earlier theologians: "the belief that a divine providence ruled over economic activity and ensured, so long as man did not presumptuously interfere, the maximum public good through the dispersed and unregulated efforts of every private, self-seeking individual."[13]

Imbedded in this common market assumption is the idea that individual workers and consumers are often more important than corporate decision makers in shaping urban patterns, because the capitalists mostly react to the demands of consumers. A study of the U.S. business creed accented this point: "One way of shedding awkward responsibility is to believe that the consumer is the real boss."[14] Such analysts accept the business view of individual consumers and workers as "voting" in the marketplace with their consumer choices: Cities are viewed as having been created by average Americans whose demands for such things as autos and single-family houses have forced developers, builders, and industrial executives to respond. Consumers are often termed "kings" and "queens" when it comes to urban development. For decades not only urban scholars but also business leaders have argued that through their consumption choices "the masses of Americans have elected Henry Ford. They have elected General Motors. They have elected the General Electric Company, and Woolworth's and all the other great industrial and business leaders of the day."[15]

One assumption in much traditional urban research is that no one individual or small group of individuals has a determinate influence on patterns of urban land uses, building, and development. Mainstream sociologists and land economists such as William Alonso and Richard Muth have argued that urban commercial and residential land markets are determined by free competitive bidding. According to these theories, thousands of consumers, and thousands of firms, are pictured as autonomous atoms competing in a market system, largely without noneconomic (for example, political) relations and conventions, atoms that have a "taste" for commodities such as more space and housing. As their incomes grow, they will seek more space. Conventional analysts offer this as an explanation of why cities grow, expand, or die. Actors in this competitive bidding are recognized as having different interests, even different incomes, which affect the bidding process. However, the fact that a small group of the most powerful decision makers (such as major developers) can do far more to shape the land

and building markets than simply outbid their competitors is not seriously analyzed. And the negative consequences of market-generated growth (for example, water pollution from sewer crises) in these same cities are seldom discussed.[16]

David L. Birch, Director of the Massachusetts Institute of Technology's Program on Neighborhood and Regional Change, has offered a worker-driven theory in explaining why many cities have had too much office space. Birch argues that the story of the current high vacancy rates in office buildings in many U.S. cities began decades ago when the "war babies" began to enter the labor force. This movement into the labor force caused a huge increase in employment. Birch argues that both sexes decided they did not want to work in factories. Rather, they "wanted to work in offices. They wanted to join the service economy, wear white shirts, and become managers or clerks."[17] According to this line of reasoning, there was only one thing for developers and builders to do; in order to satisfy this new generation of workers and consumers, "we built them offices." Yet the power of workers and consumers in shaping the urban office landscape has never been as profound as Birch and others describe. Indeed, it is the industrialists, investors, developers, bankers, and their associates who have the capital to invest in job creation and to build office buildings and other workplaces—in places they decide upon and in terms of their corporate restructuring and profit needs.

ACCENTING TECHNOLOGY AND DOWNPLAYING INEQUALITY

Traditional social scientists often view the complexity of cities as largely determined by historical changes in transportation and communication technologies, whose economic contexts, histories, and alternatives are not reviewed. Changes in urban form are explained in terms of technological transformation, including shifts in water, rail, and automotive transport systems, without reference to the decisions of powerful decision makers such as investors and top government officials. Waterborne commerce favors port and river cities, while auto, train, and truck technologies facilitate the location of cities apart from water systems. In an opening essay for a 1985 book *The New Urban Reality*, Paul Peterson views technological innovations as independent forces giving "urban development its rate and direction."[18] And in the influential book *Urban Society*, mainstream ecological researcher Amos Hawley looked at the relocation of industry from the industrial heartland to outlying areas and explained this decentralization substantially in terms of technological changes in transport and in communication.[19] Transport and communication technologies are certainly important in urban centralization and decentralization. But the corporate history and capitalistic decision-making *context* that led to the dominance of, for example, automobiles—and not mass transit—in the U.S. transport system should be more carefully examined. . . .

SOME MAJOR OMISSIONS

Missing from most traditional research on cities is a major discussion of such major factors in urban development as capital investment decisions, power and resource inequality, class and class conflict, and government subsidy programs. The aforementioned collection, *The New Urban Reality*, has important essays by prominent geographers, economists, political scientists, and sociologists on urban racial demography and the black underclass, but there is no significant discussion of capital investment decisions made by investors and developers and the consequences

of these decisions for urban development. Moreover, in the recent summary volume, *Sociological Human Ecology*, prominent ecologists and demographers have reviewed the question of how humans survive in changing social environments, including cities, but without discussing inequality, power, conflict, or the role of governments.[20] Traditional urban scholars such as the geographer Berry and the sociologist Kasarda briefly note that in market-directed societies the role of government has been primarily "limited to combating crises that threaten the societal mainstream," that government involvement tends to be incremental, and that state government dealing with the "social consequences of laissez-faire urbanization" are "ineffective in most cases."[21] In his influential urban textbook, *Urban Society*, sociologist Amos Hawley has devoted little space to the government role in city growth and decline. This neglect of the role of government has been most common among mainstream urban sociologists, geographers, and economists. As we will see, the mainstream political scientists among contemporary urban researchers have given more attention to government, but generally with a pluralistic emphasis.[22]

AN IMPORTANT GOVERNMENT REPORT

However, the federal government has used this traditional urban research for policy purposes. In the 1980s a major federal government report, *Urban America in the Eighties*, publicly articulated the traditional urban perspective for the general public. Prepared by the President's Commission for a National Agenda for the Eighties, this report called on the federal government to refrain from assisting the troubled northern cities. Free-enterprise markets are viewed as driving the basically healthy changes in urban development.

And these markets know best. The *Urban America* report's strong conclusions were publicly debated—particularly those suggesting that the federal government should neglect dying northern cities and should, at most, assist workers in leaving Frostbelt cities for the then-booming cities of the Sunbelt. Some northern mayors protested the report's conclusions, but many Sunbelt mayors were enthusiastic. While northern officials were concerned about the report's conclusions, few publicly disputed the report's basic assumptions about how cities grow or die.[23]

This market-knows-best view of the Frostbelt-Sunbelt shift in capital investment and of urban growth more generally drew on the work of traditional urban researchers. Prepared under the direction of prominent business leaders, this report conveys the view of cities found in mainstream urban research: that cities are "less conscious creations" than "accumulations—the products of ongoing change." Again, choices by hundreds of thousands of individual consumers and workers are emphasized as the fundamental determinants of urban landscapes. Changes in cities, such as the then-increasing prosperity of many Sunbelt cities, reflect "nothing more than an aggregate of countless choices by and actions of individuals, families, and firms."[24] The urban land and building market is again viewed as self-regulating; according to this theory the market efficiently allocates land uses and maximizes the benefits for everyone living in the cities. The hidden hand of the market receives heavy emphasis in this conventional accounting. In the policy-oriented conclusions, the authors of *Urban America* pursued this market logic to its obvious conclusion: Those impersonal individuals and firms actively working in cities and shaping urban space know best, and government officials should thus not intervene when impersonal decisions lead to the decline of cities in the North. Growth in, and migration to, booming cities such as those in the Sunbelt should simply be recognized, and, at most, governments should encourage workers to move from dying cities to booming cities.

Growth and Decline of Cities: The Critical Urban Perspective

BASIC THEMES IN THE NEW APPROACH

Since the 1970s the dominance of the mainstream urban research in the United States has been challenged by a critical urban perspective, called by some the "new urban sociology." Both European and American researchers have developed a critical urban paradigm grounded in concepts of capital investment flows, class and inequality, activist governments, and powerful business elites. European researchers such as Henri Lefebvre, Manuel Castells, and David Harvey had developed critiques of the traditional urban approaches by the late 1960s and early 1970s.[25] This European influence was soon felt in U.S. urban studies. By the late 1970s critical urban studies were pursued and published by Michael Peter Smith, Mark Gottdiener, Allen Scott, John Mollenkopf, Norman and Susan Fainstein, Richard Child Hill, Ed Soja, Michael Dear, Richard Walker, Allen Whitt, Todd Swanstrom, and Harvey Molotch, to mention just a few of the growing number of critical social scientists in the United States.[26] The critical urban approach accents issues neglected in most traditional sociological, economic, and political science analysis. While there is still much ferment and debate among contributors to the critical urban perspective, there is some consensus on three fundamental themes.

The first major theme is that city growth and decline, internal city patterns, and city centralization and decentralization are shaped by both economic factors and political factors.

Although some critical scholars accent the economic over the political, and others the political over the economic, in this book we will focus on both the economic and political factors. In [Figure 1] we show the economic and political influences on cities, as well as the interaction between these economic and political influences. Most Western cities are shaped by capitalistic investments in production, workers, workplaces, land, and buildings. These urban societies are organized along class (also race and gender) lines; and their social institutions are substantially shaped by the commodity production and capital investment processes. Capital investment is centered in corporations calculating profit at the firm level; this can result in major urban social costs associated with the rapid inflow of capital investment and accompanying growth and also with capital outflow (disinvestment) and accompanying urban decline. But [Figure 1] indicates that there are governmental (state) factors in urban growth, structuring, and decline as well. Governments protect the right to own and dispose of privately held property as owners see fit. Moreover, governments in capitalistic societies are often linked to business elites and the investment process; various levels of government play a part in fostering corporate profit making. But government officials also react to citizen protests, to class, race, and community-based struggles; as a result, they often try to cope with the costs of capitalist-generated growth and decline. In addition, in cities with relatively independent political organizations (for example, "machines"), politicians may develop interests of their own and work *independently* of individual capitalists and citizen groups to shape and alter cities. In the urban worlds there is much interaction between the political and economic structures and political and economic decision makers.

A second important theme to be found in many critical urban arguments has to do with

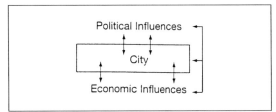

Figure 1

the central role of *space*. Some critical scholars only implicitly touch on spatial issues, while others feature the spatial dimension at the center of their city analysis. As [Figure 2] is designed to illustrate, we human beings live not only economic and political lives as workers affected by investments in markets and voters affected by political advertising, but also lives as occupiers of space, in households and families living in the home and neighborhood spaces of our cities. On the one side, we have the group of profit-oriented industrialists, developers, bankers, and landowners who buy, sell, and develop land and buildings just as they do with other for-profit commodities. Exchange value, the value (price) of commodities exchanged in markets, is usually the dominant concern in their decisions about buying and selling land and buildings. The investment actions of developers and others seeking to profit off the sale of, and construction on, land are centered in exchange-value considerations. On the other side, we have the group of American tenants and homeowners, low-income and middle-income, black and

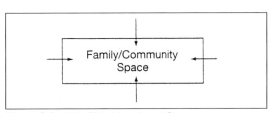

Figure 2 Capital's Global Investment Space

white, who are usually much more concerned with the *use value* of space, of home and neighborhood, than with the exchange value.

Corporate exchange-value decisions frequently come into conflict with the use-value concerns of many Americans. A concern with use value can mean that the utility of space, land, and building for everyday life, for family life, and for neighborhood life is much more important than land or building profitability. Such use-value concerns are behind the actions of neighborhood residents who have fought against numerous office buildings, malls, and redevelopment projects in order to keep them from intruding on their home and neighborhood spaces. Some zoning and other government land-use controls have thrown up barriers to the unrestrained expansion of capitalistic investment. Historically, much pressure for land-use regulation has come from worker-homeowners concerned with protecting family spaces and neighborhoods against industrial and commercial encroachment.[27]

Capitalist investors operate today in a worldwide investment space, so they may move factory and office jobs (or real estate capital) quickly from one city or country to another. However, workers and consumers generally spend their lives in more constricted family and home spaces. They often invest their lives in particular communities and cities and cannot move so easily to a city in another region or country, so they suffer when investors relocate quickly to other areas on the globe. Capital accumulation, capital investment, and the capitalistic class structure interact with space to generate urban and rural spatial patterns of production, distribution, and consumption. The aforementioned competition of local urban politicians for capital investments by corporate actors had not only job and construction effects, but also effects on the livability of local urban space. Uneven economic development also means uneven spatial development. Some places, homes and neighborhoods, stay viable and livable, while other urban communities become difficult to live in because of capital flight to other places across the nation or the globe.

A third basic theme in the new critical perspective is that of *structure* and *agency*, which is suggested in [Figure 3]. While most critical scholars tend to accent either structure (for example, institutions) or agency (for example, decision makers) in research on urban development, a number of scholars such as Lefebvre, Gottdiener, and Giddens, have called for research giving more attention to *both* dimensions. Some focus on the concrete actors involved in making cities, such as developers and business elites or citizens protesting development, while others prefer to emphasize the complex web of institutions and structures, such as state bureaucracies and capital investment circuits. . . . Economic systems and governments do not develop out of an inevitable and unalterable structural necessity, but rather in a contingent manner; they result from the conscious actions taken by individual decision makers in various class, race, gender, and community-based groups, acting under particular historical circumstances. The most powerful actors have the most influence on how our economic and political institutions develop. Yet they, in turn, are shaped by those institutions.[28]

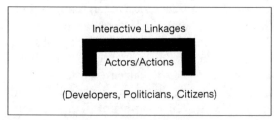

Interactive Linkages

Actors/Actions

(Developers, Politicians, Citizens)

Figure 3 Institutional Structures (Economy/State)

A STRUCTURAL DIMENSION: PRIVATE PROPERTY

The U.S. legal system, a critical part of our governmental structure, institutionalizes and protects the right to private property. Yet this legal system is critical to the perpetuation of great inequalities in real estate ownership and control. Most Americans own or control little property, other than their homes. Essential to the maintenance of inequality in land decision making is the legal protection of individualized property ownership. The rights of private property give owners, especially the large property owners, a great deal of control over land and buildings. Within broad limits land can be developed, and buildings constructed, as owners desire. This unbridled use of private property has not always been the case in the United States. The early Puritans, for example, had highly planned towns from Maine to Long Island. For two generations Puritan towns were designed by pioneers whose strong religious values influenced the layout of urban areas. The private ownership and control of property were not central; more important communal and collective goals often overrode private property interests. But the Puritan group-centered town planning soon gave way to intensified private landholding, even in New England. Fee-simple (unrestricted transfer) ownership of land became central to the expanding capitalistic system of eighteenth-century America. Early immigrants from Europe were generally hostile to landlords and vigorously sought to own their own land. Ownership of even a small piece of property was a sign of independence from landlords; many immigrants had come to the colonies to escape oppressive European landlords. Land was seen as a civil right by the many small farmers.[29]

Yet this early and heavy commitment to the sacredness of privately held property had a major negative effect on development once the United States was no longer primarily a country of small farmers. By the early decades of the nineteenth century, there were fewer landholders and ever more tenants without land. In many cases, the growing number of Americans with little or no real estate property were seen as unworthy. Yet the strong commitment to private property, on the part of both propertied and landless Americans, has continued to legitimate the private disposal of property by the powerful landowning and development decision makers. As a result, over the last two centuries control over urban land development has become more concentrated in the hands of executives of banks, insurance firms, development corporations, and industrial companies.[30] In addition, there are major social costs for a private property system that gives owners of large amounts of land the right to use the land more or less as they wish. Those who build and develop large projects on central-city land have shown that they can transfer certain social costs onto other people nearby. A good example is the modern skyscraper with its mirrored glass walls, which often generate heat problems for nearby buildings, and with its thousands of workers whose exit in the evenings can create massive traffic jams. Such social costs of skyscraper development are generally not paid for by the developers and owners of the buildings. . . .

Powerful Agents of Urban Change: Private Producers

NEGLECTING POWERFUL AGENTS

. . . Mainstream scholars often portray . . . land and building markets as "natural" markets guided by an invisible hand. But they are not natural. In reality, these markets are the creation of the most powerful players on the urban scene—the array of visible real estate decision makers in industry, finance, development, and construction. Over decades of urban development these powerful decision makers have both shaped, and been shaped by, the structures and institutions of urban real estate capitalism. Not only some of the critical analyses, such as the research of Harvey, but also traditional urban analyses, such as Berry and Kasarda's *Contemporary Urban Ecology* and Micklin and Choldin's *Sociological Human Ecology,* have largely ignored the central role of specific capitalistic and political actors in basic decisions about shaping urban land and built environments, the complex array of residential subdivisions, shopping malls, factories, warehouses, and office buildings.[31]

Among the primary decision makers in the urban real estate game are the capitalistic producers. Today real estate capitalism is organized around a complicated network of entrepreneurs and executives heading corporations of varying size. The size and complexity of the urban development industry can be seen in [Table 1], which lists major real estate and development decision makers. The categories refer to sets of major decisions that are critical to urban development.[32]

Looking at the private sector, we see that category 1 encompasses those corporate executives whose location decisions (for example, the choice of locating a factory in a northern city or a Sunbelt city) often set the other decision makers into motion. Category 2 covers the developers, land speculators, and landowners who buy, package, and develop land for use by industrial corporations and others.[33] Category 3 encompasses, among others, those bankers and financial corporations that make the loans for land purchase, construction, and related development. Category 4 includes the various design and construction actors who actually construct urban projects. And cate-

gory 5 covers a variety of supporting actors, including real estate brokers and chamber of commerce executives.

TABLE 10.1

Urban Development: Decision Categories and Selected Decision Makers

1. Industrial and commercial location decisions
   Executives of industrial companies
   Executives of commercial companies
2. Development decisions
   Executives of development companies (developers)
   Land speculators and landowners
   Apartment owners and landlords
3. Financial decisions
   Commercial bankers
   Executives of savings and loan associations ("thrifts")
   Executives of insurance companies
   Executives of mortgage companies
   Executives of real estate investment trusts
4. Construction decisions
   Builders and developer-builders
   Executives of architectural and engineering firms
   Construction subcontractors
5. Support decisions
   Chamber of commerce executives
   Real estate brokers
   Executives of leasing companies
   Apartment management firms

Today a single corporation may include subsidiaries and other organizational units involved in a variety of decisions across several categories. Within one firm there may be a development subdivision which not only develops projects but also engages in land speculation; a real estate brokerage subsidiary; and an architectural subsidiary. A major insurance company may have a lending department, as well as its own urban land development subsidiary. Large integrated real estate development companies are often involved in major decisions in more than one category. Frequently local developers, realtors, and bankers are the major decision makers in local development projects; studies of community decision makers show clearly the role and power of local business people in all types of cities in the North and South. However, major real estate decisions are made not only by local individuals and real estate companies but also by powerful regional and national firms, such as the Hines and Levitt firms cited earlier. There are complex interconnections between influential interests external to cities and those that are part of the internal power structure of a particular city. An example would be a major insurance company, such as the Prudential Life Insurance Company, which, in connection with other local and national companies, finances and owns real estate and development projects in cities across the United States. . . .

Government and Urban Development

PLURALIST AND MARKET POLITICS ANALYSES

In addition to economic structures and decision makers, we must give substantial attention to political structures and decision makers in understanding city building. Most social scientists have either neglected the role of government in city development or have assumed a pluralist or "market politics" perspective. The pluralist outlook has dominated much political science analysis of U.S. cities. Political decision makers, on the whole, promote the general welfare because their decisions result from responding to and coordinating pressures from a multiplicity of contending pressure groups. Advocates of urban pluralism see a competitive market in the urban political sphere that is analogous to the economic mar-

ket; there is a political market in which individual voters and an array of diverse interest groups, in ever changing coalitions, compete for influence on local governments within a general value consensus.[35] Yet traditional pluralists have tended to neglect private economic decision making. . . .

CRITICAL PERSPECTIVES ON GOVERNMENT

In contrast to this market-knows-best perspective on urban economics and politics, critical urban analysts note the overwhelming evidence that certain groups have *far* more power than others to shape both economic and political decisions. Just as markets generally favor powerful capitalist investors over ordinary consumers, the urban political process favors the interests of powerful business and other groups over ordinary voters. Neither U.S. markets nor U.S. political arrangements are neutral. And both economic and political arrangements are dominated by the few. Some critical social scientists emphasize the economic and political decision makers, while others accent economic and governmental structures. But all critical analysts reject the pluralist and market-knows-best perspectives. Certain critical researchers such as Ralph Miliband and G. William Domhoff have accented the importance of specific business decision makers, particularly the capitalists, in state decisions. They view powerful economic decision makers as generally dominant over governmental decision makers and their decisions. Miliband and Domhoff have emphasized the specific ties between the capitalist class and various governments, including the movement of business leaders into and out of key political positions. In the United States, at the federal and local government levels, there is the everyday reality of interpersonal connections between business leaders and governmental officials. Domhoff has demonstrated that in the United States individual capitalists and their close subordinates do in fact rule by serving in critical governmental positions at both the national and the local levels. These governmental actors generally work hard to maintain favorable conditions for capitalists' enterprises and profits.[36]

Conclusion: The Need for Public Balance Sheets

In this [excerpt] we have examined the traditional social science and governmental perspectives on urban growth and development and have seen them to be substantially grounded in neoclassical economics. These traditional perspectives put heavy emphasis on a "free" land and property market, on allegedly equal individuals competing freely, on private property, on efficient land use, and on the benefits that markets in land are supposed to bring to all urbanites. But the realities are not what these perspectives suggest. As we have seen from examples, there are no free competitive markets in cities, because corporate location, urban land purchase, and urban development are disproportionately controlled, often monopolized, by powerful capitalistic decision makers. The newer critical perspective, also described in this [selection], focuses on these power and inequality realities of city growth and decline.

For the most part, the actions of urban industrialists, developers, bankers, and their political allies are visible and quantifiable. Using the language of the accountant and the economist and calculating profit and loss on their private balance sheets, they are prepared to spell out what they see as the need for and benefits of constant urban growth. Down to the last square foot, they can tell us how much new office space is needed and how much has been created. They inform us of the number of jobs produced by their construction projects,

and, once completed, they speculate with great precision about the number of additional employees the employers in their urban monuments will require. They calculate, and often exaggerate, the expected amount of additional tax revenues their large projects will generate, and, using the concept of the multiplier effect, speculate upon the economic benefits of their actions for the city as a whole.

On the other hand, the negative fallout from urban development is noticeably absent from the industrialists' and developers' lexicon. Just as critical, and usually just as obvious, the *social costs* generated by urban growth are less studied and are sometimes more difficult to specify and quantify. For example, why do we not attempt to measure the long-term physical and psychological impact of increasing pedestrian and auto congestion on consumers and workers? How can we eliminate unsafe pollution levels and prevent health damage? How should we measure the psychological impact on urbanities of routinely being deprived of sunlight as high-rise skyscrapers obstruct the sun? And what is the total community cost of the growing numbers of the homeless and those displaced by the processes of condominium conversion and gentrification in our cities? Finally, how can we calculate the fading sense of community that is produced in many neighborhoods as constant development and redevelopment converge to constitute the modern city?

In the last few years a start on studying social costs has been made. The idea that what is efficient and rational for developers is not necessarily so for workers, consumers, and society as a whole has even been documented in a study of Phoenix, Arizona, by the Center for Business Research at Arizona State University. According to this study the benefits of Phoenix's growth to businesses included more customers, improved market potential, greater availability of labor, and higher profits; the study's research manager stated that "most businesses enjoy a substantial net benefit from urban growth." His evaluation of the net effect of urban growth for ordinary citizens was less favorable. The benefits of expanded job opportunities, a greater selection of goods, and higher incomes for some workers are offset by higher taxes, an increased cost of living, urban sprawl and traffic congestion, water and air pollution, destruction of the natural environment and depletion of resources, waste disposal, a higher crime rate, greater demand for social services, and problems such as homelessness.[37]

Industrial and real estate capitalism does indeed shape the major development projects in cities—the factories, shopping centers, suburbs, business parks, office towers, and apartment complexes. Once the decisions of the powerful are made, smaller scale builders must work around the larger-scale projects, and average workers and their families have to choose within the limits provided. Workers and consumers, especially those with inadequate economic resources, endure the brunt of many social costs of our capitalistic development system. And these costs . . . have been enormous. However, we must not forget that group struggle is at the heart of capitalist cities. Citizens' movements are pressing for the community costs of urban development and decline to be addressed and eliminated.

Notes

1. D. Lindorff, "About-Face in Santa Monica," *Village Voice* (December 2–8, 1981), 20.
2. "Who's Gone This Year," *Forbes* 140 (October 26, 1987), 308. See also H. Banks, "Real Men Don't Need Tax Breaks," *Forbes*, 135 (June 3, 1985), 78, 80.
3. H. Gans, *The Levittowners* (New York: Random House, 1967), p. 6.
4. Ibid., pp. 5–13.
5. "The Master Builder," *Newsweek* (August 31, 1981), 45; J. R. Feagin, "Sunbelt Metropolis and Development Capital," in *Sunbelt/Snowbelt: Urban Development and Regional Restructuring,* ed. L. Sawers and W. K. Tabb (New York: Oxford University Press, 1984), pp. 110–11.
6. R. E. Park and E. W. Burgess, *Introduction to the Science of Society* (Chicago: University of Chicago Press, 1924), p. 507.
7. W. P. Frisbie and J. D. Kasarda, "Spatial Processes," in *The Handbook of Sociology,* ed. N. Smelser (Newbury Park, Calif.: Sage, 1988), pp. 629–66.
8. B. J. L. Berry and J. Kasarda, *Contemporary Urban Ecology* (New York: Macmillan, 1977); M. Micklin and H. M. Choldin, eds., *Sociological Human Ecology* (Boulder: Westview, 1984); Harvey M. Choldin, *Cities and Suburbs: An Introduction to Urban Sociology* (New York: McGraw-Hill, 1985). This paragraph draws on J. R. Feagin, *Free Enterprise City: Houston in Political-Economic Perspective* (New Brunswick, N.J.: Rutgers, 1988), pp. 15–21.
9. S. E. Harris, *The Death of Capital* (New York: Pantheon, 1977), p. 64.
10. Ibid., p. 65.
11. J. Kasarda, "The Implications of Contemporary Redistribution Trends for National Urban Policy," *Social Science Quarterly,* 61 (Dec., 1980), 373–400.
12. K. Bradbury, A. Downs, and K. Small, *Urban Decline and the Future of American Cities* (Washington, D.C.: The Brookings Institution, 1982), p. 296.
13. L. Mumford, *The City in History* (New York: Harcourt, Brace and World, 1961), p. 452.
14. F. X. Sutton et al., *The American Business Creed* (Cambridge: Harvard University Press, 1956), pp. 361–62.
15. E. A. Filene, *Successful Living in the Machine Age* (New York: Simon & Schuster, 1932), p. 98.
16. W. Alonso, *Location and Land Use* (Cambridge: Harvard University Press, 1964); Richard Muth. *Cities and Housing* (Chicago: University of Chicago Press, 1969).
17. D. L. Birch, "Wide Open Spaces," *Inc.,* 9 (Aug., 1987), 28.
18. P. E. Peterson, "Introduction: Technology, Race, and Urban Policy," in *The New Urban Reality* (Washington, D.C.: Brookings Institution, 1985), pp. 2–12.

19. A. Hawley, *Urban Society*, 2d ed. (New York: Wiley, 1981).
20. Micklin and Choldin, eds., *Sociological Human Ecology.*
21. Berry and Kasarda, *Contemporary Urban Ecology*, pp. 353, 402.
22. Hawley, *Urban Society*, pp. 228–29, 262–63; see also Frisbie and Kasarda, "Spatial Processes."
23. President's Commission for a National Agenda for the Eighties, Panel on Policies and Prospects, *Urban America in the Eighties: Perspectives and Prospects* (Washington, D.C.: U.S. Government Printing Office, 1980).
24. Ibid., pp. 12, 104.
25. M. Castells, "Is There an Urban Sociology?" in *Urban Sociology*, ed. C. G. Pickvance (London: Tavistock, 1976), pp. 33–57; M. Castells, *The Urban Question* (London: Edward Arnold, 1977); D. Harvey, *The Urbanization of Capital* (Baltimore: Johns Hopkins University Press, 1985); H. Lefebvre, *La revolution urbaine* (Paris: Gallimard, 1970).
26. M. P. Smith, *The City and Social Theory* (New York: St. Martin's, 1979); S. Fainstein, N. Fainstein, M. P. Smith, D. Judd, and R. C. Hill, *Restructuring the City* (New York: Longman, 1983); R. C. Hill, "Urban Political Economy," in *Cities in Transformation*, ed. M. P. Smith (Beverly Hills: Sage, 1984), pp. 123–38; J. Allen Whitt, *Urban Elites and Mass Transportation* (Princeton, N.J.: Princeton University Press, 1982); M. Gottdiener, *The Social Production of Urban Space* (Austin: University of Texas Press, 1985); G. L. Clark and Michael Dear, *State Apparatus: Structures and Language of Legitimacy* (Boston: Allen and Unwin, 1984), pp. 131–45; J. R. Logan and H. M. Molotch, *Urban Fortunes: The Political Economy of Place* (Berkeley and Los Angeles: University of California Press, 1987).
27. Other pressures for land-use controls have stemmed from local merchants concerned with protecting their business places for profitable marketing uses. In such cases the commitment by local merchants to land is primarily to its use value as a place to make a profit. Thus we actually have three basic interests in land: (1) in the exchange value of the land itself, (2) in the use value of the land for living, family, and neighborhood; (3) in the use value of the land for local commercial or industrial profit making.

Selected Readings

Being Urban: A Sociology of City Life by David A. Karp, Gregory P. Stone, William C. Yoels.

Urban Structure: The Social and Spatial Character of Cities by Ralph Thomlinson.

Humanising the City? Social Contexts of Urban Life at the Turn of the Millennium by Anthony P. Cohen, Katsuyoshi Fukui.

Urbanization in History: A Process of Dynamic Interactions by A. M. Van Der Woude, Akira Hayami, Jan De Vries.

The Intellectual Versus the City, from Thomas Jefferson to Frank Lloyd Wright by Morton and Lucia White.

Cities in World Perspective by Ivan Light.

Cities and Citizenship by James Holston.

The Ghetto Game: Racial Conflicts in the City by Dennis Clark.

City against Suburb: The Culture Wars in an American Metropolis by Joseph A. Rodriguez.

Good Neighborhoods: A Study of the In-Town & Suburban Residential Environments by Sidney Brower.

Urban Danger: Life in a Neighborhood of Strangers by Sally Engle Merry.

Critical-Thinking Questions

1. How did Burgess and Park view the growth of urban centers?

    _____
    _____
    _____
    _____
    _____
    _____
    _____
    _____
    _____

2. How does the Contemporary View of urban development see growth?

    _____
    _____
    _____
    _____
    _____
    _____
    _____
    _____
    _____

3. How does the Conflict View see Suburbanization occurring?

    _____
    _____
    _____
    _____
    _____
    _____
    _____
    _____

CHAPTER XI

Science, Technology and Self

Science and technology in Western Culture cannot be understood without a discussion of Western reason, rationality and individuality. Science/technology and individuality are the product of two concurrent social forces, the Enlightenment period an eighteenth-century movement characterized by a spirit of skepticism toward traditional doctrines and values, and the Protestant Reformation which demystifies world occurs/events.

The Enlightenment is historically significant for Western Civilization because it has become a sociological movement, rather than a private achievement. Sociological in that the effects can be found in all spheres of life. In religion the Enlightenment meant the struggle against orthodox superstition as found in the revolt of reason; in politics the Enlightenment represented the freedom against arbitrary despotism of estates; in philosophy it meant the liberation from theological dogmatism. In short, Enlightenment required a free-thinking person to displace the irrational with a rational world-image.

Paradoxically, the concept of individualism is not a secular manifestation, but a religious movement rooted in Protestantism. Protestantism, replaced the rule of the church as the mediator between God and humankind. Specifically, the Calvinist (and a small member of other Protestant sects), eliminated all intermediary ecclesiastical and sacramental agencies between God and humanity, a process which, according to Max Weber, demagicalized the relationship between God and His human creatures. The result, science and technology through the displacement of the magical with an objective world-image.

Another paradox of the Protestant movement is a new human identity that of the economic individual, or one who seeks inner-worldly over outer-worldly rewards. This change in human identity sets into motion a series of sociological shifts. Indeed, individual free choice alters the entire social order. One salient example of this shift is free mate selection. This is especially significant for woman since for many reasons through-out human history mate selection and marriage were inextricably linked to private property. Another significant example is the conjugal family form. A momentous change for Western human autonomy, since the patriarchal family stood in the way of free expression and individualism.

Many of the men behind the sociological concept known as Critical Theory, specifically Max Horkheimer and Herbert Marcuse all understood the significance of these changes in social values, and the psychological impact science/technology has/will have on the individual. Indeed, for these men the idea of individuality, that which was rooted in the Enlightenment period, has eclipsed into social conformity and in fact a loss of individuality. As a result, science/technology is an ideology of oppression. Horkheimer and Marcuse further understood that these changes could not be fully explained by vulgar Marxism solely. That these new social, political and economic conditions needed a new sociological approach which evolved into the Frankfurt Institute for Social Research (the Frankfurt School). This new approach centers itself around four major historical and social contexts: 1) these changes are not rooted in the old bourgeois ideas; 2) these social changes are the product of technical efficiency; 3) reason or the accord and interest of all individuals is eliminated; and 4) the creation of the affirmative culture or one-dimensional ideology.

In order to analyze this heretofore new social condition, the men of Critical Theory (the concept of critical Theory stems from Kant who suggested that there are limits to rational thought) turn to Max Weber's Principle of Rationality, Karl Marx's critique of ideology and Sigmund Freud's psychological concept that humanity's instincts, wishes, and desires are the result of adaptation to the life processes and necessities, to fully understand this new social force.

Max Horkheimer

Max Horkheimer as the director of the Frankfurt School sets the tone of the Institute in his work entitled "The Dialectic of the Enlightenment" in which he argues that science/technology as a single force controls nature in the quest to better the human experience here on earth. The result is that nature becomes an object of exploitation by humanity therefore distancing itself from nature, and hence humanity itself (humanity is nature). This distancing is the product of the Enlightenment period in which reason and rationality (the intellect) must be separated from the biological function of the nature of humanity.

Therefore, science/technology's mastery and objectification of nature contradictorily leads to external control of the qualities of humanity as a biological species. On the one hand science/technology's domination of nature leads to the "good life," but it is also a mechanism for human repression. Today science/technology has been elevated from servant to master.

Horkheimer in his essay "On the Problem of Truth" questions the claim of a 'unified science'. He suggested that there are presuppositions of truth creating science as an ideology. The procedure of science/technology should never be seen as a guarantee of truth. In fact, these claims may not be identical with human progress. Indeed, "science and its interpretations are two different things" in that value-free science/technology is an 'objectivistic illusion' because values seemed to be added to, and superimposed on the facts. Horkheimer cites the following idea " . . . what is true is

that which is helpful to the condition of humanity, and none else."

Finally, Horkheimer suggests that everything changes with time, and hence all judgments are related to time. Scientific/technological 'truth' is only valid for a certain time, and changes along with history and society.

Herbert Marcuse

In "On Science and Phenomenology" Marcuse suggest that based upon the Greek concept of "reason" humans' self-determination of its own life and the understanding of its world is the result of intellectual ability. Therefore, the world and universe can be rationally understood though rational knowledge gained by science/technology. This idea according to Marcuse is exemplified in Galileo's "mathematization on nature" because it created an 'ideational world' based in mathematics as 'true reality'. However, the 'ideational veil' of mathematics falsely assumes that we take for 'true being' that which is method and not empirical reality. In other words if what is being studied does not fit what humanity believes to be true reality, that is the method of mathematization, it should not be seen as science/technology and rejected, for mathematics is value-free. However, as we have seen nothing is value-free including mathematics for it is just one method form which is limited based upon humanities intellectual understanding and limited and restricted to the human imagination.

In 1988 Stanley Aronowitz in his book *Science as Power* (The University of Minnesota Press) cites a study done by Sharon Teaweek of the culture of a major physics laboratory in which the machinery not only dictates what is scientifically discovered, but also symbolizes power within that community. There is one significant problem with machinery dictating scientific discovery, the machine acts as the means by which the scientists see the physical phenomenon, but the scientists creates the machine according to their own theoretical concepts. Perhaps suggesting Goethe's idea found in the "problem of Truth" essay that what "I have noticed that I regard as true that idea which is fruitful for me fits in with the rest of my thought, and at the same time benefits me."

Aronowitz further cites Andrew Pickering's history of the discovery of quark (an idea used within quantum physics to suggest the absence of phenomena). According to Aronowitz, when the machine changed so did what was seen. Hence, what was seen conformed to what wanted to be seen, and not the value-free scientific empirical data. Pickering and Aronowitz both are not deniers of the possibility of quarks, rather suggest that they are only one interpretation of the data collected from the man-made machine, from a host of other possibilities. Therefore, seen as arbitrary interpretation and not value-free science. As we saw within Marcuse's concept of the 'ideational veil' of mathematics, it falsely assumes that we take for 'true Being' that which is method and not empirical reality.

Finally, Herbert Marcus in "Some Implications of Modern Technology" suggested that the modern machine age with its' efficiency fetish has substituted for commodity fetish at the hands of an authoritarian state or the apparatus. The apparatus was seen by Marx as a tool of repression controlled by the 'ruling class' to further their objectives, that is the economic exploitation of society's members.

However, Louis Althusser suggests that there are two forms of apparatuses: 1) the repressive which controls coercive force, and 2) the Ideological State Apparatus which functions predominantly through ideology. Althusser identifies six areas in which this form of apparatus reproduces the current social conditions they are: 1) family, 2) religion, 3) legal system, 4) political system, 5) trade unions, and 6) the mass media.

This form of apparatus operates by presenting an imaginary relation to the real conditions of existence because the aim of the ruling class is the reproduction of the current relations and the real conditions are masked in ideologies supportive of social distinction.

Marcuse's concern for authoritarian coercive state control did not lead him to see many of the implications located within post-modern technology would be that of volunteristic behavior, mainly due to Ideological State Apparatus. Predominate among these effects on behavior is the loss of individuality, and social conformity.

Today the impact of the computer age leads to standardization of thought, social conformity, and should be seen as a volunteristic social by-product of the nature of advanced technology, and not the tool of an authoritarian state.

During the rapid, almost anomic technological advancement of post-modern society, the historical concept of individuality is lost and social conformity becomes the new form of human identity.

To clarify, consider for a moment the image of a youngster sitting at a computer attempting to learn a new computer software. The software routine demands a new understanding of the technical process which presents itself as an obstacle to gaining entry. This individual must conform to the software's demands both in language and behavior. So the youngster turns to the tech support system of the software company, where on line the "techies" in effect tell the youngster what to do and how to think in order to gain access to the program. Essentially, it is sensible for that youngster to follow another's directions in order to have use of the software.

However, during this exercise the youngster learns to accept the will of another, which also includes the computer. This volunteristic social behavior becomes even more insidious because the youngster internalizes these directions of another, as one's own thought creating a new human identity which rejects free thought and individuality by relying on the will of another.

As the youngster grows into an adult, there is the tacit understanding that the demands of the post-modern era will require consistent technical training. Consequently, there is the continuous management of autonomous individual thought by the "authority" of technology. This is an ongoing process throughout one's life.

The conscience volunteristic submission and conformity of post-modern humanity to what can be seen as the external authority of the technology has striped the individual of free thought and individuality itself. Constant exposure throughout one's life to the continuous demands of the computer age implies the continuous management of individual free thought.

This management is unavailable and inescapable in a post-modern society because it transcends technology itself and affects all segments of social life. Most notably fashion, education, business, and entertainment. In fashion there is an effort to express individuality through dress. However, because it is a fashion "trend" many dress alike, and individuality is lost. In education the curriculum stress common knowledge acquisition, but producing standardization of thought. In the business world top executives rape the wealth of the company, and others "go along to get along." In entertainment the historical "individual" was seen as the hero, but today is portrayed as a kook, and someone to be feared.

Likewise, being critical in an era which demands social conformity is irrational. Having an individual opinion which stands outside the mainstream is unreasonable. Doing the "right thing" suggests social conformity. Conformity has become reasonable and sensible behavior in the post-modern technical era.

In summary, the Frankfurt School/Critical Theory took the position that the analysis of post-modern society should critique the positive effects and the limits of rationality. Rationality has created the "good life" in terms of health and living conditions through the domination of nature. However, rational domination of nature for human benefit also leads to human domination and repression.

The Frankfurt School also suggested that science/technology in post-modern society is in fact an ideology. As a result, science and technology cannot be seen as "value-free." Consequently, all scientific methods and its products have a hidden agenda, and personal interests. Indeed, the method and technology used to prove theoretical models are made and apply by scientists and technologists leading to a conflict of interests. Moreover, the method and technology used is limited to, indeed restricted to the depths of the human imagination.

Finally, the conscience submission and conformity of post-modern humanity to what can be seen as the external authority of the technology has striped the individual of free thought and individuality itself, suggesting a tendency toward the "one-dimensional" ideology. For Marcuse the one-dimensional ideology represented the elimination of all sense of otherness, the individual, criticism of the social order, and the trajectory toward the affirmative culture in which all forms of protest and negation are senseless.

On the Problem of Truth

Max Horkheimer

Originally published in Zeitschrift für Sozialforschung, *Vol. IV (1935), Hork-heimer's essay is part of a series of critical confrontations with contemporary philosophies and their social implications.*

In a sense, the article is an exemplary exercise in a critical sociology of knowledge. Beginning with the obvious co-existence of rational and irrational human pursuits, this split itself becomes the problem, rather than remaining the factual premise, as for most of Horkheimer's contemporaries. The division has grown to the same extent that rational investigation of the world has: the more the world becomes transparent, the more the secure orders disappear and the more the need for secure orders increases. Even—and in fact especially—among the most relentless rationalists, we find the readiness to bracket out and maintain certain areas allegedly inaccessible to reason.

The philosophic thought of recent decades, shot through with contradictions, has also been divided on the problem of truth. Two opposing and unreconciled views exist side by side in public life and, not infrequently, in the behavior of the same individual. According to one, cognition never has more than limited validity. This is rooted in objective fact as well as in the knower. Every thing and every relation of things changes with time, and thus every judgment as to real situations must lose its truth with time. "Every particular entity is given to us in time, occupies a definite place in time, and is perceived as lasting for a length of time and during this time developing changing activities and possibly altering its properties. Thus all our judgments on the essence, properties, activities, and relations of particular things are necessarily involved with the relationship to time, and every judgment of this sort can only be valid for a certain time." Subjectively, too, truth is viewed as necessarily circumscribed. Perception is shaped not only by the object but by the individual and generic characteristics of human beings. It is particularly this subjective moment to which the modern science of mind has given its attention. Depth psychology seemed to destroy the illusion of absolutely valid truth by pointing out that the function of consciousness only made its appearance together with unconscious psychic processes, while sociology made a philosophically developed discipline out of the doctrine that every idea belongs to an intellectual pat-

The Essential Frankfurt School Reader Arato & Gebhardt Continuum Publishing Co. 1982

233

tern bound up with a social group, a "standpoint." Present-day relativism, in particular, has subjectivist characteristics, but it is by no means the sole representative of this period's intellectual attitude toward truth. Rather, it is opposed by the impulse to blind faith, to absolute submission, which has always been necessarily linked with relativism as its opposite, and is once again characteristic of the cultural situation today. In philosophy, a new dogmatism has emerged in the wake of the metaphysical reworking of the concept, at first strictly interpreted, of intuition of essences. This development in the history of ideas reflects the historical circumstance that the social totality to which the liberal, democratic and progressive tendencies of the dominant culture belonged also contained from its beginning their opposite compulsion, chance and the rule of primal nature. By the system's own dynamic, this eventually threatens to wipe out all its positive characteristics. The role of human autonomy in the preservation and renewal of social life is completely subordinated to the effort to hold together mechanically a dissolving order. The public mind is increasingly dominated by some rigid judgments and a few postulated concepts.

The appearance of this contradiction in our time repeats in distorted form a discord which has always permeated the philosophy of the bourgeois era. Its prototype in the history of philosophy is the linkage of Descartes' universal methodical doubt with his devout Catholicism. It extends to the details of his system. It reveals itself not only in the unreconciled juxtaposition of faith and contradictory knowledge, but in the theory of cognition itself. The doctrine of a solid *res cogitans*, a self-contained ego independent of the body, which serves as an absolute resolution of the attempt at doubt and is preserved immutable in the metaphysics of Descartes and his idealistic successors, reveals itself as an illusion, corresponding to the situation of the bourgeois individual and present before the inquiry rather than based on it. The independent existence of individual souls, the principle which for Descartes makes the world philosophically intelligible, is no easier to reconcile with the criteria and the whole spirit of the analytic geometry which he himself invented than is his proclamation of empty space as the sole physical substance with the theological dogma of transubstantiation. Complete doubt as to the reality of material truth, the constant emphasis on the uncertainty, conditional character and finiteness of all definite knowledge, immediately next to ostensible insights into eternal truths and the fetishization of individual categories and modes of being—this duality permeates the Cartesian philosophy.

It finds its classic expression in Kant. The critical method was supposed to perform the task of differentiating the purely conditional and empirical from "pure" knowledge and reached the conclusion that pure knowledge was possible only in regard to the conditions of the conditional. The system of the necessary subjective conditions of human knowledge is the exclusive goal of transcendental philosophy. To Hume's skepticism, Kant opposes nothing but the sensory and conceptual forms of knowledge and what can be deduced therefrom. But what comes into existence on the basis of these conditions, the theory of our actual world and not a merely possible one, knowledge of actual nature and existing human society, lacks for Kant the criteria of genuine truth and is only relative. Everything that we know of reality, of conditions in space and time, relates according to him only to appearances, and of these he claims to have shown "that they are not things (but only a form of representation), and that they are not qualities inherently belonging to the things in themselves." In regard to knowledge of the world, he is no less a skeptical relativist than the "mystical" and "dreaming" idealists whom he combats. In the latest phase of transcendental philosophy, this subjective relativism is clearly formulated: "In the last analysis, all being is relative (as opposed to the false ideal of an absolute Being and its absolute truth), and is nevertheless *relative in some customary sense to the transcendental subjectivity*. But this subjectivity alone is 'in and for itself.'" Along with the careful and differentiated theoretical philosophy, which did indeed keep thought rooted in the ahistorical sphere of transcendental subjectivity, there are in Kant the postulates of practical reason and—linked to them by conclusions which are in part extremely questionable—the transformation into absolute of the existing property relations under prevalent public and private law. In the *Critique of Practical Reason,* which fetishizes the concept of duty, he did not in any way overcome the need for an immovable intellectual foundation but merely met it in a way more fitting to the time than that of the rationalist ontology of the period. The theoretical philosophy itself assumes that there is absolute knowledge, independent of any sensory experience, and indeed that this alone deserves the name of truth. Even the *Critique of Pure Reason* depends on the assumption that pure concepts and judgments exist "a priori" in the consciousness, and that metaphysics not only always has been, but that it will of right exist for all eternity. Kant's work embraces in itself the contradiction between the German and English schools of philosophy. The resolution of the contradictions it produces, the mediation between critique and dogmatic system, between a mechanistic concept of science and the doctrine of intelligible freedom, between belief in an eternal order and a theory isolated from practice, increasingly and vainly occupied his own thought till the last years of his life: this is the mark of his greatness. Analysis carried through to the end and skeptical distrust of all theory on the one hand and readiness to believe naively in detached fixed principles on the other, these are

characteristic of the bourgeois mind. It appears in its most highly developed form in Kant's philosophy.

This dual relationship to truth is again mirrored in the failure of the progressive methods of the scholar to influence his attitude toward the most important problems of the time, the combination of notable knowledge in the natural sciences with childlike faith in the Bible. The association of that particularly strict tendency in modern philosophy, positivism, with the crudest superstition, has already been noted in this magazine. Auguste Comte not merely laid the groundwork for a whimsical cult, but prided himself on his understanding of the various theories of the beyond. William James turned to mysticism and even mediumism. The brain appears to him not so much to promote as to obstruct the enlightening intuitions which exist "ready-made in the transcendental world" and come through as telepathic experiences as soon as the brain's activity is "abnormally" reduced. "The word 'influx' used in Swedenborgian circles" describes the phenomenon very well. The pragmatist F.C.S. Schiller, whom James quotes, declares on this point: "Matter is not that which produces consciousness but that which limits it" and conceives of the body as "a mechanism for including consciousness." This inclination to spiritualism can be followed through the later history of positivism. In Germany, it seems to have reached its ultimate in the philosophy of Hans Driesch, in which a scientism carried to extremes goes together with unconcealed occultism in all questions of this world and the beyond. In this, the occultistic dilemma finds a grotesque expression in his logic and theory of knowledge through intentional formalism and rigidity and through the monomaniacal reference of all the problems of the world to some few biological experiments. On the other side, the misconception of a self-sufficient science independent of history appears through the pseudo-scientific dress of his barbarous errors in religion and practice.

Only in the decline of the contemporary epoch has it become the typical behavior of scholars for a person to develop high critical faculties in a specific branch of science while remaining on the level of backward groups in respect to questions of social life and echoing the most ignorant phrases. In the beginning of the bourgeois order; the turn to specific juristic and scientific studies without regard to social and religious demands immediately produced a moment of liberation from the theological tutelage of thought. But as a result of the alteration of the social structure, this sort of production without regard to the rational relation to the whole has become regressive and obstructive in all fields—in science just as in industry and agriculture. This abstractness and ostensible independence of the bourgeois science industry shows itself in the mass of isolated individual empirical studies, not related to any sort of theory and practice by clear terminology and subject matter. It is likewise visible in the efforts of scientists, without any significant reason, to divest their concepts of all empirical material, and especially in the inordinate mathematicization of many intellectual disciplines. The conventional attitude of the scholar to the dominant questions of the period and the confinement of his critical attention to his professional specialty were formerly factors in the improvement of the general situation. Thinkers ceased to be concerned exclusively with the welfare of their immortal souls, or to make concern for it their guide in all theoretical matters. But subsequently this attitude has taken on another meaning: instead of being a sign of necessary courage and independence, the withdrawal of intellectual energies from general cultural and social questions, the placing of actual historical interests and struggles in a parenthesis, is more a sign of anxiety and incapacity for rational activity

than of an inclination to the true tasks of science. The substance underlying intellectual phenomena changes with the social totality.

It is not the intention here to go into detail in regard to the historical causes of this dual relationship to truth. The competition within the bourgeois economy, in the context of which the forces of this society unfolded, produced a critical spirit which not only was able to liberate itself from the bureaucracies of church and absolutism but, driven by the dynamic of the economic apparatus, can to a fantastic degree place nature at its service. But this power only seems to be its own. The methods for the production of social wealth are available, the conditions for the production of useful natural effects are largely known, and the human will can bring them about. But this spirit and will themselves exist in false and distorted form. The concept of having power over something includes deciding for oneself and making use of it for one's own purposes. But domination over nature is not exercised according to a unified plan and purpose, but merely serves as an instrument for individuals, groups and nations which use it in their struggle against one another and, as they develop it, at the same time reciprocally circumscribe it and bend it to destructive ends. Thus, the bearers of this spirit, with their critical capacity and their developed thinking, do not really become masters but are driven by the changing constellations of the general struggle which even though summoned up by men themselves, face them as incalculable forces of destiny. This seemingly necessary dependence, which increasingly bears fruit in disruptive tensions and crises, general misery and decline, becomes for the greatest part of mankind an incomprehensible fate. But to the extent that the alteration of basic relationships is excluded in practice, a need arises for an interpretation based purely on faith. The conviction that a constricting and painful constellation is essentially unalterable prods the mind to give it a profound interpretation so as to be able to come to terms with it without despairing. Death as the inevitable end was always the basis of the religious and metaphysical illusion. The metaphysical need which permeates the history of this period stems from the fact that the inner mechanism of this society, which produces insecurity and continuous pressure, does not emerge into clear consciousness and is put up with as something necessary and eternal, rather than as an object of effective change. The firm faith which was part of the mortar of the medieval social structure has disappeared. The great systems of European philosophy were always intended only for an educated upper crust and fail completely in the face of the psychic needs of the impoverished and socially continually sinking sections of the citizenry and peasantry, who are nevertheless completely tied to this form of society by upbringing, work and hope, and cannot believe it to be transitory. This is why the intellectual situation has for decades been dominated by the craving to bring an eternal meaning into a life which offers no way out, by philosophical practices such as the direct intellectual or intuitive apprehension of truth and finally by blind submission to a personality, be it an anthroposophic prophet, a poet or a politician. To the extent to which individual activity is circumscribed and the capacity for it eventually stunted, there exists the readiness to find security in the protective shelter of a faith or person taken as the vessel and incarnation of the truth. In particular periods of the rise of contemporary society, the expectation of steady progress within its own framework reduced the need for an interpretation that would transfigure reality, and the rational and critical faculties achieved greater influence in private and public thought. But as this form of social organization becomes increasingly crisis-prone and insecure, all those

who regard its characteristics as eternal are sacrificed to the institutions which are intended as substitutes for the lost religion.

This is, to be sure, only one aspect of the social situation out of which the shaky relationship to truth in modern times arises. A fundamental analysis of the fallacious bourgeois self-perception, which preserves the ideology of complete inner freedom in the face of the dependence and insecurity of its bearers, could show that the liberal validation of alien ideas (the mark of relativism) has a common foot with the fear of making one's own decisions, which leads to belief in a rigid absolute truth: the abstract, reified concept of the individual which inescapabably dominates thought in this economic system. But here the question is less one of the derivation of the phenomenon than of its practical significance. Is there really only the choice between acceptance of a final truth, as proclaimed in religions and idealistic schools of philosophy, and the view that every thesis and every theory is always merely "subjective," i.e., true and valid for a person or a group or a time or mankind as a species, but lacking objective validity? In developing the dialectical method, bourgeois thought itself has made the most ambitious attempt to transcend this antinomy. Here the goal of philosophy no longer appears, as in Kant, to be merely the system of the subjective factors of cognition; perceived truth is no longer so empty that in practice one must take refuge in the solidity of faith. While the concrete content is perceived as conditional and dependent and every "final" truth is just as decisively "negated" as in Kant, it does not for Hegel simply fall through the sieve in the sifting out of pure knowledge. Recognition of the conditional character of every isolated view and rejection of its absolute claim to truth does not destroy this conditional knowledge; rather, it is incorporated into the system of truth at any given time as a conditional, one-sided and isolated view. Through nothing but this continuous delimitation and correction of partial truths, the process itself evolves its proper content as knowledge of limited insights in their limits and connection.

To skepticism, Hegel opposes the concept of determinate negation. The progressive recognition of partial truths, the advance from one isolated definition to another, means for him not a mere lining up of attributes but a description which follows the actual subject matter in all particulars. This critique of every concept and every complex of concepts by progressive incorporation into the more complete picture of the whole does not eliminate the individual aspects, nor does it leave them undisturbed in subsequent thought, but every negated insight is preserved as a moment of truth in the progress of cognition, forms a determining factor in it, and is further defined and transformed with every new step. Precisely because of this, the methodological form of thesis, antithesis and synthesis is not to be applied as a "lifeless diagram." If at any given time the antithesis expresses the critical and relativizing impetus in opposition to the assimilation and establishment of a pattern of thought, thesis and antithesis together immediately form a new insight, a synthesis, because the negation has not simply rejected the original insight but has deepened and defined it. Hegel does not end up with the bare assurance that all definite knowledge is transitory and unreal, that what we know is only appearance in contrast to an unknowable thing in itself or an intuitively perceived essence. If for Hegel the true is the whole, the whole is not something distinct from the parts in its determinate structure, but the entire pattern of thought which at a given time embraces in itself all limited conceptions in the consciousness of their limitation.

Since the dialectical method does not rest with showing that a thing is conditioned, but takes the conditioned thing seriously, it escapes the relativistic formalism of the Kantian philosophy. Hegel therefore does not need to make a fetish out of an isolated concept like that of duty. He recognizes the vain effort of all idealistic philosophy before him to make the whole content of the world disappear in some conceptual generalization and declare all specific differences unreal as opposed to such attributes as the infinite, will, experience, absolute indifference, consciousness, etc. The second-rate thought to which the world always appears as a mysterious presentation in which only the initiate knows what goes on behind the scenes, which sets philosophy to solving an ostensible riddle in order to know once and for all or even to despair that such a key is not to be found—this sort of dogmatism does not exist in Hegel. Rather, the dialectical method quickly led him to become aware of the stupidity of such philosophical work and to see in development and flux what presents itself as absolute and eternal.

Insofar as this method, in Hegel, nevertheless still belongs to an idealistic system, he has not freed his thought from the old contradiction. His philosophy too is ultimately characterized by the indifference to particular perceptions, ideas and goals which belongs to relativism, as well as by the transformation of conceptual structures into substances and the inability to take theoretical and practical account of the dogmatism and historical genesis of his own thought. Its dogmatic side has been especially often attacked in the critique of cognition since the middle of the nineteenth century. In place of those doctrines which made an abstract concept into substance, that is, which sought to raise this limited aspect over history as identical with being, and thus degenerated into naive faith, Hegel puts the hypostatization of his own system. In his polemic against skepticism and relativism, he himself says: "The goal is fixed for knowledge just as necessarily as the succession in the process; it is there, where knowledge no longer needs to go beyond itself, where it finds itself, and the concept fits the object, the object the concept. The progress to this end is therefore also continuous, and satisfaction is not to be found at any earlier stage." Hegel believes that he guarantees this satisfaction through the whole of his thought. For him, philosophy has the same absolute content as religion, the complete unity of subject and object, a final and eternally valid knowledge.

What man . . . ensnared on all sides in the finite, seeks, is the region of a higher substantial truth in which all the oppositions and contradictions of the finite can find their final resolution and freedom its complete satisfaction. This is the region of the truth in itself, and not of the relatively true. The highest truth, the truth as such, is the resolution of the highest opposition and contradiction. In it the opposition of freedom and necessity, of spirit and nature, of knowledge and object, law and impulse, opposition and contradiction in general, whatever form they may take, no longer have validity and force as opposition and contradiction. . . . Ordinary consciousness, on the other hand, does not get out of this contradiction and either despairs in it or discards it and helps itself in some other way. But philosophy steps into the middle of the mutually contradictory propositions, knows them according to their significance, i.e., as not absolute in their one-sidedness but self-resolving, and places them in the harmony and unity which is the truth. To grasp this concept of truth is the task of philosophy. . . . For philosophy also has no other subject than God and is thus rational theology, and by being in the service of truth is continuous service of God.

According to Hegel himself, the doctrine of an absolute self-contained truth has the purpose of harmonizing in a higher spiritual region the "oppositions and contradictions" not resolved in the world. Especially in his later lectures and writings, he stresses that "the region of truth, freedom and satisfaction" is to be found not in the mechanism of reality but in the spiritual spheres of art, religion and philosophy. He opposes this peace and satisfaction in thought not only to skeptical despair but to the active attitude which tries to overcome the incompleteness of existing conditions "in some other way."

This dogmatic narrow-mindedness is not some sort of an accidental defect of his doctrine which one can strip off without changing anything essential. Rather, it is inextricably bound up with the idealistic character of his thought and enters into all the details of his application of the dialectic. Hegel cannot be reproached for the role in his thought played by external observation, from which, as Trendelenberg points out in criticism, the basic concept of the dialectic, movement comes. He himself expounded the importance of experience for philosophy. Rather, in contemplating his own system, Hegel forgets one very definite side of the empirical situation. The belief that this system is the completion of truth hides from him the significance of the temporally conditioned interest which plays a role in the details of the dialectical presentation through the direction of thought, the choice of material content, and the use of names and words, and diverts attention from the fact that his conscious and unconscious partisanship in regard to the problems of life must necessarily have its effect as a constituent element of his philosophy. Thus, his conceptions of folk and freedom, which form the backbone of many parts of his work, are not perceived in terms of their temporal presuppositions and their transitory character, but on the contrary are, as conceptual realities and forces, made the basis of the historical developments from which they are abstracted. Because Hegel does not recognize and assert the specific historical tendencies which find expression in his own work, but presents himself as absolute mind in philosophizing and accordingly preserves on ostensible distance and impartiality, many parts of his work lack clarity and, in spite of the revolutionary sharpness and flexibility of the method, take on the arbitrary and pedantic character which was so closely bound up with the political conditions of his time. In the idealistic thought to which it owes its existence, the dialectic is beset by dogmatism. Since the abstractions at which the method arrives are supposed to be moments in a system in which thought "no longer needs to go beyond itself," the relationships comprehended by it also are regarded as unalterable and eternal. If a great deal may happen in history yet to come, even if other peoples, e.g., the Slavs, should take over leadership from those nations which have in the past been decisive, nevertheless no new principle of social organization will become dominant and no decisive change will take place in the organization of mankind. No historical change which brought about a new form of human association could leave the concepts of society, freedom, right, etc., unaltered. The interconnection of all categories, even the most abstract, would be affected thereby. Hence, Hegel's belief that his thought comprehended the essential characteristics of all being—the unity of which remained as it appeared in the system, a complete hierarchy and totality undisturbed by the becoming and passing of individuals—represented the conceptual eternalization of the earthly relationships on which it was based. The dialectic takes on a transfiguring function. The laws of life, in which according to Hegel domination and servitude as well as poverty and misery have their eternal place, are sanctioned by the fact that the conceptual interconnection in which they are included is regarded as something higher, divine and absolute. Just as religion and the deification of a race or state or the worship of nature offer the suffering individual an immortal and eternal essence, so Hegel believes he has revealed an eternal meaning in the contemplation of which the individual should feel sheltered from all personal misery. This is the dogmatic, metaphysical, naive aspect of his theory.

Its relativism is directly bound up with this. The dogmatic assertion that all the particular views which have ever entered the lists against one another in real historical combat, all the creeds of particular groups, all attempts at reform are now transcended and canceled out, the notion of the all-embracing thought which is to apportion its partial rightness and final limitation to every point of view without consciously taking sides with any one against the others and deciding between them—*this* is the very soul of bourgeois relativism. The attempt to afford justification to every idea and every historical person and to assign the heroes of past revolutions their place in the pantheon of history next to the victorious generals of the counterrevolution, this ostensibly free-floating objectivity conditioned by the bourgeoisie's stand on two fronts against absolutist restoration and against the proletariat, has acquired validity in the Hegelian system along with the idealistic pathos of absolute knowledge. It is self-evident that tolerance toward all views that are in the past and recognized as conditioned is no less relativist than negativist skepticism. The more the times demand unsparing outspokenness and defense of particular truths and rights, the more unequivocally it reveals the inhumanity immanent in it. If in spite of the lack of a conscious relationship between his philosophy and any particular practical principle, Hegel was guided in detail not simply by the conservative Prussian spirit but also by interests pushing him forward, his dogmatism nevertheless prevented his recognizing and defending these tendencies, which found expression in his science, as his own purposes and progressive interests. He seems to speak of himself when he describes how "the consciousness lets the idea of something good in itself, which as yet has no reality, go by like an empty cloak." In Hegel, as in Goethe, the progressive impulses enter secretly into the viewpoint which ostensibly comprehends and harmonizes everything real impartially. Later relativism, in contrast, directs his demonstration of limiting conditionality mainly against the progressive ideas themselves, which it thereby seeks to flatten, that is, to equate with everything already past. In his conceptual projections, the new as well as the old easily appear as simple rationalizing and ideology. Since the recognition of the truth of particular ideas disappears behind the display of conditions, the coordination with historical unities, this impartial relativism reveals itself as the friend of what exists at any given time. The dogmatism concealed within it is the affirmation of the existing power; what is coming into being needs conscious decision in its struggle, while the limitation to mere understanding and contemplation serves what is already in existence. That impartial partisanship and indiscriminate objectivity represent a subjective viewpoint is a dialectical proposition that indeed takes relativism beyond itself.

In materialism, the dialectic is not regarded as a closed system. Understanding that the prevalent circumstances are conditioned and transitory is not here immediately equated with transcending them and canceling them out. Hegel declares: "Something is only known, indeed felt, as a limit, a defect, only when one is already beyond it. . . . It is . . . simply lack of consciousness not to see that precisely the description of something as finite or limited contains proof of the *real presence* of the infinite and unlimited, that knowledge of boundaries is only possible insofar as the unbounded is here in one's consciousness." This view has as its presupposition the basic postulate of idealism that concept and being are in truth the same, and therefore all fulfillment can take place in the pure medium of the spirit. Inner renewal and exaltation, reformation and spiritual elevation, were always the solution to which he pointed. Insofar as dealing with and changing the external world was regarded as at all fundamental, it appeared as a mere consequence of this. Materialism, on the other hand, insists that objective reality is not identical with man's thought and can never be merged into it. As much as thought in its own element seeks to copy the life of the object and adapt itself to it, the thought is nevertheless never simultaneously the object thought about, unless in self-observation and reflection—and not even there. To conceptualize a defect is therefore not to transcend it; concepts and theories form an impulse to its removal, a prerequisite to the proper procedure, which as it progresses is constantly redefined, adapted and improved:

An isolated and conclusive theory of reality is completely unthinkable. If one takes seriously the formal definition of truth which runs through the whole history of logic as the correspondence of cognition with its object, there follows from it the contradiction to the dogmatic interpretation of thought. This correspondence is neither a simple datum, an immediate fact, as it appears in the doctrine of intuitive, immediate certainty and in mysticism, nor does it take place in the pure sphere of spiritual immanence, as it seems to in Hegel's metaphysical legend. Rather, it is always established by real events, by human activity. In the investigation and determination of actual conditions, and even more in the verification of theories, the direction of attention, the refinement of methods, the categorical structure of subject matter, in short human activity within the framework of the given social period, play their role. (The discussion here will not deal with the question of how far all connection with such activity is avoided by Husserl's "formal ontology" which refers "to any possible world in empty generality" or by formal apophantic, which likewise relates to all possible statements in empty generality; or by other parts of pure logic and mathematics, nor with how far they possess real cognitive value without regard to such a connection.)

If certain philosophical interpretations of mathematics correctly stress its a priori character, that is, the independence of mathematical constructions from all empirical observation, the mathematical models of theoretical physics in which the cognitive value of mathematics finally shows itself are, in any case, structured with reference to the events that can be brought about and verified on the basis of the current level of development of the technical apparatus. As little as mathematics needs to trouble itself about this relationship in its deductions, its form at any given time is nevertheless as much conditioned by the increase in the technical capacity of mankind as the latter is by the development of mathematics. The verification and proof of ideas relating to man and society, however, consists not merely in laboratory experiments or the examination of documents, but in historical struggles in which conviction itself plays an essential role. The false view that the present social order is essentially harmonious serves as an impetus to the renewal of disharmony and decline and becomes a factor in its own practical refutation. The correct theory of the prevalent conditions, the doctrine of the deepening of crises and the approach of catastrophes does, to be sure, find continuous confirmation in all particulars. But the picture of a better world that inheres in this theory and takes its departure from the assertion of the

badness of the present, the idea of men and their capabilities immanent in it, finds its definition, correction and confirmation in the course of historical struggles. Hence, activity is not to be regarded as an appendix, as merely what comes after thought, but enters into theory at every point and is inseparable from it. Just for this reason pure thought does not here give the satisfaction of having sure and certain grasp of the question and being at one with it. It is certainly impossible to speak too highly of the conquests of the human spirit as a factor in liberation from the domination of nature and in improving the pattern of relationships. Social groups and possessors of power who fought against it, all propagandists of every sort of obscurantism, had their shady reasons and always led men into misery and servitude. But if in particular historical situations knowledge can, by its mere presence, obstruct evil and become power, the effort to make it in isolation the highest purpose and means of salvation rests on a philosophical misunderstanding. It cannot be said in general and a priori what meaning and value some particular knowledge has. That depends on social conditions as a whole at the particular time, on the concrete situation to which it belongs. Thoughts which, taken in isolation, are identical in content can at one time be unripe and fantastic and at another outdated and unimportant, yet in a particular historical moment form factors of a force that changes the world.

There is no eternal riddle of the world, no world secret the penetration of which once and for all would be the mission of thought. This narrow view—which ignores the constant alteration in knowing human beings along with the objects of their knowledge as well as the insurmountable tension between concept and objective reality—corresponds today to the narrow horizon of groups and individuals who, from their felt inability to change the world through rational work, grasp at and compulsively hold to universal recipes which they memorize and monotonously repeat. When the dialectic is freed of its connection with the exaggerated concept of isolated thought, self-determining and complete in itself, the theory defined by it necessarily loses the metaphysical character of final validity, the sanctity of a revelation, and becomes an element, itself transitory, intertwined in the fate of men.

But by ceasing to be a closed system, the dialectic does not lose the stamp of truth. In fact, the disclosures of conditional and one-sided aspects of other thought and its own forms an important impetus to the intellectual process. Hegel and his materialist followers were correct in always stressing that this critical and relativizing characteristic is a necessary part of cognition. But the certitude and verification of its own conviction does not require the assertion that concept and object are here henceforth one, and thought can rest. To the degree that the knowledge gained from perception and inference, methodical inquiry and historical events, daily work and political struggle, meets the test of the available means of cognition, it is the truth. The abstract proposition, that once a critique is justified from its own standpoint it will show itself open to correction, expresses itself for the materialists not in liberality toward opposing views or skeptical indecision, but in alertness to their own errors and flexibility of thought. They are no less "objective" than pure logic when it teaches that the relativistic "talk of a subjective truth which is this for one and the opposite for another must rate as nonsense." Since that extrahistorical and hence exaggerated concept of truth which stems from the idea of a pure infinite mind and thus in the last analysis from the God concept, is impossible, it no longer makes any sense to orient the knowledge that we have to this impossibility and in this sense call it rela-

tive. The theory which we regard as correct may disappear because the practical and scientific interests which played a role in the formation of its concepts, and above all the facts and circumstances to which it referred, have disappeared. Then this truth is in fact irrecoverably gone, since there is no super-human essence to preserve the present-day relationship between the content of ideas and their objects in its all-embracing spirit when the actual human beings have changed or even when mankind has died out. Only when measured against an extraterrestrial, unchanging existence does human truth appear to be of an inferior quality. At the same time as it nevertheless necessarily remains inconclusive and to that extent "relative," it is also absolute, since later correction does not mean that a former truth was formerly untrue. In the progress of knowledge, to be sure, much incorrectly regarded as true will prove wrong. Nevertheless, the overturn of categories stems from the fact that the relationship of concept and reality is affected and altered as a whole and in all its parts by the historical changes in forces and tasks. To a large extent the direction and outcome of the historical struggle depends on the decisiveness with which men draw the consequences of what they know, their readiness to test their theories against reality and refine them, in short, by the uncompromising application of the insight recognized as true. The correction and further definition of the truth is not taken care of by history, so that all the cognizant subject has to do is passively observe, conscious that even his particular truth, which contains the others negated in it, is not the whole. Rather, the truth is advanced because the human beings who possess it stand by it unbendingly, apply it and carry it through, act according to it, and bring it to power against the resistance of reactionary, narrow, one-sided points of view. The process of cognition includes real historical will and action just as much as it does learning from experience and intellectual comprehension. The latter cannot progress without the former.

Freed from the idealistic illusion, the dialectic transcends the contradiction between relativism and dogmatism. While it does not suppose the progress of criticism and definition at an end with its own point of view, and does not hypostatize the latter, it in no way surrenders the conviction that in the whole context to which its judgments and concepts refer, its cognitions are valid not only for particular individuals and groups but in general—that is, that the opposing theory is wrong. The dialectical logic also contains the law of contradiction; but in materialism it has completely stripped off its metaphysical character, because here a static system of propositions about reality, indeed any relation of concept and object not historically mediated, no longer appears meaningful as an idea. The dialectical logic in no way invalidates the rules of understanding. While it has as its subject the forms of movement of the advancing cognitive process, the breaking up and restructuring of fixed systems and categories also belongs in its scope along with the coordination of all intellectual forces as an impetus to human practice in general. In a time which in its lack of a way out tries to make everything into a fetish, even the abstract business of understanding, and would like thereby to replace the lost divine support, so that its philosophers rejoice in ostensibly non-temporal relations between isolated concepts and propositions as the timeless truth, the dialectical logic points out the questionable character of the interest in such "rigor" and the existence of a truth apart from it which is in no way denied by it. If it is true that a person has tuberculosis, this concept may indeed be transformed in the development of medicine or lose its meaning altogether. But whoever today with the same concept makes a contrary diagnosis, and not in terms of a higher insight which includes the determination of this man's tuberculosis, but simply denies the finding from the same medical standpoint, is wrong. The truth is also valid for him who contradicts it, ignores it, or declares it unimportant. Truth is decided not by what the individual believes and thinks of himself, not by the subject in itself, but by the relation of the propositions to reality, and when someone imagines himself the messenger of God or the rescuer of a people, the matter is not decided by him or even the majority of his fellow men, but by the relation of his assertions and acts to the objective facts of the rescue. The conditions to which those opinions point must really occur and be present in the course of events. There are at present various opposed views of society. According to one, the present wretched physical and psychological state of the masses and the critical condition of society as a whole, in the face of the developed stale of the productive apparatus and technology, necessarily follows from the continued existence of an obsolete principle of social organization. According to the others, the problem is not the principle but interference with it or carrying it too far or a matter of spiritual, religious or purely biological factors. They are not all true; only that theory is true which can grasp the historical process so deeply that it is possible to develop from it the closest approximation to the structure and tendency of social life in the various spheres of culture. It too is no exception to the rule that it is conditioned like every thought and every intellectual content, but the circumstance that it corresponds to a specific social class and is tied up with the horizon and interests of certain groups does not in any way change the fact that it is also valid for the others who deny and suppress its truth and must nevertheless eventually experience it for themselves.

This is the place to define the concept of proof which dominates the logic of many otherwise opposed tendencies. Epicurus says: "Just as we do not desire the knowledge of the physician for the sake of its technical perfection itself, but consider it good for the sake of good health, and the skill of the helmsman possesses its value because it masters the methods of correct navigation but does not find recognition for its perfection, so wisdom, which must be perceived in skill in life, would not be sought after if it did not accomplish something." The motif of result and proof as criteria of science and truth has never disappeared in the subsequent history of philosophy. Goethe's line "What fruitful is, alone is true" and the sentence "I have noticed that I regard as true that idea which is fruitful for me, fits in with the rest of my thought, and at the same time benefits me," appear to imply a pragmatic theory of cognition. Many phrases of Nietzsche suggest a similar interpretation. "The criterion of truth lies in the increase in the feeling of power. . . . What is truth? Inertia; the hypothesis with which satisfaction occurs; the least use of spiritual strength, etc." "True means 'useful for the existence of human beings.' But since we know the conditions for the existence of human beings only very imprecisely, the decision as to true and untrue can, strictly speaking, only be based on success."

With Goethe and Nietzsche, it is necessary to place such views; to which contradictions exist in their own writing, in the context of their entire thought in order to comprehend their meaning properly. But a special school of professional philosophy has grown up since the middle of the nineteenth century which places the pragmatic concept of truth in the center of its system. It has developed principally in America, where pragmatism has become the distinctive philosophical tendency through William James and subsequently John Dewey. According to this view, the truth of theories is decided by what one accomplishes with them. Their power to produce desired effects for the spiritual and physical existence of human beings is also their criterion. The furtherance of life is the meaning and measure of every science. "Our account of truth is an account of truths in the plural, of processes of leading realized *in rebus,* and having only this quality in common, that they pay." If two theories are equally well fitted to produce a particular desired effect, it is at most still necessary to ask whether more intellectual energy is required with one than with the other. The proof of the idea in its working is identical with its truth, and indeed pragmatism, especially in its most recent development, places the principal emphasis not so much on the mere confirmation of a judgment by the occurrence of the predicted factual situation, as on the promotion of human activity, liberation from all sorts of internal restraints, the growth of personality and social life.

> If *ideas, meanings, conceptions, notions, theories, systems are instrumental to an active reorganization of the given environment, to a removal of some specific trouble and perplexity, then the test of their validity and value lies in accomplishing this work. If they succeed in their office, they are reliable, sound, valid, good, true. If they fail to clear up confusion, to eliminate defects, if they increase confusion, uncertainty and evil when they are acted upon, then are they false. Confirmation, corroboration, verification lie in works, consequences. . . . That which guides us truly is true—demonstrated capacity for such guidance is precisely what is meant by truth.*

This view is closely related to positivism in France. If Bergson had not taken over the pragmatically restricted concept of science from Comte, it would be impossible to understand the need for a separate, supplementary, vitalistic metaphysics. The isolated intuition is the wishful dream of objective truth to which the acceptance of the pragmatic theory of cognition must give rise in a contemplative existence. The pragmatic concept of truth in its exclusive form, without any contradictory metaphysics to supplement it, corresponds to limitless trust in the existing world. If the goodness of every idea is given time and opportunity to come to light, if the success of the truth—even if after struggle and resistance—is in the long run certain, if the idea of a dangerous, explosive truth cannot come into the field of vision, then the present social structure is consecrated and—to the extent that it warns of harm—capable of unlimited development. In pragmatism there lies embedded the belief in the existence and advantages of free competition. Where in regard to the present it is shaken by a feeling of the dominant injustice, as in the far-reaching pragmatic philosophy of Ernst Mach, the problem of necessary change forms a personal commitment, a utopian supplement with a merely external connection to the other part, rather than a principle for the development of theory. It is therefore easy to separate that ideal from the empirio-critical way of thinking without doing it violence.

There are various elements contained in the concept of proof which are not always differentiated from one another in pragmatist literature. An opinion can be completely validated because the objective relationships whose existence it asserts are confirmed on the basis of experience and observation with unobjectionable instruments and logical conclusions; and it can moreover be of practical use to its holder or other people. Even with the first of these relationships, a need arises for intellectual organization and orientation. In this connection, James speaks of a "function of guidance, which repays the effort."

He sees that this theoretical proof, the agreement between idea and reality, the portrayal, often means nothing more than "that nothing contradictory from the quarter of that reality comes to interfere with the way in which our ideas guide us elsewhere." If the difference between this theoretical verification of truth and its practical meaning, the "furtherance of life," is nevertheless often eliminated in a given moment of history, there comes into existence that idea of a strictly parallel progress of science and mankind which was philosophically established by positivism and has become a general illusion in liberalism. But the more a given social order moves from the promotion of the creative cultural forces to their restriction, the greater the conflict between the verifiable truth and the interests bound up with this form, bringing the advocates of truth into contradiction with the existing reality. Insofar as it affects the general public rather than their own existence, individuals have reason, despite the fact that proclaiming the truth can endanger them, to sharpen it and carry it forward, because the result of their struggle and the realization of better principles of society is decisively dependent on theoretical clarity. Pragmatism overlooks the fact that the same theory can be an annihilating force for other interests in the degree to which it heightens the activity of the progressive forces and makes it more effective. The epistemological doctrine that the truth promotes life, or rather that all thought that "pays" must also be true, contains a harmonizing illusion if this theory of cognition does not belong to a whole in which the tendencies working towards a better, life-promoting situation really find expression. Separated from a particular theory of society as a whole, every theory of cognition remains formalistic and abstract. Not only expressions like life and promotion, but also terms seemingly specific to cognitive theory such as verification, confirmation, proof etc., remain vague and indefinite despite the most scrupulous definition and transference to a language of mathematical formulae, if they do not stand in relation to real history and receive their definition by being part of a comprehensive theoretical unity. The dialectical proposition that every concept possesses real validity only as a part of the theoretical whole and arrives at its real significance only when, by its interconnection with other concepts, a theoretical unity has been reached and its role in this is known, is valid here too. What is the life promoted by the ideas to which the predicate of truth is to be attributed? In what does promotion consist in the present period? Is the idea to be considered valid when the individual who has comprehended it goes down while the society, the class, the public interest for which he fights strides forward? What does confirmation mean? Is the power of the slanderers and scoundrels to serve as confirmation of the assertions with whose help they attained it? Cannot the crudest superstition, the most miserable perversion of the truth about world, society, justice, religion, and history grip whole peoples and prove most excellent for its author and his clique? In contrast, does the defeat of the forces of freedom signify the disproof of their theory?

The concept of proof also plays a role in the materialistic way of thinking. Above all, it is a weapon against every form of mysticism because of its significance in the criticism of the acceptance of a transcendent and superhuman truth which is reserved for revelation and the insight of the elect, instead of being basically accessible to experience and practice. Yet as much as theory and practice are linked to history, there is no pre-established harmony between them. What is seen as theoretically correct is not therefore simultaneously realized. Human activity is no unambiguous function of insight, but rather a process which at every moment is likewise determined by other factors and resistances. This clearly follows from the present state of the theory of history. A number of social tendencies in their reciprocal action are described

there theoretically: the agglomeration of great amounts of capital as against the declining share of the average individual in relation to the wealth of society as a whole, the increase of unemployment interrupted by ever shorter periods of a relative prosperity, the growing discrepancy between the apportionment of social labor to the various types of goods and the general needs, the diversion of productivity from constructive to destructive purposes, the sharpening of contradictions within states and among them. All these processes were shown by Marx to be necessary at a time when they could only be studied in a few advanced countries and in embryo, and the prospect of a liberalistic organization of the world still seemed excellent. But from the beginning, this view of history, now in fact confirmed, understood these developments in a particular way, that is, as tendencies which could be prevented from leading to a relapse into barbarism by the effort of people guided by this theory. This theory, confirmed by the course of history, was thought of not only as theory but as an impetus to a liberating practice, bound up with the whole impatience of threatened humanity. The testing of the unswerving faith involved in this struggle is closely connected with the confirmation of the predicted tendencies which has already taken place, but the two aspects of the verification are not identical; rather, they are mediated by the actual struggle, the solution of concrete historical problems based on the theory reinforced by experience. Continuously in this process partial views may prove incorrect, timetables be disproved, corrections become necessary; historical factors which were overlooked reveal themselves; many a vigorously defended and cherished thesis proves to be an error. Yet the connection with the theory as a whole is in no way lost in this application. Adherence to its proven teachings and to the interests and goals shaping and permeating it is the prerequisite for effective correction of errors. Unswerving loyalty to what is recognized as true is as much an impetus to theoretical progress as openness to new tasks and situations and the corresponding refocusing of ideas.

In such a process of verification the individuals and groups struggling for more rational conditions might succumb completely and human society develop retrogressively, a conceivable possibility which any view of history that has not degenerated into fatalism must formally take into account. This would refute the trust in the future which is not merely an external supplement to the theory, but belongs to it as a force shaping its concepts. But the frivolous comments of well-meaning critics who use every premature claim, every incorrect analysis of a momentary situation by the adherents of the cause of freedom as evidence against their theory as a whole, indeed against theory in general, are nevertheless unjustified. The defeats of a great cause, which run counter to the hope for its early victory, are mainly due to mistakes which do not damage the theoretical content of the conception as a whole, however far-reaching the consequences they have. The direction and content of activity, along with its success, are more closely related to their theory for the historically progressive groups than is the case with the representatives of naked power. The talk of the latter is related to their rise only as a mechanical aid, and their speech merely supplements open and secret force with craft and treachery, even when the sound of the words resembles truth. But the knowledge of the falling fighter, insofar as it reflects the structure of the present epoch and the basic possibility of a better one, is not dishonored because mankind succumbs to bombs and poison gases. The concept of verification as the criterion of truth must not be interpreted so simply. The truth is an impetus to correct practice. But whoever identifies it directly with success passes over history and makes himself an apologist for the reality dominant at any given time. Misunder-standing the irremovable difference between concept and reality, he reverts to idealism, spiritualism and mysticism.

One can find in Marxist literature formulations close to pragmatic doctrine. Max Adler writes: "Theory turns directly into practice because, as Marxism has taught us to understand, nothing can be right which does not work in practice; the social theory is nevertheless only the recapitulation of the practice itself." In regard to the identity of theory and practice, however, their difference is not to be forgotten. While it is the duty of everyone who acts responsibly to learn from setbacks in practice, these can nevertheless not destroy the proven basic structure of the theory, in terms of which they are to be understood only as setbacks. According to pragmatism, the verification of ideas and their truth merge. According to materialism, verification forms the evidence that ideas and objective reality correspond, itself a historical occurrence that can be obstructed and interrupted. This viewpoint has no place for a basically closed and unknowable truth or for the subsistence of ideas not requiring any reality, but this does not mean that the concept of a conviction which, because of a given constellation of the world is cut off from verification and success, is a priori untrue. This also holds true for historical conflicts. The possibility of a more rational form of human association has been sufficiently demonstrated to be obvious. Its full demonstration requires universal success; this depends on historical developments. The fact that meanwhile misery continues and terror spreads—the terrible force which suppresses that general demonstration—has no probative force for the contrary.

The contradictions appear plainly in Max Scheler's extensive refutation of pragmatism in postwar Germany. Scheler did not fail to recognize the relative truths of pragmatism: "So-called 'knowledge for knowledge's sake' . . . exists nowhere and cannot and also 'should' not exist, and has never existed any-where in the world. When pragmatism attributes to the positive, exact sciences a primary purpose of control, it is certainly not wrong. Rather, it is vain foolishness to consider positive science too 'good' or too 'grand' to give men freedom and power, to guide and lead the world." He also understood that the criteria for practical work in this doctrine were modeled exclusively on the inorganic natural sciences and then mechanically transferred unchanged to knowledge as a whole. Had he analyzed the concept of practice itself, it would have been evident that this is by no means as clear and simple as it seems in pragmatism, where it reduces and impoverishes truth. The meaning of the criterion is indeed not developed in experiments in natural science. Its essence consists in neatly isolating assertion, object and verification. The undefined and questionable aspect of the situation lies in the unarticulated relationship between the specific scientific activity and the life of the individuals involved and people in general, in the ostensible natural and self-evident character of the theoretical act. The unresolved and problematical aspect of its relationship to the concrete historical life with which it is obviously interwoven appears as soon as one more closely investigates the controlling categories and the choice of objects and methods. Practice as verification itself leads to a critique of positivist philosophy's hypostatization of natural science and its basic concepts. The help of metaphysics is not required. However much the problems of natural science are soluble within its boundaries and with its specific means, independent of anything else, technical knowledge is in itself abstract and acquires its full truth only in the theory which comprehends natural science in this particular historical situation as an aspect of society's development as a whole. If, in addition, practice is understood as the criterion not merely in the spe-

cial case of physical science and the technique based on it, but in the theory of history, then it becomes clear without further ado that it embraces the whole situation of society at any given moment. It takes more than attention to isolated events or groups of events, or reference to general concepts such as that of progress, to apply the criterion of practice in deciding such questions as whether one or another judgment of the contemporary authoritarian states is correct; whether they can develop only in politically backward countries with strong remnants of a landed aristocracy or whether they should be regarded as an adequate state form for the present economic phase, hence necessarily to be expected in other areas; whether this or that theory of colonial expansion applies; whether, to come to more abstract problems, the progressive technical sealing off and mathematicization of logic and economics is more suited to their present situation than sticking to the development of concepts reflecting the historical situation. For this, one needs a definite theory of society as a whole, which is itself only to be thought of in terms of particular interests and tasks with one's own point of view and activity.

Scheler does not pursue this conceptual movement in which it becomes clear that practice as an abstract criterion of truth changes into the concrete theory of society and strips off the formalism in which it is clad in the undialectical thought of the pragmatic school. He does not push this category to the consequences which contradict the system of bourgeois thought in which it is firmly frozen. Instead, he opposes to the knowledge which can be verified and criticized through practice other forms of knowledge which according to him exist along with it and unconnected to it. He fails to recognize the elevation to a philosophical absolute of mechanical natural science as the ideological reflection of bourgeois society which was able to increase reason and thereby human "power and freedom" in a high degree in the technique of material production, and yet must block the ever more urgently necessary reorganization of human relations in production in accordance with its own principle. Thus it negates and destroys the same criteria of reason, power and freedom which in cognitive theory it recognizes in isolated areas. Nor does he relate the bourgeois reality and science which he combats to their own ideas and standards and thus show both society and ideas in their one-sidedness and abstraction and thus contribute to their supersession. Instead, like Bergson and other philosophers of this period, he goes on to proclaim his own special higher forms of cognition. In the face of the deepening contradictions between use in science and use for humanity, between use for privileged groups and for society as a whole, use for facilitating production and for easing life, the criterion of utility had become a dubious principle. Scheler does not further pursue the dialectic sketched out in his work, but rather places useful science at the very bottom in his ranking of knowledge. Turning back to earlier stages of human development, he advocates in opposition to "mastery or production knowledge" the two types of "cultural knowledge" and "redemption knowledge." He declares himself in complete agreement with the "new sub-bourgeois class" in the pragmatist interpretation of "the pretentious rationalist metaphysics of the bourgeois entrepreneurs," attacking most sharply classic German idealism and the historical materialism which issued from it. For him it is nonsense "that the human spirit and the ideal factors could ever control the real factors according to a positive plan. What J. G. Fichte, Hegel ('Age of Reason') and—following them, only postponed to a future point in time—Karl Marx, with his doctrine of the 'leap into freedom,' have dreamt will remain a mere dream for all time." In contrast to this freedom, in which science would in fact have an important role to play, Scheler prophesied that the world should and could expect the rise of noble and spiritually elevated groups. If bourgeoisie and proletariat are "completely uncreative of all cultural knowledge and redemptive knowledge," this will be remedied from now on by the fact "that growing and advancing capitalism will gradually again be able to produce a whole class of purely cognitive people, and likewise of such people who have broken with the authoritative class doctrines, with bourgeois and proletarian metaphysics—that is, with the absolute mechanistic view and philosophical pragmatism. In this elite and its hands alone rests the future development of human knowledge. . . . But the future will have a new independent rise of the genuine philosophical and metaphysical spirit." In connection with the passage previously cited, Epicurus defines the goal of knowledge and wisdom as the happiness and good fortune of mankind. Scheler's view and the present heralded by him are in irreconcilable opposition to this materialistic pragmatism.

In the analysis of the concept of proof and its role in open-ended, dialectical thought, it is shown that the decision on particular truths depends on still uncompleted historical processes. While progress in theory and, practice is conditioned by the fact that, in contrast to relativistic neutrality, a definite theory corresponding to the highest available level of knowledge is adhered to and applied, this application reacts on the form of the theory and the meaning of its concepts. This is not merely a question of the correction of errors. Categories such as history, society, progress, science and so on experience a change of function in the course of time. They are not independent essences but aspects of the whole body of knowledge at a given time, which is developed by human beings in interaction with one another and with nature and is never identical with reality. This also applies to the dialectic itself. It is the sum total of the methods and laws which thought adheres to in order to copy reality as exactly as possible and to correspond as far as possible with the formal principles of real events.

What are the characteristics of dialectical thought? It relativizes every many-sided but isolated definition in the consciousness of the alteration of subject and object as well as their relationship. (What results in idealism from a postulated absolute, takes place in materialism on the basis of developing experience.) Instead of ranging attributes alongside one another, it seeks to show, by analysis of each general characteristic in respect to the particular object, that this generalization taken by itself simultaneously contradicts the object, and that in order to be properly comprehended it must be related to the contrary property and finally to the whole system of knowledge. From this follows the principle that every insight is to be regarded as true only in connection with the whole body of theory, and hence is so to be understood conceptually that in its formulation the connection with the structural principles and practical tendencies governing the theory is preserved. Bound up with this is the rule that, while maintaining unswerving fidelity to the key ideas and goals and the historical tasks of the epoch, the style of presentation should be characterized more by "as well as" than "either-or." A basic principle is the inseparability of the regressive and progressive impulses, the preserving and decomposing, the good and bad sides of particular situations in nature and human history. Instead of accepting the legitimate analyses and abstractions of professional science but turning to metaphysics and religion for an understanding of concrete reality, it tries to place the analytically achieved concepts in relation to one another and reconstruct reality through them. These and all the other characteristics of dialectical reason correspond to the form of a complicated reality, constantly changing in all its details.

Such very general intellectual laws of motion, which are abstracted from previous history and form the content of dialectical logic in general, seem relatively constant and also extremely empty. But the special dialectical forms of description of a particular subject matter correspond to its characteristics and lose their validity as forms of the theory when their bases change. The critique of political economy comprehends the present form of society. In a purely intellectual construction, the concept of value is derived from the basic general concept of the commodity. From it, Marx develops the categories of money and capital in a closed system; all the historical tendencies of this form of economy—the concentration of capital, the falling rate of profit, unemployment and crises—are placed in relation to this concept and deduced in strict succession. At least in terms of the theoretical intention, a close intellectual relationship should exist between the first and most general concept, whose abstractness is further transcended with every theoretical step, and the unique historical event, in which every thesis necessarily follows from the first postulate, the concept of free exchange of commodities. According to the theoretical intention, whose success will not be examined here, knowledge of all social processes in the economic, political and all other cultural fields will be mediated by that initial cognition. This attempt to carry the theory through to the end in the closed form of an inherently necessary succession of ideas has an objective significance. The theoretical necessity mirrors the real compulsiveness with which the production and reproduction of human life goes on in this epoch, the autonomy which the economic forces have acquired in respect to mankind, the dependence of all social groups on the self-regulation of the economic apparatus. That men cannot shape their labor according to their common will but, under a principle which sets them against one another individually and in groups, produce with their labor not security and freedom but general insecurity and dependence; that they fall into misery, war and destruction instead of using the immeasurably increased social wealth for their happiness, and are the slaves instead of the masters of their fate—this finds expression in the form of logical necessity, proper to the true theory of contemporary society. It would therefore be wrong to think that events in a future society could be deduced according to the same principles and with the same necessity as the lines of development of the present one.

The meaning of the categories will change along with the structure of the society from which they are drawn and in whose description they play a role. The concept of historical tendency loses the compulsive character that it had in the present historical period, while preserving a relation to the category of natural necessity, which may indeed be narrowed but can never be transcended completely. The concept of the individual will lose the character of an isolated monad and simultaneously the unconditionally central place it has held in the system of thought and feeling in recent centuries at the moment when individual and general goals really coincide and are supported in the whole society, when man no longer merely imagines that he embodies absolute self-determination but is in reality a member of a freely self-determining society. With the ending of the situation in which the contradiction between particular and general purposes necessarily follows from the economic structure and the idea that the individualistic principle has been fully transcended rests partly on conscious deception and partly on impotent dreaming, the concept of the I loses its function of controlling the entire relation to the world and acquires another meaning. As long as the life of society flows not from cooperative work but from the destructive competition of individuals whose relationship is essentially conducted through the exchange of commodities, the I, possession, the mine and not-mine play a fundamental role in experience, in speech and thought, in all cultural expressions, characterizing and dominating all particulars in a decisive way. In this period, the world disintegrates into I and not-I as in Fichte's transcendental philosophy, and one's own death means absolute annihilation insofar as this relationship is not alleviated by metaphysical or religious faith. Like the categories of tendency and the individual, all other social concepts will be affected by the alteration of reality. The more formal categories such as the lawful nature of society, causality, necessity, science, etc., as well as the more material ones such as value, price, profit, class, family and nation, acquire a different look in the theoretical structures which correspond to a new situation.

In traditional logic, this alteration of concepts is interpreted in such a way that the original divisions in the system of classification of a field of knowledge are made more specific by subdivisions. The general concept of tendency then includes the historical tendencies of the present society as well as the possible tendencies of a different sort in a future society. In spite of all historical changes, Aristotle's definition of the polis—composed of individuals and groups and differing not only quantitatively but qualitatively from its elements—can be absorbed into a supreme formal category of society, valid for all forms of society, and thus preserved in its general validity. For Aristotle himself, slavery belonged to this highest category, while in later conceptual systems it is only one of the subcategories of society, contrasted to other definite types. The conceptual realism which dominates Platonic and in part medieval philosophy, and whose remnants have by no means yet been surmounted in modern logic (for instance, in modern phenomenology), has the character of discursive logic. It interprets all changes as mere additions of new subtypes under the universal types, made absolute and subsumed under the metaphysical view that all change is to be understood as the incarnation or emanation of permanent ideas and essences in ever-new particulars and exemplars. Thus, the essential would always remain in the old, there would be an eternal realm of unalterable ideas, and all change would affect only the lower levels of being. Indeed, it would not be genuinely real and would only exist for the dull senses of men. Since the Hegelian system hypostatizes the categories dealt with within its framework, it still preserves something of this realism and falls into the dualism of essence and appearance which it opposed so vigorously. The given fate of historically determined individuals and the changing circumstances of present and future history become null and void in comparison with the ideas which are supposed to underlie the past. The discursive logic of "Understanding" is only limited inside Hegel's system; in the sense of a metaphysical legend, it retains its reifying power over his philosophy as a whole. The logic of the Understanding abstracts from the fact that in the face of the changed content of concepts, lumping them indiscriminately with those which formerly went under the same headings can become distortion, and a new definition, a new ordering and hierarchy of concepts can become necessary. Perhaps the category of tendency later becomes so restructured as to revolutionize its relation to the concept of systematic purpose on the one hand and that of the power of nature on the other. The concept of the state alters its relation to the categories of will, domination, force, society, etc. Such definite perspectives do not flow from observation of today's valid system of classification of social phenomena, but from the theory of historical development itself, of which the former is only an ordered, abstract

inventory. The connection between the concrete movement of thought, as it develops in constant interrelation with the life of society, and the systems organized by the Understanding, is not examined in detail by traditional logic, which relegates it to a separate discipline as the subject of the history of science or culture. It itself deals with the relations of unchanging concepts: how one passes from one to another judiciously and conclusively and how one develops from each what it contains. Traditional logic is "a science of the necessary laws of thought, without which no use of understanding and reason takes place and which are therefore the conditions under which alone understanding can and should be congruous with itself—the necessary laws and prerequisites of its correct use." Their function is "to make clear concepts intelligible." This proceeds analytically, drawing out of the concept what is in it. The concept itself "remains the same; only the form is changed. . . . Just as nothing is added to a map itself when it is illuminated, so the lighting up of a concept by the analysis of its characteristics does not expand the concept itself in the least." Traditional logic has nothing to do with the alteration of the "map" and the construction of new systems of classification. But if concepts are used without being strictly tied in to the existing system of reference, in which all previous discoveries of the branch concerned have been arranged, if they are used without that correct reading of the "map" which is required by the laws of logic, every intellectual outline remains blurred, or rather meaningless. The accurate description of the object results from the methodical collaboration of all cognitive forces in the theoretical construction. Aside from the table of contents for this content, which it does not itself produce, "the tabular understanding" also gives conceptual material. From time to time "the empirical sciences," investigation and analysis, "have contradicted the material" of the dialectical description "in finding general uniformities, classifications, and laws." The real significance of this work, the cognitive value of understanding, rests on the fact that reality knows not only constant change but also relatively static structures. Because development proceeds not gradually but in leaps, there are between these junctures, leaps and revolutions periods in which the tensions and contradictions trying to break through appear as elements of a relatively closed and fixed totality, until the particular form of being turns into another. This determinate and organized state is therefore a necessary condition of truth but not its real form, movement and progress. Thus, traditional logic is inadequate for, and comprehends only individual aspects of, the historically conditioned alteration of the fundamental categories and every thought process about the subject matter. Since a concept plays a determinate role in the dialectical construction of an event, it becomes a non-autonomous aspect of a conceptual whole which has other qualities than the sum of all the concepts included in it. This whole, the construction of the particular object, can indeed only come into existence in a way appropriate to the existing knowledge if the concepts are interpreted in the sense that belongs to them in the systems of the individual sciences, in the systematic inventory of scientifically based definitions, insofar as it is a question of concepts for which special branches of science exist. In *Capital*, Marx introduces the basic concepts of classical English political economy—value, price, labor-time etc.—in accordance with their precise definitions. All the most progressive definitions drawn from scientific practice at that time are employed. Nevertheless, these categories acquire new functions in the course of the presentation. They contribute to a theoretical whole, the character of which contradicts the static views in connection with which they came into being, in particular their uncritical use in isola-

tion. Materialist economics as a whole is placed in opposition to the classical system, yet individual concepts are taken over. The dialectical forms of the movement of thought show themselves to be the same as those of reality. A hydrogen atom observed in isolation has its specific characteristics, acquires new ones in molecular combination with other elements, and displays the old ones again as soon as it is freed from the combination. Concepts behave in the same way; considered individually, they preserve their definitions, while in combination they become aspects of new units of meaning. The movement of reality is mirrored in the "fluidity" of concepts.

The open-ended materialistic dialectic does not regard the "rational" as completed at any point in history and does not expect to bring about the resolution of contradictions and tensions, the end of the historic dynamic, by the full development of mere ideas and their simple consequences. It lacks the aspect of the idealistic dialectic which Hegel described as "speculative" and at the same time as "mystical," namely, the idea of knowing the ostensibly unconditioned and thereby being oneself unconditioned. It does not hypostatize any such universal system of categories. To attain the "positively rational," it does not suffice to resolve and transcend contradictions in thought. It requires the historical struggle whose guiding ideas and theoretical prerequisites are indeed given in the consciousness of the combatants. But the outcome cannot be predicted on a purely theoretical basis. It will be determined, not by any firmly outlined unity such as the "course of history," the principles of which could be established indivisibly for all time, but by human beings interacting with one another and with nature, who enter into new relationships and structures and thereby change themselves. The resolution of contradictions in subjective thought and the overcoming of objective antagonisms can be closely intertwined, but they are in no way identical. In a particular historical period, a free society in the sense of the free development of the individual and in the sense of free enterprise on the basis of inequality will be conceptually and actually full of contradictions. The resolution in terms of ideas occurs through the concept of a differentiated higher form of freedom. It has a decisive voice in the real overcoming, but in no way coincides with it and predicts the future only abstractly and inexactly. Since the logic of the open-ended dialectic allows for the possibility that change will affect the entire present content of the categories, without therefore considering the theory formed from it as any less true, it corresponds exactly to the Hegelian conception of the difference between dialectic and understanding without overlaying it with a new dogmatism. "The intelligible exists in concepts in their fixed definition and differentiation from others; the *dialectical* shows them in their change and disintegration." To be sure, the first is immanent in the second; without the definition and organization of concepts, without understanding, there is no thought and also no dialectic. But the understanding becomes metaphysical as soon as it absolutizes its function of preserving and expanding existing knowledge, of confirming, organizing and drawing conclusions from it, or the results of that function as the existence and progress of truth. The revolutionizing, disintegration and restructuring of knowledge, its changing relation to reality, its changes of function resulting from its intertwinement with history, fall outside the thought processes which traditional logic, whose theme is understanding, comprehends. Taken by itself, it leads to the erroneous concept of a detached thought with fixed, eternal and autonomous results. Nietzsche said that a great truth "wants to be criticized, not worshipped." This is valid for truth in general. He might have added that criticism includes not only the negative and skeptical impulse but also the inner independence not

to let the truth fall but to remain firm in its application even if it may sometime pass away. In the individual, the process of cognition includes not only intelligence but also character; for a group, not merely adaptation to changing reality but the strength to declare and put into practice its own views and ideas.

The initially discussed division in the bourgeois spirit with regard to truth, in contrast to dialectical thought, finds especially clear expression in the attitude toward religion. In the face of the primitive materialism which dominates economic life, it has become more and more internalized. The practice of general competition which characterizes contemporary reality was pitiless from the beginning, and with the exception of a few periods, has become increasingly inhuman. Its means and consequences, which at particular historical moments have led to domination by small economic groups, the abandonment of power to the most culturally backward elements of society, and the extermination of minorities, notoriously contradict the basic teachings of Christianity. In a period in which, despite great resistance, reading and writing had to become common skills for economic reasons, and the contents of the Bible could not remain a permanent secret from the masses, it had long been inevitable that the opposing principle of Christianity would be openly sacrificed to reality, and the vulgar positivism of bare facts along with the worship of success, immanent in this life-style, propagated as the exclusive and highest truth. But the gross contradiction that existed was really understood within the bourgeoisie only by religious outsiders such as Kierkegaard and Tolstoi. The monistic propaganda of Strauss and Haeckel, who proclaimed it on the basis of scientific research, saw only the difference which it implied between natural science by itself and revelation and misunderstood both the spirit of the Gospels and historical reality. These materialists on the basis of natural science had to remain sectarians, for religion was indispensable for the social groups to which they belonged. The predominant intellectual attitude in recent centuries was not that of exposing the split. Instead, religion was so robbed of any clear and definite content, formalized, adapted, spiritualized, relegated to the innermost subjectivity, that it was compatible with every activity and every public practice that existed in this atheistic reality.

Since individuals began to think more independently, that is, since the rise of the new economic order, philosophy in all fields has ever more clearly fulfilled the function of erasing the contradiction between the dominant way of life and Christian or Christian-oriented theoretical and practical doctrines and ideas. The reason for this coincides with the root of bourgeois dogmatism in general. The isolated individual, who is simultaneously regarded as free and responsible, is in the present epoch necessarily dominated by anxiety and uncertainty. In addition to this inner need, which is directly grounded in the atomistic principles of the existing order, the external concern for social peace has led to great efforts to gloss over the irreconcilability of modern science and the way people conduct their lives with the religious views on the origin and structure of the world as well as the ideas of love for one's neighbor, justice and the goodness of God. Troeltsch, a typical philosopher of religion in prewar Germany, openly states what he fears:

> To anyone even moderately acquainted with human beings, it will be inconceivable that divine authority could ever disappear without damage to the moral law, that the generally coarse-thinking average man could do without this supplement to the motivation of morality. The abstraction of a self-validating law will be forever unrealizable for him; in connection with law, he will always have to

think of the lawgiver and watcher. He may think of this a bit coarsely, but not so irrationally. . . . Where atheistic morality has undone divine authority among the masses, experience shows that there is little sense of that law left. A fierce hatred of all authority and an unbounded unchaining of selfishness as the most obvious thing in the world has been, with few exceptions, the easily comprehensible logical consequence.

A social situation in which there would be no "watcher," either in the form of a transcendent being or "a self-validating law," to hold the "unbounded" selfishness of the masses in check, is something he cannot conceive of. Dogmatic adherence to the inherited conceptual world seems to him a self-evident proposition, a *thema probandum.* Nevertheless, he also sees

> that the Protestant-confessional axiom must be self-revised and more freely interpreted; that its accomplishments must find a broader, more general basis and make themselves far more independent of immediate clerical reality; that its style must leave room for detailed historical research and the definitive results of natural science, and be constantly prepared for new revisions on the basis of this work. Indeed, the possibility exists that eventually Christianity itself will cease to be axiomatic.

The axioms to which earlier liberal theology could reach back have meanwhile been overturned. "Kant and Schleiermacher, Goethe and Hegel, still lived under the influence of an axiomatic validation which no longer exists." He therefore recommends resorting to Kant's critical philosophy "which undertakes to discover the ultimate presuppositions in the organization of consciousness instead of metaphysics." He seeks refuge in a "critique of religious consciousness" and hopes

> *to find a firm footing through a general theory of religion and its historical development. But this theory itself would have to be rooted in a transcendental theory of consciousness and to answer, from this ultimate basis of all scientific thinking, this ultimate and correct presupposition, two questions: the question of the justification of religion in general, and that of the difference in value between its historical forms. Theology is thereby referred to the philosophy of religion. On this basis only will it be able so to construe the essence and validity of Christianity as to satisfy the modern spirit of taking nothing for granted. The ultimate presuppositions lie in the philosophy of transcendentalism. . . .*

According to this, the "justification of religion in general" and even the advantages of Christianity are still the question, and the whole uncertainty, the relativistic readiness for concessions not to the selfishness of the masses but to ostensibly non-axiomatic science, becomes clear. Only one thing is preserved at any cost: "In all change there must be a permanent truth. This is a requirement of that ideal faith, to renounce which would be to renounce the meaning of the world." If this so necessary faith only remains attached to an eternal meaning, one can come to terms with idealistic philosophy, Judaism, Islam, Confucianism, Brahmin and Buddhist ideas of salvation.

This ambiguous relationship to religion characterizes the whole period, and only finds a particularly clear ideological expression in phenomena like Troeltsch. It is an aspect of the objective dishonesty which, despite the good conscience of the participants, dominated the spiritual atmosphere. If one looks closely at previous history, the fact that in many areas of public discussion the crude and obvious lie is now treated with honor represents no incomprehensible change. The situation of the bourgeoisie has resulted in the setting aside of intellectual development in moral and religious questions and the keeping in twilight of central areas, as if by tacit agreement. The religious philosophy of the middle ages outlines the spiritual horizon which corresponded to society at the time. Its most important results therefore form historical evidence of obvious greatness. Since the irreligion immanent in modern natural science and technology, these specifically bourgeois achievements, has found no corresponding place in the general consciousness, and the conflicts that this involves have not been arbitrated, official spirituality is characterized by hypocrisy and indulgence toward particular forms of error and injustice, and this has eventually spread over the cultural life of entire peoples. The only great spirit who, in the face of the gross thickening of this fog which has taken place since the middle of the last century, has achieved the freedom from illusion and the comprehensive view which are possible from the standpoint of the big bourgeoisie, is Nietzsche. It must indeed have escaped him that the intellectual honesty with which he was concerned did not fit in with this social standpoint. The reason for the foulness against which he fought lies neither in individual nor national character, but in the structure of society as a whole, which includes both. Since as a true bourgeois philosopher he made psychology, even if the most profound that exists today, the fundamental science of history, he misunderstood the origin of spiritual decay and the way out, and the fate which befell his own work was therefore inevitable. ("Who among my friends would have seen more in it than an impermissible presumption, completely indifferent to happiness?")

The philosophically mediated dishonesty in questions of religion cannot be eliminated by psychological or other explanations. Whereas Nietzsche makes the religious question and Christian morality negatively central and thereby makes an ideologue of himself, this aspect of the existing situation also can only be eliminated by transcending it through higher forms of society. In dialectical thought, religious phenomena too are related to knowledge as a whole and judged at any given time in connection with the analysis of the whole historical situation. As important as it is to see the incompatibility of the religious content with advanced knowledge, the present shows that making religious questions central to the whole cultural problem can be foolish. One can find more penetrating analysis of bourgeois society in the literature of the Catholic counterrevolution in France, in Bonald and de Maistre and the writings of the Catholic royalist Balzac, than in the critics of religion in Germany at the same period. The devout Victor Hugo and Tolstoi have more nobly depicted and more vigorously fought the horrors of existing conditions than the enlightened Gutzkow and Friedrich Theodor Vischer. In the practical questions of daily life, efforts guided by dialectical thought can lead to temporary collaboration with religiously motivated groups and tendencies and radical opposition to anti-religious ones. The complex of historical tasks which is decisive for an illusion-free and progressive attitude today does not divide people primarily on the basis of their religious preference. Groups and individuals may be characterized more quickly today on the basis of their particular interest (theoretically explicable, to be sure) or lack of interest in just conditions which promote the free development of human beings, in the abolition of conditions of oppression which are dangerous to and unworthy of mankind, than by their relation to religion. It follows from the differing cultural levels of social groups, the miserable state of education on social problems, and other factors, that religion can mean altogether different things for different classes and different ways of life. It requires not merely experience and theoretical education but a particular fate in society to avoid either inflating thought into the creation of idols or devaluing it as the sum total of mere illusions, making it an absolute lawgiver and unambiguous guide for action, or separating it from the practical goals and tasks with which it interacts. It is a utopian illusion to expect that the strength to live with the sober truth will become general until the causes of untruth are removed.

On Science and Phenomenology

Written at a time when, following Thomas Kuhn's The Structure of Scientific Revolutions, *the philosophy of science was rediscovering the historical contingency of its paradigms, Marcuse here focuses on the central presuppositions of the category of "reason." Reason had not always been defined as a mere tool to devise efficient means to implement values, which themselves remain beyond rational discussion and challenge. Rather, it was once the distinguishing mark of reason to formulate, examine, implement and modify the ends on the basis of emerging historical possibilities. It was this usurpation of substantive reason, its reduction to paradigmatic rules of deductive inference that the critical theorists consistently fought. Intended as a critique of a position that has recently again received attention, the essay unfolds the historical origins and manifestations of the concept of reason, from the days of reason as the basis for transforming the world which gave rise to science to the point where the structuring ends and objectives have been exiled from the self-awareness of science.*

The Crisis of European Science and Transcendental Phenomenology is Husserl's last work. Written in the thirties, the first part was published in 1936, the second part only after Husserl's death.

I would like to indicate first where I see the general historical locus of this work. It seems to me that we have to place it into the context of the radical reexamination of the Western concept of Reason, of Western rationality that begins in the last decades of the nineteenth century and to which so essentially different thinkers as Bergson, Dilthey, Max Weber . . . Spengler, Piaget and Bachelard belong: All of them have in common this questioning of the very idea which has guided Western thought since its Greek origins, i.e., the rationality typical of the occident. It seems to me that Husserl is the last in this group, and in a certain sense, (which may strike you as strange) the most radical of these re-examiners. In Husserl, it is modern science itself, this most sacrosanct child of Western rationality, that is questioned. In this reexamination, modern science appears as the end of a fateful development which begins with Greek thought, that is, with the origins of Western thought it-self—as the "end" of this development in the twofold sense of termination and of fulfilling the *telos,* the purpose, the objective of this thought.

According to Husserl, science—modern science, Galilean as well as post-Galilean—originates in the Greek idea of knowledge and truth and comes to rest in a scientific rational-ity in which truth and validity contain in themselves illusion and repression. Before I try to present Husserl's radical thesis, I have to stress that it is not the result of a sociological analysis or of a sociology of knowledge. It is precisely the fascinating aspect of Husserl's work that it is a *philosophical* analysis within the academic framework of intellectual his-tory, even within the academic division of la-bor. Husserl emphasizes philosophy as *Beruf,* as calling, and that philosophy is done in the *Berufszeit,* that is to say, in the time reserved, in the academic division, for such investiga-tions. Husserl adds (and this is important: I come back to it at the end) that the calling of the philosopher is a unique calling because (and I quote him)

> *this calling is linked with the "possibility of a radical transformation of human-ity," and not only a radical transforma-tion of humanity but also a "liberation," and this possibility makes the calling of the philosopher unique within the divi-sion of labor.*

In the course of such a philosophical un-dertaking (philosophical also in the sense of a discipline!), in the course of its own inner de-velopment, Husserl's analysis transcends itself, or rather it, descends from the pure theoretical to the impure pre-theoretical, practical dimen-sion. Better—the pure theoretical analysis discovers its own internal impurity, but only to return from this impure sphere to the still pure theoretical dimension of transcendental phe-nomenology as constituent of the practical,

pre-theoretical dimension, the *Lebenswelt.* (I use the German term *Lebenswelt.* The literal translation "life-world" is too large and too vague in this context; what Husserl means is our own empirical day-to-day world as it is given in immediate experience, practical and other—the world of life and death, in our em-pirical reality. So I will use either *Lebenswelt* or "empirical reality").

I will now devote some time to presenting Husserl's own thesis (the work is not fully translated; we only have Gurwitsch's excellent abstract of it), but I shall focus it in such a way that the critical problems stand out. Husserl begins with a very brief description of what he considers the Greek concept of Reason, namely the idea of human being as self-deter-mination and determination of its world by virtue of man's intellectual faculties, the con-cept of Reason, according to which man's in-tellectual faculties are at the same time capable of determining his own life and of determin-ing, defining and changing the universe. This conception presupposes that the universe it-self which is thus rationally comprehended is in its very structure a rational system and therefore accessible to knowledge and change on the grounds of man's own rational knowl-edge. In other words, Reason for the Greeks is objective and subjective at one and the same time, and on this basis. Reason is the subjec-tive as well as objective instrument for chang-ing the world in accord with man's rational faculties and ends. But in this process, Reason itself as *theoria* is and remains the basis of the transformation of the world. Philosophy is thus established as *science,* and as the first, most excellent and general science, which must give direction and the end to all other sciences.

What are the implications of this original concept of Reason? First, it implies a supra-factual, supra-temporal validity of Reason, so that the really real as discovered and defined by Reason is rational as *against* the immediately given fact. Reason establishes an authority and reality which is in this way antagonistic to the immediately given facts. Second, true being is ideational being (a conclusion from the first implication), not being as we experience it immediately in the flux of our empirical, practical world. Thus "Platonism" is the basis of all scientific knowledge. Thirdly, objectivity is necessarily correlated with subjectivity, again the subjective as well as objective structure of Reason. Husserl here gives a formulation which, in an entirely different context, recaptures the very question and thesis with which Western philosophy began, namely, the final identity of Being and Reason. He says:

> *Can Being and Reason be separated if cognitive Reason determines (the essence of being?)*

So we find at the very beginning and at the late stage of western philosophy this almost literal identity in the formulation of the basic problem, the mysterious union and even identity of Reason and Being, Knowing and Being. Now this concept of Reason, which is theoretical and practical Reason in one, is understood by Husserl as a *project*. I use the term here as it was elaborated in the philosophy of Sartre "project" in the sense that this idea of rationality and its application is a specific way of experiencing, interpreting, organizing and changing the world, a specific historical project among other possible ones, not the only, necessary project. This project, according to Husserl, came to fulfillment with the foundation of modern science, namely, in Galileo's mathematization of nature. Galileo's mathematization of nature established that purely rational, ideational system which was the dream of all Platonism; Galileo established the ideational world mathematically as the true reality, substituting this scientific universe for the only given reality, namely, our empirical *Lebenswelt.* But the very fulfillment

of this project was also its collapse, according to Husserl. For this scientific rationality, this idea of Reason and its application, proved successful only in the positive sciences and in the technological conquest of Nature, while the original foundation of this entire science, that which originally was supposed to constitute the very structure, content and end of science, namely, philosophy, remained an impotent, abstract, meaningless metaphysical sphere of knowledge and continued in this impotent form a hopeless academic existence which, in addition, was more and more dissolved into psychology. Thus separated from the basic philosophy which, according to the original ideas of Reason, was supposed to give the ends, the objectives, the meaning of science, separated from this basic philosophy which was supposed to provide the truly universal concepts, Reason was at the same time divorced—and this is decisive for Husserl—from that rational *humanitas* envisaged in the original philosophical project. Scientific, technological rationality became reason *kath' exochen.* Divorced from the validating "ends" set by philosophy, the rationale set by science and the rationale of its development and progress became that of the *Lebenswelt* itself, in which and for which this science developed. Instead of rationally transcending the *Lebenswelt,* science comprehended, expressed and extended the specific rationale of the *Lebenswelt,* namely, the ever more effective mastery of the environment *(Herrschaft über die praktische Umwelt),* including the ever more effective mastery of man. But that was not the inherent *telos* of science, which was first and foremost, and not only in a chronological sense, the *telos* defined by the empirical reality in which science developed. Thus, theoretical Reason, pure Reason, without losing its scientific character as theory, becomes practical Reason. Theory, by virtue of its internal dynamic rather than on external grounds, becomes a specific, historical practice. But (and this is decisive for Husserl and the justification of his own subsequent phenomenological reduction) this entire development, this entire transformation of Reason, this essential, structural, internal commitment of pure Reason, pure theory and pure science to the empirical reality in which they originated, this entire transformation *remains hidden to science itself,* hidden and unquestioned. The new science does not elucidate the conditions and the limits of its evidence, validity and method; it does not elucidate its inherent historical denominator. It remains unaware of its own foundation, and it is therefore unable to recognize its servitude, unable to free itself from the ends set and given to science by the pre-given empirical reality. I should like to stress again, because these formulations can be easily misunderstood, that it is not a sociological relation which is here established between an empirical reality and the pure science which develops in this empirical reality. Husserl's concept goes much farther. He maintains that the empirical reality is the framework and dimension in which the pure scientific concepts develop. In other words, the empirical reality constitutes, in a specific sense, the very concepts which science believes are pure theoretical concepts.

Before I go on with Husserl's interpretation of this development, I would like to reformulate and to extend his thesis in a way which may bring out its provocative implications. What happens in the developing relation between science and the empirical reality is the abrogation of the transcendence of Reason. Reason loses its philosophical power and its scientific right to define and project ideas and modes of Being beyond and against those established by the prevailing reality. I say "beyond" the empirical reality, not in any metaphysical but in a historical sense, namely, in the sense of projecting essentially different, historical alternatives.

Now back to Husserl's interpretation.

The new science (by which he understands mainly Galilean science) establishes a rational "infinite" universe of Being (I follow his words here literally), systematically organized and defined by science itself. Within this universe, every object becomes accessible to knowledge, not incidentally, in its contingent, particular occurrence, but necessarily and in its very essence. Thus, it becomes object of scientific knowledge, not as this individual object but as exemplification of general objectivity (the falling feather as *res extensa* in motion). That is to say, the concrete and particular object, the Aristotelian totality is no longer the *Wesen,* the essence; Platonism supersedes Aristotelianism, not only in physics, but in the very concept of scientific rationality. And concomitant with this de-individualization, which is the pre-requisite for the quantification of the scientific universe, is the familiar reduction of secondary to primary qualities, devaluation of the inexorably individual sense experience as nonrational.

As a result of this twofold process, reality is now idealized into a "mathematical manifold": everything which is mathematically demonstrated with the evidence of universal validity as a pure form (*reine Gestalt*) now belongs to the true reality of nature. But (and here is the great gap which separates the new science from its classical original) in contrast to the ideational forms of Plato, the ideational forms of mathematical physics are freed from any substantive connection with other than mathematical ends. The ideational realm of Galilean science no longer includes the moral, esthetic, political Forms, the *Ideas* of Plato. And separated from this realm, science develops now as an "absolute" in the literal sense no matter how relative within its own realm it may be, absolved from its own, pre-scientific and nonscientific conditions and foundations. According to Husserl, the absolute evidence of mathematics (which as we shall see we question) was for Galileo so self-evident that he never asked for the actual foundation of its validity, for the validating ground of this evidence, and of its extension to the whole of nature. Thus, the validation of the new science remained in the dark; its own basis never became the theme of scientific inquiry; science, contained an unmastered, unscientific foundation. This is of the utmost importance for *the validity of science* itself, because the relation between science and the pre-scientific empirical reality is for Husserl not an external one but one which affects the very structure and meaning of the scientific concepts themselves.

Now according to Husserl, where is this pre-scientific validating ground of mathematical science? It is originally in geometry as the art of measuring (*Messkunst*) with its specific means and possibilities. This art of measuring in the empirical reality promised and indeed achieved the progressive calculability of nature, subjecting nature to the ever more exact "foresight" in mastering and using nature. (Foresight—*Voraussicht*, perhaps better translated as projection and valid, rational anticipation). Foresight and anticipation, rational anticipation can then guide the practical orientation in and the transformation of the empirical *Lebenswelt*, without however (and this is decisive) setting or defining or changing the goals and ends of this transformation. Geometry can and does furnish (and the same holds true for the extension of geometry, mathematics) the methods and ever more exact, ever more calculable approaches for the transformation and extension of the established *Lebenswelt*, but remains forever incapable of defining, anticipating or changing, by its own concepts, the ends and objectives of this transformation. In its method and concepts, the new science is essentially non-transcendent. This is what I consider as Husserl's key sen-

tence: Science "leaves the *Lebenswelt* in its essential structure in its own concrete causality unchanged."

As to the interpretation of this paradoxical and provocative thesis (so obviously paradoxical since we are used to seeing in science one of the most dynamic forces in the world): In my view, what is at stake is not the more or less external relation between science and society, but the internal conceptual structure of science itself, its pure theory and method which Husserl now reveals in their essential historicity (*Geschichtlichkeit*), in their commitment to the specific historical project in which they originated. Pure science retains, *aufgehoben* (to use Hegel's term now), the practice out of which it arose, and it contains the ends and values established by this practice. The empirical reality thus performs the *sinngebende Leistung* (constituent act): It is constitutive of scientific truth and validity. Science is *Aufhebung der Lebenswelt*

(1) inasmuch as science cancels the data and truth of immediate experience,
(2) inasmuch as science preserves the data and truth of experience, but
(3) preserves them in a higher form, namely in the ideational, idealized form of universal validity.

And this threefold process takes place in the scientific abstraction. The quantified ideational forms are abstracted from the concrete qualities of the empirical reality, but the latter remains operative in the very concepts and in the direction in which the scientific abstraction moves.

In this way, the pre-scientific, pregiven empirical reality enters the scientific enterprise itself and makes it a specific project within the pre-established general project of the empirical reality. However, the abstract, ideational, mathematical form into which science transforms the empirical conceals this historical relation:

> The Ideenkleid *(the ideational veil) of mathematics and mathematical physics represents and [at the same time] disguises the empirical reality and leads us to take for True Being that which is only a method.*

This is perhaps the most effective and lasting mystification in the history of Western thought! What is actually only one method appears as the true reality, but a reality with a *telos* of its own. The mathematical ideation, with all its exactness, calculability, foresight, leaves a void *(Leerstelle)* because the objectives and ends of this calculability and anticipation are not scientifically determined. This void can thus be filled by whatever specific end the empirical reality provides, the only condition being that it is within the range of scientific method. This is the famous neutrality of pure science which here reveals itself as an illusion, because the neutrality disguises, in the mathematical-ideational form, the essential relation to the pregiven empirical reality.

In Husserl's terms: The objective a priori of science itself stands under a hidden empirical a priori, the so-called *lebensweltliche* a priori. Moreover, as long as this empirical a priori remains hidden and unexamined, scientific rationality itself contains its inner and own irrational core which it cannot master. According to Husserl, modern science thus operates like a machine which everyone can learn to handle without necessarily understanding the inner necessity and possibility of its operation. In other words, pure science has an inherently instrumental character prior to all specific application; the Logos of pure science is technology and is thus essentially dependent on external ends. This introduces the irrational into science, and science cannot overcome its irrationality as long as it remains hidden from science. In Husserl's words: Rea-

son is Reason only as manifest Reason *(Offenbare Vernunft)*, and Reason "knows itself as Reason only if it has become manifest." Inasmuch as Reason remains non-manifest in science, scientific rationality is not yet the full rationality of science. How can Reason become conscious of itself?

Husserl proposes to break the mystification inherent in modern science by a phenomenological analysis which is in a literal sense a *therapeutic* method. Therapeutic in the sense that it is to get behind the mystifying concepts and methods of science and to uncover the constitutive *lebensweltliche* a priori under which all scientific a priori stands. This is to Husserl first a methodological problem. The pregiven empirical reality as a whole must become the object of the philosophical analysis, otherwise the a priori prior to the scientific a priori could never come to light. But obviously philosophy itself is part of this empirical reality and philosophy itself stands under the a priori of the empirical reality. The circle is to be broken by a dual phenomenological reduction (suspension, *epoche*): First the suspension of the objective a priori; the suspension of scientific truth and validity; secondly the suspension of the *lebensweltliche* a priori, of the *doxa* and its validity.

Now what do we retain, what remains as the residuum of this twofold suspension? In the first *epoche*, "we put in brackets" (that is to say, we do not deny but simply suspend judgment on) scientific truth and scientific validity. What remains as the residuum is (a) the entire general structure of the empirical reality, the infinite manifold of things in time and space, the orta, and (b) the world itself in which all these things necessarily appear—the world as the universal, unsurpassable horizon of all particular objects. But this first *epoche* is not sufficient: it cannot do what it is supposed to do, namely, break through the mystification and uncover the ultimate foundation of scientific truth. It cannot do this because with this first "bracketing" we are still on the basis (*auf dem Boden*) of the empirical reality within the "natural position" of our day-to-day experience. A second *epoche* is necessary which "at one stroke" leads to a total alteration of the "natural position" of experience, to the suspension of the natural validation of everything that we naturally accept as valid in our immediate experience. Once we have suspended these judgments too, we reflect no longer on the pregiven world and the particular objects appearing in it, but on *how* these objects appear, on the *modes* in which this entire world is given to us. The residuum of this *epoche* is thus the world as correlate of a totality of *modes of consciousness*, as a "synthetic totality." What we have now as residuum is the *transcendental* subjectivity, and to this transcendental subjectivity the world is now given as phenomenon of and for an absolute subjectivity. This transcendental subjectivity is no longer any particular or individual or group subjectivity. It is "absolute" because whatever object or object-relation may appear, now appears as necessarily constituted in specific acts of synthesis which inseparably link objectivity and subjectivity. In other words, we have now what we might call the absolute original experience: the experience which is at the origin of and is constitutive of any possible objectivity that can ever become the object of scientific and of any other thought. The phenomenological reduction has now opened the dimension in which the original and most general structure of all objectivity is constituted.

I shall add only a few critical remarks. The breakthrough to the transcendental subjectivity is supposed to be the road to uncover the foundation on which all scientific validity rests. I ask the question: can the reductive phenomenological analysis ever attain its goal, namely, to go behind scientific, and pre-scientific, validity and mystification? I shall offer three suggestions.

First: The phenomenological analysis is confronted with the fact of reification (Husserl does not use this term). Reification is a form which is usually not examined. Scientific as well as pre-scientific experience are false, incomplete inasmuch as they experience as *objective* (material or ideational) what in reality is subject-object, objectivation of subjectivity. In founding the analysis on the constitutive subject-object correlation, Husserl's dual *epoche* does go behind the reification—but so does all transcendental idealism. Thus far we are, in my view, in no way beyond Kant. I know Husserl's own interpretation of the difference between phenomenology and Kant; I think that in the context of my criticism this difference is not very relevant. My point is that the phenomenological breakthrough stops short of the *actual* constituent subjectivity. Husserl transcends the objective a priori of science in the first *epoche* and the empirical a priori in the second *epoche*. He thus creates a conceptual metalanguage for the critical analysis of the empirical reality. But my question is does this conceptual metalanguage really come to grips with the constituent subjectivity? I think not.

Second: The phenomenological reduction arrives at a subjectivity which constitutes only the most general forms of objectivity, for example, the general form of appearing as object, changing as object, being related to other objects. But does this subjectivity give us "manifest Reason" behind the disguising Reason, the validation of scientific truth? Can this transcendental subjectivity ever explain—and solve—the crisis of European science? Husserl's transcendental subjectivity is again a pure cognitive subjectivity. One does not have to be a Marxist in order to insist that the empirical reality is constituted by the subject of thought *and* of *action*, theory and practice. Husserl recognizes the historical subjects in its *sinngebende Leistung*; but then, by suspending, bracketing it, the phenomenological analysis creates its own a priori, its own ideation, and its own ideological veil. Pure philosophy now replaces pure science as the ultimate cognitive lawgiver, establishing objectivity. This is the *hubris* inherent in all critical transcendentalism which in turn must be cancelled. Husserl himself seems to have been aware of this *hubris*. He speaks of the philosopher as *"urquellend fungierende Subjektivität"*: the philosopher functions as the primordial source of what can rationally be claimed as objective reality.

I come to the conclusion and leave it as a question. Husserl recognizes the fetishism of scientific universality and rationality by uncovering the specific historical-practical foundations of pure science. He sees that pure science is in its very structure technological—at least potentially applied science. The scientific method itself remains dependent on a specific *Lebenswelt*. This is the hidden irrational element in scientific rationality. Husserl finds the reason for this dependence in the loss of the philosophical dimension, which was originally the basic dimension of science. Classical philosophy defined the method and function of science in terms of an idea of Reason which claimed higher truth and validity than those embodied in, and established by, the given empirical reality. This validating idea of Reason was that of the *telos* of man as man, the realization of *humanitas*. According to Husserl, the humanistic structure of Reason collapses with the release of science from this philosophical foundation. This would imply that humanism becomes an ideology at the very time when modern humanism is born. In other words, the birth hour of humanism itself would be the degradation of humanism to a mere ideology. Apparently there must be something wrong with this formulation. The fact remains that humanism is still today an ideology, a higher value which little affects the inhuman character of reality. The question with which I would like to conclude is this: Is philosophy entirely innocent of this development, or does it perhaps share the *hubris* of science? Does it share the reluctance to examine its own real foundation and function and is it therefore equally guilty of failing in the task of *Theoria*, of Reason—to promote the realization of *humanitas*?

Some Social Implications of Modern Technology

Herbert Marcuse

First published in Studies in Philosophy and Social Sciences Vol. IX (1941), the article is a large-scale investigation of that "fetish" of technique, or technical efficiency, which, after 1941, represented for critical theory, especially for Marcuse, the key ideological replacement of the commodity fetish under modern industrialized authoritarian states. With respect to Marcuse's better-known later position, the essay incorporates two anomalous attitudes: the ultimate political neutrality of technique as such (even the existing technologies) and the possibility of progressive utilization of techniques (even bureaucratic ones) through democratic reform. Nevertheless, Marcuse, in an extremely clear fashion, specifies all those dimensions of technical reason open to repressive and ideological utilization in the hands of authoritarian regimes.

In this article, technology is taken as a social process in which technics proper (that is, the technical apparatus of industry, transportation, communication) is but a partial factor. We do not ask for the influence or effect of technology on the human individuals. For they are themselves an integral part and factor of technology, not only as the men who invent or attend to machinery but also as the social groups which direct its application and utilization. Technology, as a mode of production, as the totality of instruments, devices and contrivances which characterize the machine age is thus at the same time a mode of organizing and perpetuating (or changing) social relationships, a manifestation of prevalent thought and behavior patterns, an instrument for control and domination.

Technics by itself can promote authoritarianism as well as liberty, scarcity as well as abundance, the extension as well as the abolition of toil. National Socialism is a striking example of the ways in which a highly rationalized and mechanized economy with the utmost efficiency in production can operate in the interest of totalitarian oppression and continued scarcity. The Third Reich is indeed a form of "technocracy": the technical considerations of imperialistic efficiency and rationality supersede the traditional standards of profitability and general welfare. In National Socialist Germany, the reign of terror is sustained not only by brute force which is foreign to technology but also by the ingenious manipulation of the power inherent in technology: the intensification of labor, propaganda, the training of youths and workers, the organization of the governmental, industrial and party bureaucracy—all of which constitute the daily implements of terror—follow the lines of greatest technological efficiency. This terroristic technocracy cannot be attributed to the exceptional requirements of "war economy"; war economy is rather the normal state of the National Socialist ordering of the social and economic process, and technology is one of the chief stimuli of this ordering.

In the course of the technological process a new rationality and new standards of individuality have spread over society, different from and even opposed to those which initiated the march of technology. These changes are not the (direct or derivative) effect of machinery on its users or of mass production on its consumers; they are rather themselves determining factors in the development of machinery and mass production. In order to understand their full import, it is necessary to survey briefly the traditional rationality and standards of individuality which are being dissolved by the present stage of the machine age.

The human individual whom the exponents of the middle class revolution had made the ultimate unit as well as the end of society stood for values which strikingly contradict those holding sway over society today. If we try to assemble in one guiding concept the various religious, political and economic tendencies which shaped the idea of the individual in the sixteenth and seventeenth century, we may define the individual as the subject of certain fundamental standards and values which no external authority was supposed to encroach upon. These standards and values pertained to the forms of life, social as well as personal, which were most adequate to the full development of man's faculties and abilities. By the same token, they were the "truth" of his individual and social existence. The individual, as a rational being, was deemed capable of finding these forms by his own thinking and, once he had acquired freedom of thought, of pursuing the course of action which would actualize them. Society's task was to grant him such freedom and to remove all restrictions upon his rational course of action.

The principle of individualism, the pursuit of self-interest, was conditioned upon the proposition that self-interest was rational, that is to say, that it resulted from and was constantly guided and controlled by autonomous thinking. The rational self-interest did not coincide with the individual's immediate self-interest, for the latter depended upon the standards and requirements of the prevailing social order, placed there not by his autonomous thought and conscience but by external authorities. In the context of radical Puritanism, the principle of individualism thus set the individual against his society. Men had to break through the whole system of ideas and values imposed upon them, and to find and seize the ideas and values that conformed to their rational interest. They had to live in a state of constant vigilance, apprehension, and criticism, to reject everything that was not true, not justified by free reason. This, in a society which was not yet rational, constituted a principle of permanent unrest and opposition. For false standards still governed the life of men, and the free individual was therefore he who criticised realization. The theme has nowhere been more fittingly expressed than in Milton's image of a "wicked race of deceivers, who . . . took the virgin Truth, hewd her lovely form into a thousand peeces, and scatter'd them to the four winds. From that time ever since, the sad friends of Truth, such as durst appear, imitating the careful search that Isis made for the mangl'd body of Osiris, went up and down gathering up limb by limb still as they could find them. We have not yet found them all, . . . nor ever shall do, till her Master's second coming . . . —To be still searching what we know not, by what we know, still closing up truth to truth as we find it (for all her body is homogeneal and proportional)," this was the principle of individualistic rationality.

To fulfill this rationality presupposed an adequate social and economic setting, one that would appeal to individuals whose social performance was, at least to a large extent, their own work. Liberalist society was held to be the adequate setting for individualistic rationality. In the sphere of free competition, the tangible achievements of the individual which made his products and performances a part of society's need, were the marks of his individuality. In the course of time, however, the process of commodity production undermined the economic basis on which individualistic rationality was built. Mechanization and rationalization forced the weaker competitor under the dominion of the giant enterprises of machine industry which, in establishing society's dominion over nature, abolished the free economic subject.

The principle of competitive efficiency favors the enterprises with the most highly mechanized and rationalized industrial equipment. Technological power tends to the concentration of economic power, to "large units of production, of vast corporate enterprises producing large quantities and often a striking variety of goods, of industrial empires owning and controlling materials, equipment, and processes from the extraction of raw materials to the distribution of finished products, of dominance over an entire industry by a small number of giant concerns. . ." And technology "steadily increases the power at the command of giant concerns by creating new tools, processes and products." Efficiency here called for integral unification and simplification, for the removal of all "waste," the avoidance of all detours, it called for radical coordination. A

contradiction exists, however, between the profit incentive that keeps the apparatus moving and the rise of the standard of living which this same apparatus has made possible. "Since control of production is in the hands of enterprisers working for profit, they will have at their disposal whatever emerges as surplus after rent, interest, labor, and other costs are met. These costs will be kept at the lowest possible minimum as a matter of course." Under these circumstances, profitable employment of the apparatus dictates to a great extent the quantity, form and kind of commodities to be produced, and through this mode of production and distribution, the technological power of the apparatus affects the entire rationality of those whom it serves.

Under the impact of this apparatus, individualistic rationality has been transformed into technological rationality. It is by no means confined to the subjects and objects of large scale enterprises but characterizes the pervasive mode of thought and even the manifold forms of protest and rebellion. This rationality establishes standards of judgment and fosters attitudes which make men ready to accept and even to introcept the dictates of the apparatus.

Lewis Mumford has characterized man in the machine age as an "objective personality," one who has learned to transfer all subjective spontaneity to the machinery which he serves, to subordinate his life to the "matter-of-factness" of a world in which the machine is the factor and he the factum. Individual distinctions in the aptitude, insight and knowledge are transformed into different quanta of skill and training, to be coordinated at any time within the common framework of standardized performances.

Individuality, however, has not disappeared. The free economic subject rather has developed into the object of large-scale organization and coordination, and individual achievement has been transformed into standardized efficiency. The latter is characterized by the fact that the individual's performance is motivated, guided and measured by standards external to him, standards pertaining to predetermined tasks and functions. The efficient individual is the one whose performance is an action only insofar as it is the proper reaction to the objective requirements of the apparatus, and his liberty is confined to the selection of the most adequate means for reaching a goal which he did not set. Whereas individual achievement is independent of recognition and consummated in the work itself, efficiency is a rewarded performance and consummated only in its value for the apparatus.

With the majority of the population, the former freedom of the economic subject was gradually submerged in the efficiency with which he performed services assigned to him. The world had been rationalized to such an extent, and this rationality had become such a social power that the individual could do no better than adjust himself without reservation. Veblen was among the first to derive the new matter-of-factness from the machine process, from which it spread over the whole society: "The share of the operative workman in the machine industry is (typically) that of an attendant, an assistant, whose duty it is to keep pace with the machine process and to help out with workmanlike manipulation at points where the machine process engaged is incomplete. His work supplements the machine process rather than makes use of it. On the contrary the machine process makes use of the workman. The ideal mechanical contrivance in this technological system is the automatic machine." The machine process requires a knowledge oriented to "a ready apprehension of opaque facts, in passably exact quantitative terms. This class of knowledge presumes a certain intellectual or spiritual attitude on the part of the workman, such an attitude as will readily apprehend and appreciate matter

of fact and will guard against the suffusion of this knowledge with putative animistic or anthropomorphic subtleties, quasi-personal interpretations of the observed phenomena and of their relations to one another."

As an attitude, matter-of-factness is not bound to the machine process. Under all forms of social production men have taken and justified their motives and goals from the facts that made up their reality, and in doing so they have arrived at the most diverging philosophies. Matter-of-factness animated ancient materialism and hedonism, it was responsible in the struggle of modern physical science against spiritual oppression, and in the revolutionary rationalism of the Enlightenment. The new attitude differs from all these in the highly rational compliance which typifies it. The facts directing man's thought and action are not those of nature which must be accepted in order to be mastered, or those of society which must be changed because they no longer correspond to human needs and potentialities. Rather are they those of the machine process, which itself appears as the embodiment of rationality and expediency.

Let us take a simple example. A man who travels by automobile to a distant place chooses his route from the highway maps. Towns, lakes and mountains appear as obstacles to be bypassed. The countryside is shaped and organized by the highway. Numerous signs and posters tell the traveler what to do and think; they even request his attention to the beauties of nature or the hallmarks of history. Others have done the thinking for him, and perhaps for the better. Convenient parking spaces have been constructed where the broadest and most surprising view is open. Giant advertisements tell him when to stop and find the pause that refreshes. And all this is indeed for his benefit, safety and comfort; he receives what he wants. Business, technics, human needs and nature are welded together into one rational and expedient mechanism.

He will fare best who follows its directions, subordinating his spontaneity to the anonymous wisdom which ordered everything for him.

The decisive point is that this attitude—which dissolves all actions into a sequence of semi-spontaneous reactions to prescribed mechanical norms—is not only perfectly rational but also perfectly reasonable. All protest is senseless, and the individual who would insist on his freedom of action would become a crank. There is no personal escape from the apparatus which has mechanized and standardized the world. It is a rational apparatus, combining utmost expediency with utmost convenience, saving time and energy, removing waste, adapting all means to the end, anticipating consequences, sustaining calculability and security.

In manipulating the machine, man learns that obedience to the directions is the only way to obtain desired results. Getting along is identical with adjustment to the apparatus. There is no room for autonomy. Individualistic rationality has developed into efficient compliance with the pregiven continuum of means and ends. The latter absorbs the liberating efforts of thought, and the various functions of reason converge upon the unconditional maintenance of the apparatus. It has been frequently stressed that scientific discoveries and inventions are shelved as soon as they seem to interfere with the requirements of profitable marketing. The necessity which is the mother of inventions is to a great extent the necessity of maintaining and expanding the apparatus. Inventions have "their chief use . . . in the service of business, not of industry, and their great further use is in the furtherance, or rather the acceleration, of obligatory social amenities." They are mostly of a competitive nature, and "any technological advantage gained by one competitor forthwith becomes a necessity to all the rest, on pain of defeat," so that one might as well say that, in the monopolistic system, "invention is the mother of necessity."

Everything cooperates to turn human instincts, desires and thoughts into channels that feed the apparatus. Dominant economic and social organizations "do not maintain their power by force . . . They do it by identifying themselves with the faiths and loyalties of the people," and the people have been trained to identify their faiths and loyalties with them. The relationships among men are increasingly mediated by the machine process. But the mechanical contrivances which facilitate intercourse among individuals also intercept and absorb their libido, thereby diverting it from the all too dangerous realm in which the individual is free of society. The average man hardly cares for any living being with the intensity and persistence he shows for his automobile. The machine that is adored is no longer dead matter but becomes something like a human being. And it gives back to man what it possesses: the life of the social apparatus to which it belongs. Human behavior is outfitted with the rationality of the machine process, and this rationality has a definite social content. The machine process operates according to the laws of mass production. Expediency in terms of technological reason is, at the same time, expediency in terms of profitable efficiency, and rationalization is, at the same time, monopolistic standardization and concentration. The more rationally the individual behaves and the more lovingly he attends to his rationalized work, the more he succumbs to the frustrating aspects of this rationality. He is losing his ability to abstract from the special form in which rationalization is carried through and is losing his faith in its unfulfilled potentialities. His matter-of-factness, his distrust of all values which transcend the facts of observation, his resentment against all "quasi-personal" and metaphysical interpretations, his suspicion of all standards which relate the observable order of things, the rationality of the apparatus, to the rationality of freedom,—this whole attitude serves all too well those who are interested in perpetuating the prevailing form of matters of fact. The machine process requires a "consistent training in the mechanical apprehension of things," and this training, in turn, promotes "conformity to the schedule of living," a "degree of trained insight and a facile strategy in all manner of quantitative adjustments and adaptations. . ." The "mechanics of conformity" spread from the technological to the social order; they govern performance not only in the factories and shops, but also in the offices, schools, assemblies and, finally, in the realm of relaxation and entertainment.

Individuals are stripped of their individuality, not by external compulsion, but by the very rationality under which they live. Industrial psychology correctly assumes that "the dispositions of men are fixed emotional habits and as such they are quite dependable reaction patterns." True, the force which transforms human performance into a series of dependable reactions is an external force: the machine process imposes upon men the patterns of mechanical behavior, and the standards of competitive efficiency are the more enforced from outside the less independent the individual competitor becomes. But man does not experience this loss of his freedom as the work of some hostile and foreign force; he relinquishes his liberty to the dictum of reason itself. The point is that today the apparatus to which the individual is to adjust and adopt himself is so rational that individual protest and liberation appear not only as hopeless but as utterly irrational. The system of life-created by modern industry is one of the highest expediency, convenience and efficiency. Reason, once defined in these terms, becomes equivalent to an activity which perpetuates this world. Rational behavior becomes identical with a matter-of-factness which teaches reasonable submissiveness and thus guarantees getting along in the prevailing order.

At first glance, the technological attitude rather seems to imply the opposite of resignation. Teleological and theological dogmas no longer interfere with man's struggle with matter; he develops his experimental energies without inhibition. There is no constellation of matter which he does not try to break up, to manipulate and to change according to his will and interest. This experimentalism, however, frequently serves the effort to develop a higher efficiency of hierarchical control over men. Technological rationality may easily be placed into the service of such control: in the form of "scientific management," it has become one of the most profitable means for streamlined autocracy. F. W. Taylor's exposition of scientific management shows within it the union of exact science, matter-of-factness and big industry: "Scientific management attempts to substitute, in the relation between employers and workers, the government of fact and law for the rule of force and opinion. It substitutes exact knowledge for guesswork, and seeks to establish a code of natural laws equally binding upon employers and workmen. Scientific management thus seeks to substitute in the shop discipline, natural law in place of a code of discipline based upon the caprice and arbitrary power of men. No such democracy has ever existed in industry before. Every protest of every workman must be handled by those on the management side and the right and wrong of the complaint must be settled, not by the opinion either of the management or the workman but by the great code of laws which has been developed and which must satisfy both sides." The scientific effort aims at eliminating waste, intensifying production and standardizing the product. And this whole scheme to increase profitable efficiency poses as the final fulfillment of individualism, ending up with a demand to "develop the individuality of the workers."

The idea of compliant efficiency perfectly illustrates the structure of technological rationality. Rationality is being transformed from a critical force into one of adjustment and compliance. Autonomy of reason loses its meaning in the same measure as the thoughts, feelings and actions of men are shaped by the technical requirements of the apparatus which they have themselves created. Reason has found its resting place in the system of standardized control, production and consumption. There it reigns through the laws and mechanisms which insure the efficiency, expediency and coherence of this system.

As the laws and mechanisms of technological rationality spread over the whole society, they develop a set of truth values of their own which hold good for the functioning of the apparatus—and for that alone. Propositions concerning competitive or collusive behavior, business methods, principles of effective organization and control, fair play, the use of science and technics are true or false in terms of this value system, that is to say, in terms of instrumentalities that dictate their own ends. These truth values are tested and perpetuated by experience and must guide the thoughts and actions of all who wish to survive. Rationality here calls for unconditional compliance and coordination, and consequently, the truth values related to this rationality imply the subordination of thought to pre-given external standards. We may call this set of truth values the technological truth, technological in the twofold sense that it is an instrument of expediency rather than an end in itself, and that it follows the pattern of technological behavior.

By virtue of its subordination to external standards, the technological truth comes into striking contradiction with the form in which individualistic society had established its supreme values. The pursuit of self-interest now appears to be conditioned upon heteronomy, and autonomy as an obstacle rather than stimulus for rational action. The originally identical and "homogenous" truth seems to be split into two different sets of truth values and two

different patterns of behavior: the one assimilated to the apparatus, the other antagonistic to it; the one making up the prevailing technological rationality and governing the behavior required by it, the other pertaining to a critical rationality whose values can be fulfilled only if it has itself shaped all personal and social relationships. The critical rationality derives from the principles of autonomy which individualistic society itself had declared to be its self-evident truths. Measuring these principles against the form in which individualistic society has actualized them, critical rationality accuses social injustice in the name of individualistic society's own ideology. The relationship between technological and critical truth is a difficult problem which cannot be dealt with here, but two points must be mentioned. (1) The two sets of truth values are neither wholly contradictory nor complementary to each other; many truths of technological rationality are preserved or transformed in critical rationality. (2) The distinction between the two sets is not rigid; the content of each set changes in the social process so that what were once critical truth values become technological values. For example, the proposition that every individual is equipped with certain inalienable rights is a critical proposition but it was frequently interpreted in favor of efficiency and concentration of power.

The standardization of thought under the sway of technological rationality also affects the critical truth values. The latter are torn from the context to which they originally belonged and, in their new form, are given wide, even official publicity. For example, propositions which, in Europe, were the exclusive domain of the labor movement are today adopted by the very forces which these propositions denounced. In the fascist countries, they serve as ideological instruments for the attack on "Jewish capitalism" and "Western plutocracy," thereby concealing the actual front in the struggle. The materialistic analysis of present-day economy is employed to justify fascism to the German industrialists in whose interest it operates, as the regime of last resort for imperialistic expansion. In other countries, the critique of political economy functions in the struggle among conflicting business groups and as governmental weapon for unmasking monopolistic practices; it is propagated by the columnists of the big press syndicates and finds its way even into the popular magazines and the addresses to manufacturers associations. As these propositions become part and parcel of the established culture, however, they seem to lose their edge and to merge with the old and the familiar. This familiarity with the truth illuminates the extent to which society has become indifferent and insusceptible to the impact of critical thought. For the categories of critical thought preserve their truth value only if they direct the full realization of the social potentialities which they envision, and they lose their vigor if they determine an attitude of fatalistic compliance or competitive assimilation.

Several influences have conspired to bring about the social impotence of critical thought. The foremost among them is the growth of the industrial apparatus and of its all-embracing control over all spheres of life. The technological rationality inculcated in those who attend to this apparatus has transformed numerous modes of external compulsion and authority into modes of self-discipline and self-control. Safety and order are, to a large extent, guaranteed by the fact that man has learned to adjust his behavior to the other fellow's down to the most minute detail. All men act equally rationally, that is to say, according to the standards which insure the functioning of the apparatus and thereby the maintenance of their own life. But this "introversion" of compulsion and authority has strenghthened rather than attenuated the mechanisms of social control. Men, in following their own reason, follow those who put their

reason to profitable use. In Europe, these mechanisms helped to prevent the individual from acting in accordance with the conspicuous truth, and they were efficiently supplemented by the physical control mechanisms of the apparatus. At this point, the otherwise diverging interests and their agencies are synchronized and adjusted in such a manner that they efficiently counteract any serious threat to their dominion.

The ever growing strength of the apparatus, however, is not the only influence responsible. The social impotence of critical thought has been further facilitated by the fact that important strata of the opposition have for long been incorporated into the apparatus itself—without losing the title of the opposition. The history of this process is well known and is illustrated in the development of the labor movement. Shortly after the first World War, Veblen declared that "the A.F. of L. is itself one of the Vested Interests, as ready as any other to do battle for its own margin of privilege and profit. . . . The A.F. of L. is a business organization with a vested interest of its own; for keeping up prices and keeping down the supply, quite after the usual fashion of management by the other Vested Interests." The same holds true for the labor bureaucracy in leading European countries. The question here pertains not to the political expediency and the consequences of such a development, but to the changing function of the truth values which labor had represented and carried forward.

These truth values belonged, to a large extent, to the critical rationality which interpreted the social process in terms of its restrained potentialities. Such a rationality can fully develop only in social groups whose organization is not patterned on the apparatus in its prevailing forms or on its agencies and institutions. For the latter are pervaded by the technological rationality which shapes the attitude and interests of those dependent on them, so that all transcending aims and values are cut off. A harmony prevails between the "spirit" and its material embodiment such that the spirit cannot be supplanted without disrupting the functioning of the whole. The critical truth values borne by an oppositional social movement change their significance when this movement incorporates itself into the apparatus. Ideas such as liberty, productive industry, planned economy, satisfaction of needs are then fused with the interests of control and competition. Tangible organizational success thus outweighs the exigencies of critical rationality.

Its tendency to assimilate itself to the organizational and psychological pattern of the apparatus caused a change in the very structure of the social opposition in Europe. The critical rationality of its aims was subordinated to the technological rationality of its organization and thereby "purged" of the elements which transcended the established pattern of thought and action. This process was the apparently inevitable result of the growth of large-scale industry and of its army of dependents. The latter could hope effectively to assert their interests only if these were effectively coordinated in large-scale organizations. The oppositional groups were being transformed into mass parties, and their leadership into mass bureaucracies. This transformation, however, far from dissolving the structure of individualistic society into a new system, sustained and strengthened its basic tendencies.

It seems to be self-evident that mass and individual are contradictory concepts and incompatible facts. The crowd "is, to be sure, composed of individuals—but of individuals who cease to be isolated, who cease thinking. The isolated individual within the crowd cannot help thinking, criticizing the emotions. The others, on the other hand, cease to think: they are moved, they are carried away, they are elated; they feel united with their fellow members in the crowd, released from all inhibi-

tions; they are changed and feel no connection with their former state of mind." This analysis, although it correctly describes certain features of the masses, contains one wrong assumption, that in the crowd the individuals "cease to be isolated," are changed and "feel no connection with their former state of mind." Under authoritarianism, the function of the masses rather consists in consummating the isolation of the individual and in realizing his "former state of mind." The crowd is an association of individuals who have been stripped of all "natural" and personal distinctions and reduced to the standardized expression of their abstract individuality, namely, the pursuit of self-interest. As member of a crowd, man has become the standardized subject of brute self-preservation. In the crowd, the restraint placed by society upon the competitive pursuit of self-interest tends to become ineffective and the aggressive impulses are easily released. These impulses have been developed under the exigencies of scarcity and frustration, and their release rather accentuates the "former state of mind." True, the crowd "unites," but it unites the atomic subjects of self-preservation who are detached from everything that transcends their selfish interests and impulses. The crowd is thus the antithesis of the "community," and the perverted realization of individuality.

The weight and import of the masses grow with the growth of rationalization, but at the same time they are transformed into a conservative force which itself perpetuates the existence of the apparatus. As there is a decrease in the number of those who have the freedom of individual performance, there is an increase in the number of those whose individuality is reduced to self-preservation by standardization. They can pursue their self-interest only by developing "dependable reaction patterns" and by performing pre-arranged functions. Even the highly differentiated professional requirements of modern industry promote standardization. Vocational training is chiefly training in various kinds of skill, psychological and physiological adaptation to a "job" which has to be done. The job, a pre-given "type of work . . . requires a particular combination of abilities," and those who create the job also shape the human material to fill it. The abilities developed by such training make the "personality" a means for attaining ends which perpetuate man's existence as an instrumentality, replaceable at short notice by other instrumentalities of the same brand. The psychological and "personal" aspects of vocational training are the more emphasized the more they are subjected to regimentation and the less they are left to free and complete development. The "human side" of the employee and the concern for his personal aptitudes and habits play an important part in the total mobilization of the private sphere for mass production and mass culture. Psychology and individualization serve to consolidate stereotyped dependability, for they give the human object the feeling that he unfolds himself by discharging functions which dissolve his self into a series of required actions and responses. Within this range, individuality is not only preserved but also fostered and rewarded, but such individuality is only the special form in which a man introcepts and discharges, within a general pattern, certain duties allocated to him. Specialization fixates the prevailing scheme of standardization. Almost everyone has become a potential member of the crowd, and the masses belong to the daily implements of the social process. As such, they can easily be handled, for the thoughts, feelings and interests of their members have been assimilated to the pattern of the apparatus. To be sure, their outbursts are terrifying and violent but these are readily directed against the weaker competitors and the conspicuous "outsiders" (Jews, foreigners, national minorities). The coordinated masses do not crave a new order but a larger share in the prevailing one.

Through their action, they strive to rectify, in an anarchic way, the injustice of competition. Their uniformity is in the competitive self-interest they all manifest, in the equalized expressions of self-preservation. The members of the masses are individuals.

The individual in the crowd is certainly not the one whom the individualist principle exhorted to develop his self, nor is his self-interest the same as the rational interest urged by this principle. Where the daily social performance of the individual has become antagonistic to his "true interest," the individualist principle has changed its meaning. The protagonists of individualism were aware of the fact that "individuals can be developed only by being trusted with somewhat more than they can, at the moment, do well"; today, the individual is trusted with precisely what he can, at the moment, do well. The philosophy of individualism has seen the "essential freedom" of the self to be "that it stands for a fateful moment outside of all belongings, and determines for itself alone whether its primary attachments shall be with actual earthly interests or with those of an ideal and potential 'Kingdom of God.'" This ideal and potential kingdom has been defined in different ways, but it has always been characterized by contents which were opposed and transcendent to the prevailing kingdom. Today, the prevailing type of individual is no longer capable of seizing the fateful moment which constitutes his freedom. He has changed his function; from a unit of resistance and autonomy, he has passed to one of ductility and adjustment. It is this function which associates individuals in masses.

The emergence of the modern masses, far from endangering the efficiency and coherence of the apparatus, has facilitated the progressing coordination of society and the growth of authoritarian bureaucracy, thus refuting the social theory of individualism at a decisive point. The technological process seemed to tend to the conquest of scarcity and thus to the slow transformation of competition into cooperation. The philosophy of individualism viewed this process as the gradual differentiation and liberation of human potentialities, as the abolition of the "crowd." Even in the Marxian conception, the masses are not the spearhead of freedom. The Marxian proletariat is not a crowd but a class, defined by its determinate position in the productive process, the maturity of its "consciousness," and the rationality of its common interest. Critical rationality, in the most accentuated form, is the prerequisite for its liberating function. In one aspect at least, this conception is in line with the philosophy of individualism: it envisions the rational form of human association as brought about and sustained by the autonomous decision and action of free men.

This is the one point at which the technological and the critical rationality seem to converge, for the technological process implies a democratization of functions. The system of production and distribution has been rationalized to such an extent that the hierarchical distinction between executive and subordinate performances is to an ever smaller degree based upon essential distinctions in aptitude and insight, and to an ever greater degree upon inherited power and a vocational training to which everyone could be subjected. Even experts and "engineers" are no exception. To be sure, the gap between the underlying population and those who design the blueprints for rationalization, who lay out production, who make the inventions and discoveries which accelerate technological progress, becomes daily more conspicuous, particularly in a period of war economy. At the same time, however, this gap is maintained more by the division of power than by the division of work. The hierarchical distinction of the experts and engineers results from the fact that their ability and knowledge is utilized in the interest of autocratic power. The "techno-

logical leader" is also a "social leader"; his "social leadership overshadows and conditions his function as a scientist, for it gives him institutional power within the group . . .," and the "captain of industry" acts in "perfect accordance with the traditional dependence of the expert's function." Were it not for this fact, the task of the expert and engineer would not be an obstacle to the general democratization of functions. Technological rationalization has created a common framework of experience for the various professions and occupations. This experience excludes or restrains those elements that transcend the technical control over matters of fact and thus extends the scope of rationalization from the objective to the subjective world. Underneath the complicated web of stratified control is an array of more or less standardized techniques, tending to one general pattern, which insure the material reproduction of society. The "persons engaged in a practical occupation" seem to be convinced that "any situation which appears in the performance of their role can be fitted into some general pattern with which the best, if not all, of them are familiar." Moreover, the instrumentalistic conception of technological rationality is spreading over almost the whole realm of thought and gives the various intellectual activities a common denominator. They too become a kind of technique, a matter of training rather than individuality, requiring the expert rather than the complete human personality.

The standardization of production and consumption, the mechanization of labor, the improved facilities of transportation and communication, the extension of training, the general dissemination of knowledge—all these factors seem to facilitate the exchangeability of functions. It is as if the basis were shrinking on which the pervasive distinction between "specialized (technical)" and "common" knowledge has been built, and as if the authoritarian control of functions would prove increasingly foreign to the technological process. The special form, however, in which the technological process is organized, counteracts this trend. The same development that created the modern masses as the standardized attendants and dependents of large-scale industry also created the hierarchical organization of private bureaucracies. Max Weber has already stressed the connection between mass-democracy and bureaucracy: "In contrast to the democratic self-administration of small homogeneous units," the bureaucracy is "the universal concomitant of modern mass democracy."

The bureaucracy becomes the concomitant of the modern masses by virtue of the fact that standardization proceeds along the lines of specialization. The latter by itself, provided that it is not arrested at the point where it interferes with the domain of vested control, is quite compatible with the democratization of functions. Fixated specialization, however, tends to atomize the masses and to insulate the subordinate from the executive functions. We have mentioned that specialized vocational training implies fitting a man to a particular job or a particular line of jobs, thus directing his "personality," spontaneity and experience to the special situations he may meet in filling the job. In this manner, the various professions and occupations, notwithstanding their convergence upon one general pattern, tend to become atomic units which require coordination and management from above. The technical democratization of functions is counteracted by their atomization, and the bureaucracy appears as the agency which guarantees their rational course and order.

The bureaucracy thus emerges on an apparently objective and impersonal ground, provided by the rational specialization of functions, and this rationality in turn serves to increase the rationality of submission. For, the more the individual functions are divided, fixated and synchronized according to objective and impersonal patterns, the less reasonable is it for the individual to withdraw or withstand. "The material fate of the masses becomes increasingly dependent upon the continuous and correct functioning of the increasingly bureaucratic order of private capitalistic organizations." The objective and impersonal character of technological rationality bestows upon the bureaucratic groups the universal dignity of reason. The rationality embodied in the giant enterprises makes it appear as if men, in obeying them, obey the dictum of an objective rationality. The private bureaucracy fosters a delusive harmony between the special and the common interest. Private power relationships appear not only as relationships between objective things but also as the rule of rationality itself.

In the fascist countries, this mechanism facilitated the merger between private, semi-private (party) and public (governmental) bureaucracies. The efficient realization of the interests of large-scale enterprise was one of the strongest motives for the transformation of economic into totalitarian political control, and efficiency is one of the main reasons for the fascist regime's hold over its regimented population. At the same time, however, it is also the force which may break this hold. Fascism can maintain its rule only by aggravating the restraint which it is compelled to impose upon society. It will ever more conspicuously manifest its inability to develop the productive forces, and it will fall before that power which proves to be more efficient than fascism.

In the democratic countries, the growth of the private bureaucracy can be balanced by the strengthening of the public bureaucracy. The rationality inherent in the specialization of functions tends to enlarge the scope and weight of bureaucratization. In the private bureaucracy, however, such an expansion will intensify rather than alleviate the irrational elements of the social process, for it will widen the discrepancy between the technical character of the division of functions and the autocratic character of control over them. In contrast, the public bureaucracy, if democratically constituted and controlled, will overcome this discrepancy to the extent that it undertakes the "conversation of those human and material resources which technology and corporations have tended to misuse and waste." In the age of mass society, the power of the public bureaucracy can be the weapon which protects the people from the encroachment of special interests upon the general welfare. As long as the will of the people can effectively assert itself, the public bureaucracy can be a lever of democratization. Large-scale industry tends to organize on a national scale, and fascism has transformed economic expansion into the military conquest of whole continents. In this situation, the restoration of society to its own right, and the maintenance of individual freedom have become directly political questions, their solution depending upon the outcome of the international struggle.

The social character of bureaucratization is largely determined by the extent to which it allows for a democratization of functions that tends to close the gap between the governing bureaucracy and the governed population. If everyone has become a potential member of the public bureaucracy (as he has become a potential member of the masses), society will have passed from the stage of hierarchical bureaucratization to the stage of technical self-administration. Insofar as technocracy implies a deepening of the gap between specialized and common knowledge, between the controlling and coordinating experts and the controlled and coordinated people, the technocratic abolition of the "price system" would stabilize rather than shatter the forces which stand in the way of progress. The same holds true for the so-called managerial revolution. According to the theory of the managerial revolution, the growth of the apparatus entails the rise of a

new social class, the "managers," to take over social domination and to establish a new economic and political order. Nobody will deny the increasing importance of management and the simultaneous shift in the function of control. But these facts do not make the managers a new social class or the spearhead of a revolution. Their "source of income" is the same as that of the already existing classes: they either draw salaries, or, insofar as they possess a share in the capital, are themselves capitalists. Moreover, their specific function in the prevailing division of labor does not warrant the expectation that they are predestined to inaugurate a new and more rational division of labor. This function is either determined by the requirement of profitable utilization of capital, and, in this case, the managers are simply capitalists or deputy-capitalists (comprising the "executives" and the corporation-managers); or it is determined by the material process of production (engineers, technicians, production managers, plant superintendents). In the latter case, the managers would belong to the vast army of the "immediate producers" and share its "class interest," were it not for the fact that, even in this function, they work as deputy-capitalists and thus form a segregated and privileged group between capital and labor. Their power, and the awe which it inspires, are derived not from their actual "technological" performance but from their social position, and this they owe to the prevailing organization of production. "The leading managerial and directional figures within the inner business sancta . . . are drawn from, or have been absorbed into, the upper layers of wealth and income whose stakes it is their function to defend." To sum up, as a separate social group, the managers are thoroughly tied up with the vested interests, and as performers of necessary productive functions they do not constitute a separate "class" at all.

The spreading hierarchy of large-scale enterprise and the precipitation of individuals into masses determine the trends of technological rationality today. What results is the mature form of that individualistic rationality which characterized the free economic subject of the industrial revolution. Individualistic rationality was born as a critical and oppositional attitude that derived freedom of action from the unrestricted liberty of thought and conscience and measured all social standards and relations by the individual's rational self-interest. It grew into the rationality of competition in which the rational interest was superseded by the interest of the market, and individual achievement absorbed by efficiency. It ended with standardized submission to the all-embracing apparatus which it had itself created. This apparatus is the embodiment and resting place of individualistic rationality, but the latter now requires that individuality must go. He is rational who most efficiently accepts and executes what is allocated to him, who entrusts his fate to the large-scale enterprises and organizations which administer the apparatus.

Such was the logical outcome of a social process which measured individual performance in terms of competitive efficiency. The philosophers of individualism have always had an inkling of this outcome and they expressed their anxiety in many different forms, in the skeptical conformism of Hume, in the idealistic introversion of individual freedom, in the frequent attacks of the Transcendentalists against the rule of money and power. But the social forces were stronger than the philosophic protests, and the philosophic justification of individualism took on more and more of the overtones of resignation. Toward the end of the nineteenth century, the idea of the individual became increasingly ambiguous: it combined insistence upon free social performance and competitive efficiency with glorification of smallness, privacy and self-limitation. The rights and liberties of the individual in society were interpreted as the rights and liberties of privacy and withdrawal from society. William James, faithful to the individualistic principle, asserted that, in the "rivalry between real organizable goods," the "world's trial is better than the closest solution," provided that the victorious keep "the vanquished somehow represented." His doubt, however, as to whether this trial is really a fair one seems to motivate his hatred of "bigness and greatness in all their forms," his declaration that "the smaller and more intimate is the truer,—the man more than the home, the home more than the state or the church." The counterposition of individual and society, originally meant to provide the ground for a militant reformation of society in the interest of the individual, comes to prepare and justify the individual's withdrawal from society. The free and self-reliant "soul," which originally nourished the individual's critique of external authority, now becomes a refuge from external authority. Tocqueville had already defined individualism in terms of acquiescence and peaceful resignation: "a mature and calm feeling, which disposes each member of the community to sever himself from the mass of his fellow-creatures; and to draw apart with his family and his friends; so that, after he has thus formed a little circle of his own, he willingly leaves society at large to itself." Autonomy of the individual came to be regarded as a private rather than a public affair, an element of retreat rather than aggression. All these factors of resignation are comprehended in Benjamin Constant's statement that "our liberty should be composed of the peaceful enjoyment of private independence."

The elements of restraint and resignation which became increasingly strong in the individualist philosophy of the nineteenth century elucidate the connection between individualism and scarcity. Individualism is the form liberty assumes in a society wherein the acquisition and utilization of wealth is dependent on competitive toil. Individuality is a distinct possession of "pioneers": it presupposes the open and empty spaces, the freedom of "hewing out a home" as well as the need to do so. The individual's world is a "world of labor and the march," as Walt Whitman says, one in which the available intellectual and material resources must be conquered and appropriated through incessant struggle with man and nature, and in which human forces are released to distribute and administer scarcity.

In the period of large-scale industry, however, the existential conditions making for individuality give way to conditions which render individuality unnecessary. In clearing the ground for the conquest of scarcity, the technological process not only levels individuality but also tends to transcend it where it is concurrent with scarcity. Mechanized mass production is filling the empty spaces in which individuality could assert itself. The cultural standardization points, paradoxically enough, to potential abundance as well as actual poverty. This standardization may indicate the extent to which individual creativeness and originality have been rendered unnecessary. With the decline of the liberalistic era, these qualities were vanishing from the domain of material production and becoming the ever more exclusive property of the highest intellectual activities. Now, they seem to disappear from this sphere too: mass culture is dissolving the traditional forms of art, literature and philosophy together with the "personality" which unfolded itself in producing and consuming them. The striking impoverishment which characterizes the dissolution of these forms may involve a new source of enrichment. They derived their truth from the fact that they represented the potentialities of man and nature which were excluded or distorted in the reality. So far were those potentialities from their actualization in the social consciousness that much

cried out for unique expression. But today, *humanitas*, wisdom, beauty, freedom and happiness can no longer be represented as the realm of the "harmonious personality" nor as the remote heaven of art nor as metaphysical systems. The "ideal" has become so concrete and so universal that it grips the life of every human being, and the whole of mankind is drawn into the struggle for its realization. Under the terror that now threatens the world the ideal constricts itself to one single and at the same time common issue. Faced with fascist barbarism, everyone knows what freedom means, and everyone is aware of the irrationality in the prevailing rationality.

Modern mass society quantifies the qualitative features of individual labor and standardizes the individualistic elements in the activities of intellectual culture. This process may bring to the fore the tendencies which make individuality a historical form of human existence, to be surpassed by further social development. This does not mean that society is bound to enter a stage of "collectivism." The collectivistic traits which characterize the development today may still belong to the phase of individualism. Masses and mass culture are manifestations of scarcity and frustration, and the authoritarian assertion of the common interest is but another form of the rule of particular interests over the whole. The fallacy of collectivism consists in that it equips the whole (society) with the traditional properties of the individual. Collectivism abolishes the free pursuit of competing individual interests but retains the idea of the common interest as a separate entity. Historically, however, the latter is but the counterpart of the former. Men experience their society as the objective embodiment of the collectivity as long as the individual interests are antagonistic to and competing with each other for a share in the social wealth. To such individuals, society appears as an objective entity, consisting of numerous things, institutions and agencies: plants and shops, business, police and law, government, schools and churches, prisons and hospitals, theaters and organizations, etc. Society is almost everything the individual is not, everything that determines his habits, thoughts and behavior patterns, that affects him from "outside." Accordingly, society is noticed chiefly as a power of restraint and control, providing the framework which integrates the goals, faculties and aspirations of men. It is this power which collectivism retains in its picture of society, thus perpetuating the rule of things and men over men.

The technological process itself furnishes no justification for such a collectivism. Technics hampers individual development only insofar as they are tied to a social apparatus which perpetuates scarcity, and this same apparatus has released forces which may shatter the special historical form in which technics is utilized. For this reason, all programs of an anti-technological character, all propaganda for an anti-industrial revolution serve only those who regard human needs as a by-product of the utilization of technics. The enemies of technics readily join forces with a terroristic technocracy. The philosophy of the simple life, the struggle against big cities and their culture frequently serves to teach men distrust of the potential instruments that could liberate them. We have pointed to the possible democratization of functions which technics may promote and which may facilitate complete human development in all branches of work and administration. Moreover, mechanization and standardization may one day help to shift the center of gravity from the necessities of material production to the arena of free human realization. The less individuality is required to assert itself in standardized social performances, the more it could retreat to a free "natural" ground. These tendencies, far from engendering collectivism, may lead to new forms of individualization. The machine individualizes men by following the physiological lines of individuality: it allocates the work to finger, hand, arm, foot, classifying and occupying men according to the dexterity of these organs. The external mechanisms which govern standardization here meet a "natural" individuality; they lay bare the ground on which a hitherto suppressed individualization might develop. On this ground, man is an individual by virtue of the uniqueness of his body and its unique position in the space-time continuum. He is an individual insofar as this natural uniqueness molds his thoughts, instincts, emotions, passions and desires. This is the "natural" *principium individuationis*. Under the system of scarcity, men developed their senses and organs chiefly as implements of labor and competitive orientation: skill, taste, proficiency, tact, refinement and endurance were qualities molded and perpetuated by the hard struggle for life, business and power. Consequently, man's thoughts, appetites and the ways of their fulfillment were not "his," they showed the oppressive and inhibitive features which this struggle imposed upon him. His senses, organs and appetites became acquisitive, exclusive and antagonistic. The technological process has reduced the variety of individual qualities down to this natural basis of individualization, but this same basis may become the foundation for a new form of human development.

The philosophy of individualism established an intrinsic connection between individuality and property. According to this philosophy, man could not develop a self without conquering and cultivating a domain of his own, to be shaped exclusively by his free will and reason. The domain thus conquered and cultivated had become part and parcel of his own "nature." Man removed the objects in this domain from the state in which he found them, and made them the tangible manifestation of his individual labor and interest. They were his property because they were fused with the very essence of his personality. This construction did not correspond to the facts and lost its meaning in the era of mechanized commodity production, but it contained the truth that individual development, far from being an inner value only, required an external sphere of manifestation and an autonomous concern for men and things. The process of production has long dissolved the link between individual labor and property and now tends to dissolve the link between the traditional form of property and social control, but the tightening of this control counteracts a tendency which may give the individualistic theory a new content. Technological progress would make it possible to decrease the time and energy spent in the production of the necessities of life, and a gradual reduction of scarcity and abolition of competitive pursuits could permit the self to develop from its natural roots. The less time and energy man has to expend in maintaining his life and that of society, the greater the possibility that he can "individualize" the sphere of his human realization. Beyond the realm of necessity, the essential differences between men could unfold themselves: everyone could think and act by himself, speak his own language, have his own emotions and follow his own passions. No longer chained to competitive efficiency, the self could grow in the realm of satisfaction. Man could come into his own in his passions. The objects of his desires would be the less exchangeable the more they were seized and shaped by his free self. They would "belong" to him more than ever before, and such ownership would not be injurious, for it would not have to defend its own against a hostile society.

Such a Utopia would not be a state of perennial happiness. The "natural" individuality of man is also the source of his natural sorrow. If the human relations are nothing but human, if they are freed from all foreign standards, they will be permeated with the sadness of their singular content. They are transitory and irreplaceable, and their transitory character will be accentuated when concern for the human being is no longer mingled with fear for his material existence and overshadowed by the threat of poverty, hunger, and ostracism.

The conflicts, however, which may arise from the natural individuality of men may not bear the violent and aggressive features which were so frequently attributed to the "state of nature." These features may be the marks of coercion and privation. "Appetite is never excessive, never furious, save when it has been starved. The frantic hunger we see it so often exhibiting under every variety of criminal form, marks only the hideous starvation to which society subjects it. It is not a normal but a morbid state of the appetite, growing exclusively out of the unnatural compression which is imposed upon it by the exigencies of our immature society. Every appetite and passion of man's nature is good and beautiful, and destined to be fully enjoyed . . . Remove, then, the existing bondage of humanity, remove those factitious restraints which keep appetite and passion on the perpetual lookout for escape, like steam from an overcharged boiler, and their force would instantly become conservative instead of destructive."

The Science of Sociology and the Sociology of Science

Stanley Aronowitz

Earlier in this book, I introduced a concept of epistēmē as a way of seeing that is specific to a historical period but that is, at the same time, discontinuous in time and space. When explicating the intellectual and cultural influences in the development of quantum mechanics in the 1920s, we saw that what might be called a modernist discourse permeates parts of western and central Europe from the middle of the nineteenth century into our own time. The crucial features of this discourse are: the renunciation of foundationalism in ethics and epistemology; skepticism regarding the unified field in "nature" as an ontologically certain entity; and the positing of discontinuity as the chief characteristic of both the historical process and the physical field.

The possibility of human and social sciences independent of physics and biology becomes a major problematic in the late nineteenth century. Inundated by the will to scientificity that pervades all intellectual culture (even the use of the term "science" signifies the degree to which scientific ideology remains hegemonic), those who would found sciences of history, culture, and society are faced with three nagging and apparently unsolvable puzzles. First, can human (social) relations be "reduced" to physical or biological laws? Those who followed Francis Galton and Herbert Spencer held to the primacy of biological "nature" in considerations governing human relations. Later, some American sociologists sought to employ mathematical and other methods borrowed from physics and chemistry in the study of social relations. For American social science of the first half of the twentieth century, either the intellectual orientations of a biologically rooted "organicism" projected in terms of a social "system" whose elements are functionally interrelated, or the postulate of social physics which derives generalizations from quantitatively adduced "data" culled from surveys, qualified as first steps on the long road to genuine science.

Second, midcentury leaders of American sociology such as Robert Merton and Talcott Parsons never tired of reiterating the problematic character of social knowledge, because of both its relative infancy compared to the "hard" sciences and the impossibility of replicating the experimental method in the social sphere. Controlled experiments may be conducted in psychology, but history, economics, and sociology do not lend themselves to such methods because the social cannot be fixed in space and time.

A third debate concerns the "specificity" of the social in comparison to other fields of inquiry. To what does social inquiry refer? Is there a social "system" that integrates culture and personality systems, as Parsons attempted to theorize? Does the "social" consist in a particular series of problems unified only by scientific method modified to the specificity of predefined social problems? In this mode, Robert Merton, perhaps the most influential theorist on the practice of social science in the last half of the twentieth century, argued for the proposition that social theories could only be of the "middle range," by which he meant a sphere of generality whose boundary condition was that statements be subject to empirical test. Thus, Merton rejects the arguments of his teacher, Parsons, that theory could make statements for which "data" did not (yet) exist; where Parsons's intellectual orientation was speculative, even as it purported to refer, in the last instance, to empirical reality, Merton insists that such speculation be suspended until the maturation of sociology as a cumulative science permits empirical or logical proofs. However, what unites both writers is their common "frame of reference," a *system of action* in which the postulate of methodological individualism may be made. That is, for the preponderant American sociological community the social system is built inductively from units involving social actors. The action *situation* in which "ego" confronts "alter" is the primary unit of analysis. Moreover, analytic methods borrowed from philosophy and mathematics are the privileged mode of theorizing for this school. Underlying the action situation is a normative or cultural system that motivates and sets boundaries of the choices actors will make. These are variable and ultimately indeterminate because the cultural system is not unified but is constituted as a typology of orientations, the choice from which depends in the last analysis on the vicissitudes of the personality system that in the Freudian transmutation is called a psychic structure and is by definition undecidable. Or, to cite Pareto, the subject matter of sociology is nonlogical actions. American sociology constructs its axiomatic structure in almost explicit opposition to two alternative paradigms: Marxism, by which it understands the underlying concept that the mode of produc-

tion of material life constitutes the unit of analysis, and psychologism, which reduces social action to the propensities of individuals. What Merton designates as middle-range issues are, for Marxism, derivative of the forces and relations of production. In opposition to this Marxism, Parsonian/Mertonian sociology follows Weber by insisting that "ideas" have material effectivity, particularly those that may be named intellectual and moral norms guiding action. Parsons never doubts that the economic sphere is central to human life and that, consequently, the rules governing action are instrumental/rational. But "interests" are by no means the only orientation governing action. The personality system conceived as a wild card in action systems, introduces nonlogical considerations; actors may cathect on objects that do not correspond to their cognitively rational motives. Parsons's categories of affectivity, expressive modes of action, and the frank employment of the psychoanalytic term "cathexis" are amendations to Pareto's category of nonlogical behavior, which accounts for the indeterminacy of the choices made by actors in any given situation and may produce instability of the social system.

Parsons holds the cultural system constant and posits its integration under equilibrium conditions into the social system. Thus, even if the personality system may disrupt the reproduction of the social system, the normative order remains the countervailing structure that ensures stability. In turn, this normative system is transmitted to individuals institutionally through family, school, church, and law, in the so-called socialization processes.

Now, since Weber posited the action system as the scene of sociological investigation, theorists have recognized that social equilibrium (the term is Parsons's) remains problematic. Socialization is a process that owes its existence to the lack of a monochronic general action system. Its three components obey different regularities, or laws, and their mutual integration is always questionable, both because of the fact that their mutual integration must be reestablished in every action situation and because of their logical distinction. Yet, the probability of equilibrium in any given space/time continuum is established by the assumed complicity of the cultural system with the social system. Since individuals are formed in and through institutions that are the material repositories of the normative order, only the vicissitudes of the personality have the capacity to disrupt the social system.

For Merton, the scene of action is not the social system. Rather, actors form relations in the context of *communities,* which, at a higher level of abstraction, are linked to a larger society. Yet, because of his invocation that propositions refer to an empirical frame of reference subject to confirmation or infirmation, we are advised to say nothing of such phenomena as production *in general,* social relations *taken as a whole,* or the *totality of social structures.* The best we can do is find the homologies between distinct spheres of human action. By rigorously employing scientific methods such as modeling, the hypothetic/deductive system, and verification, we can be reasonably sure that our investigations lead to solid knowledge.

This is not to suggest that Merton and his school are empiricists as well as positivists. On the contrary, Merton makes a crucial distinction that enables the investigator to deal with the complexity of objects, which cannot be sensibly apprehended. It is that between manifest and latent functions. The manifest function of an element of a (sub) system does not exhaust its effectivity, according to Merton. What we see is not altogether what we get. The interaction of elements of a system of action have consequences that are often unexpected in terms of the empirical world as perceived on the surface. These consequences are indeterminate from the perspective of the investigator at the outset of the inquiry. Having

discovered that they have shown themselves in the course of interaction, the investigator may infer that these functions are part of the system; their latency cannot be posited a priori but can be established only retrospectively.

Thus, the object of social investigation is to discover functional elements of a given system of action which do not appear to observation until the completion of the given interaction. This is surely a "speculative" element in the Mertonian paradigm and is borrowed from Durkheim's work on suicide. Recall Durkheim's view that while suicide is an apparent sign of social disequilibrium because it violates the cultural system, which commands that suicide be abhorred as an antisocial act, it may simply reinforce the solidarity of the community, which now rededicates itself to life and the tasks the community has not yet fulfilled. Further, suicide functions to spur reform in the rules governing social action if it has not been determined that the individual is deviant. In either case suicide reintegrates the society rather than results in its dismemberment. A similar argument is made about crime which contrary to common sense (which understand it as antagonistic to social and cultural integration) is, for Durkheim, a necessary referent for law and instruments of social order. The criminal validates the system of justice; deviance turns out to be the mirror image of norms.

Writing in the 1930s and 1940s, Parsons was influenced by the burgeoning prominence of psychoanalysis, both as a therapeutic practice and as a mode of social explanation. His designation of the "personality system" as one of the three principal components of the general system of action and as constituting, therefore, an independent variable in determining the social system, was not followed by most sociologists, who stayed close to Merton's adoption of only the elements of Parson's paradigm which remained useful for middle-range theorizing. Nevertheless, Merton joined

Parsons in rejecting the Hegelian concept of "totality," which posited the eventual unity of subject and object. Nor did sociology enter the deep waters of epistemological inquiry. Instead, action systems were studied at a "distance." The postulate of action as a mode of interaction between self and other was supplemented by the notion of symbolic communication as the chief mechanism by which culture is reproduced. I would argue that despite the considerable debt sociology in its American manifestation owed to some of its European forebears, especially Weber and Durkheim, the central intellectual orientations of American sociology are pragmatism and physics. The main concurrences of social theory to the pragmatic reading of scientific method are as follows.

1. The statement that the social system is constituted primarily by the interaction of two actors and that what we mean by the "social system" is induced from the multiplicity of situations in which actors engage each other.

2. The concept of latent functions that derive from unintended consequences of social action. As with Dewey, the object, therefore, is eventual and cannot be specified a priori. All social knowledge is a project whose object is the indeterminate system of action between ego and alter.

3. The only a priori is the methodological postulate of empirical verification, a social adaptation to the experimental method.

4. The organicist presuppositions of Dewey's naturalism are embedded in the structure/functionalism of the mainstream of American sociology, as is the notion of the social system as an unstable equilibrium constituted by its elements.

5. As with Thomas Kuhn's idea of normal science, day-to-day American sociology consists in puzzle solving within the paradigm of social action as the unit of analysis. The concept of puzzle solving corresponds to the problem-solving approach of pragmatism that rejects the search for grand theory, which in physics as well as social sciences is regarded as metaphysics. As we saw in Chapter 9, Dewey's commentary on Heisenberg's uncertainty relation is that it verified the particular nature of the object of scientific discovery. But mainstream sociology has not adopted Dewey's other postulate—that the object is constituted by inquiry, that its results are consequent of the relations between the knower and the known. The epistemological stance of sociology has been to take social action at a distance, to forget that the question asked in a survey constitutes the response and that "observation of fact" is itself problematic. To be sure, some critical schools in American sociology, such as ethnomethodology, make this problem the object of knowledge; the investigator is an element of the investigation, whose intervention is part of the field.

Sociology is mindful of Weber's admonition that fact must be separated from value, that to be a scientist means to expel the bias that may be present in sociologists' interests. It is widely believed that such methodological devices as multivariate regressions, modeling and rigorously maintaining the empirical referent to theorizing constitute a check on the value orientations of the investigator. But, with few exceptions, these methodological failsafes are relied on to validate the results, which, in relation to the frame of reference, are considered valid.

American social science, therefore, has followed the Popperian invocation of method to make knowledge "objective." Its assumptions, however, are by no means as sophisticated as those of physical science, for which mathematical precision has become its intellectual ideal. For whereas physical science, as we have seen, has been prepared to recognize the indeterminacy of its results and the relativity of its theory, social science is still embarked on the quest for certainty.

However, in many other respects, American sociology is a discourse that constitutes an element of postmodern epistēmē. For methodological foundationalism is by no means as secure as the epistemological variety. Further, social sciences as a set of disciplines are plagued by the plurality of paradigms that compete at both margins and center for intellectual space. For, even if the premise of methodological individualism and the rule that theories be of the middle range (and consequently subject to empirical reference and test) dominate the field, the leading paradigms within the sociological community have been unable, as in physics and chemistry, to impose their paradigm on others. That is, the positivists do not enjoy effective control over the system of rewards, including recognition of what constitutes true sociology, except in the United States.

That is not to claim that no elite exists in the discipline. The leading university departments of sociology, even in Europe, East and West, are predominantly but not exclusively dominated by positivists, but by no means are they only of the quantitative variety. In social science, not only is the discipline divided by a social division of labor, that is, by field (deviance, medical, educational, community, urban, political, etc.), but there is also a technical division between theorists and investigators. Social theorists, as in physics, enjoy higher status, and, among these, mathematical modelers and other quantitative methodologists do not (yet) occupy a space of privilege. Rather, the high-status theorists are analytic, i.e., those who interrogate, critically or otherwise, the categories of the discipline. Like other sciences, social sciences are preoccupied with metascience but reserve the privilege of this activity for a select few. To-

day, most investigative social scientists practice normal science, working in one or another positivist paradigm.

Thus, even American social science, which has an international reputation for its methodological orientation and, as Mannheim remarked more than fifty years ago, seems to have forgotten the "substantive" side of sociological theorizing, has recently discovered its own theoretical poverty. With the recent infatuation with some European social theorists, such as Anthony Giddens, Michel Foucault, Pierre Bourdieu, and particularly Jurgen Habermas (whose Weberian premises make American sociologists feel they are on familiar ground when reading him), a new generation of social theorists may arise in this country.

I would not want to make too much of the parallel between the interwar rise of the United States to global supremacy and the emergence of a social science that was concerned not with the dynamics of historical transformation but with the conditions for social equilibrium; and I would insist that the epistēmē of this period exhibits features not directly attributable to the economic and political position of the United States in world affairs. Nonetheless, the effect of microinteractionist sociology, in the interwar and post-World War II periods, was to shift the paradigmatic weight from questions of historical transformation to problems of social integration. Moreover, these problems were taken in their specificity, abstracted from systematic considerations. In this respect, Merton's functionalism represents a retreat from the Parsonian *system*, which, contrary to the accusations made against it by C. Wright Mills and Alvin Gouldner, was deeply influenced by the imperative to explain the causes of social change. Even Merton, who took sociology into the less ambitious territory of "social problems," attempts in one place in his magnum opus to argue that Marxism is fully compatible with functionalist explanation. Indeed, for Merton and his associates such as Paul Lazersfeld, the major fault of Marxism is not its materialist explanation of history with its emphasis on the mode of production. Rather, like the analytic Marxists who repeat Merton's objections thirty years later, he merely wants to purge social theory of its speculative elements and place its axiomatic and propositional structure on firm empirical grounds. And this course is to correspond to the analytic philosophical conception of science offered by the Vienna circle, Carnap and Reichenbach, Hempel, and, in a different register, Karl Popper. As we shall see, the sociological study of science forms the backdrop of the effort to turn sociology into a science.

Parsons's conception of the social system retained a considerable portion of the scaffolding inherited from the German conception of the human sciences. "Interpretive understanding" (*Verstehen*) is the core of the action situation. Actors do not simply enter into relations within a given situation on the basis of their "interests" or the propensities imposed on them by their (mostly) nonlogical personality system. They interpret the behavior of the other and reflexively endow *meaning* to both their own behavior as well as the outcome of the interaction. In this sense, despite his growing distance after the 1930s from this hermeneutic vision of the human sciences (for example, his organicism mainly displayed in his anticipation of systems theory), Parsons's work may be considered continuous with the European, particularly Kantian, perspectives on the possibility of the human sciences.

The American reduction of this tradition took the form of reliance on survey research: investigators take seriously what actors say, especially their accounts of both situations and beliefs. However, this apparent opening to subjectively meaningful utterance is limited by its quantifiability, and interpretation is left to the investigator. Thus, under the impact of the will to (natural) scientificity, sociologists, in the name of the empirical reference and the primacy of methodology, become enslaved to the structured interview, aggregation, and statistical averaging as mechanisms of generating social knowledge. Similarly, "normal" political science is nearly entirely encompassed by survey methods. Its frankly behaviorist orientation focuses on voting, aggregated attitudes toward specific issues and events. To determine the character of American political culture, it is sufficient, for many investigators, to aggregate the results of a structured interview with a cross section of voters, segregated by class, race, gender, age, occupation, region, and such other variables as provide a simulated totality. The key task is to predict and control election outcomes on the basis of voter attitudes and beliefs about issues and events and its corollary, to reduce the margin of error by perfecting the algorithms of research.

In this social paradigm, "action" is reduced to passively induced attitudes which manifest themselves in the voting booth or, alternatively, the reluctance to vote. This research aims at abstracting the relevance of the interview situation from the object of inquiry and attempts thereby, to get back to the things themselves, at least in relation to the electoral context within which all questions are asked. Needless to say, the aspiration to accurate prediction is often frustrated in an increasingly unstable national political system which fails to account for volatility in voting behavior. In recent years, the study of American politics, with the notable exception of some theorists such as Walter Dean Burnham, has abandoned explanation in favor of description culled from aggregate surveys. In effect, there is a merger between political journalism, which in the United States reduces new analysis to data, and some branches of political science, which are content to *construct* a model of behavior generalized from survey data. Of course, construction is never innocent for several reasons:

1. The data themselves are constructed within a framework of implied theories of social structure. The categories employed to select respondents not only are statistically derived from the demographic characteristics of the country but adopt an implicit conception of the social order. The lower one goes in the investigative hierarchy, the more stratification theory is taken for granted. Moreover, the stratification system is taken as an objective system in which individual membership is largely involuntary.

Yet, true to the indeterminacy of social theory, the categories employed in the survey sample are not presumed to offer predictive material to link social identification with either attitudes or behavior. The stratification system is employed primarily to ensure that the sample of individual interviews is broadly representative of the voting population or the otherwise relevant group. Analytic techniques may provide means for testing hypotheses about correlations between status attitudes and behavior, if voting for the choices offered by the political system is reflective of the latter.

2. The questions asked are constructed by the investigator. That is, the meanings imputed to action are transfigured by the interview situation into a series of structured, imposed questions that may or may not be of interest to the interviewee. Weberian conceptions of the action situation presuppose that actors have both cognitive and affective interest in interaction and that the situation is constructed, in part, by their intentions. In contrast, the interview situation is typically constituted by the interviewer's interests, whereas the interviewee may or may not perceive the encounter subjectively. Upon this shaky "unit," much political science and empirical sociology are constructed.

The tradition that American social science explicitly rejects treats the study of social phenomena from premises that can only be called philosophical. In the latter half of the nineteenth century, the question was posed in Kantian fashion: social relations exist, how are they possible? Historical and social sciences were constituted by this question. Lacking a failsafe method of verification and a controlled experimental situation within which to make observations, the social sciences are obliged to acknowledge, with Weber, that social knowledge is an interpretation among other interpretations which may also be valid. Not only is this condition produced by the infancy of these sciences; social behavior being "meaningful" is, thereby, always subject to the understanding of the investigator as well as the sometimes ambiguous self-interpretation of the actor(s). Peter Winch, accepting this unique character of social relations, has argued that Wittgenstein's philosophy of languages provides an important methodological amendment to other sociological methods: "If social relations between men exist only in and through their ideas, then, since the relations between ideas are internal relations, social relations must be species of internal relations too." In Winch's model, the relations between ideas are logical relations, so the rules governing logic should govern social relations as well. Winch's position "conflicts, of course, with Karl Popper's 'postulate of methodological individualism'" whose fundamental tool is models. Popper is, perhaps, the most outspoken nominalist in the philosophy of science, and his postulate of methodological individualism is still dominant in Anglo-American social science. Its origin is undoubtedly derived from the eighteenth-century economists' presupposition that economic relations spring from the actions of self-interested, rational actors. Even though Popper dispenses with the normative requirement of "rational actors," admitting that individuals may harbor nonrational expectations and attitudes, he stands with those, including Merton and Parsons, who would hold up the criterion of natural sciences to the social sciences, replicating, where possible, what they understand as the presuppositions of modern particle physics. Winch's argument is that the objects of social scientific inquiry are the logical relations between ideas that discursively constitute the social. Here Winch demarcates the social field from physics: "social action can more profitably be compared to the exchange of ideas in conversation than to the interaction of *forces* in a physical system" [my emphasis]. Consequently, among the objects to be investigated are language systems in use within a given social context, although these do not exhaust the material of social relations.

Thus, like Rorty's program in which philosophy becomes interpretive conversation in the European mode, sociology's objects are the regularities exhibited by the exchange of ideas between speakers starting from somewhat different premises. Winch's program is remarkably similar to that of the ethnomethodology school, which insists that the exchange of meaningful discourse is really *the* object of sociological inquiry. For both positions, relations, not individuals, are the methodological a priori and "conversation," not aggregated and reduced attitudes and expectations, are the material from which interpretive understanding is culled.

Harold Garfinkel tells us that if we want to find how relations are constituted, the "observer" disrupts everyday life to find out how it is constituted again. For without intervention, without participating in the exchange, social relations remain opaque to social inquiry.

One of the distinguishing features of Winch's and Garfinkel's critiques of positivist sociology is their insistence that the social world is constituted by actors *reflexively*. How we act entails evaluation of the consequences of our prior actions. So, rules of conduct are constantly being challenged, modified, resisted by actors for whom they are no longer self-evident. Wittgenstein regards the "given" as a mode of life which under ordinary conditions translates into rules of interaction. Following rules is what we mean by social life, because they define not only what people must do in a specific social context, but what is a mistake and under what conditions people may seek to change the rules, i.e., transform the social context of interactions. Rules may refer to the boundary conditions of exchange of ideas, the use of language, procedures governing conduct, and so on. What is clear about them is their social, not individual, character; they define what it means to be a member of a "given" community and what it takes to be excluded from it. However, one may not choose to be excluded from the language community, which is the ineluctable feature of social life.

Obviously, to know the rules implies that community members are more than habitual in their action. Rule making and rule breaking are both conscious actions and subject to evaluation. This is the sense in which every community is a discursive formation impelled by consent as well as necessity. For if necessity were the only constraint to action, social relations would be merely epiphenomena of biological relations. Production, in this model, becomes *social* reproduction, a permanent analogue to biological reproduction.

Underlying this approach to social science is the concept that individuals are inducted into the social world through language/discourse and that our mutual relations are regulated through exchange. It may be inferred that Winch's idea of a social science is really the addition of Wittgenstein's concept that discourse is the social mode of life, to Weber's theory of action, which always includes subjectively meaningful understanding.

The positivist and nominalist perspectives have become so powerful in social sciences that the Weberian program has been largely confined to a relatively marginal subdiscipline in sociology, that which addresses the social determinants of knowledge. The sociology of knowledge is by no means a *generally* accepted subdiscipline in social sciences. Or, to be more accurate, what is meant by the sociology of knowledge is often construed to refer to the ways in which knowledge *communities*, rather than what counts as scientific knowledge itself, are mediated by discourse, language use, rules of interaction, and so forth. This paradigm shift away from subjectively meaningful interaction, initiated by Merton in the late 1930s, addresses not the relation of science to ideology, since physical sciences are presumed to be ideology-proof by way of method. Merton asks questions that are quite distinct from the social constitution of knowledge; for example, the degree to which intellectual orientations may be permeated by extrascientific interests that have effectivity in the character of knowledge itself. Rather, his work sidesteps the question of the social determinants of scientific knowledge and focuses instead on two ancillary issues. The first is the normative structures within a society that may foster or hinder the pursuit of pure science. His specific question is, what are the values that must be present in society that lead to support for the scientific community? These include such norms as skepticism, without which new discoveries would bow to dogmatism, and universalism, by which is meant the commitment to seeking truth that is in turn free of particular social interests. Therefore, disinterestedness does not refer to the absence of the universal aims of science as an interest, but to particular interests that might impede discovery; and, finally, "communism," that is, commitment to collective and congenial work—the view that the discoveries made by an individual contribute to the progress of the community as a whole and must be understood as a contribution to the larger project of seeking universal truth. Merton equates these values with those of democratic societies, which are the only context within which scientific truth must be pursued.

Of course, this is not necessarily true. Although his essay on the democratic prerequisites for free science was composed in the midst of the rise of fascism, it would have to be assumed that Soviet and Nazi ideology, with their (differing) doctrines of the internal relation of knowledge and interest, the Soviet concept of dialectics as a metascience unifying others and its partisanship rather than skepticism, would be inimical to scientific "progress." Although doctrinal considerations play a role in Soviet science, they are also present in the formation of public recognition of American, and West European sciences. It is not difficult to cite examples that show partisanship and interestedness as universal traits, within both society and the scientific community. No science is free, even relatively speaking, of interest, and Merton's norms, however widely held among both scientists and others, are merely one set of operators in the scientific enterprise.

Second, Merton wants to discover how rewards work in the scientific community, and more especially, how scientists are created in the education system, laboratories, and professional associations. Scientists are found to quarrel over who first discovered a particular scientific phenomenon; they race to publish their results before another investigator beats them to the punch. In short, the scientific "community" is marked by intense competitiveness, even in "big sciences" such as high energy physics and molecular biology.

Careers are built by getting there first, including winning Nobel prizes with all the prestige and power that accrue to those who win them. This focus on the internal struggles within the scientific community dominates much of Merton's later work on science and constitutes the real paradigm of what became a genuine subdiscipline of sociology, the study of scientific communities. Just as sociology studies geographic, professional and demographic communities, so science becomes a legitimate community exhibiting the characteristics of any sociological object. What we want to know, according to Merton and his followers, is how scientists behave in their professional lives, what are the relations of power and privilege within the community, and how the scientific elites are formed and reproduced.

Merton's studies of the politics of the scientific community devolving around "reward" structures could provide a link with his earlier interest in the bearing of socioeconomic factors on selection of scientific problems. However, this is not the direction of his later work. Instead, Merton interprets the reward system in terms of the "institutional norms of science." Competitiveness is not the product of so-called human nature or personal ego, on the one hand; nor does Merton again refer to the socioeconomic influence. Now, the institutional norms of originality, role performance, etc., take precedence over other influences. In effect, the scientific community becomes the context to which the social study of science refers. And it is a context that begins to resemble a discursive formation in Wittgenstein's sense more than a power/knowledge axis, in the manner of Foucault's understanding of discourse. Norms are not free-floating ideas but are integrated institutionally by being linked to professional reward structures such as recognition and career advancement.

This emphasis represents a departure from Merton's early work in which scientific studies are considered from the point of view of the sociology of knowledge. What Merton wanted to know in the 1930s was not only which value systems were compatible with the process of scientific development, but also the influence of the context within which sci-

ence is produced on the forms of knowledge. His assumption, which pioneers of the sociology of knowledge such as Karl Mannheim were unwilling to make, is that science is not to be exempted from the general proposition that knowledge is mediated by the social context within which it functions, especially the intellectual orientations, the social or class interest of knowledge producers, and the value systems that accompany knowledge production. This perspective, most forcefully presented by Hessen's study of Newton's *Principia,* deeply influenced Merton's work. Both in his first book, *Science, Technology and Society in 17th Century England,* and in his defense of Hessen against G. N. Clark's critique of "The Social and Economic Roots of Newton's *Principia*" as crude economic determinism, Merton shows considerable appreciation of the central argument of Hessen's work—that technology influences the content of science, and that economic and ideological influences cannot be divorced from scientific discovery. In short, the social context considered in its totality influences the nature of scientific knowledge.

To be sure, in the mid-1930s, Merton is already developing his concern with the normative character of science and its relation to democratic culture. But his concerns embrace the influence of practical problems of navigation on fields of science such as astronomy. His corroborative case studies of transport, the military, and mining provide empirical verification for Hessen's thesis that, in Merton's words, "the range of problems investigated by 17th century scientists was appreciably influenced by the socio-economic structure of the period."

Yet, Merton stops short of endorsing Hessen's insistence that the content of scientific knowledge is linked to the socioeconomic structure, but confines his concerns to the *selection* of scientific problems. I can find no extended discussion in Merton's writings on science that explores the relations of scientific knowledge itself to the technical, economic, or value issues that surround it. Here, Merton does part company with Hessen and adopts the Mannheimian position on the sociology of knowledge: science *itself* must be exempt from the statement that knowledge is mediated by social interest. Rather, economic and technical considerations contribute to determining what problems will be studied, for, as Marx remarks in the famous *Preface to the Contribution to the Critique of Political Economy,* humans take up only those problems "for which the material conditions for their solution are already present," and this includes questions bearing on our knowledge of the external world. There is, according to Merton, a scientific ideology corresponding to different historical periods. But this ideology tells us only the general intellectual orientation of scientists toward research, even if it does not originate in the scientific community but is embedded in social structure. Thus, Merton finds that the value system we generally associate with the Enlightenment is also intrinsic to democratic societies. Science is linked to its social context through a common ideology, but if we follow Merton's work carefully, this influence is felt most strongly in the area of *method.* Such characteristics as skepticism, disinterestedness, etc., are safeguards against the influence of social interest on the content of science. So, a specific methodological ideology is the way to separate fact from value at the level of scientific theory.

Between World War II and the mid-1960s, the sociology of science is dominated by Merton's program. Studies of the scientific community, the influence of military and other social consideration on the selection of scientific problems, and the normative relation of science to the social order are the three legitimate areas of scholarship in social studies of science. Efforts to trace the social constitution of scientific facts are considered marginal to or are excluded altogether from mainstream considerations.

Merton's enduring contribution to the sociology of science, then, is his insistence that a politics of science exists, that the scientific community reflects, in deep ways, the normative order, not only its positive features that promote the search for dispassionate truth but its "sordid" aspects such as conflicts over the priority of scientific discovery. Moreover, the link between the socioeconomic structure and the selection of appropriate problems for investigation has opened the way for an enormously fruitful and detailed account of the ways that the state and large corporations have intervened in science to determine what is to be studied.

To be sure, the most important work in the politics of science has been performed by journalists such as Dan Greenberg and David Dickson, whose comprehensive studies of the close links of the scientific community with political and economic power, especially in the United States, show clearly what Merton indicated only programmatically earlier in his work. Or scientists themselves, notably Joel Primack and Frank Von Hippel, have argued that even when the formal machinery exists for the participation of scientists in shaping national policy in science and technology, corporate and political establishments, which control the use of science in industry and as instruments of foreign and military policy, usually ignore their advice. Merton's own students and colleagues have focused, instead, on the internal workings of the scientific community considered as a political arena. After the 1960s, American sociology of science has virtually ignored the part of Merton's program that calls for the exploration of the relation of the socioeconomic structure to the selection of scientific problems. One can only speculate about the reasons for this silence, perhaps suggesting that the selection of sociological problems is influenced by the political context as well.

Despite the ambiguity of Kuhn's *Structure of Scientific Revolutions* for a specifically social theory of science, its reception resulted in a sharp turn from the dominant paradigm. Although first published in 1962 in what retrospectively must be understood as a much longer wave of critical studies of the history and philosophy of science, the full impact of Kuhn's account was not really evident until the latter years of the decade, when Imre Lakatos organized a major symposium whose focus was the contrast between the Kuhnian and Popperian images of science. By the time of its publication, it was evident that the truth status of scientific facts was in contention. Nor could the experimental method be relied upon to vitiate the argument of the cultural conditioning of these facts. Significantly, in the 1970s, Merton himself joined forces with Kuhn to assist in the translation and publication of a long neglected study in the sociology of science, Ludvik Fleck's study of the origin and development of the modern concept of syphilis, originally published in 1934, coincidentally the year that Karl Popper's *Logic of Scientific Discovery* made its appearance. Fleck argues that the substance of scientific knowledge is culturally and socially "conditioned," that the facts adduced are constructed historically and cannot be understood as simply the result of observation and experiment. What Fleck calls "thought collectives" (the scientific community) adopt "thought styles" (paradigms of knowledge) that enframe the ways in which observations are assimilated into explanations. Thought styles tend to be "structurally complete and closed systems of opinion" which offer enduring resistance to anything that contradicts it. Therefore, "1) a contradiction to the system appears unthinkable, 2) what does not fit into the system re-mains unseen, 3) alternatively, if noticed, it is kept secret, and 4) laborious efforts are made to explain an exception in terms that do not contradict the system," and the exception is reconstrued, explained, and described in a way that tends to corroborate the system. Moreover, conceptions and evidence have no logical relation since there are many possible "correct" conceptions that can be derived from the same evidence.

Fleck's work may or may not have been known to Merton in the early years of the 1930s. Whatever the case, his mid-1970s collaboration with Kuhn and others to bring Fleck's work to English readers signaled the changing mood of social inquiry into science. For Fleck's study foreshadowed the new sociology of science, which was inspired by Kuhn's refutation of the Popperian objectivist concept of scientific discovery and explicitly criticized Merton's studied avoidance of the issues of the social relations of scientific knowledge. In the early 1970s, a relatively small group of (primarily) British sociologists and anthropologists undertook, simultaneously, to critique the Mertonian conception of the sociology of science and to study the social influences on scientific knowledge. Among the strongest contributions to this critique was Ian Mitroff's attack against Merton's argument for social norms as the chief regulative device for ensuring the progress of science. On the basis of interviews with scientists, he discovered that such phenomena as organized skepticism and disinterestedness are combined with the reverse. Mitroff argues:

> *that the norm of emotional neutrality is countered by a norm of emotional commitment. Thus, many scientists ... said that strong, even 'unreasonable' commitment to one's ideas was necessary in science, because without it researchers would be unable to bring to fruition lengthy and laborious projects or to*

withstand the disappointments which inevitably attend the exploration of the recalcitrant empirical world. Similarly, the norm of universalism appears to be balanced by a norm of particularism. Scientists frequently regard it as perfectly acceptable to judge knowledge-claims on the basis of personal criteria.

And "Mitroff produces evidence to show that the ideal of common ownership of knowledge is balanced by a norm in favor of secrecy." According to Michael Mulkey, "Mitroff's central argument, then, is that there is not one set of norms in science but two norms." Of course, Merton implicitly acknowledged this argument in 1957 in his study "Priorities in Scientific Discovery," where the sordid issues were, to some extent, sorted out. However, there is no doubt that the few instances where the politics of the community are understood to contradict the normative order are viewed by Mertonians, not as evidence of dual norms, but as ways in which "scientists are human," that is, emotional deviations from recognized standards. And Merton himself insisted that "competition" rather than communism in scientific discovery is a product of another institutional norm, the commitment to progress.

But the new sociology of science does not stop with the effort to revise Merton's program. Within this group, a branch known as the Edinburgh School, associated with the work of Barry Barnes and David Bloor, advances a new, "strong" program for the discipline. In Bloor's words: "The sociologist will be concerned with beliefs which are taken for granted or institutionalized, or invested with authority by groups of men. . . . The sociology of knowledge focuses on the distribution of belief and the various factors that influence it." And, for Barnes and Bloor, social interest is among the influences on belief as well as on what counts as scientific knowledge. Their

major innovation is to regard science as subject to these assumptions, rebuking the arguments emanating from Mannheim that science is not socially mediated knowledge. The program addresses the question of the social causes of scientific knowledge, including sociology: "In principle, its patterns of explanation would have to be applicable to sociology itself."

Bloor is careful to acknowledge the forebears of this renovation. Durkheim's call for impartiality "with respect to truth and falsity, rationality and irrationality, successor or failure" would be strictly observed. This ensures that sociology could study marginalized as well as mainstream science and would not make the a priori presupposition that mainstream scientific knowledge is always the rational choice from data. Further, Bloor wants to follow social theory's invocation to the primacy of method. In short, the sociology of science would maintain the commitment to accepted science rather than constituting itself as a counterscience.

In fact, there is considerable continuity between the "new" sociology of science and the "old" model. For the most part, the site of social studies of science remains the scientific community. However, evidence for this community is not found chiefly in journals or in professional associations but in the laboratory. The crucial study that adopts this perspective, Bruno Latour and Steve Woolgar's *Laboratory Life*, follows Bloor's defense of empirical knowledge. The laboratory is selected as the site of social relations of science, not only because this is where scientific knowledge is produced, but also because it is where the interactions among scientists engaged in production may be observed. The "observability" of scientific work consists in three artifacts: (1) the written results of scientific inquiry designated as "inscriptions"; (2) scientists' conversations recorded on video- or audiotape, which provide "reasoning . . . displayed in the midst of orders of intersubjectively accountable details," that is, the order of spoken utterances by different parties in conversation; (3) the compositional order of manipulated materials at the laboratory.

These are the "data" of social scientific investigation into scientific inquiry. By paying "painstaking" attention to the details, especially the temporal ordering of materials, conversations, and inscriptions, the *informal* versus the formal procedures are revealed. This program of ethnomethodology, when applied to scientific work, provides a close reading of the labor process of knowledge production and is expected to show the degree to which a second normative set is produced by the multiplicity of interactions. It is precisely in the ordinariness of scientific work that investigators expect to discover how science is done. The assumption is not that scientists do not mean what they say, but that human praxis obeys rules that reveal the variability of scientific methods and are not present unless the most minute details are attended. Further, since the "object" in mathematical and physical inquiry but also in biochemistry is rarely "seen" but must be inferred indirectly, the process of inferential consensus becomes for some in the new sociology of science a central object of inquiry. Rather than presupposing "interest" as a component of knowledge, investigators hope by "thick" description to make visible what goes on. What goes on, in the first place, is talk, or, in Bloor's terms, negotiation as to what is "seen," what to make of it, and how to inscribe it in writing.

For some investigators, the "it" represents something of a mystery. For example, Woolgar, reflecting in 1983 on the development of this field, expresses confusion about whether his earlier study *Laboratory Life* discovered that the new reality was constituted by interactions among scientists in the Salk laboratory or whether it was *uncovered*. This issue reflects the difficulties in sorting out the constructivist

and realist theories of science. Negotiation among scientists takes place to name, describe, and represent the significance of the scientific "fact." But, asks Woolgar, are the constructivists guilty of a priori judgment? Perhaps the accounts by scientists *uncover* rather than *produce* the objects?

Of course, the ethnomethodological approach to scientific practice cannot accept the strong program since it presupposes a set of relationships that, although embedded in practices, are understood as relatively autonomous. That is, knowledge presupposes social contexts, which according to Edinburgh theorists include the socioeconomic structure and "interests." Garfinkel remains neutral on these questions, which, in any case, cannot be settled in advance. Nor, I may add, does the construction of the object of inquiry permit such issues to intervene in the accounts. By adopting a perspective on what constitutes a proper social scientific object, namely, the "local" production of scientific knowledge, the laboratory, and confining the "data" to conversation, the ordering of manipulated materials (what is, in Heidegger's terms, "at hand"), and inscriptions, ethnographers cannot resolve the debate between the concept of knowledge as socially constructed through interaction and its "objective" character. In Woolgar's terms, the irony of social studies of science that commit themselves to get as close as possible to the site of production is that this issue becomes undecidable.

However, more recent studies have moved further in the direction of validating the argument that science in action is science constructed by discourse, technology, and power. Sharon Traweek's study of the culture of a major research laboratory in physics argues that machinery not only mediates what is seen in the course of scientific experiment, but becomes a signifier of power both within the research community and between science and society. She demonstrates by empirical inquiry the problematic character of observation. In her account, the machine constitutes, in part, the object. In turn, the machinery is built by scientists according to their own theoretical models.

Andrew Pickering's history of the quark in quantum physics shows that the theoretical models adopted determine the selection of the objects. For example, "from the experimental point of view . . . two key differences between the new (quark) physics and the old physics which preceded it were: an emphasis on the use of lepton rather than hadron beams; and, within hadron-beam physics, an emphasis on hard rather than soft scattering achieved through novel combinations of detectors." As machines change, so do physical objects and vice versa. This account differs from the traditional view of machinery as a tool of experimental physics. Like Traweek, Michael Lynch, et al., Pickering is concerned to show that the construction of machines that conform to a model of physical reality themselves play a role in the construction of the object. But his account goes further: like Quine's rueful discussion of the indetermination by experience of scientific propositions. Pickering's argument is that each step in the development of the concepts underlying the quark is indeterminate from the experimental data, and that quarks remain to this day only one possible inference among other choices which would be consistent with what scientists agree is observed. I think it is safe to say that the *form* of scientific facts is socially determined and reflects "interest." Thus what counts as science today is the "useful," the quantitative, the formula. This limitation may be so narrow that within it the data *do* often dictate only one possible inference. Pickering says that even if we accept science on its own terms (and he appears afraid to do otherwise), the data are consistent with many inferences, so that the inference we make is in a sense arbitrary. But this may not be true, and per-

haps it need not be true for us to say that such an inference is socially determined. The inference is forced by the narrow, socially determined boundary conditions that define what is acceptable as science. Why should we accept science on its own terms? For Pickering, the new physics is a worldview, and he disputes the scientists' own accounts of the evolution of the quark as an inescapable conclusion derived from experimental facts. Instead, Pickering asserts that these facts are actually "judgments" which are obscured by inscriptions made by scientists themselves. In other words, he argues that the presuppositions of realist theories disguise the construed character of physical reality. Having discovered this unremarkable (at least from the point of view of the new sociology of science) manner in which scientific fact is asserted, he goes further: the changes in high energy physics were culturally bound by research traditions and "shared sets of research resources" among actors. Moreover, these traditions constitute the conditions under which certain inferences, rather than others, are made from data. Pickering's account of the preferred research tradition in physics not only emphasizes the familiar, that is, types of explanation and the procedures used to verify them, but also argues that simplicity governs preference. In his account, quarks are the name assigned to (absent) phenomena that cohere with particle rather than field theories, which, in each case, offer different, although equally plausible, explanations for the same (inferred) observation. That the majority of the scientific community chose one over another is a function of scientists' preference for the tradition rather than the validity of explanation.

However, Pickering does not reach back far enough into the history of physics to find the basis of the research tradition from which the quark explanation emanates. It may not be found inside the tradition but in the ideology of science, in the differences behind field versus particle theories, simple versus complex explanations, the bias toward certainty rather than indeterminateness. But this might take the social investigator outside the laboratory and even beyond the scientific community. This might entail a critique of research tradition as a kind of ideology that guides interpretation, since the discourses of interpretation depend on but are not governed by facts adduced by experiment.

Third, Bruno Latour, whose pioneering earlier work with Woolgar asserted the social construction of scientific facts as the outcome of interactions among those performing scientific work, has made two significant amendments: that what counts as scientific knowledge achieves this status by linking itself to power—the power of leading figures in the scientific community and the state, and that of corporations that sponsor and transform research into technology. In both his historical study of Pasteur's discovery of a serum for curing anthrax and his more recent study of three major contemporary discoveries, he insists that an examination of scientific discourse is necessary but insufficient to establish the mode by which experimental results are converted into accepted truth; and that the laboratory has become a new center of power and is a model for society. Latour accepts the argument that a discourse analysis of science is needed to understand how social context is embedded in practice. Indeed, his close reading of both scientific and technological discoveries reinvents a *rhetorical* approach to the analysis of texts. Where Pickering's inferences from this type of analysis remain always implicit because, following the post-structuralist understanding of language, he holds that discursive formations are identical to what we mean by the social context, Latour says explicitly that the development of knowledge as a productive force, and of science as the core knowledge determining technology in all its manifestations, changes our understanding of

the significance of scientific research. The laboratory is now the late capitalist factory, its productive apparatus is no longer a reflection of social relations that lie outside it, but has become the set of internal relations that constitute what we mean by society. Pickering's slogan to epitomize his findings is that science is "opportunism in context"; Latour's is "Give me a laboratory, I will raise the world."

Latour provides the first account of science in terms of Foucault's declaration that knowledge/power is the object of inquiry, where power is constituted discursively through rhetoric, negotiation and inscription, but also by the political alliance of the scientists, the state, and capital. He offers examples of Merton's sordid politics of the scientific community, especially the competition between Watson/Crick's postulate that the structure of DNA is represented in the metaphor of a double helix and that of Linus Pauling, who offered a triple helix view. Moreover, he is among the few social investigators who has refused to accept the distinction between the power relations that constitute scientific facts and those of technology. And he draws the firm conclusion that nature is constituted in and through culture, including language, so that discourse must be taken as an object of inquiry. This will lead, no doubt, to fruitful studies of the texts of the traditions of which Pickering speaks.

But, at a deeper level than these conclusions, I must note the superficial resemblance, in some respects, between the new and the old sociology of science, or, more to the point, the degree to which the presuppositions of the positivist tradition still form the backdrop of this discourse. Although the new and the old paradigms differ as to expected findings, that is, differ as to whether the point of the study is to determine the degree to which scientific fact is constituted socially, with few exceptions each side expects to find answers in an examination of the ethnographic data. The sociology of knowledge is construed as an empirical study that fits neatly into Merton's program for middle-range theory (here, ethnomethodology parts company by bracketing the question of theory since any "explanations" contaminate the purpose for which the study of scientific work is conducted: to make visible that which is disguised by discourse). On a deeper level, the new sociology of science tends to confine its study to the laboratory, for the reasons given by Latour, which, in any case, are retrospectively adduced, and because it accepts the argument that scientific discovery is underdetermined not only by the "facts" since these are in turn constructed, but by the socioeconomic structure as well. Augustine Brannigan states the case best: "Language, as philosophers like George Herbert Mead and the phenomenologists Husserl and Heidegger have noted, not only communicates information, it constitutes and forms the social relations of its speakers." His reference is to Wittgenstein's translator and a leading commentator, G. E. M. Anscombe. Discussing to the concept of causality, Anscombe argues "how we come by our primary knowledge of causality" is that "in learning to speak we learned the linguistic representation and application of a host of causal concepts." Language discourse is the primary socializer into the scientific worldview. Thus, Brannigan adapts Wittgenstein's model of language as a mode of life to explain science. The process of scientific discovery is understood as meaningful action determined not by the nature of the object but by the conventions that are culturally acquired, especially in terms of the language games that constitute interaction.

However, in the final account, science is understood as Parsons and Weber understand all action—as socially meaningful. In turn, scientists inherit their presuppositions from the socializing work of language, which embodies folk and other cultural traditions. The accounts scientists make of their own discoveries, which are invariably framed in causal discourse, are seen by Brannigan as instances of folk reasoning rather than as representations of natural events.

From the perspective of traditional sociology, the main contribution of the new work in the social study of science is in no way a challenge to the basic paradigm of the sociology of knowledge: it merely insists that scientific discovery not be exempted from rules governing investigations into knowledge in which interest, culture, and power are recognized as mediations. Brannigan's treatment of science is parallel to the sociological study of religion developed in Weber's *Economy and Society,* and this is, of course, a scandal given that social science, no less than physics or biology, dedicates itself to finding Truth, defined in this context as rationally adduced knowledge that combines observation and experiment, rather than relying on intuition, revelation, or transcendence. To place science on the same plane as folk religion is surely controversial, but it must be recognized that Bloor and Brannigan, perhaps the most forthright and philosophically inclined among social theorists of science, are careful to associate themselves with the dominant paradigm in sociology, precisely in terms of its axiom that the social system is constructed from units of action, that actors interpret action-situations teleologically, that is, in accordance with their own purposes, but also with their unconscious motives that intrude in scientific discovery; and, equally important, that the cultural system, conceived here as intellectual orientations, is integrated into what counts as knowledge.

Perhaps Latour has gone the farthest in implementing Winch's program for social science. I would argue that what is lacking in the social studies of science is a way to make the power/knowledge link commensurable with the idea of science as a discursive formation. Foucault's argument that the "social" may be considered only as a series of discursive formations surely has advantages over the older base/superstructure models or theories in which action and communication are considered separately.

The knowledge/power axis in Foucault's archaeology, implies that power relations cannot be subsumed under discourse, even if discourses always embody power. For, even in Latour's study of the emergence of Pasteur's laboratory as a new power center, this development resulted from the authority the latter's discoveries received from state/corporate power: "He (Pasteur) transfers himself and his laboratory into the mist [sic] of a world untouched by laboratory science. Beer, wine, vinegar, diseases of silk worms, antisepsy and later asepsy, had already been treated through these moves. Once more, he does the same with a new problem: anthrax." In the case of anthrax, Pasteur moves his laboratory onto a farm site. "They learn from the field of veterinary, translating each item of veterinary science into their own terms so that working on their terms is also working on the field." This *positioning* of the laboratory in the field of production follows the fact that "it is in laboratories that most new sources of power are generated." The laboratory becomes the new social context as well as the site of knowledge production. The traditional distinction between inside and outside (the famous "externalist or internalist" accounts of the process of scientific discovery) is overcome.

Surely, Latour is right to insist that the laboratory is a site of power, constituting both text and context and also a new model for society. And it may also be said that knowledge producers in this new social paradigm *impose* a new regime upon production. But sociology still has to account for other power centers that may not be the repositories of scientific knowledge themselves, but that still command knowledge as a (crucial) resource for the reproduction of their institutional power.

It would be interesting to apply Latour's model to the study of the relation of the American military to the scientific community. The military is a discursive formation with its own language, rules of action, and priorities. Its connection to knowledge has become absolutely fundamental for the maintenance of its power, and it does not directly incorporate science institutionally, except in selected fields such as civil engineering, ordinance and strategy and tactics, and other questions bearing on organization. In relation to the development of modern weaponry, it is certainly dependent on relatively autonomous knowledge, which, even if financed by public (military) funds, remains separate. Could it be argued, as Latour appears to do, that the military is subsumed under science and technology since laboratories are now the "new" sources of power?

As we have seen in Soviet science, if one accepts the postulate that the scientific/technological nexus is today the major new source of power, the capacity of scientific communities, by their assent or refusal, to determine the configuration of other discursive formations, to become the core constituent of action situations in all spheres, brings into existence new relations of domination and subordination.

Latour has adopted, even if unwittingly, STR (the Scientific-Technological Revolution) as the leading postulate of a new sociology of science. To push the argument further, he wants to argue that the sociology of science is not merely a subdiscipline of social science, but has become the heart of the discipline. "Lab studies" are "the key to a sociological understanding of society itself" because "it is time for sociology of science to show sociologists and social historians how societies are displaced and reformed with and through the very contents of science." The laboratory has burst the boundaries of its technical funding and the "future reservoir of political power is in the making."

This is the *strongest program* for the sociology of science, but its validity is not an empirical question. At stake is the claim not only that knowledge has become the leading productive force, but that scientific knowledge contexts are displacing other power centers, making them contingent. Whereas Marx assimilates knowledge to intellectual labor, which is, in modern capitalism, subsumed under capital, especially in the labor process, Latour claims this relation is in the process of being "reversed" and argues for the materiality and effectivity of its discourse.

How does this occur? Here, Gouldner's point becomes relevant. When knowledge producers develop their own culture of critical discourse and generalize it as a social model, science is positioned to impose this social model because its method is reflexive. The "interests" underlying scientific discovery are not extrinsic to the ordinary normative and experimental structures of the community, but are embedded in both ideology and procedures. If science is organized around the principle of reflexive self-understanding which goes beyond skepticism, we can expect that its relations with other power/discursive formations cannot be reduced to its subsumption but must be termed "alliances" in which dominance and subordination are not determined in advance.

This hypothesis implies that at least on the level of the elite, scientists are conscious of the power/knowledge axis, and it is a choice rather than a relation of coercion that cements the links between physics and chemistry and the military, biology and large medical corporations, geology and the oil industry, sociology and the social policy apparatus of the state. Thus, from a subdiscipline of social science, social studies of science become a way to study and understand power, especially class relations.

Whether the scientific community constitutes itself as a class is an empirical, historical, and theoretical question. The empirical/historical dimension depends, in the last instance, on how classes are theorized. If the classes are conceptualized as self-constituted historical actors, the argument that intellectuals, particularly scientists, are a class in formation is entirely plausible. But this concept is not necessarily compatible with the Marxist expectation that rising classes are historically progressive. For the centrality of science and technology to capitalist and really existing socialist formations suggests only that the power/knowledge axis becomes a crucial problematic for the survival of old classes and ruling groups of these formations. One must allow for the possibility that the bearers of knowledge as historical agents may forge compromises with the old hegemonies, rather than acting independently to challenge that power. This possibility assumes what Marxism has been unwilling to admit: the capacity of the traditional bourgeois or even postbourgeois discourses and power centers to assimilate new power centers into their fold, or even to negotiate the terms of a settlement.

This model predicts neither contradiction nor integration, only that both are possible. It retains the indeterminacy of the postmodern epistēmē without positing complete deterritorialization in which power is so dispersed as to become unintelligible. Further, it retains the crucial idea of agency, even if no longer lodged in the old actors. Or, at least, it enlarges the range of historical actors to include not only the new social movements not directly linked to class positions but also new classes whose identity springs not from relations of ownership or even control of the means of production, even if they are crucial to production itself. The concept of the formation of the intellectuals as a class relies heavily on the relatively autonomous mode of discourse as social object, the knowledge/power axis, and the economic/social formation, without establishing in advance the priority of one over the other.

The empirical/historical question is how discursive formations position themselves in these relations, what is their political effectivity, and which alliances do they choose to make in their own interest or in relation to the (conflictual) structures that have formed them and reproduced them?

This perspective differs from the recent tendency of some, like Ernesto Laclau and Chantal Mouffe, Latour and others, to collapse social relations into discourse. In the first place, arguments for the disappearance of the social as a category independent of discursive formations tend to read the knowledge/power link into history in a way that becomes ahistorical. The historical argument, which asserts that this link has been made under specific conditions, is far more persuasive, even though Foucault's studies demonstrate, I think convincingly, that knowledge is connected to power prior to the late nineteenth century. But his studies sidestep the question of class formation. Instead, Foucault means to show that moral discourses contain a profoundly political content, and that the position of a discursive formation relative to others influences its effectivity. Laclau and Mouffe generalize this amendment to the study of social power and, in the process, abolish classes. Refusing the reduction of the social to discursive formation denies not the validity of such categories, but that only discourse encompasses all relations. Post-Foucaultian social theory has assimilated his work to a centralizing postulate that is unwarranted. Surely, economic and political relations are constituted through language, and in this sense, examinations of inscriptions, conversations, and of the position of knowledge in the power matrix are extremely important, especially because these studies are virtually absent from social sciences. That social studies of science have entered this research will prove rewarding for clarifying the way in which scientific knowledge is constituted as power.

Second, one would not wish to deny the materiality of language/knowledge, and thereby reduce either to a function of the socioeconomic structure. And it may prove to be true that the socioeconomic structure is constructed from the laboratory, the knowledge-factories upon which it increasingly depends, especially in advanced industrial societies, in both East and West. The question is whether the older socioeconomic structure, which is based on the state-capital conjuncture, dissolves into discourse? Or, whether the scientific labor process and its procedures dominate all production? We might want to adopt, provisionally, a threefold structure of social action in which the old mode of production, including the classes and institutions tied to it, retains considerable power, including its claims on knowledge production. That it is forced to give ground in the wake of the emergence of a scientific/technical social category seems unassailable.

What needs to be avoided is the tendency to displace classes by discourse and thereby to establish a new universal. For the value of Foucault's archaeology consists precisely in its antiessentialism, its ideas of dispersal, deterritorialization, and its refusal to designate, in advance, univocal motor forces that propel history. We can fruitfully adopt the concept that institutionalized knowledge is, *sui generis*, a new power center which inscribes the social without retrospectively reading this relation into the past. Instead, we may understand the position of science and its apparatus in the social formations as historically specific, as constituting a new and undeniable problematic of these formations whose consideration makes them intelligible.

This formulation avoids the tendency, characteristic of a considerable portion of contemporary social theory, to assert scientific and/or technological determinism, or, to be more exact, the determination of knowledge, over all other discourses and social relations. Rather, I want to advance the postulate that knowledge is a discursive formation that, at the same time, constitutes itself and its agents as new historical actors. That science has become indispensable for virtually all social formations in the late twentieth century and has established its hegemony on the ideological plane seems unexceptionable. That it is required to connect itself to the capital/state axis threatens to undermine its autonomy, although what we mean by these other formations cannot be separated from the will to scientificity. (The examples are almost too numerous to mention, but it is enough to recall that the concept of the scientific management of society has become the ideal of this axis. What is meant by this slogan varies according to time and place. But the desire to transform politics and economics into sciences, rather than keep them as arts, is nearly universal.)

The real question is whether the culture of critical discourse is a leading ideology of the social categories that surround science as a discourse, not the least of which are the scientists themselves. We may read Popper's corpus as an effort to establish the hegemony of his conception of critical science over the entire enterprise. In a different register, Kuhn's internal referent for paradigm shifts leans in the same direction. For if science is not subject to the fundamental influence/determination of other power centers and their discourses, we may assert the autonomy of science and its effectivity without positing its subsumption under capital, not only with respect to the selection of problems to be studied, but with respect to the contents of scientific discoveries.

If science is a discourse whose status as privileged inquiry within the social formation is historically rather than naturally constituted, its autonomy is always mediated and therefore relative to its position within the social formation of which it is a part. Its place is constantly renegotiated with other power centers, and the degree of its "freedom" is always understood in context.

Toward A New Social Theory Of Science

Stanley Aronowitz

It remains for me to show *how* science is social relations. For even if Marcuse has already argued for the ineluctability of the relation between science, technology, and social domination, he has not provided a systematic, detailed explanation of the way in which, by virtue of its own concepts and methods, scientific practices promotes a universe in which domination of nature is linked to the domination of humans, or the way in which science is a form of power. The fundamental argument advanced by Horkheimer and Adorno concerning the presumptions of science and technology refers to the Enlightenment's transformation of nature into an object, the simultaneous estrangement of nature by taking it as an antagonist rather than a partner of human culture and the organization of production and the state by bureaucratic management. Thus, "rationality" itself becomes inextricably linked to domination. The division of labor is now conceived as the segmentation of tasks and their performance by qualified persons who have found their place in the order of nature and society by purely individual talents, while, conforming to the pregiven organizational chart that defines the boundaries of their authority and has the status of a natural fact.

The imputation to nature of characteristics that are nothing more than the objectivization of the table of organization of the social world has imparted to both the appearance of natural facts as well. On the one hand, nature is taken as external to human consciousness, a hallmark of the scientific attitude since the sixteenth century. On the other hand, as we have seen, humans have attempted to make their world "scientific," to organize economic, political, and social life according to a system of rationality that is understood as consistent with natural law. The point made by Critical Theory is that society has reified nature and its own relations. Although external to consciousness, we have imposed our own class-dominated, bureaucratically organized division of labor on the external world, which, in contemplation, appears at once lawlike in its structure, chaotic. For the floods, torrential rains, snows, earthquakes, as much as disease, in short, the unexpected "revolts" of nature have become phenomena to be controlled; these events define the task of science, the horizon in the quest for domination. Just as nature is understood as subject to subsumption under human powers, so humans themselves are increasingly regarded as controllable. The "sciences of man" have been mobilized in the drive for social and psychological domination; the instincts, according to B. F. Skinner, the latest of the behavior managers, must be directed, lest the famous "war of all against all," that is, the freedom of the marketplace, result in the destruction of the human species itself. Of course, Skinner is just the most "humanistic" of the scientific managers of human behavior. At a more global level, governments have now recruited social science in a wide-ranging effort to manage international relations and biology to "manage" human reproduction.

For in late industrial societies, east and west, the fear of nature has been projected onto the fear of humans, a fear of their psychic structure as much as their command over the material means of destruction. And, of course, the object of economic science throughout most of the twentieth century has become the uncontrolled vicissitudes of civil society that lead to inexplicable crises or wars. Economics is now nothing but a technology masked as social theory for assisting the state, in both East and West, in managing the economy, or, to be more precise, in displacing contradictions from the relations of material production to other institutions and countries.

We have already seen that the choice of scientific inquiry is now subject to corporate and state determination, not necessarily by coercion or even material incentives of a crude type, but in virtue of the capital requirements of the apparatus of scientific work. For the costs of scientific research (at both "natural and social levels") have made it virtually impossible for the aristocratic scientists to pursue their labors in the privacy of their estates. Nor can scientific work proceed on the basis of patronage by aristocrats and prosperous business persons. The days are over when Frederick Engles, for example, a Manchester textile employer, could slip an occasional twenty pounds to his friend Karl Marx so that the progress of the development of a science of society would not be disrupted by Marx's need to write a few pieces for the *New York Tribune* to keep family and body together. Now the patron has become a corporate foundation established as a tax dodge and to provide a bureaucracy for the conduct of research that appears independent of corporate sponsorship. The state, too, insofar as its veneer of ideological and economic neutrality has become a major support for research, is a crucial patron. And corporations, confined for the most part by their emphasis on "applied" research (a euphemism for technological development), help define the parameters of the financing of all sciences.

The state and the large corporate foundations claim that their grants are free of political influence and that they have created a mechanism for bringing members of the scientific community into decision making, to legitimate their claims to neutrality. Many scientists believe that such measures safeguard the integrity of "pure" scientific research. However, it must be noted that leading scientists and technologists are increasingly integrated into the management of the state. When Harold Brown, president of the California Institute for Technology, a major scientific and technical research and educational center, became Jimmy Carter's Secretary of Defense, it was a sign that the scientific establishment had achieved considerable status in the commanding heights of political power in America. For it is one thing to place scientists high in the councils of the National Science Foundation, a government agency that funds research, and quite another to acknowledge that science is no longer a "servant of power" (in Loren Baritz's terms). Science and power are now in the process of merging, a frightening verification of the theoretical appraisal that the division between the state and civil society is undergoing a collapse, if it has not already been accomplished. From the political and ideological perspective, the control of scientific research by the guardians of "normal" science ensures, in the first place, that the *choice of the field for scientific inquiry* will remain subject to the determination of those who are considered mainstream scientists. By bringing them into the apparatus of government and the corporation foundations, as well as the large corporations (which perform about one-third of all scientific research), the social system legitimates its own claim to neutrality from the conflicts of civil society and makes sure that science reproduces a certain direction of inquiry. It is true that the Department of Defense finances "pure" research, that the Department of Health and Welfare is interested in biological sciences, not only those fields subject to immediate application, but also more long-range and theoretical areas. The vast sums of money appropriated by the state and private foundations each year are subject to the priorities of Congress, the executive branch of government, and economic considerations. It is not that the government and corporate foundation bureaucracies *consciously* believe in the subordination of science; on the contrary, many if not most are persuaded that the autonomy of research ought to be maintained "in the national interest." But the management of science by leading scientists and scientific bureaucrats (those who were scientists, but have become managers of research projects and institutions such as universities that manage research) has an ideological content, insofar as science is itself a "normative" activity. (1) Theory and method, (2) the form of result, (3) field of inquiry, and (4) the constitution of the scientific object are categories within which norms are established and normative activity defined. To the extent that the norms within these categories are part of the taken-for-granted assumptions of science, coercive control by the state and corporate apparatuses becomes more or less unnecessary; scientific culture (the matrix of conventions of inquiry, social and political networks among scientists, the language and institutions of science) is usually the sufficient condition for bringing science within the apparatus politically and for reproducing ideologies in which the domination of nature, already a normatively constructed practice, is linked to the domination of humans.

Beyond the social determination of the field of inquiry, the *constitution of the scientific object of knowledge of inquiry is linked to the prevailing social and technical division of labor.* At the level of the so-called social division of labor, science itself is constituted by various distinct fields or practices whose demarcation has purely historical roots. Or, the rationality that informs the division of conventional scientific fields may be shown to conform to systems of classification that have historical origins. There is a *social logic* of the classification of the sciences, rather than a logic that is "given" by nature.

It is by now commonplace to remark that the relation of magic, science, and philosophy is an internal, rather than external, conjunctural phenomenon. Historians of science have pointed out that science breaks from magic and religion and becomes a secular philosophy only during the Athenian city-state, and breaks with philosophy during the Renaissance period, during the development of capitalism. These breaks are accompanied by mutations in the logic of natural and social inquiry whose relationship to changes in the concept of rationality is intimate. Yet, the logic of science is continuous as well. This continuity may be traced, in part, to Aristotle's invention of a binary structure for classifying *levels* of material things. Aristotle presented the system of classification according to which physics, astronomy, biology, and other sciences were arranged as an outcome of the logic of identity and exclusion. This logic proceeds from a system of binaries (the either/or) in which the exclusion of oppositions within the thing (an explicit repudiation of Heracleitus and the other pre-Socratic philosophers) is taken as the foundation. The principle of classification also contains the concepts of levels, according to which reality is arranged hierarchically in a series of mutually excluding layers of object-classes.

Aristotle deals in both a theory of "natural causes" and a theory of the "prime mover" —God. There is both a scientific and a religious element in his theory, and the religious side gets bracketed by modern science; but the logic of noncontradiction and hierarchy remains central to both stages of the history of sciences. Thus, even if we may sidestep for now the question of whether ancient and medieval sciences were dedicated to empirical observation as the ground for their theoretical formulations (as Feyerabend claims), the foundation of modern science accepted much of

Aristotle's classification system, because the *logic* of scientific inquiry remained largely intact until the nineteenth century. We may speak of an *Aristotelian* revolution as the genuine epistemological break between what is called science and prior forms of natural inquiry, because it is he who divides the natural as well as the social world and thus defines the scientific object as one level of that world.

The concept of levels of material existence was at first integrated into "natural philosophy" only implicitly. But, by the sixteenth century, it was clear that a hierarchy of sciences had already taken shape. Mathematics, of course, was the "queen" of the sciences, because its object had the greatest degree of generality and was not confined to any one science. Physics was privileged among the so-called empirical sciences because it attempted to find the most fundamental unit of matter to which all other levels could be reduced and to discover the laws of material motion and transformation. Astronomy was similarly important but, as we have already seen, lived in the intersection of practical concerns such as navigation and the ideal of knowledge for its own sake. In a sense, it was not a separate field of science because it was subsumed, from the beginning of the modern era, by physics. Chemistry, biology, and psychology are sciences whose separation from philosophical speculation came only with the period of industrialization. The development of psychology as an independent discipline really came out of the mind/body split introduced by Cartesian metaphysics and the British empiricists. As a branch of biology, the field had been dominated by the reduction of mental phenomena to properties that could be traced to physical and chemical causes. As late as the time of Freud, the conflict between the concept of the mind as a legitimate object of knowledge and its reduction to the instincts, which were supposed to possess a bioenergic character, made the object of knowledge ambiguous.

The division among the sciences into fields of inquiry was generated by the adaptation of the rules of formal logic to systems of classification, the concept of levels in nature, which is grounded in (1) the logical principle of boundaries or exclusion, where a thing is only what it is and excludes another, and (2) the principle of contradiction, which asserts the separability of a thing from anything else, or a determinate other. *A* and *B* exclude each other by definition but may be arranged in a grid as binary oppositions or vertically as an ordered discourse. The concept of hierarchy, in which these defined sciences are arranged in vertical order, is presented in Aristotle, and in the modern era, legitimated by the social organization of sciences as if these are a property of nature.

The concept of levels in vertical ascending or descending order presupposes the formal rationality of Aristotelian philosophy and cannot be taken as an observation from nature. In turn, this type of rationality, challenged in the modern period by Vico and Hegel, has remained hegemonic in the constitution of the fields of scientific inquiry, determining the relative weight, both within the scientific community and in society at large, of the various disciplines. I call these divisions *social* because they correspond to various branches of industry under capitalism, which are similarly historically formed—as industry is formed. In place of steel, automobiles, electronics, retail, public sector, etc., science is organized into various fields that are considered as separate discourses corresponding to separate levels of reality.

But science is also organized according to a technical division of labor in two ways: first, the distinctions between pure and applied sciences, and second, between these and "technology," appear to be objectively rooted in the nature of the objects. Scientific workers in these three fields acquire a common education only at the beginning of their training; occupational nomenclature as well as prescribed curriculum vary depending on which of the fields is pursued. The applied scientist may develop new types of cosmetics, synthetic fibers, or artificial fertilizers, but not concern himself/herself with the physical chemistry of matter except insofar as it relates to the development of a product. The character of the scientific object here is socially determined, more specifically, has to do with the difference between the pure researcher, who is engaged in making discoveries about the "nature" of the material world, apparently with no ulterior purpose beyond the discovery itself, and the applied researcher, who is part of the system of rational-purposive action: knowledge is gained about the material world, indeed, the object of knowledge is clearly defined in terms of its commercial, industrial, or social uses. Society has placed an ideological premium on the acquisition of knowledge for its own sake and an economic premium on the practical, i.e., technical outcomes of knowledge. In this respect, the technical division of labor masks the fact that both types of knowledge depend on historical and social context—particularly the way in which the relation of the state, the economy, and the ideological forms divides scientific labor. The parameters of the object of knowledge are socially prescribed depending upon this context, and are given significance by their respective institutional frameworks. Thus, discoveries made in each sphere that do not conform to the teleological presuppositions of that sphere may be suppressed. Even though the pure scientist may discover a practical use for his/her theory, such applications would tend to be "forgotten," laid aside, regarded as either inappropriate or trivial because intervention may not bring prestige with the community of pure science. Conversely, the industrial laboratory is not considered a place for "pure science." The applied scientists' work must yield a marketable product, that is, a product which can yield at least the average rate of profit.

The technical division of labor *appears* to be normal, a division of branches of scientific labor, just as any other two branches of the same industry seem naturally divided according to types of tasks. But this logic masks the hierarchical character of the divisions; the ideological outcome is to preserve the notion of a pure science unsullied by the marketplace. At the same time, the difference between "pure" and "applied" science retains the concept of the neutrality of at least one branch of scientific research.

The organization of scientific research takes place on the same basis as the organization of industrial labor. At the pinnacle of a research project or institution there is a manager; in the university, the site of much of what is called pure science, this person is a professor and is considered a working scientist and teacher. But, as a manager, this individual has a specific set of responsibilities that correspond to those of any other superintendent: raising funds for the research, hiring and firing professional and technical staff, and equally important, maintaining relations with the administration of the university, the funding source, and the scientific community at large. He is an administrator/politician whose skills range from those of persuasion to repression. Often, he becomes a manager as a result of his stature in the field of inquiry, usually gained years before his academic ascendancy. Thus, he becomes the logical person for the managerial function because he belongs to the social network called the scientific community and the academic community. His ability to maneuver within bureaucracies is made possible by years of sitting on committees, including review panels for the National Science Foundation and other agencies where he has gained contacts. When he writes a research proposal, scientific bureaucrats and university administrators are inclined to accept it because they know him to be a *normal* scientist who is also an effective negotiator and operator.

I have already remarked that scientific research is no longer the province of individuals; it is now a vast social, economic, and political enterprise. In the first place, it is located in mainstream institutions of society: the universities, corporations, and "independent" institutes, often connected to both schools and business. The nature of the research process in both the pure and applied branches is connected to the use of high technology equipment amounting to several million dollars for even modest projects. Often the equipment is nontransferable, that is, cannot be used for other projects because it is designed for specific experiments, by scientists working on the project. It is not unusual for many projects to be funded as joint ventures among several institutions who are similarly connected to government agencies and the scientific establishment.

Each project is organized as a job hierarchy below the principal investigator, or manager of the project. Research scientists fall into two distinct groups within universities: the academic faculty, whose major responsibility is to work on the project and whose ancillary task is teaching, and a growing number of researchers hired for the individual project, possessing no academic standing. These are usually postdoctoral fellows or migrant employees who are hired on contract and who perform their duties at the direction of the faculty members or directly under the principal investigator. Often their activities do not differ from those of other researchers on the university faculty, but even if they are included as authors when the results of the project are published, this may not be significant for their careers.

The homology between migrant construction or farm workers and many scientific researchers does not refer to the type of work they perform, but to their *social position* within the scientific project. Even if highly paid, they are never integrated into the "scientific community"; their relationship to the institutions of primary research is always tenuous because they are only part of the "team" for the life of the contract. Thus, their influence is usually confined to the single project. They are often assigned specific tasks within a much larger investigation, which, however complex and based on their sophistication about the major issues in the field, is largely controlled by those with stable ties to the scientific establishment, including those institutions charged with the bulk of research.

Graduate students in physics, chemistry, and biology occupy an ambiguous position with respect to research. Typically, their work is linked to their doctoral dissertation. In turn, the choice of both field of inquiry and object is defined by their thesis director, who may be either an academic member of a research team or a manager. The function of the doctoral study in the sciences, as in the social sciences and humanities; remains primarily to constitute a *rite of passage* into the field. But the natural sciences, and increasingly the social sciences, possess more power than other disciplines to ensure that the candidate has internalized their ideological precepts. Since the process of knowledge acquisition is far more collective, the research project is the scene for the reproduction of the scientific laborer as much as the production of knowledge. The graduate student is obliged to accept a thesis director who not only advises on intellectual issues connected to the research topic, but selects the topic, supervises the methodology of inquiry, and manages the process itself. The graduate student is often completely under the domination of faculty, which not only approves the results, but intervenes at every step of the research to ensure that the intellectual canons of the scientific community are observed.

Thus, the process of paradigm maintenance is built into the training of the graduate student in the sciences, since the student is already a regular member of the research team and the dissertation consists in little more than a report of results of one segment of the project, reconceptualized in academic terms so as to meet the requirements of the university. This merging of the academic process in the sciences with the research functions of the university serves to undermine any critical function of the academy at its foundations, because the social organization of scientific labor at the micro level conflates learning with performance. The concept of critical distance associated with the acquisition of theoretical knowledge is foreshortened by the increasing tendency of social and natural scientific graduate study to be integrated with research projects that are commissioned by the government and by private foundations or are indirectly (or directly) associated with product development for private industry. In many sciences where the experimental activity depends on the availability of fairly expensive equipment, the learning process for students takes place within the framework of research projects even if the research takes place on the university site. Access to up-to-date equipment is limited to those who participate as members of the research team.

This rule is equally true for the social sciences which increasingly employ computers for calculation and data gathering. As quantitative methods become more "normal" in the social sciences in comparison to older qualitative research methodologies such as ethnography, the whole enterprise of social scientific research, in both universities and private or government research institutions, is bound up with norms of natural science. Although it is still possible for students to enter the social sciences without being committed to its positivist objectives, it is increasingly difficult to complete graduate degrees in most major universities without participating in funded research projects. It is not only that the student is obliged to learn certain methods that imply scientific ideologies or paradigms. The basis upon which degrees are granted is increasingly bound up with such research as is currently funded by the government or private foundations. In sociology, economics, and political science, most funded research contains explicit or implicit policy outcomes. The mobilization of the social sciences for purposes of helping to shape and evaluate social policy has become characteristic of research since World War II. The research is linked with instrumental ends that become disturbing for the social sciences, and much of the research is fragmented, narrow, and, in the last analysis, remains part of system maintenance. It is not uncommon for large grants to be made for social research on drug abuse, alcoholism, child abuse, and criminal behavior. These areas are selected by funding agencies on a relatively arbitrary basis: the topic has become politically significant; the "public is clamoring" for solutions. Federal, state, and local governments are under pressure to "do something." The task of research is either to *legitimate* a series of preselected responses by providing a "scientific" veneer for policies, or to help guide political and social agencies in the selection of options.

Very little of this applied research has the time, the money, or the inclination to challenge the presuppositions of these topics, although individual researchers sometimes become critics of the categories and institutions associated with these practices. For example, can the causes of crime be discovered on the basis of data that focus on individuals, or even local environments such as neighborhoods? Or, to be more far-reaching, does crime have a cause? Or, do we have an adequate definition of what we mean by crime, that is, is it a discontinuous set of behaviors and attitudes that can be separated out from the complex of activities that make up daily life within society?

Social research devoted to discovering the causes for criminal behavior often selects the wrong object (the individual), makes the assumption that crime can be abstracted from a larger series, and that the medical model (treatment) may be applied to its cure. Thus, much of the debate in what is called in sociology "deviance" centers on options that are circumscribed by these viewpoints. Students who select "deviance" as their area of sociological study are provided with funds to complete their dissertation through their participation in projects supported by government agencies. In many cases, their adviser is principal investigator for the project and, as in physics and biology, sets the parameter for the student's research; the student is then assigned to a particular segment of the project. Without this opportunity to work on the project, the student would be obliged to teach in undergraduate programs in order to earn sufficient money to write. Since many departments of sociology are oriented nearly completely to policy research, this student might not find an adviser, a necessary requisite for the dissertation. And, even if such a person could be found from among senior faculty, the burdens of being a teaching assistant or an adjunct for several courses might prove too difficult to allow the student to do much writing and research. The induction of social scientists into paradigm maintenance, while not yet as overwhelming as in the natural sciences, is becoming increasingly common.

The managers, of course, are responsible for another, equally central function of research. They define or supervise the *definition of the object of knowledge.* Their position in the specialized field of inquiry is such as to enable them to determine what is an appropriate object of investigation as well as a fundable field of inquiry. This object is often tech-

nically divided, not only by the broad divisions such as between chemistry and physics, but even more narrowly. Within each scientific discipline, which defines the *level* of the scientific object, there are subdisciplines that define the field within the level. Examples of such subdisciplines are quantum theory, high energy physics, and cosmology, and even these have further divisions. Some scientists are trying to determine the properties of causality in relation to these fields, others to determine the properties of specific metals, particles, or waves, to predict their behavior and control their action in a field.

From the cognitive perspective of scientists, these fields appear to be a logical set that is generated by the progressive march of science. One "problem" is solved and another arises as a side effect of the solution. As we gain more knowledge, so many scientists believe, we are able to pose new questions that are now capable of solution by virtue of our prior knowledge. But even if this tells one part of the story, it remains an incomplete account. The division of scientific labor into sets of problems to be solved already implies that such categories of "prediction and control" form the presupposition of science. Its *purity* is mediated by the rational-purposive character of the scientific labor process. Problem-solving approaches to science are forms of fragmentation of the object. The subject, the scientist, has inserted herself/himself into the field of observation from the outset. Thus, science is a form of purposive action that proceeds from a rationality that is conventional, but that appears to have the force of natural fact. The progressive subdivisions within each level, or scientific discipline, already embodies the history of scientific interventions into nature. Nature has now been defined and subdivided in accordance with the social will of the scientific community as well as the corporations and the elite sciences, is organized within the boundaries of the social and technical division of labor analogous to any industrial enterprise. The organization of scientific labor is not a socially neutral process. And the determination of the object of knowledge presupposes this division of labor, the technical parameters of which correspond to those of any other branch of the labor process. Just as the assembly line is organized according to definite rules, preeminently that work is divided into a series of discrete, repetitive operations, and the function of management appears merely that of coordination of these fragmented tasks, so scientific labor is organized in terms of an object of knowledge that remains discrete and fragmented and is given significance only by its managers.

If Althusser is correct that theories, experimental method, and technique constitute the mechanism of scientific knowledge—its internal apparatus, which becomes the criterion, in the last instance, of the truth of its discoveries—then one of the crucial tasks for an argument that wishes to oppose the separation of science, ideology, and social relations is to show the ideological character of the *experimental method*. The Copernican revolution has been supposed by most writers to consist in the first place in taking account of the observation of nature in the development of scientific theory. Its *sufficient* contribution to the history of science has been traditionally understood as the insistence that a scientific proposition can be verified (falsified) only by means of experiment. However, the experiment is an ambiguous activity.

The presupposition of all science, according to Karl Popper, is that no proposition may be said to be scientific unless it can be falsified by observation or experiment. Thus, no statements about the material or social world may be taken seriously if it cannot be reduced to a form that may permit the methods of experimental science to operate. This a priori is part of the apparatus of modern science, is closely

linked to what contemporary sciences mean by theory: a theory is a proposition that can be verified (falsified) by experiment/observation.

Now, "observation" is not the same as "experiment" in the commonsense use of these terms. Observation usually implies the reception by the senses of external phenomena. But, for science, the term "observation" is linked to experiment; the scientist observes effects of experiments, or to be more typical, records results of experiments in numerical form. A theory is merely a hypothesis that can be quantified by means of observing effects recorded in numerical form. In these terms, the scientific observation of human behavior, no less than the observation of subatomic particles, is concerned with effects that are presumed to be accurate reflections of the intrinsic properties of the object.

The ambiguity of the experimental method becomes apparent when we remember that its preconditions include decisions about how the object of knowledge is to be constituted, not only by its classification according to levels and fields, but also in the setting up by the scientist of the *boundaries* of the experimental field. It is commonplace among scientists to reduce the number of variables to be observed to the *least number possible* because the ability to make sense of the observations is understood to be a function of this reduction. Thus, the second condition, after its definition, is to delimit the observational field by decontextualizing the object so as to facilitate the project of predicting and controlling behavior. I do not wish to dispute this procedure for the moment, merely to point out that such decontextualization implies that the category of interpretability has already changed the concept of observation to conform to the requirement of prediction and control. What is observed is the effects of an experiment on an object under certain conditions determined by the scientist and his/her apparatus. Of course, the investigator knows that decontextualization limits the claims resulting from the experiment. He/she often tries to model the environment within which the organism or object interacts within the framework of experiment. But the requirement for at least *statistical probability* for prediction and control restricts the degree to which the experimental method may be taken as an "objective" mechanism of knowledge.

Experiment is a type of human activity that is an *intervention* by the investigative team into "objective" processes. The forms of intervention entail the establishment of the context within which the object is observed; the machinery employed to produce the effects from which inferences are made according to theoretical presuppositions and from the rational-purposive basis of all modern knowledge. Werner Heisenberg's indeterminacy principle attempted to preserve the objectivity of scientific theory by inserting the observer into the observation field and arguing for a science that recognized the problematic character of the results and included these in its calculations, procedures, and results. The instrument of observation must be taken into account in the measurement of the object as well as in the determination of its position, according to Heisenberg.

The philosophical implications of this argument have disturbed scientists and philosophers because claims of science to precise calculation of the movement of particles, and the integrity of the experimental method itself have been challenged by the revelation that the object of knowledge may be our relation with the object, not the thing itself. Most physicists as well as philosophers have now been obliged to acknowledge that nature offers more than one option, depending on the theoretical framework in which the experiment is conducted. There is said to be a "degree of truth" in these determinate options, now called interference of possibilities. The framework adopted by the scientist to understand the results of experiments will make the result itself.

Largely because of the development of quantum theory, modern theoretical physics, at least, has been forced to work with uncertainties. The experiment is one valid means of knowing the external world, *provided* we understand that knowledge depends on its theoretical presuppositions, which are taken as no more than possible explanations for the characteristics of matter.

The crisis in science has occurred because of the challenge posed by Heisenberg and others to its positivist assumptions, particularly the notion that the relation of the observer to the observed is unproblematic. When Heisenberg reduced to mathematical language the simple notion that what is observed depends on the apparatus of observation, that is, depends on experiment, the scientificity of science was thrown into question. In the 1930s and 1940s, some, like James Jeans and Arthur Eddington, took these discoveries to mean that nature was, at the bottom, a mental construct, or at least was unknowable. Others understood Heisenberg's principle as an invocation to further limit the variables, to further narrow their field of observation, or to calculate the impact of the mechanism of experiment and make their results more probabilistic.

Since we can only calculate effects and infer causes, control and predict behavior by constituting the object of knowledge theoretically and changing it in the process of our intervention, I argue that the so-called laws of nature are better described as *laws of science*. Scientific theory describes the relation of humans to the object of knowledge, not the objects themselves, taken at a distance. Further, our knowledge of effects is always mediated by the logic of scientific discovery, e.g., by its concepts of causality as a part of the apparatus of discovery.

Linear causality assumes that the relation of cause and effect can be expressed as a function of temporal succession. Owing to recent developments in quantum mechanics, we can postulate that it is possible to know the effects of absent causes; that is, speaking metaphorically, effects may anticipate causes so that our perception of them may precede the physical occurrence of a "cause." The hypothesis that challenges our conventional conception of linear time and causality and that asserts the possibility of time's reversal also raises the question of the degree to which the concept of "time's arrow" is inherent in all scientific theory. If these experiments are successful, the conclusions about the way time as "clock-time" has been constituted historically will be open to question. We will have "proved" by means of experiment what has long been suspected by philosophers, literary and social critics: that time is, in part, a conventional construction, its segmentation into hours and minutes a product of the need for industrial discipline, for rational organization of social labor in the early bourgeois epoch. To be sure, we may discover that time's arrow is inverted and that the evolutionary assumption of the progressive nature of time possesses only a "degree of truth" insofar as it is *one possible option* in answer to the question about the complexity of temporality. But so was the older theory of time and causation "experimentally" verified.

Since our knowledge of the external world is gained principally by theoretical construction and experiment, and since the purpose of experiment is not the verification of hypothesis in an abstract sense but the prediction and control of external phenomena, the masked basis of experiment is domination of nature and of humans. Prediction and control are presupposed in the language of science-mathematics and statistics. Mathematics is understood by scientists to be necessary to remove the ambiguities of ordinary language, to gain a degree of precision in the description of re-

sults and the inferences about the internal construction of the objects of knowledge. There is an "intrinsic uncertainty in the meaning of words," in Heisenberg's view, a conclusion that already prompted Aristotle's solution to this problem by investigating the formal structure of language and "conclusions and deductions" independent of the content. Aristotle thought that formal logic would lay the "solid basis for scientific thinking." That "solid basis" could be obtained only when form was abstracted from content and when the relations of these forms were expressed symbolically. The separation of quantity from quality is instrinsic to the constitution of the physical and chemical object in the reduction of all observations to their mathematical, that is, symbolic, form. I have argued that the logic of these relations has historically obeyed rules that are not ideologically innocent: they are linked to the attempt to achieve dominion over nature in order to satisfy human ends. In turn, these ends are mediated by social relations, by the further mediation provided by the scientific community, which operates according to rules of evidence and canons of truth that are part of the legacy of Western logical thought.

The implications of modern developments in theoretical physics have called into question the logical tradition because new ideas such as "coexistent states" and "uncertainty of possibilities" seem incongruous with the loss of contradiction and mutual exclusion. Heisenberg has discovered that the logical principles that underly mathematical symbolization are no longer in a relation of simple correspondence to nature. The concepts derive from the theoretical ambiguity of physics, its noncorrespondence with nature, which Heisenberg has called the "limits of the correlation" between the older languages of classical physics and the new concepts soluble only if

> *one confines the language to the description of facts, i.e., experimental results.*

However, if one wishes to speak of the atomic particles themselves, one must either use the mathematical scheme as the only supplement to natural language or one must combine it with a language that made use of a modified logic or of no well defined logic at all.

When science digs into the areas of "potentialities or possibilities," it has left the world of experimentally adduced facts or things, and the old logic must be abandoned.

If natural language is filled with meanings that defy precision and thus make control and prediction difficult, the language of control, mathematics, contains within it a limit on science. The questions within scientific theory that imply a logic that defies the formal categories of space and time and that have renounced, however implicitly, the rational-purposive, i.e., experimental, basis of investigation, lead to the discovery that ordinary language, precisely because of its undecidability, is more suited to these issues. Experimental methods, the results of which are formulated in purely quantitative terms, may not be abandoned but must be placed in a subordinate position to speculative science frankly concerned with a reconceptualization of all the fundamental presuppositions of the old science.

Despite his intentions to preserve the heuristic value of experimental mathematical science, Heisenberg opened a Pandora's box: he began the process by which physical science must become reflexive, that is, must recognize its own presuppositions as interested, that is, as ideological. A scientific practice that forces research to subordinate itself to a normative a priori of prediction and control is prevented from reformulating the object of knowledge in ways that may be suggested by the anomalies arising from its own methodology. The presence of measurement in the observational field, that is, the objectivity of mediation, the challenge to time's forward direction, which

questions conventional theories of cause and effect as a temporal series, the self-limiting character of quantitative a prioris to research—these may not result in the formulation of a new paradigm as long as science remains entwined with the requirements of domination. Such questions will remain on the margins of normal science, relegated to the purgatory of projects that are poorly funded, or worse, regarded as secondary priorities in the organization of scientific research subordinate to defense requirements, or the construction of bigger and more efficient machinery to "treat" conditions such as heart disease and cancer that have become a concomitant of industrialization. Of course, the establishment of priorities for scientific research is common to all nation-states that manage science and technology. These priorities embody the economic and political programs of these states, are formulated in terms of technical problems that require solution for the benefit of the entire society. But, as certain branches of science stumble on anomalies that cannot be fitted into the existing *ideological* presuppositions of science, not merely the particular paradigm, the question of the internal processes by which new paradigms are formulated is thrown into doubt.

Take the question of medical science. In the United States, millions of dollars every year are appropriated by government and private corporations to find "treatments" for diseases whose "causes" are related to the entire matrix of social existence within our society. The object of knowledge is defined as the human body not principally the quality of social life. Research institutions employ a virtual army of scientists, engineers, and technicians to discover chemical treatments for these diseases. The experimental method dictates that medical treatments be tested on animals under laboratory conditions. Researchers also test hypotheses about the causes of the diseases under the same conditions. Causal factors stemming from the "external" environment, such as the relationship of cigarettes and industrial pollution to cancer and the relationship of stress produced by insecurity and tension arising from working conditions to heart disease, are acknowledged but studiously avoided as the object of knowledge. The scientific object is the *effects* of these conditions on the human body, which, in the last instance, constitutes the limit on scientific inquiry related to medicine. For medical science is confined to the study of the human body, even if practitioners may take external factors into account. Thus, the question of defining the causes and cures of infirmities finds its parameters within the characteristics of the body itself. As a result, medical science, more or less willfully, defines its tasks in terms of ameliorating the effects of a social system that produces disease. In effect, within a system where rationality is determined, in part, by the criterion of capital accumulation, the rationality of scientific research on disease cannot be in conflict with the larger rationality without risk.

Even late capitalist and state socialist science has been required to study the degree to which the rationality of capital accumulation affects the physical environment. But, because of the social divisions within the sciences, these questions are not the province of medical research. If studies of the impact on the biosphere of the use of some types of spray cans show that these devices should be banned, government regulation may prevent the entire species from becoming extinct. Yet, medical science may not adequately study the degree to which repetitive labor performed at a killing pace should be stopped to prevent heart disease, or whether certain materials that pollute the work environment with carcinogens, such as some types of plastics, should be declared illegal. Funds for medical research dealing with the prevention of disease by social means are far less available than funds for research treating the individual as the object of knowledge. Medical research in the United States is confined almost wholly to discovering treatments for diseases already presumed inevitable. Occupational health-related research comes regularly under severe political attack by large corporations that may be forced to change labor processes and equipment, both with respect to what is produced and with respect to how production is conducted. Managers of medical research projects internalize the attacks by avoiding such subjects as may be considered unlikely by funding sources, by media, and finally by their own professional communities.

Nevertheless, some preventive medical research goes on, and its results are published and sometimes disseminated beyond the networks of professional science. But environmentally related research of all types occupies the margins of medical science. It is not considered "sexy," except when its results show that specialization and segmentation have gone too far, that it is sometimes in capital's interest to pull back, either because popular movements have exerted political pressure or because the legitimacy of the state and the corporations has been undermined, as was the case with the food scandals of the early twentieth century.

The case of medical science illustrates the ideological content of science, the degree to which science is constituted by social relations. First, the object of knowledge perpetuates the division between the body, the mind, and the external environment. Second, the technical division of labor within medicine segments parts of the body so that research is often directed to discrete characteristics of each part that may be susceptible to disease, without considering the relationship between these and the body taken as a whole. There are exceptions to the extreme rationalization of the body into fragments for the purposes of study; but, for the most part, medical science accepts the invocation to reduce the number of variables within its experimental methodology to a minimum. This reduction of variability of course becomes ideological insofar as it induces an epistemological perspective which does not conform to the way in which the human being acts in the world, but which sets internalist boundaries that conform to the precepts of normal scientific inquiry. Thus, the chemistry of the body is a legitimate object, the work environment is not.

Third, medical science, by dealing with effects of absent causes, produces treatments that are often detrimental to the rest of the body. The "side effects" of medication are understood by specialists as unintended consequences of certain remedies. Since the object has been so narrowly construed, chemical treatments often produce more problems than they resolve. And, since the mind/body split has, for the most part, been preserved in medical research, or, to be more precise, the problems of the mind are increasingly reduced to the body, mental illness is treated as a problem of chemical imbalances, skewed metabolism, nutritional aberrations, or some other type of physical mutation. For a brief period after World War II, when ego psychology became fashionable among middle strata groups, the reverse tendency was observed. For numerous physicians as well as social workers, teachers, and nonprofessionals, many diseases could be traced to "psychosomatic" causes. The psyche was believed to produce everything from the common cold to heart disease. But this psychological reductionism was just the other side of physical reductionism.

Of course, there is a great deal of validity in both perspectives. The division of labor within science has blinded each to the dialectical relation of the body to the mind, their indissolubility. Most medical research cannot conceptualize the notion of a body-subject, that is, a body that acts in the world and has both conscious/unconscious sides which constitute physical as well as mental functions. Even if such "unscientific" conceptions could be formulated, research that began from this relationship would encounter difficulties gaining support, because of the difficulty in reducing such conceptions to discrete experiments and in quantifying the results.

Yet, the consequence of our understanding of pathology resulting from the mind/body split, the methods of normal contemporary science, and the reductionist ideologies has been to perpetuate the "mysteries of the organism." Despite the fact that billions of dollars are allocated for research that seeks to develop elaborate chemical treatments, which may disturb the internal relations within the body, or to construct machines to deal with symptoms, medical science is imprisoned by its own ideology. It still operates on the basis of linear causality and has been unable to find "cures" for diseases that have no simple origin. Yet, there is no prospect for immediate change: large-scale research will continue to search within the fragmented body for the secrets of disease, for the one vaccine or chemical cure for our maladies, in the hopes of avoiding social or preventive medicines.

Of course, as critics have shown, the expansion of a misdirected medical research establishment is predicated upon the political pressure of large drug and machinery corporations, in alliance with hospital associations, research institutes, and the dominant forces in the medical profession who control these medical institutions. Yet, it would be a mistake to attribute *all* the problems of scientific research to the power of these institutions. Political and economic power must be linked to the preproduction of an ideology of science, in this case ideological presuppositions for the discovery of causes and treatments of diseases. For, even if "profit" was taken out of medicine, it does not follow that science would immediately turn to a more integrated, dialectical view of its object. As the experience of those countries in which the private ownership of capital has been abolished shows, the transformation of science and technology entails the transformation of the epistemological as well as the material foundations of science.

It is time to summarize the discussion of the relation of science and ideology. I shall follow it with a discussion of the problem of the truth in relation to ideology. My central thesis that science may not be considered a separate discourse from ideology depends on the following propositions:

1. The concept of the science/ideology antinomy is itself ideological because it fails to comprehend that all knowledge is a form of social relations and is discursively constituted. Within late capitalism and state socialism, these relations are organized according to a division of labor (principally the division between intellectual and manual labor). The rational-purposive basis of social production under both capitalism and state socialism means that science is a labor process as well as an ideology whose truth claims are entwined with the interest of domination. This ideological function is revealed in at least five ways:

a. The choice of the object of knowledge or inquiry is determined by the complex of economic and political alliances made between scientific institutions, corporations, and the state. These have a virtual monopoly of the means of scientific production and dictate, more or less completely, those projects that may be supported. This monopoly does not preclude funding occasional projects that depart, in one way or another (although never in toto), from the canon of normal science. But these are always relegated to exceptions, whose function is to legitimate normal, incremental science. Contrary to Kuhn's ascription of paradigmatic change to internal developments within science, particularly the relation of experimental results to accepted scientific laws, since science as well as technology are

entwined with the relations of power, these changes will always be constrained and configured by social and political influences.

b. But although the end of the alliance of science with corporate and state institutions and technology is a necessary condition for an emancipatory scientific theory and practice, it is not a sufficient condition. As Marcuse has reminded us, after centuries of reproduction of society according to division of classes and the division of labor, we have internalized, even introjected, domination. Specifically, this means that the *object of knowledge* has been constituted according to the social division of scientific labor (physics, chemistry, biology, psychology, and human sciences), and these categories are considered separate objective levels of natural and social reality, rather than necessary but partial abstractions from the totality of social existence.

Second, the object is constituted by a technical division of labor, where specialization of tasks within a field determines the perception of the investigator, such that a fragment is defined as the object, taken out of its natural context for the purposes of study. The result of this fragmentation is to impute characteristics to an object, discovered under certain circumstances but taken as intrinsic to the object.

c. Ways of knowing in contemporary science are discursively produced. The experimental method is not an "observation of nature" free of presuppositions. It assumes (i) that the abstraction of the object from its natural context is unproblematic, (ii) the intervention of the observer into the observed both by measurements that produce certain "effects" from which inferences are made, and by producing "causes" of the effects, such as by applying electrical currents of certain frequencies and magnitudes in physics, by inoculating animals to produce symptoms from which causes are inferred, and so on. The assumption of *intervention* is only part of the reflexivity of science to the extent that it tries to "correct" for its ingression. But the experimental method must be recognized as informed by its presupposition of intention, that is, the control of nature and humans so that their action may be predicted. Its claim to value neutrality is vitiated by the degree to which behavioral hypotheses or symptomatic readings are endemic to scientific inquiry.

d. *The form of the results* of science is historically located in the formal logic of Aristotle, which tried to understand forms of nature irrespective of their particular content. Galileo's doctrine that the "book of nature" was written in the language of mathematics was the logical culmination of this attempt to reduce nature to a form that permitted its predictability and control. But mathematics as the hegemonic form of scientific discourse constitutes a boundary to science. To the extent that knowledge is inextricably linked to language discourse, it generates a set, an internal unity that excludes those questions that require natural language and do not rationalize anomalies in terms that reduce *signification* to their technological dimensions. The separation of quantity from quality is linked to the divorce between means and ends. For example, a society wishing to "use" the results of science to serve class-determined or class-mediated human ends requires science to take a form in which it may be infinitely fungible. Even if the ostensible purposes of research are not instrumental in the immediate uses of results, the quantification of results lends technical significance to the research. Under present conditions, such technical uses are almost always connected to social and natural domination or profit.

e. The development of conventions that are legitimated and reproduced within the scientific community determine what is called truth, and what is acceptable as science. These conventions are not separate from the paradigms of scientific knowledge, which may be

seen as both the presuppositions and the outcome of the systemic requirement that certain traditions of inquiry, methods, and forms of results be followed. The observance of the conventions is just the other side of the rituals and credentials that are preconditions for entrance into the scientific community. Thus, no less than any other specialization in the division of labor, the scientific community regulates entrance requirements, conditions for membership maintenance, and power relations within the community. Since the entire machine of scientific investigation presupposes the social relations of the prevailing mode of production, the project of transforming science must be consonant with the project of transforming social relations.

2. The struggle for the transformation of ideology into critical science is a project in our period which is made possible by recent philosophical work. It proceeds on the foundation that the critique of all presuppositions of science and ideology must be the only absolute principle of science. Thus, a reflexive science is radically opposed to "normal" science that takes its ethical, epistemological, and methodological foundations for granted. Althusser's Freudian metaphors have validity insofar as change can take place only when what occurs behind our backs is brought to our conscious view, that is, when science takes itself as its object.

Since the turn of the century, when it became apparent that capitalism had undergone a fundamental transformation in its structure and material/ideological practices, those who wished to preserve Marxism as a living socialist philosophy and critique of capitalist society have tried to comprehend the character of the changes and to discover their implications for Marxism itself. The Frankfurt School, which tried to integrate Freud and Weber with a Marxist framework, made a serious effort to challenge the theoretical presuppositions of Marxism in the light of historical changes.

More recently, others have claimed that the historical conditions that produced Marxism have been surpassed by the integration of the working class into late capitalist society. As I have shown above in my critique of Habermas, such positions do not constitute a critique of Marxism from within but abolish its foundations by constituting a new scientific object. At the same time, whether in its French manifestations (the new philosophers) or its German expression, post-Marxism, since it cannot identify the motive force of history because it has abandoned the category altogether, is left with a new positivism. For those who have abandoned agency as a vital historical category, there are no conditions for the transformation of society. All critical theory may do is refine the categories of the eternal, reified present and wait for the "will" of humans to take care of the rest. But Gouldner is right to point to the historicity of Marxism, especially its nineteenth-century insistence on the autonomy of science. For a critical theory cannot be critical of itself if its highest aspiration remains to achieve scientificity in the traditional sense. It is this aspect of Marxism that has generated the post-Marxist antinomies as much as the changed social conditions within late capitalism and the deformations of state socialist societies.

Historical agents are not necessarily personified in particular social categories, for example, industrial workers, scientists, or women. To approach the question in this way ignores the critique made by contemporary philosophy and social theory of Marxism, or, to be more exact, merely replaces workers with women, the Third World, or whatever. What is at issue here is the discovery that agency is produced discursively and that people attach themselves to certain discourse because these offer a vision of an alternative to the system of production and reproduction of social life. I hope to show in a future work that the emergent agency today

defines itself against the prevailing rationality, not within it, and this characteristic precludes the substitution of one group of personified agents for another, or the reform of the management system governing the production of either knowledge or things. For what is at stake in the struggle over historicity is the challenge to the dual system of domination over nature and humans, of which the prevailing division of labor is a crucial element, but also the entire system of social production and appropriation.

In short, the discourse we need to elaborate is already present in the various critiques of Marxism, liberalism, and conventional science.

3. Science and ideology have the same object—the material world and social relations that have been produced by social labor considered historically. All relations with this world are mediated by material and social structures and the concept of unmediated relations that may produce knowledges that are independent of the social processes by which they were acquired is the ideology of science that draws its inspiration from the bourgeois protest against feudalism. Since the relations of science, magic, and religion are internal to each other because they all purport to offer adequate explanations for natural and social phenomena, it is rank ethnocentrism to claim that one may be privileged over the others without specifying the social-historical setting which under capitalism tends to subsume all discourse under its system of rational-purposive action. Within this framework, modern science becomes a partner of industrialization, whose social consequences have both liberated us from the brute struggle with nature, but only partially, and imprisoned us in a logic of domination and degradation.

4. If science is ideological, what is truth? My argument leads to the conclusion that truth is the critical exposition of the relations of humans to nature within a developing, his-

torically mediated, context. Within this critical project, the form of appearance of social relations is a unidimensional rationality that implies particular conceptions of space and time, causality, and construes the object of knowledge both discursively and socially. Thus, the laws of science are the laws of nature, providing one specifies the system of rationality within which they are discovered. Their reified "natural" appearance remains opaque without the weapons of criticism: we can discover the external world as a product of the collective labor of centuries, not by observation, but by the construction of a series of concepts that are contradictory to the certainty of the senses that only report the surfaces. I am not claiming that critical science exists. Normal science, particularly the study of microphenomena, has also contained a critical dimension but is not, itself, critical, especially of its own presuppositions, for example, the discovery of the atom, which was theorized long before it was "observed," and the hypothesis of the psychic structure, whose existence could only be inferred from a "reading" of symptoms. In the study of society, Marx's theory of surplus value is, above all, a logical discovery; examples given to illustrate it are mostly "made up." This does not imply that Marx failed to do detailed historical and empirical economic research. My point is that Marx's theoretical framework was constituted by the relation of history to its conceptual foundations in dialectical philosophy.

But normal science is enslaved by its positivist presuppositions. Its *structure* of inquiry as much as its picture of the world makes it *positive* and *descriptive* rather than critical. For science and technology within its current framework to challenge its foundations would be tantamount to its self-immolation because it would be required to separate itself from the economic, social, and political conditions for its work as much as its epistemology.

5. What we call science and what we call ideology are distinguished *in practice* by the degree to which the acceptance of the ideology of science exempts it from being called ideology. "Ideology" is the general form of all human thought because social relations coded as discourse not only mediate but constitute thought itself—the forms of discourse refer to the material world in ways that are demarcated from each other yet all appear as truth. The various moments of discourse appear as common sense. Ideology, in general, takes the form of discursive hegemony. The most general sense in which hegemony is exercised is the internalization of an entire conception of the material and social world by the population of a given social formation. The most powerful form of hegemony is inscribed in science, which is constituted both by its paradigms at the theoretical level and by the complex of institutions and material practices that are reproduced as self-focused and self-evident facts. Scientific ideology refers to a totality of forms of conceptualization that not only are reproduced as knowledge of the material world but take on the appearance of the material world, such that the opacity of things has the force of nature. The laws of science are perceived as properties of nature, bereft of their material and historical determinations and mediations.

Some Theses on Science and Technology

1. There are three key aspects of capitalism as a social formation: the universalization of the commodity form over all production; that is, production for exchange and for profit becomes the dominant rationale for investment of labor and money capital; the Industrial Revolution, in which machines become the central productive force, together with the

technologies of the organization of labor; and urbanization, which is usually distinguished from medieval or ancient cities which were centers for regional and world trade in food. The modern city, now a site of industrial production, becomes the space of accumulation of capital whose main form is *fixed* capital, or machines and buildings.

Although scientific and technological knowledge play a crucial role in the development of capitalism, it is not until the mid-nineteenth century that intellectual labor (whose sole possession is knowledge) becomes a major productive force, partly displacing both craft and unskilled types of manual labor. In his *Grundrisse,* Marx already takes notice of this shift, which is still nascent even in England. The first half of the twentieth century is marked by the ascendancy of knowledge (if not of a new intellectual class) as the premier productive force. This transformation is manifest not only in the rise of the engineer as a key player in production, but by the advent of *scientific* management which seeks to both subordinate the manual labor force to its direction, and to impose systematic methods of control and organization over the state and the corporations. Management is an *ideology* to the degree that it seeks power on the basis of a new rationality that claims the mantle of science in affairs outside the laboratory and other traditional sites of scientific work; it is also a potentially competing community that challenges the hegemony of capital and the state, or, to be more exact, wants to impose its unique discourse on these hitherto autonomous sites.

By the first half of the twentieth century, neither science and technology nor management, the two most important forms of intellectual labor, had as yet captured more than the workplace, more than the sphere of production of things. Still to be conquered are the military and other state institutions, the crucial economic institutions of capital, principally financial agents and, more globally, cultural life.

2. The past thirty years have been characterized by the emergence of technology as the discursive formation that constitutes the dominant space of dispersion in industrial society. This entails massive impositions in (nearly) all social relations or discursive formations. Here, I define "discursive formation," following Foucault; as *a group of statements that form a unity.* These statements include the formation of the knowledge object, the rules for investigation as well as the specific claims about the objects. To say that the discourse of technology is dispersed everywhere does not signify a kind of technological determinism in the older meaning of the term; what is commonly understood as "technology," namely, machines or tools, do *not* constitute the determining element of social life. I am not arguing that means constitute ends in the modern world, or that the forces of production determine social relations. Instead, I understand technology as a constituted totality that drives production; more broadly, it is a type of rationality that (in Heidegger's felicitous phrase) "enframes" scientific thought and also constitutes a *sensorium,* a field of perception. Further, technology is not merely an extension of human powers, "mediating" our relation to the external world, or nature, but has penetrated human character structure. That is, one may not sharply distinguish "emotions," "feelings," and other terms of interiority from the technological sensorium, just as science has become virtually identical with technology. This statement implies that we are *wired*, that the mass communication media, perhaps the most powerful technological achievement of this century, are neither extensions of collective human powers, nor an awesome otherness standing against us, but occupy the space of social life such that no relations—those within the psychic structure, or between individuals, or among and between collectivities—can escape the enframing of technology.

3. Technology is not an epistēmē alone, although it is surely entwined with all forms of knowledge, including language and art; it is the discourse that modifies, when it does not entirely shape, objects as well as the rules of knowledge formation.

4. Thus, to speak of technology is to speak of culture; for the objects of the social world are not only constituted socially, in the sense that "natural" objects have been so severely mediated that to speak of physics, biology, etc., as direct causal agents in the social matrix appears naive. More to the point, technology as discourse defines social construction.

5. In turn, natural objects are also socially constructed. It is not a question of whether these natural objects, or, to be more precise, the objects of natural scientific knowledge, exist independently of the act of knowing. This question is answered by the assumption of "real" time as opposed to the presupposition, common among neo-Kantians, that time always has a referent, that temporality is therefore a relative, not an unconditioned, category. Surely, the earth evolved long before life on earth. The question is whether objects of natural scientific knowledge are constituted outside the social field. If this is possible, we can assume that science or art may develop procedures that effectively neutralize the effects emanating from the means by which we produce knowledge/art. Performance art may be such an attempt. The artist foregoes the use of tools—brushes, chisels, cameras, as well as the raw materials (paper, stone, film) upon which are inscribed shapes, colors, lines. Performance art, like more conventional theater, attempts to restore to the body its autonomous space. Communication is no longer mediated by things. This might satisfy the antitechnological impulse were it not for the body itself, which is already incorporated into the technological sensorium. Movement is never natural; it is enframed in technology.

6. Science invented the algorithm of reproducible, testable experiments to screen out the social world, including the prejudices of the investigator, relations of domination and subordination in the laboratory, the pressures of the scientific community to conform to established paradigms, and so on. In short, the progress of science is presumed guaranteed by the requirement that any statement about the object be falsifiable by standard experimentation (Popper). However, if it can be shown that the experimental method presupposes a technological telos, the effort to achieve value neutrality in the sciences is unachievable unless this telos is, itself, considered value neutral.

7. The fact is, science and technology have been constituted as discursive formations, which, by definition, exclude the social and cultural world as relevant influences in knowledge production. Gaston Bachelard and Louis Althusser go so far as to claim that science is constituted by its separation from common sense (even though Stephen Toulmin defines science as "organized common sense"). If organization may be related to technology as one of its modes of existence, science becomes a kind of technology. Popper's definition, cited earlier, is to specify the criticism through organization as the metarule for achieving scientific truth, if by that term we mean knowledge uncontaminated by ideology. This is nearly identical to Bachelard's program for verification, although Bachelard adds the requirement that criticism extend to the axiomatic foundations of science, not merely to theories operating within a given paradigm. But, unlike Bachelard, Popper in his later work abandons the traditional epistemological assumption that knowledge is constituted through the interaction of objects to be known and the knower. For Popper, while this process may be entirely accurate as a description of how knowledge is gained, the "third world"

of theories and propositions, which he calls epistemologies, stands independent of both the objects and the subjects who know them. Knowledge takes on an ontological existence and thereby itself becomes *objective*. This is, for Popper, the most reliable of the three worlds because its existence no longer depends on the fallible processes of acquisition. The theories have been tested, and the results have become autonomous. Clearly, Popper hopes to avoid the messiness of epistemological questions. By separating the processes of the production of scientific knowledge from their structure, Popper wants to remove behaviorist or psychological aspects from judgments about the contents of scientific knowledge. But, as David Bloor has pointed out in his critique of Frege, psychology is not really at issue when addressing the production of knowledge. More to the point is the question of social determinants, mediations, etc., of scientific knowledge. What we want to know is whether the products of the knowledge process, the representations called theories, propositions, and statements, can be shown to be independent of discourses of the social, cultural, ideological. We want to ask whether the products of science, notwithstanding the social processes that combine to construct them, are true. That is, can the thesis of realism be maintained with respect to scientific knowledge? The issue is not whether theories refer to an object. The question is whether that object is free of social construction, which, even if admitted, leaves no traces.

Bloor focuses his argument on mathematics, which Frege, following Kant, regards as not an abstraction from objects but as derived from pure intuition. Popper, following Brouwer's suggestion, disputes this by asserting that mathematics uses discursive, particularly logical, thought. He has not escaped Kant's invocation of the mental sources of mathematical knowledge. Bloor's argument is that while Frege is right to reject the contention that the products of mathematics are derived by abstraction from material objects (such as pebbles), he also rejects the idea that arithmetic has no source outside mind. Bloor substitutes social for psychological and "material" determination of matematical knowledge. He adduces several examples culled from the literature on the philosophy of mathematics to show that many ideas correspond not to scientific necessity but to cultural influences. In this, he follows Spengler's and Wittgenstein's concept that different cultures will produce different mathematical concepts. We can show that evolving concepts in the theory of numbers as well as other branches of mathematics vary according to influences already present in a culture. Taking the evidence of Evans-Prichard's famous study of the Azande, Bloor disputes the idea that there can be only one logic. He argues that the refusal of the Azande to acknowledge the contradiction in their culture between the assumption that all are witches and the fact that this is not the case is not due to "a lack of theoretical interest" in the subject of logical contradictions. Rather, according to Bloor, the "logic" of the Azande in deflecting the contradiction is no different from "Western" logic that regularly denies that bomber pilots are murderers even though a murderer is defined as someone who deliberately kills someone else. From the point of view of the society within which pilots function, they are seen as persons who perform their duty out of loyalty to the government. From the point of view of the victim, however, they are murderers since the victim experiences only the danger of death without the referent of duty to government. Bloor invokes this example to demonstrate that social interest mediates logic, and that the assumption that there is a "pure" logic separate from culture is false.

We don't have to stop with Bloor's perspectivist refutation of the notion of objective knowledge. Scientific experiment may be shown to derive from a specific conception of "value," that of intervention into nature as the road to reliable knowledge. Or we might cite the problematic object of scientific knowledge, that the construction of the object has both cultural and political presuppositions. The point is that neither logic nor mathematics escapes the "contamination" of the social. What remains to be discovered is the nature of that contamination, its relation to the truth value of scientific propositions, and, most particularly, the role of science and technology in the social world.

8. Whatever our solution to the problems posed in Thesis 7, we are faced with the fact that science and technology remain subjects for intense discussion and disputation. These debates must be explained, for, since the nineteenth century, the advances in scientific knowledge have been supposed to eliminate the need for metaphysics, including a metaphysics whose field of discourse is science. Science should be able to "speak for itself" if its objects and methods preempt metacommentaries. All we need do, according to the most optimistic advocates of this position, is *do science.* Problems posed in the course of scientific inquiry/discovery should be subject only to solutions arrived at by those qualified to perform scientific activity. It is true that after Kant, with the exception of ethics, all philosophy is a discourse on science. Moreover, with the advent of logical empiricism and logical atomism, schools associated with the rise of what is sometimes called nonclassical physics—the physics associated with relativity theory and quantum mechanics, although by no means identical with them—problems in philosophy existed only to clarify the actual results of scientific inquiry at the level of language and discourse.

The distinction between philosophy, long viewed as a speculative inquiry, and natural science, in which speculation is strictly limited by scientific method to preexperimental hypothesis, has become increasingly blurred.

For, just as philosophers have confined their work to interpreting scientific outcomes, scientists have felt constrained to become philosophers to make sense of their own work. Apart from a few relatively isolated figures (Alfred North Whitehead comes to mind), philosophy has been transformed into metascience, illuminating the most general principles that are said to derive from scientific practices. Philosophy is no longer magisterial in its ambition to be the most general of the sciences; philosophers either have become metamathematicians insofar as logical inquiry defines their intervention, or have tried to enter the still unresolved disputes within science.

Speculative philosophy refuses to go away, despite its intentions, because physics, mathematics, and biology, the three sciences that have generated the controversy, are themselves rent. Nonclassical physics continues to make discoveries, but the actors cannot agree on what they have found. Or, to be fair, they are unable to render clearly the significance of the products of scientific discovery because the framework of understanding is in contention.

This framework is by no means self-evident: in the torrent of commentaries on the significance of quantum mechanics and relativity theory, one may discern wide differences, even among those most responsible for the discoveries. This is another way of saying that science proves incapable of speaking for itself with a unified voice. This is not particularly new. Since the so-called Copernican revolution, both philosophers and scientists have felt the need to interpret the results of inquiry.

9. Their central interpretations are these:

a. Scientific theories are descriptions dictated by the real world. Taken together, they constitute a picture of the world as it actually exists "in nature." The quotation marks are used because there is a question concerning what we mean by nature. Since Copernican/Newtonian science insists that objects and relations must be explained by purely natural causes, the conception of nature means simply the object of scientific knowledge taken in its totality. For these purposes, we need not address whether the real is identical with something called "material" reality. For realists who have gone beyond the naive implications of materialism, the main requirement is that a theory refers to something outside itself. Referentiality is regarded as the *sine qua non* of theorizing.

b. There are no laws of nature, only laws of science. In this way of seeing, science is defined by the rules of inquiry, mediated by the level of development of (i) its theoretical apparatus and (ii) the material apparatus, i.e., technologies of inquiry. Since these mediations inevitably overdetermine what we mean by fact (that is, facts are always both theory and technology dependent), no individual fact can be falsified/verified by means of experiment without taking into account its referent(s) which constitute themselves as traditions that have become conventions of inquiry.

c. The significance of quantum mechanics and relativity theory is that scientific theories refer to the relation between the "field" of inquiry and the tools of measurement, on the one hand, and to subject/object relations, on the other. The first formulation takes the position that theory is "objective" knowledge in Popper's mode; the second reformulates the proposition in terms of interaction and mutual determination, in the manner of hermeneutic/dialectical analysis. In either case, the intervention of the "observer" is inescapable in the constitution of the field (I use the term "field" rather than "object" because "facts" refer to relations and relations of relations, rather than things). The second and third interpretations assume that uncertainty, which results from overdetermination, is both the consequence of shifting referentiality of the field and the refer-

ent of the social mediated by the subjects who engage in the process of scientific inquiry. That scientific facts are constituted socially as well as technologically infers that science is an *intervention* in both senses. This means that the object is constituted as a relation between the ends of scientific inquiry and its means. As Fleck demonstrates, facts are produced, not discovered.

10. To the degree that human sciences aspire to scientificity, they have felt obliged to parallel the epistemological and methodological norms of natural science. But what these are is in dispute within the human sciences. Weber adopted the probabilistic, uncertain stance of his contemporaries in theoretical physics. His theory of unintended consequences and his reflexive methodological comments were enframed by the same epistēmē that gave rise to relativity. In his *Protestant Ethic,* he protested against historical materialism's a priorism in accounting for both periodicity and change. Weber contended that each historical situation manifested its unique determinations depending on the conjuncture of discourses. Thus, he introduces the "principle" of historical specificity, which would argue, in terms of relativity theory, for the significance of the signifier as well as the referent in determining the nature of social relations. At the same time, Weber holds to the view that rationalization is the distinctive characteristic of modern scientific/technological society, including its thought forms. As Mannheim points out, this is a universalistic, quantitatively determined thought mode and is identified with the Enlightenment. In consequence, *science* is posed against magic and religion, which become marginalized in the bourgeois world.

Mannheim argues that the Counter-Enlightenment, or romanticism, is a deeply conservative movement. But its insistence on the return of the suppressed cannot succeed in resuscitating the "irrational" dimension and making a place for it in the modern world without, at the same time, unwittingly rationalizing this dimension. For, to consider the so-called irrational and expose the elements of its reason as *system* is already to submit to the scientific worldview, since the process of legitimation nearly always entails demonstrating that the "other" conform, at least in a great degree, to science. In this connection, one may cite the experience of parapsychology, psychoanalysis, and other suspect sciences. In both of these cases, the controversy surrounding their findings turns on whether they can be shown to conform to the canon of experimental method and deductive/inductive reason. Consequently, their advocates are obliged to argue that the discovery of the "irrational" can take place only by means of normal, enlightenment science. Only a few of their proponents, especially of psychoanalysis, insist on the methodological validity of hermeneutic/dialectic procedures of investigation.

Durkheim introduces a classical conception of society in his insistence that it be treated as a fact, that is, as indivisible object. Rules for sociological method are construed *objectively*, with the investigator standing outside the field of vision.

This dispute has set the terms of theoretical development in the social sciences since the turn of the twentieth century. Needless to say, "normal" Anglo-American social science follows the objectivist account of Durkheim rather than the hermeneutic or dialectical accounts of Weberian and phenomenological paradigms, whether neo-Marxist or not. On the other hand, recent social theory in France, Italy, and Germany roughly follows the prescriptions of relativity and quantum theory in their respective insistences on temporal discontinuities, spatial indeterminacy, and historical construction of discursive formations in social phenomena.

11. If this is so, we can reconstruct the concept of the unified field, that elusive goal of the sciences, in another way. The relation among physical, life, and human sciences is not one of determination, even in the last instance, of the physical and biological over the social. Rather, each achieves unities within macrospheres and microspheres but not necessarily between them. Further, there is an epistēmē that spans different discourses within a specific historical era.

12. Anthony Giddens has proposed that ideology be disconnected from the "philosophy of science" in favor of a concept of ideology considered "as a positive term, meaning something like an all-embracing and encyclopedic form of knowledge." Yet, he goes on to urge that ideology "should be reformulated in relation to a theory of *power* and *domination*." I take this to be another sense in which the term "ideology" may be employed. A third is to define it as lived experience, the unmediated formulation of judgment—practical, "useful," interested, but surely not "false consciousness" or "bad" science in contrast to truth.

We have three meanings of ideology. The first, against which Giddens poses ideology/power/domination, is entwined with the problem of demarcation, how to distinguish science (truth) from nonscience (myth, religion, etc.). I entirely agree that this *should* be a nonproblem. But it is not so simple: science and technology legitimate their privileged place by claiming to be the single source of reliable knowledge; their power/domination emanates from establishing demarcation. An enterprise that wishes to call attention to the character of science as a constituted discourse must address the problem of the elements that make up science—not only its "ideology" in the sense of worldview, but the neutrality of its practice in relation to issues of power/domination. If my thesis is right that, as Giddens says, the mode of signification is "incorporated within systems of domination to sanction their continuance," then science cannot be exempted from this study.

13. Science is a language of power; and those who bear its legitimate claims, i.e., those who are involved in the ownership and control of its processes and results, have become a distinctive social category equipped with a distinctive ideology and political program in the post-war world. The relation of science to the state is still one of subordination in both capitalist and state socialist formations, but this relation is now under attack by knowledge communities which increasingly perceive, even if they have not yet theorized, the elements of their autonomy. That science communities routinely declare their neutrality on political matters, especially on questions affecting the content of scientific knowledge, demonstrates not only the character of scientific and professional ideology, but a studied naïveté concerning the implications of accepting resources made available by the state for research and their own role in establishing priorities.

At the level of the economy, it has been apparent for the last century that science is central for the processes of economic reproduction, the manifestation of which, as the recent development of the high temperature superconductor demonstrates, is the intimate link between the motivation for scientific discovery and the desire for technological application. A similar example is provided by the current AIDS crisis with respect to medical research. From a small group of underfunded scientists, AIDS is rapidly becoming the hottest property in the medical field as the state mobilizes scientists to deal with the crisis. As with military-related research, state priorities have the force of inexorability: the recalcitrant independent scientist had better be prepared to sacrifice her/his career or work in some subfield for which only marginal support is required.

The scientist wants his/her work to be thought of as both esoteric and socially useful in the long run. Esoteric work carries status probably because it symbolizes freedom—in the form of distance from the dictatorial marketplace. It is more difficult to get a position as a theorist in an esoteric subfield where only modest support is required (mainly just a salary; perhaps some computer time too) than it is to get a position in a subfield more immediately connected to technology, where heavy support is required. Compare solid-state physics and cosmology, for example. One third of the 11,000 physics graduate students in the United States are in the single subfield of solid state physics, and all of them will be able to get jobs in that subfield. Even though there are only a handful of cosmologists, they will have a harder time finding jobs.

14. In turn, we may not theorize the character of the state without understanding that science is the discourse of the late capitalist and the "socialist" state. Science is rapidly displacing, as dominant discourse, the old ideologies of the liberal state—chief among them, possessive individualism, which was based on the dominance of the market in the economy and the conduct of political affairs. This development coincides with the consolidation of bureaucratic power, whose rationality parallels that of science, or, to be more precise, is the ostensible social form of scientific rationality. Therefore, an alternative science would have to imagine, as a condition of its emergence, an alternative rationality which would not be based on domination.

Some Implications of Modern Technology: Revisited

Steven Gerardi

Abstract

Although first published in 1941 Herbert Marcus' "Some Implications of Modern Technology" (published in Studies in Philosophy and Social Sciences) *suggested that the modern machine age with its efficiency fetish has substituted for commodity fetish at the hands of an authoritarian state. A typical Marxist ideology of the old left during that period of time.*

However, many of the implications located in postmodern technology Marcus failed to see as a volunteristic behavior, mainly due to the time span between the modern and postmodern age. Predominate among these effects is the loss of individuality.

Today the impact of the computer age leads to standardization of thought, social conformity, and should be seen as a volunteristic social by-product of the nature of advanced technology, and not the tool of an authoritarian state.
© 2006 Elsevier Inc. All rights reserved.

1. Background

Historically, in Occidental Culture, science/technology and individuality are the product of two concurrent social forces, the Enlightenment period an 18th-century movement characterized by a spirit of skepticism toward traditional doctrines and values, and the Protestant Reformation which demystifies world occurs/events.

The Enlightenment is historically significant for Western Civilization because it became a sociological movement, rather than a private achievement. Sociological in that the effects can be found in all spheres of life. In religion the Enlightenment meant the struggle against orthodox superstition as found in the revolt of reason; in politics the Enlightenment represented the freedom against arbitrary despotism of estates; in philosophy it meant the liberation from theological dogmatism. In short, Enlightenment required a free-thinking person to displace the irrational with a rational world-image.

Paradoxically, according to the sociologist Max Weber (1854–1920) the concept of individualism is not a secular manifestation, but a religious movement rooted in Protestantism.

Protestantism, Weber argued, replaced the rule of the church as the mediator between God and humankind. Specifically, the Calvinist (and a small member of other Protestant sects), eliminated all intermediary ecclesiastical and sacramental agencies between God and humanity, a process which, according to Weber, demagicalized the relationship between God and His human creatures. The result, free choice, free thought, and oddly enough, science and technology because of the displacement of the magical mystical with an objective and empirical world-image.

Another paradox of the Protestant movement according to Weber, was the economic individual, or one who seeks in-worldly rewards. Most of the worlds religious doctrines suggest that humanity cannot serve God and money simultaneously. But the Protestant movement suggested that humanity can serve God through wealth by providing "good works" here on earth.

This change in human identity, that of free choice, free individual thought, the individual accumulation of wealth and technology all set into motion a series of sociological shifts. Indeed, individual free choice alters the entire social order. One salient example of this shift is free mate selection. This is especially significant for woman since for many reasons throughout human history, mate selection and marriage were inextricably linked to private property. Another significant example is the conjugal family form. A momentous change for Western human autonomy, since the patriarchal family stood in the way of free expression and individualism itself.

To sum up, concurrently the Enlightenment period and the Protestant Reformation had an important sociological impact on Western Culture. Simultaneously, the power of these ideas have changed Western Civilization and the world.

2. Postmodern Era

During the rapid, almost anomic technological advancement of postmodern socicty, the historical concept of individuality is lost and social conformity becomes the new form of human identity.

To clarify, consider for a moment the image of a youngster sitting at a computer attempting to learn a new computer software. The software routine demands a new understanding of the technical process which presents itself as an obstacle to gaining entry. This individual must conform to the software's demands both in language and behavior. So the youngster turns to the tech support system of the software company, where on line the "techies" in effect tell the youngster what to do and how to think in order to gain access to the program. Essentially, it is sensible for that youngster to follow another's directions in order to have use of the software.

However, during this exercise the youngster learns to accept the will of another, which also includes the computer. This volunteristic social behavior becomes even more insidious because the youngster internalizes these directions of another, as one's own thought creating a new human identity which rejects free thought and individuality by relying on the will of another.

As the youngster grows into an adult, there is the tacit understanding that the demands of the postmodern era will require consistent technical training. Consequently, there is the continuous management of autonomous individual thought by the "authority" of technology. This is an ongoing process throughout one's life.

Illustratively, let us examine Franz Kafka's (1883–1924) "Metamorphosis." Gregor Samsa, the protagonist, awakes one morning transformed into a gigantic, hideous multi legged insect. In this perceived temporal state, Gregor must conform to social forces around him by confining himself to his room, only to be seen by his family. He becomes dependent on his family for every necessity of life. He comments: "what an exhausting job I picked on . . . Its much more irritating work than doing actual business in office . . . worrying about train connections, irregular beds and meals, casual acquaintances . . . the devil take it all!" Gregor's metamorphosed state is a volunteristic autonomous decision to reject self in an effort to recapture his individuality. But this rejection implies for him rejecting his individuality, his autonomy, indeed his human form.

Similarly, the conscience volunteristic submission and conformity of postmodern humanity to what can be seen as the external authority of the technology has stripped the individual of free thought and individuality itself. Constant exposure through out one's life to the continuous demands of the computer age implies the continuous management of individual free thought. This management is unavailable and inescapable in a postmodern society because it transcends technology itself and effects all segments of social life. Most notably fashion, education, business, and entertainment. In fashion there is an effort to express individuality through dress. However, because it is a fashion "trend" many dress alike, and individuality is lost. In education the curriculum stress common knowledge acquisition, but produces standardization of thought. In the business world top executives rape the wealth of the company, and others "go along to get along." In entertainment the

historical "individual" was seen as the hero, but today is portrayed as a kook, and someone to be feared.

Likewise, being critical in an era which demands social conformity is irrational. Having an individual opinion which stands outside the mainstream is unreasonable. Doing the "right thing" suggests social conformity. Conformity has become reasonable and sensible behavior in the postmodern technical era.

Selected Readings

Aronowitz, S. (1988). *Sciences as power*. Minneapolis: University of Minnesota Press.

Descartes, R. (1965). *Discourse on method*. NY: Dutton.

Gerth, H. H., & Mills, C. W. (1986). *From Max Weber*. Oxford University Press.

Kafka, F. (1968). *The penal colony and short pieces*. NY: Schocken Book.

Kant, I. (1969). *Critiques of pure reason*. NY: Dutton.

Locke, J. (1955). *Human understanding*. London, Dent: NY.

Marcuse, H. (2006). Some implications of modern technology. In A. Arato & E. Gebhardt (Eds.), *The essential Frankfurt school reader*. NY: Continuum.

Weber, M. (1958). *The protestant ethic and the spirit of capitalism*. NY: Charles Scribner's Sons.

Critical-Thinking Questions

1. What is the Dialectic of the Enlightenment?

2. What is science/technology an "ideological veil" ?

3. How is the loss of individuality associated with technology?

CHAPTER XII

The Family

Humanity is the creator of society, and at the same time, society is the creator of humanity. Man is a social and cultural being. Society and culture form who we are through the constant interplay between the human mind and society. There is a continuous reciprocal interaction between the human mind and society, a back-and-forth relationship molding the human into a social being. We are first and foremost a social animal. Society and culture are always forming our personalities, our ability to cope with social tensions, pain, age transitions, work, play, identification, life cycles, sexual aggression, and social adaptation. Society and culture set the scene for socialization, and at the same time, they mold and define society and culture. Socialization is the means by which values, norms, and rules for behavior of a society are transmitted to the young. Socialization is a universal process: it is found everywhere in human society; it is the process by which we become social animals, and how we acquire culture-specific behavioral patterns. As Max Weber once noted in *The Spirit of Capitalism*, the ecological, economic, technological, and political social conditions of modern life were the product of the institutionalization and the transmission of values, norms, and rules for behavior to each succeeding generation of the Protestant Reformation, creating Occidental society as we know it today. The primary socialization agent in human society is the family.

Family Forms

Family is defined as a set of people related by blood, marriage, or adoption. They share responsibility for the reproduction, care, protection, and socialization of the young. There are at least five major family forms, and are as follows: (1) the nuclear family, which is a modern Western concept where there is usually a mother, father, and children living under one "roof." Generally, the nuclear family can be any size as long as the family supports itself, and is neo-local. In the United States (until recently) this form has featured a mother, father, and 2.5 children, although about 75 percent of today's American children spend time in a single-headed household. In the United States the Ideal Type (Max Weber) nuclear family, which is seen as the proper and legitimate form, is one in which there is an exclusion of relative and kin networking, neo-local in which marriage members move to a new location, free mate selection based upon mutual attraction, and marriage is based on "love," not economics or arrangement; (2) the extended family form is a concept generally associated with several generations of relatives living together. During adulthood and marriage children generally do not establish separate living arrangements. Rather, they stay with the extended family. It is a patriarchal society; (3) the complex family is thought of as any extended family in a group marriage or polygamous relationship. This form can contain one man with two or more wives (polygyny) or one woman with two or more husbands (polyandry); (4) The joint family, or Hindu Undivided family, where all members of a family line are descended from a common ancestor. A daughter is no longer a member of her father's family when she is married, she becomes her husband's family; and (5) the free family form, in which offspring know their mothers, but do not know their biological fathers. This family form is generally found in primitive tribes where there are Hunters and Gatherers.

Tasks of Socialization

As was mentioned earlier, the one factor leading to our humanity is is the process of socialization. There are ten tasks of socialization that every society demands of the family. They are as follows: (1) the channeling of the member's libidinal forces. What is the appropriate sexual behavior? Where, when, and with whom?; (2) dealing with the unconscious, which means evaluating the social issues arising during our social experiences and life; (3) dealing with anxiety as a result of life conflicts; (4) dealing with aggression by channeling behavior into acceptable forms; (5) life-cycle progressions, moving through the age stages of life; (6) role learning, how we assess our position in the social order; (7) self-identity: who we think and feel we are as individuals; (8) internalization of the "Social Contract"; (9) diversity and variability of the roles we play throughout our lives; and (10) integration into the social life.

This book has examined the two predominate schools of thought within Sociology: Functionalism and Conflict view. As we saw in many of the previous chapters, these two concepts are considered sociological opposites; and hence, the issue of family will be no different, as we shall see during the next phase of this chapter.

Functionalism

The main designer of Functionalism is Talcott Parsons. Functionalism is an American sociological concept that was created by an American. Parsons began his career as a medical student, changing to Engineering, and later becoming the Chair of the Sociology Department at Harvard University. As was mentioned earlier, we are all products of our social environment. Hence, Parsons brought to Functionalism the medical concept known as homoeostasis, or harmony, found in the human body. From his engineering background came the need to learn how structures operate, and plotting such operations through schematics. Therefore, the sociological intent of Functionalism is found within the institutions and parts

of society that operate in the society as a system creating social balance and equilibrium. Functionalism is defined as the parts of society that are structured to maintain social equilibrium or balance. They contribute to the well operation of the system in general. If a part of society is not maintaining social homeostasis, it is referred to as dysfunctional. Furthermore, all other parts of society that are connected to this part are likewise dysfunctional. Therefore, a dysfunctional school system is the outcome of dysfunctional family life, because the family does not support the goals of education, or does not understand the importance of education in our post-modern society. The children will on average not perform well in school.

Parsons' development of this theory is based upon a voluntaristic social action, and is a synthesis of theories of Durkheim, Weber, and Pareto. The functionalist approach tends to argue that there is a consensus or agreement within the social system, through the process of individual behavior governed by social norms and values that are generally held, accepted, and agreed upon. Hence, Durkheim argued that religion, philosophy, ideas, and morals are products of the social condition of humanity, and are expressed as social realities. These social concepts are seen by Durkheim as a "conscience collective" of a clan or group, because they correspond to, and are at the root of each member's judgments and actions. Thus, producing social cohesiveness of collectives assures that social systems operate effectively.

Max Weber's concept known as the Ideal Types is also used by Parsons. Weber suggested that society has sets of values that are revered and supported through social life.

Pareto influenced Parsons because he was the first to use the term "social system" to describe the general state of human society. The chief task of sociology according to Pareto is to investigate the nature and property of social systems, the transformations they undergo, and the relationship between these elements, which produce social equilibrium.

Parsons' sociology transforms these ideas into a set of analytical tools for interpretation and comparative study of social systems known as "pattern variable," commonly referred to as the AGIL scheme. The AGIL scheme consists of adaptation, goal attainment, integration, and latency. The **Adaptation** cell contains those instrumental actions and capacities toward the means and selection, and cognitive symbolization for adaptation and change. Intrinsic to this cell is the concept of homeostasis, or harmony and balance within social systems, and most importantly, harmonious social change.

Parsons further argued that the actor as a biological entity is always interacting and adapting to his or her environment. The **Goal attainment** cell contains consummatory needs, selection, and expressive symbolization for action toward goal attainment. The **Integration** cell contains affiliations, the ability for integration based on moral evaluations, and responsible action. The **Latency** cell contains normative commitment to the ideals of balanced social change.

Although Functionalism has been critiqued for not explaining how social change occurs, that simply is incorrect. Social change occurs throughout the AGIL scheme, with the major work happening in the I and L cells. In the I cell, new social values and norms become generalized and institutionalized. Located in the L cell is system solidarity, system membership, inclusion, and acceptance. Hence, in terms of the assimilation of the so-called out group, functionalists suggest that social actors are always adapting to cultural traits of the out group in the I cell, and in the L cell, the gap between the out group and in group is continuously narrowing to a point of no difference.

In terms of the acceptance of new technology, in the I cell more and more individuals are employing this technology, and in the L cell, this new technology becomes commonplace.

Family from the functionalist perspective has six ideal type characteristics of the nuclear or conjugal family form which is seen as the proper and legitimate in the United States: (1) family should be exclusive of kin networks or extent family type; (2) neo-local residence, married couples should relocate from their parents; (3) free mate selection without parental interference; (4) courtship based upon mutual physical attraction; (5) marriage should be based upon romantic love, and not on economics; and (6) the number of children found in the American family generally is 2.5. This is seen as social balance by the functionalist, because the son and daughter within the family are seen as replacing the parents. Hence, zero population growth is another form of social balance.

As a result of social upheaval of the 1970s, functionalism became unpopular within the sociological community because: (a) it was used by power elite to justify social inequalities, and (b) to force the internalization of established values based upon consensus simply supported the social order. Secondly, the neo-Marxist feminists of the time suggested that Functionalism provided an inadequate explanation for woman's role in society. As a result of a work by Fredrick Engels entitled *The Origins of the Family, Private Property and the State*, published in 1884, it was suggested that the social relations of power and control over material resources was the true factor of the development of the modern family referred to as the Resource Power Theory. Thus, the Conflict view of the family was born.

Conflict View

Engels' *The Origins of the Family, Private Property and the State* suggested that throughout history the relationship between males and females and family historically has not always been as we see them today. Engels argued that what are at work within these areas are the historical changing modes of production is the key to social change. When there is a change in the mode of production there is a corresponding change in the Resource Power Theory, which changes family form and male/female relationships.

The first mode of production according to Engels is Savagery, or what today we refer to as Hunters and Gatherers. During this period there is no private property, and males and females equally share the responsibility of the health and welfare of the family. Engels suggests that both males and females are equal, with a free family form.

The second mode of production is Barbarism or Agriculturalism. During this period humans learned to breed domestic animals and to practice agriculture, and acquire methods of increasing the supply of food products. During this period private property arises, and males, because of their physical strength, controlled all wealth and status; including the family and all women. All property was therefore passed on to the oldest male heir in the family.

The third mode of production is Civilization or Industrialization. Within this period humanity mastered advanced mechanical forms of work. Within this mode of production, it is still a male-controlled period. Engels suggested that it was in fact a continuation of the pervious mode of production.

In the last stage, Engels suggested that there would be a workers revolution, which would render male and female, and the family, free and equal. Today we refer this period as the Post-Modern period in which education is required. Although in the United States there has not been a workers revolution, there has been a social revolution in which there is a greater number of females being educated;

hence, women are becoming more and more socially equal to men.

Hence, as a result of Engels' work, many Conflict sociologists began viewing the family as containing all of the antagonism within society and the state. They often refer to the Latin definition of family as "slaves belonging to one individual." Indeed, Marx maintained that the family was an economic institution with hierarchical structures, which allows for humanity to internalize submissiveness to authority, obedience, possessiveness, inequality, jealousy, sexual repression, competition, and rivalry. Subsequently, neo-Marxist alternative forms of family forms have come into being. The two forms this chapter will look at are the early American Oneida alternative, and the Israeli agricultural collective known as the Kibbutz.

Marxist Alternative Family Forms

John Humphrey Noyes, in 1848 in central New York State, created a social community known as the **Oneida Group**. This community attempted to establish an economic community in which everyone was equal. The philosophy of this group was to bring an end to competition, discrimination, and social inequality. This was accomplished through eliminating social differences. Everyone ate the same food, wore the same clothing, and lived in the same kind of housing, with the rotation of work.

Moreover, even the laws and law enforcement agents were eliminated, for they were seen as controlled by an elite social group. Rather, a concept known as **"Mutual Criticism"** was created. Mutual Criticism was the means by which the members of this collective community were punished if they committed transgressions against the community's policies. This committee of peers was established to discuss the infraction with the offender in the hope that he or she would see the errors of their ways.

Noyes further tried to eliminate jealously, hypocrisy, selfishness, exclusiveness, and personal possessiveness through his concept known as **Complex Marriage**. Noyes believed that romantic love encapsulated all of the conditions mentioned above. Complex Marriage would eliminate the possessiveness of romantic love through the establishment of a Marriage Committee. This committee would arrange all sexual relationships by conveying the male's wishes to the female. If the female approved, the committee granted the couple two hours together for this union.

In 1869 the group embarked on a **Eugenics program** based upon superior physical and intellectual abilities. Hence, a committee was established to oversee this program. If a couple wished to have children, they were required to submit an application to this committee. If the committee felt that this couple did not meet the physical and intellectual characteristics needed to have children, they were denied. The criteria the committee used were that of Noyes' physical and intellectual characteristics. Therefore, for a couple to have children they must possess some of, or all of, Noyes' characteristics. Over the ten-year period that this program was in effect, Noyes fathered fifty-eight children. In 1877, because of this program, the Oneida Group came to an end.

Israeli Kibbutz

The Kibbutz began as a social experiment in which the intelligentsia employed advanced social thought to guide them through what they believed to be a remedy for the negative effects of the alienating, private property driven institution of the capitalist order known as the family. This group believed that the nuclear family created an "unhealthy" relationship between family members, which limited social justice and human potential. Furthermore, the way to the elimination of all forms of social injustice is found in the family's child rearing practices. Hence, the forefathers of the Kibbutz established a completely new and unusual form of child rearing, which is still in use today.

Child Rearing Practices

The first stage of the Kibbutz is that of "**Infancy**," the first six months of life. During this period all infants must live in a common nursery cared for by female nurses. However, the biological mother can breast feed the child. The second stage is "**Infancy**," six months to one year of age. The infant still remains in the "**Infant House**" cared for by the nurses. However, now the parents can visit and take the child back to their apartment, but must be returned to the Infant House at the end of the day. The third stage is that of "**Toddles**," ages one to four. Now the children are moved into the "**Toddlers House**" or the "**Kevutza**" and remain together for the rest of their childhood. Parents continue to visit and bring them back to their apartment, and return them at the end of the day. The fourth stage is "**Kindergarten**," ages four to seven. The children are placed in "**Kindergarten Groups**" of eight and are cared for by one nurse. Parents still visit, take the children home, and return them to the group at the end of the day. Stage five is that of "**Grammar School House**," ages seven through twelve. During this stage the children live in a dormitory with a new nurse and a school teacher. Again there are evening visits with parents, and they are returned at the end of the day. Stage six is "**High School**," ages twelve to eighteen. The children now live in a new dormitory, where for the first time they have male teachers, and they must work on the farm collective.

There is a major transition upon **graduation from high school**. All must go into the army, and they are required to work outside the Kibbutz for at least one year. If they wish to return to the Kibbutz, they must apply to a committee. If they are accepted back into the community, they are assigned work based upon their ability and skills.

If couples wish to marry, they also must apply to a committee. If the committee votes in their favor, and the couple is married, they are assigned a room, which is referred to as a **"Couples Room."**

In summary, the functionalists see the nuclear family as the part of society that maintains social balance and homeostasis in American society. By contrast, the Conflict sociologists view the family as a tool of the capitalist order, creating discord and competition within society.

Critical-Thinking Questions

1. What are the forms of family?

_____

_____

_____

_____

2. What are the Tasks of Socialization?

_____

_____

_____

_____

3. What are the Ideal Types of the nuclear family?

_____

_____

_____

_____

4. How does the Oneida Group eliminate inequity in the family?

_____

_____

_____

_____

5. How does the Kibbutz eliminate inequality in the family?

_____

_____

_____

_____

Index

Tocqueville 280
toddler 340
Toddlers House/Kevutza 340
Tolstoi 255, 258
Toulmin, Stephen 324
Toward a new theory of science 305
transcendental idealism 265
transcendental subjectivity 235, 265
Transcendentalists 280
Traweek, Sharon 297
Troeltsch 256
truth 229, 230, 233, 234, 235, 237, 238, 239,
    241, 243, 244, 245, 246, 247, 248, 249,
    254, 255, 257, 266, 268, 269, 273, 274,
    281, 292, 294, 295, 296, 299, 300, 304,
    308, 313, 314, 320, 322, 326, 328

U

unconscious 337
use-value 43, 218

V

validity of science 263
Veblen 270, 274

Vischer, Friedrich Theodor 258
vocational training 276, 277, 279
volume 2, 3, 45, 73, 215
voluntaristic social action 337
volunteeristic 330, 332

W

Weber, Max 21, 22, 25, 27, 34, 37, 110, 226,
    228, 259, 278, 285, 287, 290, 300, 320,
    327, 328, 330, 337
Western Culture, science and technology
    in 228-231
Western philosophy 261
White 127
White, David Manning 183, 187
Whitehead, Alfred North 326
Whitman, Walt 281
Winch, Peter 290, 291
wisdom, goal of 250
Wittgenstein 291, 293, 300, 325
Woolgar, Steve 296, 297
World War II 288